Women and Revolution
in Iran

Westview Replica Editions

The concept of Westview Replica Editions is a response to the continuing crisis in academic and informational publishing. Library budgets for books have been severely curtailed. Ever larger portions of general library budgets are being diverted from the purchase of books and used for data banks, computers, micromedia, and other methods of information retrieval. Interlibrary loan structures further reduce the edition sizes required to satisfy the needs of the scholarly community. Economic pressures on the university presses and the few private scholarly publishing companies have severely limited the capacity of the industry to properly serve the academic and research communities. As a result, many manuscripts dealing with important subjects, often representing the highest level of scholarship, are no longer economically viable publishing projects--or, if accepted for publication, are typically subject to lead times ranging from one to three years.

Westview Replica Editions are our practical solution to the problem. We accept a manuscript in camera-ready form, typed according to our specifications, and move it immediately into the production process. As always, the selection criteria include the importance of the subject, the work's contribution to scholarship, and its insight, originality of thought, and excellence of exposition. The responsibility for editing and proofreading lies with the author or sponsoring institution. We prepare chapter headings and display pages, file for copyright, and obtain Library of Congress Cataloging in Publication Data. A detailed manual contains simple instructions for preparing the final typescript, and our editorial staff is always available to answer questions.

The end result is a book printed on acid-free paper and bound in sturdy library-quality soft covers. We manufacture these books ourselves using equipment that does not require a lengthy make-ready process and that allows us to publish first editions of 300 to 600 copies and to reprint even smaller quantities as needed. Thus, we can produce Replica Editions quickly and can keep even very specialized books in print as long as there is a demand for them.

About the Book and Editor

Women and Revolution in Iran
edited by Guity Nashat

Iranian women acquired greater legal, social, and economic opportunities during the past three decades than in any other period of history, yet they participated in large numbers in the 1979 revolution to overthrow Shah Mohammad Reza Pahlavi. Ironically, they may have lost more than any other group from the changes introduced and stand to lose even more from changes contemplated by leaders of the current regime.

The role of women in the revolution, the reasons for their participation, and their subsequent fate are documented in this volume. The authors examine the status of women in prerevolutionary society, the ways in which their lives were affected by Islamic principles, and the changes that occurred throughout the twentieth century as increasing numbers of women entered the labor force and public life. They then turn to recent political events, describing the participation of working-class, rural, and educated women and activists from both the right and left. Finally, they consider the implications of recent government politics aimed at limiting women's activities outside the home and encouraging a return to more traditional roles.

Dr. Nashat teaches Middle Eastern history at the University of Illinois, Chicago Circle. She is the author of Beginnings of Modern Reform in Iran.

Women and Revolution in Iran

edited by Guity Nashat

Westview Press / Boulder, Colorado

A Westview Replica Edition

Copyright © 1983 by Westview Press, Inc.

Published in 1983 in the United States of America by
     Westview Press, Inc.
     5500 Central Avenue
     Boulder, Colorado 80301
     Frederick A. Praeger, President and Publisher

Library of Congress Cataloging in Publication Data
Main entry under title:
Women and revolution in Iran.
     (Westview replica edition)
     1. Women--Iran--Addresses, essays, lectures.
2. Women in politics--Iran--Addresses, essays,
lectures. 3. Women, Muslim--Iran--Addresses, essays,
lectures. 4. Revolutions--Iran--Addresses, essays,
lectures. I. Nashat, Guity, 1937-   .
HQ1735.2.W65 1983   305.4'0955   83-10286
ISBN 0-96531-931-6

Printed and bound in the United States of America.

10 9 8 7 6 5 4 3

Contents

viii

Preface

This volume has been a collective effort by many individuals who shared my interest and concern about the impact of the Iranian Revolution on women. I am grateful to the contributors, without whom this volume would not have come into being. Nikki Keddie, who generously read every chapter of the volume and offered valuable suggestions, deserves my special thanks. I would also like to thank Ervand Abrahamian, Robert Michael, and Judy Becker for their help with several chapters. Madeleine Veldhoven assisted with preparation of the index. Finally, I would like to thank Gary S. Becker for all his encouragement and moral support.

The transliteration system used in this volume is a simplified version of the method used by the International Journal of Middle Eastern Studies. Most names and words of Middle Eastern origin have been transliterated in the Persian manner. To assist readers interested in primary sources, diacritical marks have been used in the footnotes, bibliographies, and index.

Guity Nashat

Introduction

The papers in this volume deal with an important but neglected aspect of the recent revolution in Iran: the role of women. Although women's participation in the events leading to the February 11 revolution was instrumental in its success, most studies have not addressed the reasons for their involvement or their contribution. When mentioned at all, women have been treated as merely one of the components that contributed to the making of the revolution.

However, two considerations justify a separate treatment of women. The first and more fundamental is the seeming contradiction between an active participation of women and their subservient and passive role in Iranian society for many centuries. Such a role has been supported by a fully developed religious doctrine which has enjoined women to be servile and to accept an inferior position to men and to concern themselves only with the affairs of the household. A second consideration also initially raises doubt and surprise about their participation. Women appeared to be one of the important beneficiaries of the policies enacted by the Pahlavis (1925-1978). The regime of the late Shah especially tried to use its policies toward women as a sign of progressiveness and as a tool for denouncing the ulama, particularly Ayatullah Khomeini. But women in general, including the most Westernized individuals and groups, came out strongly against a regime that purportedly was helping free them from the bonds of oppression. A large faction of women actually supported a regime that avowedly and openly opposed the policies that had given women a greater role in society outside the home.

Yet the paradoxes related to women's participation are more apparent than real, and there are excellent reasons why women widely supported and participated in the revolution in significant numbers. The main contribution of the studies in this volume will be to aid our understanding of women's support for the revolution in spite of the effort of the regime of the Shah to champion

1

the cause of women and in spite of the Islamic religious
limitations imposed on the role of women outside the
household

The chapters of this book are organized into three
parts. Part I offers a general historical perspective of
women's role and their status in the teachings of Islam.
In the first chapter I describe briefly the evolution of
the position of women in society. I explain that the
subservient role of women in Iran and other Middle Eastern countries that share its Islamic heritage evolved in
response to social and economic conditions prevailing in
the region over several millenia and preceded the advent
of Islam in the seventh century. Thus only in the twentieth century when social and economic conditions changed
sufficiently could women's status begin to change. The
next two chapters provide two different religious perspectives on the status of women. Fazlur Rahman analyzes
the position of women in the Qur'an, the primary source
of law in Islam. He shows that many disadvantages from
which women have suffered in Islamic society did not
originate with the Qur'an but rather resulted from the
interpretation of certain Qur'anic passages in later
periods. Adele and Amir Ferdows, on the other hand,
examine the status of women in the works of Allameh
Muhammad Baqir Majlisi, a seventeenth century theologian
regarded by many as the most influential thinker of popular Shi^{c}ite Islam. Majlisi's opinions supply the basis
for the theological arguments about the position of women
in society to this day.

The chapters in part II focus on more recent changes
in women's role and the reasons for the participation of
women from urban and from rural areas in the revolution.
S. Kaveh Mirani provides a general perspective on changes
in the role of women during the 1960s and 1970s. The
traditional status of women was being transformed by
rapid social and economic changes that improved the educational and employment opportunities for women during
these decades. The changing status of urban and rural
women affected how women perceived their role in society.

Marcia Hermansen analyzes Ali Shari^{c}ati's writing
on women. She shows that his immense popularity among
younger educated women stemmed from his ability to answer
their deeply felt need for a new definition of their
roles. The chapters by Anne Betteridge and Eliz
Sanasarian shed more light on the gradual politicization
and revolutionary activity of the younger educated women
from both traditional and more secular backgrounds.
Farzaneh Milani focuses on the transformation of a leading female poet, Saffar-Zadeh, from a fearless iconoclast
to a fervent religious zealot. The next two chapters
examine the participation of lower class women. Janet
Bauer focuses on several age groups of mostly poor
migrant women in Tehran, while Mary Hegland describes a

similar social group in a village near Shiraz in southern
Iran.
    The chapters in Part III examine the condition of
women since the revolution and some of the policies
enacted by the current regime. The ideological foundation and the policies instituted are discussed by Nashat.
Erika Friedl discusses how women in a particular village
in central Iran have fared since the revolution, and also
reports on their attitudes toward the new regime. Shahla
Haeri presents an overview of mut^{c}a [temporary marriage]
and discusses its revival under the present regime.
Yasmin Mossavar-Rahmani describes the efforts of the
leaders of the regime to encourage marriage and procreation. Cynthia Dwyer visited Iran during the hostage
crises and was jailed on charges of spying. She recounts
her observations about life inside Evin Prison in the
early days of the revolution. A brief epilogue sums up
the volume.

1
Women in Pre-Revolutionary Iran: A Historical Overview

Guity Nashat

In the twentieth century, the old traditions governing the lives of women in Iran (and in other Middle Eastern countries) gradually began to be transformed as women's perceptions of themselves and men's attitudes toward women changed. These transformations and the changes they affected were the result partly of increased contacts with the West and conscious efforts to imitate the West, and partly of changes within Iranian society generated by new economic and social conditions. To appreciate the depth and magnitude of the changes in women's lives, it is useful to examine briefly the traditional status and role of women.

The central feature of life for women was that the rules by which they lived were determined largely by men. Men set the standards of propriety for women's behavior, their role in society, and the kind of punishment meted out to women who did not abide by the social norms set for them. This was to some extent also true for women in other societies until recently, but only in Iran and the Middle East were the social norms so exclusively determined by men.

The male dominance of women was symbolized by the seclusion of women. Seclusion was enforced outside the house by the wearing of the veil, which insured and perpetuated the separation of the worlds of men and women. Despite their seclusion and their similar appearance from wearing the veil, all women did not have the same life style, as has sometimes been assumed. Their life styles differed radically and were determined by social class, locale, and geographic conditions. Social differences cut across geographical boundaries. Thus the life styles of the urban, rural, and tribal women varied more greatly than those of the women of various urban centers. Even the seclusion of a woman and the degree to which she observed the veil was much greater in urban areas than it was in the rural or tribal areas. Furthermore, despite the fact that women's activities were confined to the home, women were far from the victims they have been por-

trayed in many Western works in the past, or the idle
sexual objects of many Hollywood films.[1] To be sure, at
the two ends of the spectrum those types of women existed, but most women played useful roles within their
homes.

Despite the prevailing belief among many Muslims and
Westerners that women's seclusion was ordained by Islam,
this practice grew out of the social and economic conditions of the region rather than the early teachings of
the Islamic religion. The reason for this misconception
among both the Western critics of the practice and its
Muslim advocates is not difficult to understand. Because
Islam developed extensive laws to regulate the entire
life of the believer, it was easy to assume that laws
pertaining to women and their role in society also had
religious origins. However, closer inspection shows that
it was in large part the social conventions of the Sasanian and Byzantine empires, which adopted Islam later,
that influenced the position of women in Islamic law and
required their seclusion.

In Arabia, the birthplace of Islam, veiling and seclusion of women were not widely practiced in the early
decades of the seventh century when Islam was revealed.
Although settled life was known in the small oasis towns
of Mecca, Ta'if, and Yathrib (later named Medina in honor
or the Prophet), most Arabs led nomadic lives and lived
in tents. Hence, the requirement of the veil and the
seclusion of women were not compatible with their way of
life.[2] Women, even in the towns, enjoyed a degree of
freedom unknown in the more culturally developed Sasanian
and Byzantine empires, which had long-standing urban
traditions and complex agricultural economies. Women of
some Arabian communities could choose their husbands
and could divorce without being socially ostracized.
Women also participated in communal life. They accompanied the men on their raids, encouraging them from
behind the lines to exert their best efforts. Women took
care of the wounded, were in charge of the water and provisions, and occasionally put a captive wounded enemy to
death. In the only form of cultural activity enormously
popular among the Arabs, the art of poetry, some women
attained a high degree of excellence. Women's opinions
and criticism were also prized and taken seriously by
the men.[3] Nevertheless, women suffered from serious
drawbacks, the most important of which was the lack of
any laws delineating their role and position in the patriarchal society. Although some beautiful women were
praised highly by their suitors and admirers, many female
infants were buried alive at birth. The proper woman
married only one man,[4] whereas her husband could marry as
many women as he wished. Sometimes, the status of children was uncertain where there were multiple marriages.
Furthermore, a woman did not automatically enjoy freedom
of choice in marriage. It was normally her father or her

male guardian who decided for her, without her consent,
and he was entitled to the full bride price. Usually a
dead man's heir would inherit his wife or wives. The
heir could either marry such wives or exchange them with
another man in return for a different wife. Only those
women who went home to their tribes or clans before the
heir had disposed of them could decide their own destiny.[5]
Women who were divorced received no compensation, and they
did not inherit when they were widowed.

The teachings of Islam improved women's condition.
Women were granted economic, religious, and civil rights,
although in economic and civil areas their rights were not
equal to men's. Another important result of the Islamic
teachings was that the social foundation of society was
transformed from an emphasis on loyalty to the tribe to an
emphasis on fellowship in the general community of believers. Equally important was the emphasis placed on the
accountability of the individual rather than of the tribe
as a whole. Consequently, the emphasis shifted from the
tribe as the basic social unit to the family as the basic
unit of society. This meant that both men and women as
members of the unit and as individuals had more defined
rights and responsibilities. These developments are
reflected in the provisions of the Qur'an with regard to
marriage, divorce, inheritance, and the relationship of
men with women. In addition to stipulating that women had
a legal right to inherit from parents, spouse, children,
and siblings, the right of women to own and dispose of
their own property was strengthened. A woman did not need
her husband's permission to manage her own property; in
fact, he needed her permission to touch it. The law also
made the husband responsible for the wife's support. This
mitigated the apparent discrimination in inheritance--a
woman could inherit only half as much from her father as
her brothers could. So while the wife shared in the husband's wealth, he did not share in hers, except with her
permission. Also, the mahr [bride price] legally belonged
to her rather than to her father or guardian under Islamic
law. Even more important was the requirement that a woman
give her consent to her marriage. The law did not do away
with polygamy, but it limited the number of wives and improved the condition of women in polygamous households by
stipulating that each wife must be treated equally. If a
husband failed in any of these points, then the wife could
seek divorce. The husband was also required to pay for
the support of their children while they lived with her.[6]

Much evidence from early biographical or literary
sources indicates that women continued to participate in
the life of the community after the advent of Islam and
that women were not secluded. However, within two centuries the law books began to contain provisions requiring
the seclusion of women. What was the reason for such a
development?

Women in Pre-Islamic Iran

Although some aspects of the impact of the political
thought and artistic and intellectual heritage of the
older civilization on the rise and development of Islamic
civilization have received attention,[7] the influence of
these older cultures on other important areas has not been
sufficiently recognized. One area where continuity with
the pre-Islamic tradition of the region is strikingly
apparent is in the role of women in society and the attitude of society toward women. To fully appreciate this
continuity with pre-Islamic cultural attitudes toward
women, it is important to mention briefly women's condition in the territories conquered by early Arab Muslims
after the death of the Prophet in 632. I will concentrate
primarily on the Sasanian empire, both because the center
of the empire, later Iraq, became one of the major centers of legal development and because the Sasanians were
the forebears of the present-day Iranians. A more detailed account of women in pre-Islamic Iran must await further
study.

The fact that two women reigned briefly in the late
Sasanian period has led some modern Iranian historians to
assume that women in that empire enjoyed full political
and social rights.[8] However, Puran and Azarmidukht were
among twelve members of their dynasty who ascended the
throne during the chaotic four years between the assassination of Chosroes II, in 628, and the accession of the
last Sasanid king, Yazdgird III, in 632. Clearly, these
two women, like their brief-ruling male relatives, were
merely manipulated by various rival factions within the
court; they were used to advance one position or another
in the struggle for power. Therefore, their reigns were
not necessarily recognition of women's political rights:
rather it was the absence of more qualified candidates
that led to their choice.[9]

A closer examination of the existing sources suggests
that in the seventh century women occupied a servile position in society and enjoyed few rights or privileges.
Social rules and religious teachings demanded absolute
obedience of the woman to her husband. An important
religious work of the late Sasanian period stated, "those
[women] who practiced acquiescence and conformity, reverence and obedience to their husbands and lords" would be
rewarded with eternal salvation.[10] A woman was to regard
her husband as lord and sovereign over her.[11] Women who
showed the slightest sign of defiance, recalcitrance, or
disobedience were threatened with eternally "licking a hot
oven with their tongues, and having their hands perpetually burnt under an oven in hell."[12] Similar punishment
awaited women who refused the sexual demands of their
husbands.[13] In addition to being her husband's humble and
obedient servant, a woman's other major duty was child
care. Those who neglected this task were condemned to

everlasting hell fire. Women who neglected their own
children by being nursemaids to the children of others
would be punished in Hell by "ever dig[ging] a hill with
their breasts and by being kept perpetually thirsty and
hungry."14
   While social norms required of women total obedience
to their husbands and complete devotion to raising children, they do not seem to have rewarded women for their
obedience. Women were considered inferior to men. They
were said to lack wisdom, and men were told not to trust
any of their secrets to their wives. For this reason,
women's testimony in a court of law was not to be accepted. Another important religious text states that whereas
the duty of a man was to pray three times a day, the
prayer of a proper woman consisted of approaching her husband three times a day with folded hands and seeking to
know his will, to carry it out obediently.15
   The laws of marriage and divorce were designed for
men's convenience. Men could marry as many women as they
could afford, and the men of the ruling class were known
to have large harems, where women spent their lives, many
in idleness.16 Women, on the other hand, could marry
only one husband. Furthermore, divorced women were not
allowed to remarry while their former husbands lived.
However, the right to divorce seems to have been limited
to men.17
   Some type of veiling and segregation of women was
prevalent in Sasanian society. Upper class women were
veiled and secluded to protect them from the glances and
contact with commen men; it is not known to what extent
women in the lower strata of society observed the veil.18
   The role of women in Sasanian society had derived
from earlier practices in the region. A detailed discussion of the origins and development of their subordinate
position and seclusion is beyond the scope of this chap-
ter.19 Briefly, women's lower status seems to have been
caused by childbearing, which kept women tied to the home
while men's freedom from pregnancy and nursing allowed
them to develop their abilities as hunters and fighters.
Eventually, this greater mobility enabled men to play a
more important role in gathering food and in engaging in
agriculture. It also made it possible for men to allocate
to themselves a greater share of the products of society's
labor.20 This development occurred gradually and was by
no means uniform, and it was only after the rise and development of urban life that women could successfully be
confined to activities within the household.
   Side-by-side with the gradual seclusion of women,
certain attitudes and assumptions about women also began
to appear. Men's work began to be valued more than
women's work, and men began to be viewed as more intelligent than women. As the value of women's work outside the
house diminished, the home based activities began to be

regarded as more significant, and women's role as sexual
objects with a procreative role began to assume greater
importance. In turn, as individual and social wealth increased, the desire of individuals to insure their lineage
became important. With the development of urban areas, it
was less costly to confine women to the home because it
was not easy for urban women to combine childcare with
activities outside the home, whereas in rural areas it was
still possible for women to combine childcare with lighter farmwork. Women's confinement in the house also meant
that they were more dependent on men for their subsist-
ence. Consequently, men could more readily bring pressure
to bear on women and treat them as property.

Because men controlled the resources of society, they
could devise its moral code. Nowhere are these moral
values more strikingly indicative of the male bias and
convenience than in the laws that regulate sexuality and
the relationship between men and women. The importance of
lineage in the distribution of wealth and power gave rise
to requirements for the women's virginity before marriage
and their continued fidelity thereafter. Women who deviated were threatened with severe punishment in this life
and the next. Further to protect the purity of the male
line, women were required to stay home. Because these
requirements were reinforced by religious teaching, women
began to internalize these views and to judge themselves
by the standards set for them by men. These attitudes
toward women and the role they should play in society
developed in Mesopotamia over several millenia, and
spread from there to the rest of the region. Because they
had resulted from the particular social and economic
factors peculiar to the region, the rise and fall of
dynasties and the arrival of new groups to the region did
not fundamentally alter them. It was only in the late
nineteenth century, when socio-economic conditions altered
radically, that women's status and their role began to
show signs of transformation.

When the Sasanians (208-651 A.D.) came to power in
the region, these attitudes toward women were fairly well
established and survived the Sasanian downfall and the
arrival of the Arab Muslim conquerors. Because these
attitudes about women's inferiority were long-standing
and were reinforced by socio-economic peculiarities of the
region, the early, more liberal teachings of Islam and the
freer practices of the pre-Islamic Arabs could not easily
alter them. On the contrary, because the Arab conquerors
were much fewer in number and were culturally not as advanced as their subjects, the Arab's less rigid attitudes were easily overcome by the cultural attitudes of
their subjects. Furthermore, as the masses of population
outside of Arabia began to convert to Islam, they began
to interpret the teachings of Islam in a way that was compatible with their own preferences and prejudices. It was

in this manner that many of the earlier attitudes about
women reappeared in the religious law books in an Islamic
guise. For instance, a statement in a Sasanian religious
work which advised men not to entrust their secrets to
women was later attributed to the Prophet.

Women in the Middle-Islamic Period

Certain developments within Islamic society accelerated trends which encouraged the further seclusion of
women and offset the impact of the egalitarian teachings
of Islam. One of these developments was the expansion of
urban life in the early centuries of the Islamic period.
The spread of urban life, in turn, led to the confinement
of many more women within the house. The fact that slaves
were so plentiful that even the average family could own
one or two might have made it easier for the married
Muslim woman to avoid going out by making use of slave
girls for doing errands outside the house. Another factor
which probably encouraged the seclusion of women and helped spread the veil was the practice of the early Arab
conquerors of treating the conquered peoples as war booty.
It is likely that many families kept wives and young girls
at home or veiled them in public to keep them from being
taken by some of the Arabs, whose religious conviction in
Islam was at that time rudimentary.[21]

These social developments readily became a part of
Islamic law because they occured in the early centuries
of the Muslim era, when the law was being vigorously
developed. By the beginning of the tenth century, Muslim
jurists reached an unofficial consensus which regarded
the whole body of religious law, like the principles from
which it emanated, as immutable. Thus, the laws governing
women's activities and their role in society were held to
have been ordained by God. This sealed the fate of women
in Islamic society. Seclusion within the house and the
necessity of the veil began to be regarded as the hall-
marks of women's life in Islam; marriage and motherhood
were the quintessential manifestations of that way of
life. For centuries to come these requirements led to
complete separation of the worlds of men and women in
Islamic society, including Iran.

The triumph of norms demanding seclusion of women
rendered useless the opportunities Islam had provided to
them. Therefore, while there were no laws against women
engaging in trade, and, in fact, some women did, the
veil and seclusion impeded most women from seriously
pursuing careers. In education, an area where women
could have excelled, a few women were able to accomplish
a great deal, but these were the exceptions rather than
the rule.[22]

In addition to the biases that discouraged women
from participating in activities outside the home,
society also developed positive incentives that rewarded
women for marrying and raising children. Increasingly,

marriage came to represent a female rite of passage from
being a nonperson to being a person. The arrival of chil-
dren--especially boys--further enhanced a woman's status;
even in the absence of sons motherhood was insurance for
old age. These factors contribute to the high incidence
of marriage in the Middle East to this day.[23]

Although the veil and the seclusion of women were
at first urban phenomena, they gradually spread to the
countryside. It is difficult to say when they began to
be widely present in rural areas, but during the thirteenth century, when Ibn Battuta traveled from one extreme
corner of the Islamic world (Morocco) to the other
(China), the only unveiled women he encountered were the
Berber women in North Africa.[24] Unaccustomed to seeing
women in public, Ibn Battuta was surprised by the equality
and freedom women enjoyed among the non-Muslim Turkic
nomadic tribes. His surprise also indicates the spread
in the Islamic world of cultural biases which held women
inferior to men.

Other contemporary sources confirm the complete
separation of the social life of men and women by the
thirteenth century in the central lands of Islam, including the Iranian world. The great historian Rashid ud-Din
apologized to his readers for including an account of
awrat [women] in his history of the Mongols. He justified
this departure from the norm by explaining that the Mongols accord their women equal treatment.[25] The term he
used in references to women, however, was the same indirect term used in polite company to refer to male geni-
tals. By this time even the mention of a wife's name had
become tantamount to dishonoring her. Other terms that
were in use were za^{c}ifeh [the weak female] and manzil
[home].

The above comments also reveal the greater role
women played in the Turco-Mongol societies. We learn
from Rashid ud-Din's work that neither the gradual arrival
of the Turks beginning in the ninth century nor the massive invasion of the Mongols during the thirteenth century substantially changed the position of women in the
central lands of Islam, including Iran. On the contrary,
those Turks and Mongols who settled in towns adopted the
life style of the sedentary population. However, among
those groups which continued to live as nomads and roam
the large plains or the mountainous and hilly regions of
the central lands, women continued to be active in communal life even after their conversion to Islam. Furthermore, women of the Turko-Mongol ruling class retained
some of the higher status they had enjoyed during their
nomadic past. The fact that many of the dynasties that
came to power in Iran after the decline of the main Mongol dynasty, the Ilkahnids, were either of Turko-Mongol
origin or relied heavily on tribal support meant that the
contact between the ruling elite and their more nomadic
supporters never ceased, and the elite class was continu-

ally replenished with fresh nomadic recruits. Consequently, nomadic attitudes survived among the elite, albeit in
diluted form.

During the Safavid period (1501-1724) the present
Iranian state emerged. The imposition of Shi^Cism as the
state religion on the largely Sunni population of Iran by
Isma^Cil, the founder of the dynasty, was one of the important factors in creating a sense of loyalty to the
state among the diverse population. The introduction of
Shi^Cism also resulted in the incorporation of many popular folk beliefs into the tenets of Shi^Ci Islam.[26] In
this manner, attitudes and practices about women that had
seemed too alien to the spirit of Islam to be acceptable
to early jurists began to appear in Shi^Ci religious
works.

The works of the popular seventeenth century Shi^Cite
theologian Muhammad Baqir Majlisi (d. 1699) represents
the culmination of this development. As Amir and Adele
Ferdows point out in this volume, Majlisi elevated
obedience and subservience of the wife to her husband as
her main religious duty. However, similar statements in
religious works of the late Sasanian period, which preceded the time of the Prophet and the imams suggest that
these statements did not originate with the teachings of
Islam. Nevertheless, because Majlisi attributed his
statements and injunctions to the Prophet and the imams,
the attitudes they inculcated acquired much greater force
over the minds of men and women. Furthermore, to this
day, religious authorities use these same statements in
their arguments delineating the position of women.

Religious legitimization of women's servility does
not seem to have diminished the role played by the women
of the ruling class. Undoubtedly, the heavy reliance of
the Safavid Dynasty on Turkic tribal elements accounts
for the great influence women exerted in national affairs,
at least from time to time, at a period when the status
of urban women had reached its lowest ebb. One of the
notable examples of women who played an active role in
the Safavid state was Parikhan Khanum, the daughter of
Shah Tahmasb (1526-1576), the second ruler of the dynasty.
During her father's lifetime, "She was highly esteemed by
her royal father . . . and had great influence. Anyone
in great difficulties referred to her for advice and took
refuge in her. Her great intelligence and knowledge made
of her a consultant to the king."[27]

She played an active role in the struggles for the
throne that followed her father's death, and her support
for one of her brothers, Isma^Cil, was instrumental in his
success. It was also she who finally rid the country of
this troubled and ill-fated ruler when her influence over
him had waned. Her efforts to maintain her influence
over the new ruler, Muhammad Khudabandeh, caused his wife
to have Parikhan Khanum assassinated.[28]

This queen, Mahd-i Ulya, was a woman of great ability. She was made regent because of her husband's blindness and her sons' minority. During the two years of her
regency, her seal appeared on government decrees, and she
ran the affairs of the kingdom with great determination.
However, despite her great efficiency and courage, she
was unable to heal the rift that had occurred in the
Safavid empire after Tahmasb's death; she was engulfed in
the struggle between various powerful tribal factions and
was eventually assassinated. But her courage and
strength are revealed in her reaction to news that her
side had lost in the contest for power. When she learned
that the victors demanded that she either withdraw from
her role as regent or be killed, her husband expressed
willingness to abdicate to save her life. But she opposed such a step despite the danger to her life and
declared:

> As long as I live I will not change my ways and
> will not digress from what I pursued. If the
> Qizilbash [her opponents] out of impudence and
> lack of respect for the king, commit this crime
> against the wife of their sovereign and kill me,
> then I will defer judgement to the Almighty God.
> I am the mother of four young princes, and I
> will defer the revenge for my blood to them.[29]

Women in the Nineteenth Century

During the Qajar period (1794-1925) women played a
larger role in society and became more visible. Among
the ruling class women, this development can be partly
explained by the prevalence of strong tribal influence
on the dynasty. Several other factors also slowly began
to affect social attitudes toward women.

The most important factor was Iran's greater involvement with the West. Iran's initial contact was the result of a series of military defeats early in the nineteenth century. This was followed by steadily growing
civilian contacts. Iranians, particularly students and
diplomats, travelled to Europe, and Europeans came to
Iran. The greater exposure to Europe and Europeans made
Iranians aware of the decline of their country, resulting
in an uncritical admiration for European civilization and
its material achievements. Some Iranians, primarily the
secular members of the ruling and upper middle classes,
began to believe that Iran's salvation rested in emulating the West. They advocated adoption of Western military techniques and institutions, including opening
modern schools and teaching European languages.[30] Although these efforts during most of the nineteenth century were made sporadically and in piecemeal fashion,
they nevertheless brought about some changes in the life
style, attitudes, and beliefs of the social groups that
were affected by them. One of these changes was in the

treatment of women, which made them more visible. The
change can be detected in the mention of women in the
newer types of literary works that were being written
under Western impact. Whereas traditional chronicles
were reluctant to supply much detail about even royal
women, many of the newer writers began to supply detailed
information about women. For example, autobiographers
discussed their wives and other female relatives in their
books.

Furthermore, an increasing number of men became
advocates of modern education, either because they had
modern educations or because they could perceive its
benefits. They saw to it that their daughters as well
as their sons learned about the world beyond their
doorsteps. However, it was necessary to teach the girls
at home because there were no schools for them. It was
not until the twentieth century that there were schools
for girls. Although the girls who were thus educated
were relatively few in number, most of them became pioneers of modern education for women. Some of them later
wrote about their lives, so there are actual records of
what life was like for them.

Another source that furnishes useful information
about women is the works of European travelers to Iran.
Some of these travelers were women who wrote about their
observations of Iranian life; others were men who passed
on the insights into the lives of Iranian women they
received from their wives who accompanied them. These
European accounts, of course, must be approached with
caution since they are sometimes colored by value judge-
ments about the culture and especially about Islam.
Nevertheless, some of these provide information not
available elsewhere.

Some Iranian women learned about the West in a more
direct fashion than through education by meeting the
wives of the European diplomats and others who came to
Iran. Although the contacts between Iranian women and
European women were largely limited to members of the
royal family on one side and diplomats and aristocrats
on the other, there was some opportunity for interchange
of ideas. The account of Lady Sheil, wife of the British
Minister, reveals that Iranian women showed great curios-
ity about the life of women in Europe.[31] Although these
contacts were limited, and the number of Europeans in the
whole of Iran was very small, this channel was important
because the Iranian women who acquired knowledge of
European life were the trendsetters in their society,[32]
and, like the men, they wanted to emulate the European
way of life, which they believed to be superior.

Finally, we must mention a related development: the
expansion of European capitalism, which eventually caused
Iran to become integrated into the world market. Although Iran was not formally colonized, it nevertheless
felt the impact of this worldwide development. One

aspect which eventually touched the lives of women in
rural and tribal areas was the greater demand for agricultural products and handicrafts, particularly rugs. The
rising demand for textiles and rugs, which were primarily
produced by women, affected the women's life-style.
Although the precise nature of this effect has not been
fully studied, it is possible to make tentative suggestions. In all likelihood, women who produced for the
market did not enjoy the fruits of their labor directly
but as members of their families, which were made better
off by the increased income. Furthermore, their added
contribution to the market put a greater burden on them
than before since they continued their traditional roles
as mothers and wives. Nevertheless, their increased contributions may well have raised their power within the
family and lessened the degree of their seclusion.[33]

These changes did not begin to have a direct bearing
on the lives of women in general until the latter part of
the nineteenth century, but due to some of the other
developments discussed above we are able to construct a
much clearer picture of how women lived even before they
were directly affected by these changes.

Because of the strong tribal influence, the women of
the ruling class were allowed a greater role outside the
confines of the home. Fath-Ali Shah, the second Qajar
ruler (1797-1834), relied on his daughters: Khazin ud-
Dowleh was guardian of the crown jewels, Anis ud-Dowleh
took care of his important correspondence,[34] and Zia us-
Saltaneh was his most trusted advisor.[35]

The desire of some of the strong-willed royal women
to extend their authority beyond the harem sometimes
clashed with prevailing social mores which considered
household matters the only legitimate activities for
women. On occasion this conflict developed beyond the
persons directly involved and became a matter of concern
to the State. Since even the highly intelligent women
embroiled in these conflicts lacked sufficient exposure
to the outside world, they gave personal considerations
greater weight than matters affecting the country.

The life and activities of Malikjahan Khanum (1220-
1290/1805-1872), better known as Mahd-i Ulya exemplifies
the consequences of such subjectivity. Today she is
remembered and reviled for the role she played in the
removal and murder of the most popular nineteenth century
Iranian statesman, Amir Kabir. But as a female, she was
also a victim of prevailing conditions. Her correspondence reveals her intelligence and shrewdness. In 1234/
1821, at the age of sixteen, she was married to her
cousin Muhammad Mirza, the future king (1249-1264/1834-
1838), who was two years younger than she. Her son,
Nasir ud-Din, was not born until 1247/1832. Contemporary
historians mention the great antipathy her husband felt
toward her; this may have been the reason for the long
delay between her marriage and the birth of her son. It

may also explain, although not justify, her alleged in-
fidelities. But despite her husband's dislike of her,
she was able to insure the succession of her own son,
whose prospects were endangered by the son of a more
favored wife. She was also able to make her presence
felt during her husband's final years, when his ability
to govern was weakened by illness.

During the six critical weeks following her husband's
death, she maintained calm in the capital and in the nearby provinces, allowing her son time to reach the capital
from the city of Tabirz, where he had resided as crown
prince. When the young king arrived, however, he soon
banished his mother on the advice of his prime minister,
Amir Kabir; later she was forbidden most contact with the
outside world. Rumors circulated that Amir Kabir had
advised the king to kill her by faking an accident.
Although she was temporarily cast aside, she ultimately
succeeded in bringing about Amir's downfall and install-
ing her own candidate, Mirza Agha Khan Nuri, as prime
minister. Her success deprived the country of one of its
most able statesmen, and it helped bring to power a man
who was hesitant to be prime minister for fear of losing
British protection.[36]

Another influential royal woman was Fatimeh, better
known as Anis ud-Dowleh, whom Nasir ud-Din Shah married
in 1276/1859. She was a poor but attractive peasant girl
from a small village northeast of Tehran. She had come
to the harem as a servant of Jairan, the Shah's favorite
wife. After Jairan's death in the same year, Anis ud-
Dowleh began to rise in the Shah's favor. Despite keen
competition from other wives (who totalled 85 when Nasir
ud-Din was assassinated) she remained his favorite until
the end. She was the only wife who normally sat down to
meals with him, and she joined him at bedtime every night,
after he had spent an hour or two with this or that other
woman. She was also the only woman who could reprimand
the Shah publicly and who could assuage his anger.[37]
Because of her influence with the Shah, various individuals and groups appealed to her for aid. In 1873 she was
drawn into a struggle between two factions within the
court. Her siding with one group weakened the attempts
of Mirza Husain Khan Sipahsalar to pursue his reform policies. Her opposition and hostility to Mirza Husain Khan
was prompted by his advice to the Shah not to take Anis
ud-Dowleh on his European trip.[38]

But generally her efforts to intercede with the Shah
were motivated by desire to protect the unfortunate from
the vagaries of despotism, which could victimize even
those closest to the Shah. The workings of the system
and the way she attempted to help where she could are
exemplified in a letter she wrote to the Shah requesting
him not to remove his brother, Rukn ud-Dowleh, from the
governorship of Shiraz. "By God. I was very surprised,"
she wrote, "Rukn ud-Dowleh has been there a mere seven

months and he has suffered much financial hardship."
She then suggested that the Shah ask his brother to give
him an additional amount of tribute rather than try to
get that new amount by appointing a new governor. Her
concern, however, was not merely to protect Rukhn ud-
Dowleh, but the ultimate victims of the system, the population, who would have to bear the brunt of a more rapa-
cious individual. Therefore, she advised Nasir ud-Din to
retain his brother as governor, "This is how the poor
subject is exploited, and he is reduced to being a pauper.
After all the new governor does not pay the additional
amount [you are requesting] from his own pocket. It is
totally ungenerous. The poor [subjects] have had it
completely."[39] Anis ud-Dowleh's great influence is
revealed in the Shah's response, which he jotted on the
margin of her letter. It said, "Rukn ud-Dowleh remains
governor. We responded to his petition by telegram.
There is no more to be said."[40]

Nasir ud-Din Shah's remaining wives were not so
fortunate. Their way of life was more representative
of the life of women of their class. This ruler took
full advantage of the Shi^{c}ite religious sanction and had
four permanent and eighty-one temporary wives. All these
women lived within the inner section of the palace, in
the harem, cut off from the outside world by walls and
the watchful eyes of ninety eunuchs. The permanent wives
and the favorite temporary wives had apartments of their
own, but the other wives had to share apartments, sometimes even the same room. These wives had few domestic
responsibilities; twelve hundred employees, including
three hundred female slaves and a large number of domestic servants, cooks, and scullery maids took care of
their daily needs. They were also free of childcare
since the children were entrusted to wet nurses, nannies,
and tutors. The Shah's wives each received a monthly
allowance, which varied according to their rank, ranging
from 100 to 750 tumans per month. The favorite wife,
Anis ud-Dowleh, was assigned revenues from several dis-
tricts.[41]

The main energies of these women were spent in maintaining the interest of Nasir ud-Din Shah, who liked to
spend an hour of his leisure time with them after dinner
and choose one or two of them to keep him company at bedtime. Competition among the lesser wives to attract the
king's attention was keen, and some resorted to witch-
craft or other strategems to revive his interest. The
lesser wives also tried hard to find favor with the more
important wives. What they did with the remainder of
their time was aptly explained by one woman. "We do nothing but eat, sleep, and wonder what we will have for the
next meal."[42]

The interest of women only in idleness and conspicu-
ous consumption was not due to lack of training and education. An observer noted that:

Women of the higher classes frequently acquire
a knowledge of reading and writing, and of the
choice poetical works in their native language;
as well as the art of reading, though perhaps
not understanding, the Koran. In the royal
family, in particular, and among the ladies of
the tribe of Kajjar, these accomplishments are
so common that they themselves conduct their
correspondence without the customary aid of a
meerza, or secretary.[43]

Early marriage, often between ages nine and twelve
usually ended the education of most women; and the lack
of any opportunities for work outside the house discouraged those interested in learning from continuing their
education after marriage. A woman's life was centered
on marriage, and mothers prepared for their daughters'
marriages at birth. "To remain unwedded seems to a Persian woman a sin, a thwarting of the divine purpose of
her nature." After marriage, the concern of a woman, no
matter what her social class, was to maintain her husband's satisfaction. "She occupies the position of a
slave to man's pleasure and comfort, and aspires to
nothing more."[44] This message was drummed into girls
by their mothers from an early age. The price for those
who failed to secure a husband's total satisfaction was
high: a rival wife or even divorce. Both polygamy and
divorce were common in urban areas.

However, there were some exceptions. A small number
of well-to-do women used their privileged position to
increase their knowledge. Anis ud-Dowleh and a few other
royal wives took daily religious lessons; some of Nasir
ud-Din Shah's daughters became accomplished poets and
writers. The best known of these were Fakhr ud-Dowleh
and Taj us-Saltaneh. Fakhr ud-Dowleh wrote excellent
poetry and is credited with transcribing several popular
romances, including Amir Arsalan.[45] Taj us-Saltaneh, who
will be discussed in more detail below, wrote a memoir
remarkable for its frank criticism of conditions her own
father had helped create. But the most unusual woman of
nineteenth century Iran was Qurrat ul-Ain, the first
woman in the modern history of Iran to openly rebel
against the conventions of her time.

Fatimeh, better known as Qurrat ul-Ain, (1814-1852)
was born in Qazvin, to a family of ulama. Education was
relatively common among the middle class, especially in
the households of the ulama; she received her early education at home from her father before taking courses in
various branches of theology from other relatives. She
attained sufficient expertise in religious matters to be
able to participate in theological discussions with
religious authorities, to teach, and to write a treatise
on a religious subject. She married her cousin; they had
two sons and a daughter, all of whom she was forced to

abandon, along with the rest of her family, when she joined the Babi movement.

In 1844 Ali-Muhammad Bab (1819-1850) proclaimed himself the Bab [Gate] to the long-awaited twelfth imam and called for radical religious and social change. The Bab's advocacy of better treatment of women may have been an important reason for Qurrat ul-Ain's attraction to the new creed; she used the new movement to achieve her emancipation from the bonds imposed on her in the name of Islam. Thus she became the first Iranian woman in recent times to appear without the veil before the mixed audience gathered to hear her teach. A recent study suggests that she also played a leading role in the development of Babism.[46]

Her steadfast adherence to Babism ultimately resulted in her death. She was arrested and killed after an unsuccessful attempt in 1852 to assassinate the Shah. Before her death she had suffered from persecution not only as a Babi, but also as a woman who disregarded the conventions of her time, particularly for her refusal to wear the veil.

The efforts of Qurrat ul-Ain to improve the conditions of the women of her generation did not bring about any immediate change. Women continued to lead segregated social lives and to occupy subordinate positions. The separation of women from men was reinforced not only by veiling but even by the style of their dwellings. Their confinement to the home symbolized their subjugation to men. Houses were built with an inner courtyard [andarun] and an outer courtyard [birun]; these two parts were connected only by a corridor so that no strange male visiting the outer courtyard would see any of the women by accident. The men of the household had their midday meals either in the outer courtyard or in their shops and workplaces. Even when a husband ate at home, the wife did not eat with him; she waited on him.

Women were generally responsible for the activities that took place within the house, including management of the household's finances. The most time-consuming daily activity of the average household was preparation of meals. Women did not go to stores for provisions. Rich women sent their servants, and poor women bought what they needed from street vendors who went around the quarters from door to door.

Women, however, if properly attired in their all enveloping costumes, did go out to the bath, to the shrines of saints, or to the bazaar. Ironically, however, even their nearest relations could not recognize them when they were so dressed. Even young girls had to put on this costume when they went out. The requirement of complete covering of women was much stricter in Iranian cities than in either the Ottoman or Arab provinces.[47]

Women in rural areas or among the nomadic tribes were not required to cover themselves so completely. By the

mid-nineteenth century, rural women were seen unveiled in
the fields, working alongside the men. According to Lady
Sheil, "Their interests are identified with their husbands'; divorce is rare; and the number of wives does not
exceed one."[48]

In the last decade of the nineteenth century, the
forces discussed earlier exerted a slow but steady influence. At first only a handful of women were affected,
but gradually the lives of many women were touched. By
the end of Nasir ud-Din Shah's reign, a noticeable change
had occurred within the court and the elite class. Even
royal women enjoyed greater freedom of movement by the
end of this period. The practice of keeping a harem well
stocked with women went out of style; few men of the ruling class married more than two wives simultaneously.

The memoirs of Taj us-Saltaneh, a daughter of Nasir
ud-Din Shah, reflects this new trend. She was born in
1301/1884. Her education included the study of French,
and she read contemporary European novels. Unlike the
men of her class, she did not visit Europe personally,
but she idealized Europe and the European way of life.
She romanticized the lives of European women; it was
her opinion that "They [European women] are able to seek
their rights, defend themselves, and they demand the
franchise. They seek the right to participate in politics, and they have succeeded." Life for Iranian women,
in her view, was a prolonged and hopeless existence.
"They [Iranian women] are separated from humanity and
are classified along with wild beasts and savages."[49]

The beginnings of a change in women's perception of
themselves, their awareness of the world outside the
harem, and their frustration with their lifestyle are
reflected in the writing of this same woman. Discussing
the backward state of the country, she condemned the sel-
fish thoughtlessness of the men of her class and wistful-
ly conjectured that if women were allowed a greater role
in society, the country would benefit because women like
her would not sell the country's resources to foreign
powers but instead would develop its goods and its trade,
improve its agriculture, and increase the cultivable
land. She concluded, "As a result, I would have benefitted and lived comfortable without resorting to stealing,
and the people would have benefitted from [my] services
and efforts.[50]

Women in the Twentieth Century

Taj us-Saltaneh and like-minded women were able to
vent their frustrations by playing an active role in the
civil war which broke out after the ratification of the
Constitution on 30 December, 1906. The country acquired
its constitution without much bloodshed, but the death
of the mild-tempered Muzaffar ud-Din Shah five days after
ratification of the document suddenly changed the picture.
The new king, Muhammad-Ali, had made no secret of his

aversion to a constitutional government. He lost no
time in exerting pressure on the members of the new
parliament to bring about the demise of the Constitution.
During the next four years the fate of the Constitution
seemed uncertain. It was during these critical years
that a small but dedicated group of women, mainly from
upper and upper-middle-class families, including daughters and wives of several prominent ulama, became actively involved on the side of the Constitutionalists. They
compensated for their small numbers by their vigor.
Using their veils as protection, they acted as couriers
for transfer of messages and arms between various revolutionary hideouts. They formed several secret societies
for enlightening their fellow women and for generating
more support for the Constitution. The two most important societies were the Women's Freedom Movement [Anju-
man-i Azadi-yi Zanan] and the National Ladies Society
[Anjuman-i Mukhadarat-i Vatan]. Each society had a membership of about sixty women.
     The most dramatic event of the four-year struggle
was the women's response to the Russian ultimatum of 29
November, 1911--a threat to invade Iran if it rejected
Russia's terms. The Russian government had taken advantage of the Constitutional crisis to enhance its political influence in Iran by supporting the king's effort to
crush the Constitution. When it became apparent that the
king had lost his struggle, the Russian government presented the Parliament with demands which were in clear
violation of Iran's integrity, but which Iran was not
strong enough to turn down. The aim of the Russian
government was to discredit and weaken the Iranian Parliament. When the ultimatum was scheduled to be discussed
in Parliament, the National Ladies Society called for a
public meeting outside the house of Parliament. Thousands of veiled women responded. One woman activist
ascended a rostrum and recited a poem in which she
reprimanded the men for being "unworthy sons of our
fathers," and reminded them that "death is better than
life without honor." Finally, she enjoined the men and
women not to fear Russia, but

        Let us fight like lions, like heroes
        Let us adorn this age with repute.[51]

     Following her recitation, the crowd began to chant,
"independence or death." Later, several hundred women
marched into the public galleries and threatened to shoot
any deputy who would acquiesce to the Russian ultimatum
with pistols they had hidden under their veils.[52]
     The Parliament had no choice but to comply with the
terms of the ultimatum to avert the threat of Russian
invasion, but subsequent events inside and outside of the
country safeguarded Iran's territorial integrity. However, the women activists were not so fortunate. Their
efforts and sacrifices did not win them any immediate

returns or the gratitude of their contemporaries. The
climate of opinion within the country toward women's
activities outside the house was so hostile that even the
mere mention of franchise for women by a sympathetic
deputy caused an uproar in the Parliament. Calm was
restored only after the unfortunate man had been thrown
out of the session.[53] This same general hostility toward
the activists prevailed among the general masses of men
and women, who considered the women activists "immoral,"
"wanton," "Babi," or even "apostates."

However, in the long run these efforts were not
completely wasted. They created much greater awareness
among a small but growing number of families of the need
to educate their daughters. Secularly-oriented male
writers and intellectuals began to espouse the cause of
women's education; they decried the attitudes which considered women inferior and their education a waste. Many
of these men argued that ignorant mothers could only
bring up ignorant sons, and the only way to improve the
country and arrest its decline was to educate its women,
i.e., its future mothers.[54]

Many of the women activists also had reached this
conclusion, realizing that the greatest obstacle to
removing the injustices from which women suffered was
their own ignorance, which caused them to be hostile to
those who tried to improve their lot. The activists
devoted their energies to enlightening Iranian women.
They began their effort by opening schools for upper-middle-class and middle-class students. They hoped a good
education would teach the younger generation of women to
use their minds and not waste their intelligence in the
pursuit of men. Moreover, education would enable these
women to become useful members of society and would provide future recruits for the women's movement.[55]

Until the Constitutional period, the only modern
schools for girls were those opened by American mission-
aries in Riza'iyeh in 1835 and in Tehran in 1875. The
government had stipulated that no Muslim girls be allowed
to enter these schools, which accordingly admitted only
students from Christian backgrounds. By the 1890s, a
handful of Muslim girls had quietly been enrolled in the
missionary schools. The first school devoted to the
education of Muslim girls was a school opened in 1906 by
Mr. Richard, an Iranian of French origin, who taught
at Dar-ul-Funun. Another pioneer of women's education
was Mrs. Tuba Azmudeh, who founded the Namus School in
1907. Another Constitutionalist, Mrs. Safiyeh Yazdi,
opened Iffatiyeh soon thereafter. Although the founders
of these schools were Muslims, and there was a great
emphasis on religious teaching in their curricula, the
women were invariably harassed and intimidated by various
religious figures. The religious authorities denounced
the founders of the schools in sermons and incited the
populace to attack the teachers and students and to des-

troy the school buildings. These schools were regarded
as a means of "luring Muslim girls and leading their
minds astray and turning them into unbelievers and wan-
tons by pretending to give them lessons."[56]

Because of this religious hostility, the founders of
these schools were subjected to severe harassment and
persecution even if they came from prominent religious
families. Shortly after the first school for girls in
Isfahan was founded in 1917, its principle, Mrs. Badr-
uduja Dirakhshan, was arrested, beaten by the authorities,
and imprisoned for three months. She was released only
after her family promised not to allow her to reopen the
school. The founder of the school, Sadiqeh Dowlatabadi,
was forced to leave the city. Mrs. Safiyeh Yazdi, the
founder of Iffatiyeh school, was the wife of Shaikh
Muhammad Husain Yazdi, a leading religious authority and
an active Constitutionalist; she was repeatedly harassed,
despite her husband's support of her endeavor.[37]

Sometimes these dedicated women were harassed by
members of their own families, as was the case of Mrs.
Mahrukh Gowharshinas, the founder of the Taraqqi school
in 1911. This was a secondary school, and the founder
took pains to insure that bright girls from poorer families gained admission. However, she had to keep this
activity from her husband, who was opposed to her progressive ideas. When he found out her secret, he beat
himself on the head, saying, "How shall I reply to your
father in the next world when he asks why I did not
restrain the daughter he had entrusted to me from carrying on a sinful anti-religious activity and thus ruining
his respectability?"[58]

Until the outbreak of World War I, these and a few
other schools that were opened in Tehran, Shiraz and
Isfahan were the only schools available to girls. The
efforts of these courageous women paid off, however, and
by 1918 the idea of modern education for girls was
generally accepted. The first public school for girls
opened in 1918, and gradually many of the early private
schools were incorporated into the Ministry of Education.

Publication of newspapers and periodicals was another method undertaken by the women activists to enlighten women, to combat superstition, and to enlarge
the horizons of Iranian women. One of the earliest publications, Shukufeh [Blossom], declared its aim in the
following manner: "This is a newspaper dealing with
literature, morality, health, children, and housekeeping.
Its philosophy is to enlighten the young misses and to
purify the character of the ladies and to inform them
about education of women."[59] The various publications
were usually short-lived but exceedingly popular; most
students and young urban women subscribed to them. The
most important one was Zaban-i Zanan [The Women's Voice],
founded by Sadiqeh Dowlatabadi in 1918.

Mrs. Dowlatabadi was one of the leading women acti-

vists; she devoted herself to improving the rights of
women until her death in 1967. This courageous woman was
born into a prominent ulama family in Isfahan. Her
strong character and will enabled her to overcome many
obstacles and hardships resulting from her attempts to
improve the condition of women. She was able to free
herself from a marriage that her family had arranged for
her when she was sixteen, so that she could devote herself to her cause. She began publication of Zaban-i
Zanan in 1918 in Isfahan, where she had also founded the
first modern school for Muslim girls. However, her
efforts to rally the women and the founding of the school
aroused the hostility of a large number of religious
fanatics, and she was forced to move to Tehran. She
was one of the first Iranian women to study at a European
university; she studied educational psychology in Paris
in the 1920s. When she returned to Iran in 1927, she
often appeared in public, especially in the northern
section of Tehran, without her veil, another daring step.

Sadiqeh Dowlatabadi was active in organizing various
formal and informal gatherings for women for the purpose
of enlightening them. Organization of this type of meeting by women had begun during the Constitutional Revolution. One of the earliest societies for women was
organized by Mrs. Muhtaram Iskandari, a Qajar princess
married to one of the leading socialists of the time,
Sulaiman Iskandari. The organization of societies and
meetings for women was interrupted by World War I. Despite its neutrality, Iran was invaded by the armies of
various countries, and its society and economy were
severely disrupted. At the end of the war the country
was plunged into anarchy and chaos; various separatist
movements in Azerbaijan, Gilan, Khurasan, Kurdistan, and
Khuzistan threatened its survival. The fear of the
country's disintegration prepared the people for the
coup d'etat of February, 1921, which brought Riza Khan
to power. By 1925, Parliament proclaimed Riza Kahn king;
thus began the reign of the Pahlavi Dynasty. After con-
solidating his political control, Riza Shah initiated a
series of reforms aimed at creating a strong central
government free of clerical, nomadic, and foreign control,
characterized by European-style institutions and life
style, including activity for women outside the home.[61]

Some of the policies enacted by Riza Shah helped
attain the goals that women activists had set for themselves. The spread of public education for girls is a
case in point. Although the Constitution had enshrined
the principle of public education for girls in 1907, the
first public school for girls did not open until 1918.
It was only after Riza Shah had consolidated his power
that the law began to be seriously implemented. The
opening of an increasing number of secondary schools
paved the way for women to enter the newly-formed Tehran
University in 1935 as well as enabling them to take at

least token jobs in government service.

The rise in standards of hygiene benefitted women as did the reform of the judicial system and civil code. The age of marriage for girls was raised to fifteen and for boys to eighteen, and registration of all marriages was required. These were important steps in reducing child marriage. It also made the practice of mut^{c}a [temporary marriage], popularly referred to as sigheh, much more difficult. This latter practice, discussed in detail elsewhere in this volume, allowed the marriage of adult men to girls, sometimes as young as nine years of age, for brief periods. Often, poor families would offer their young daughters to rich older men in return for money. To many women activists and educated men this was the worst type of abuse and exploitation of women. However, since Shi^{c}i religious law recognized this practice, parents could not perceive the harm it would cause their young daughters. Although the civil code did not ban this practice, the registration requirement and the fact that only permanent marriage was recognized as legitimate made it more difficult for men to contract a mut^{c}a relationship. Consequently, mut^{c}a began to be regarded as a shameful type of relationship by many lower class families and acquired a status not too far from prostitution.

The step that was hailed by many educated women as freedom from oppression, however, was the abolition of the veil. To many women activists and their male supporters, the veil was the principle cause of women's backwardness and the symbol of their subjugation. Many leading poets and intellectuals, such as Iraj, Arif, and Ishqi, had denounced wearing of the veil in their poetry and writing. Some upper-middle class women had begun to appear unveiled in private gatherings. In the late 1920s, several leading women activists, such as Mrs. Sadiqeh Dowlatabadi and Shams ul-Muluk Javahirkalam, stopped wearing the veil in public. Some of these women taught in girls schools; they encouraged their students to cast off their veils also. However, resistance to unveiled women was strong, and women who dared take off their veils in the north parts of Tehran had to put them back on when they went to the southern parts.

It was after his visit to Turkey in June, 1934 that Riza Shah decided to abolish the veil in Iran; however, he did not issue the proclamation until February 1, 1936. Although he had already assumed full dictatorial power, the unveiling plan was unfolded with caution, and steps were taken to prepare the public. During the interval, newspaper articles discussed the disadvantages of the veil and praised its disappearance in other Muslim countries. The newly-founded Tehran University began admitting women students during this time. A small group of women, mainly high school teachers, were commanded by Riza Shah to organize the Ladies Center (Kanun-i Banuvan), a social and cultural organization which held lectures at which both men and women were present, held exhibitions of various types, and sponsored sports events for women. Mrs. Tarbiat, the leading woman activist, was chosen president of the center, which acted as a vanguard for the coming unveiling. Many of the lecturers recommended to the audience that women cast off their veils; women were encouraged not to wear veils while attending the meetings. Police protection was given to those who did cast off their veils, since unveiled women were usually harassed verbally and even physically outside the confines of the Center building, not only by men, but often by veiled women.[62]

As rumors about the impending government decision to ban the veil circulated, signs of unrest surfaced. Demonstrations broke out in Tabriz but were so quickly and ruthlessly put down that public opposition subsided. The women activists hailed the proclamation of unveiling as a major turning point in the life of Iranian women. Parvin I[c]tisami, the leading woman poet, wrote a poem commemorating the event, likening the lives of women under the veil to being held in a cage and calling the veil the primary cause of women's ignorance. She proclaimed that the abolition of the veil "gave the women of Iran a chance to live."[63]

However, the number of women sharing this feeling of liberation was quite small; primarily they were educated women of the upper and middle classes, mainly in Tehran and a few other major cities. For the majority of Iranian women, removal of the veil meant committing a major sin and disgrace. For these women the veil was not a symbol of backwardness, as the educated women proclaimed, but a sign of propriety and a means of protection against the menacing eyes of male strangers. Many of these women subsequently chose to stay home rather than risk having their veils pulled off by police, who had orders to treat harshly any woman who dared go out wearing anything other than a European style hat or hatless. Even wearing a scarf was not permitted. It is not surprising then that after Riza Shah's abdication in 1941 this law was abandoned and many women resumed wearing the veil.

The forcible banning of the veil was a typical example of many of the reforms enacted. A recent observation on Riza Shah's policies[64] also holds true for his policies for women: while they accomplished some limited objectives, they suffered from serious drawbacks as well. For example, the ban made it possible for a small group of women to cast aside the veil, but the majority had to be harshly forced to do so. Therefore, it created a great deal of resentment among most women and made them suspicious of reform and modern ideas.

More importantly, the force and repression that accompanied the enactment of his policies hurt the cause of women's advance because it stifled the development of

a political culture and experience among women. The fate
of the Patriotic Women's League illustrates this point.
The League was formed in 1922 by a group of women with
socialist tendencies who had been active in the Constitutional Revolution. Through its founder, Muhtaram Iskandari, the wife of Sulaiman Iskandari, the leader of the
Socialist Party, the women's league was affiliated with
the Socialist Party, which had resumed its activities in
the 1920s. Riza Shah used the various political groups
at the beginning of his rise to power to consolidate his
hold over the political system. However, once he had
established firm control, he began to eliminate and dis-
band any groups with any semblance of independence. Although the aim of the Women's League was merely to
"emphasize respect for the laws and rituals of Islam, to
promote the education and moral upbringing of girls, to
encourage national industries, to spread literacy among
adult women, to provide care for orphaned girls, etc.,"[65]
it was not allowed to survive and was closed in 1932.
Its successor, the Ladies Center, which was formed in
1935, came into existence by fiat, and even then it
could only tread the thin line defined for it by the
government. Therefore, no personal or group initiative
could develop under such artificial circumstances.
    Although the policies of Riza Shah helped a small
group of women, they failed to win the support of the
majority of women because they were not in step with the
needs and realities of Iranian society at that time. The
absence of social and economic conditions that could support those policies ensured that once force was removed
they would be abandoned. After Riza Shah's abdication in
1941, a backlash set in and almost destroyed the meager
gains made by women during the previous few decades.
    The backlash was led by the religious authorities,
who had lost much of their power and prestige during the
reign of Riza Shah. The ulama were concerned with
reasserting their control over society by "what may be
termed Shi'i public morality and culture."[66] One of the
quickest and most obvious ways of reassertion was the
restoration of the veil. But the repeal of the ban on
the veil was not even necessary--many women in urban
centers, including Tehran, seemed to be more than willing
to answer the call of the ulama to resume the veil. However, the veil that reappeared was lighter and less cum-
bersome than the all-enveloping shroud and face mask of
previous years. As a result of the ulama's opposition to
the education of women, a number of schools for girls in
provincial towns and the capital were closed down on
minor pretexts.[67] The religious authorities also launched a campaign to close down the remaining schools.[68]
    Despite the ulama's success in regaining much of
their lost power, they were not fully able to reverse the
clock for women. In fact, several forces set in motion
in Iranian society helped accelerate the attainment of

the goals the early feminists of the Constitutional period had set for themselves. These were the political freedom and the flowering of political activity that resulted
from the lifting of severe censorship of Riza Shah's
period and the rapid socio-economic development of the
late 1950s, 1960s, and 1970s.

     The factor that immediately counterbalanced the
effort of the religious authorities to completely push
the women back into the home was the atmosphere of freedom that replaced the total censorship of Riza Shah following his abdication. The communist Tudeh party launched the most consistent campaign advocating women's rights
and was the most successful in attracting students, teachers, and modern, educated women to its ranks. Some of
the earlier women activists joined the ranks of the Tudeh
party and, in cooperation with some of the newer recruits
and sympathizers, formed the Society for Democratic Women
in 1949. The group published a journal, Bidari-yi Ma
[Our Awakening]. The Society campaigned for extension of
suffrage to women, and it encouraged creation of educational clubs for women, equal pay for equal work, and
expansion of public education for girls.[69] It was also
the Society of Democratic Women which demanded the extension of suffrage to women in 1952 on the 45th anniversary of the Constitutional Revolution. The party was
able to collect 100,000 signatures for the extension of
the vote to women. The Constitutional amendment was discussed in Parliament, but the prime minister, Dr. Muhammad
Musaddiq, had to withdraw the bill under pressure from
religious authorities.[70]

     After the CIA-inspired coup d'etat of August, 1953,
and the overthrow of the government of Premier Muhammad
Mussadiq, much of the previous decade's political freedom
was curtailed. Meanwhile, Muhammed Riza Shah began to
rule with increased authoritarianism. Although this
development put an end to the Tudeh and other opposition
parties and their affiliate organizations, including the
Society for Democratic Women, it did not destroy the
aspiration of many women who had been active in or had
supported the campaign for women's rights. Furthermore,
the rise of the new authoritarianism adversely affected
the ulama's power and prestige for the rest of the decade,
silencing the main group opposing suffrage to women, at
least temporarily. This provided a favorable climate in
which individuals and small groups of women could step up
their efforts to improve women's rights. Many of the
older pioneers of the women's movement, such as Mrs.
Sadiqeh Dowlatabadi, Muhajir Tarbiat, Badr ul-Muluk Bamdad, Shams ul-Muluk Musahab, Dr. Mihrangiz Manuchihrian,
Farrukhru Parsa, and Batul Sami^ci, devoted their full
time to this effort.

     These women founded two major women's organizations,
The Women's Party [Hizb-i Zanan] and the Women's League,
later renamed The Women's League of Supporters of Human

Rights; both organizations were actively involved in
working for women's rights. The ceaseless campaign of
many of the older women and younger recruits--hundreds of
women professionals, teachers, and students--was instrumental in having suffrage for women included as one of
the six points of the White Revolution. Later, the
regime of the Shah tried to claim all the credit for the
extension of the right to vote to women. It is doubtful
that without the support of the regime in the face of
the mounting opposition of the religious authorities, the
franchise for women would have been enacted into law.
But, above all, it was the tireless effort of hundreds of
committed women for more than fifty years that finally
brought about the passage of this law.

This same tireless dedication was responsible for
bringing about the passage of the Family Protection Law
in 1967 and its amendment in 1973. Many critics have
repeatedly underestimated and underrated the significance
of the passage of these two laws in improving the status
of women. The extension of franchise has been dismissed
as merely giving men an additional vote. Others have
criticized the Family Protection Law as insufficient and
mere window dressing. Although the arguments contain
some truth, they nevertheless miss an important point.
The first group fails to recognize that the extension of
the franchise to women was an important and fundamental
departure from the traditional view of women as a man's
possession. It is recognition, at least on paper, of the
personhood of women and of their equality with men in
national and political matters. The second group of
critics fail to recognize that many hundreds of women had
been pressing for the passage of laws similar to those
passed in the Family Protection Law. Although the Act
did not do away entirely with all the injustices perpe-
trated against women in Iranian society, it was an important first step. While the law did not give equal
rights to women in divorce and polygamy, it made it harder
for a man to desert his wife and children or to use the
threat of divorce and loss of custody of their children
as a perpetual threat over his wife's head. The law was
slow to gain national acceptance, but as some of the
chapters in this volume indicate, information about
the Family Protection Law was beginning to reach even the
most remote areas of the country.[71] Given time and the
opportunity, the law could have benefitted women all over
Iran.

Two related developments reinforced these legal
gains in the status of women. The accelerated rate of
economic development caused by the increased oil revenues
following the nationalization of the oil industry began
to create radical changes in the Iranian economy. Although in some ways the changes increased social inequality, and much of the resulting capital was squandered, all
segments of society were affected by it. The introduc-

tion of large amounts of capital created many more jobs,
and this in turn provided employment opportunities for
qualified women, from factory workers to top level professionals. As greater numbers of women entered the work
force, the social mores against women's involvement in
activities outside the home began to change. Many men
discovered that women could be as efficient and productive
as members of their own sex. By the end of the seventies,
some women engineers could claim that men no longer looked
at the sex of the person doing a particular job but at how
well it was done.[72]
    The increase in the country's revenue and the avail-
ability of jobs also had an impact on the education of
women. Although the rate of the G.N.P. spent on education was insufficient (about 4.5 percent in the 1970s),
both the quality and quantity of women's education improved. Some of the benefits of the increased spending
could be seen in the rise in the level of literacy among
women in urban areas, which reached 46 percent, and in
rural areas, where it reached 18 percent. However, even
more important for women and their future role in society
was that the increased opportunities for women's employment helped overcome the reluctance of many families to
permit their daughters to receive higher education. Consequently, many young women from more traditional families entered secondary schools and even universities.
    It would be safe, then, to state that during the
twentieth century, especially during the last two decades
before the revolution, the attitude of Iranian society
toward its women underwent a slow but fundamental change.
The change affected women in the urban centers more than
those in the rural areas; it affected those who adopted
a Western style of life and those who led more traditional
styles of life. It was manifested in the options that
were available to women. Marriage was still the ultimate
goal, but working outside the home and alongside men,
before and even after marriage, became acceptable in many
families. Just as important was the increasing recognition that women could play useful social roles outside
their homes without compromising the time-honored traditions of society.
    The participation of women--both the young, politi-
cally active and the traditional--in the massive demonstrations against the Shah's regime in the final months
of 1978 and early months of 1979 is testimony to the new
consciousness among women that their role did not have to
be confined to activities within the house and that being
out there on the streets beside the men was also their
duty as Muslims and as Iranians.

NOTES

    1. For a typical Western view, see Dr. and Mrs.
Samuel M. Zwemer, Moslem Women (West Medford: The Central

32

Committee on the United Study of Foreign Missions, 1926),
p. 5. For the Muslim view, see Abul-Ala al-Mawdudi,
Purdah and the Status of Women in Islam (Lahore: Islamic
Publications Ltd., 1972).
    2. V.R. and L. Beran Jones, Women in Islam (Lucknow:
The Lucknow Publishing House, 1941), p. 8.
    3. B. Bizergan and E. Fernea, eds., Middle Eastern
Women Speak (Austin: University of Texas Press, 1976),
pp. 3-4.
    4. In some forms of marriage, a woman could marry
more than one man. The limit was ten, but the practice
seems to have been uncommon in the seventh century.
    5. Jones, Women in Islam, pp. 23-24.
    6. For more on the status of women in Islam, see the
chapter by Fazlur Raman in this volume.
    7. For a comprehensive account, see Marshall S.G.
Hodgson, The Venture of Islam (Chicago: University of
Chicago Press, 1974), pp. 103-147.
    8. Badr al-Moluk Bamdad, From Darkness into Light:
Women's Emancipation in Iran, F.R.C. Bagley, trans.
(Hicksville, N.Y.: Exposition Press, 1977), p. 7;
Ghulamriza Isfahanpur, Qudrat va Maqam-i Zan dar Tarikh
[The Power and Status of Women in History] (Tehran, 1346/
1967), pp. 53-62.
    9. R. Girshman, Iran from the Earliest Times to the
Islamic Conquest (New York: Penguin Books, 1978), p. 308.
    10. Martin Haug and E.W. West, trans., The Book of
Arda Viraf (Bombay: Government Central Book Depot, 1872),
p. 162.
    11. Haug, Arda Viraf, p. 162.
    12. Haug, Arda Viraf, p. 187.
    13. Haug, Arda Viraf, pp. 187, 191.
    14. Haug, Arda Viraf, p. 200.
    15. Haug, Arda Viraf, p. 59.
    16. Girshman, Iran, p. 302.
    17. Farrukhru Parsay, Huma Ahi, and Malikeh Taliqani,
Zan dar Iran-i Bastan [Women in Ancient Iran] (Tehran:
Uffsit Press, 1346/1977), pp. 123-55.
    18. Parsay, Zan dar Iran, pp. 123-55.
    19. For a brief and excellent account, see Lois Beck
and Nikkie Keddi, eds., Women in the Muslim World (Cambridge: Harvard University Press, 1978), especially pp.
21-24. Much of the discussion would also be true for
Iran.
    20. Beck and Keddie, Women. See fn. 19.
    21. Hodgson, Venture of Islam, I, p. 198-99.
    22. I.C. Dengler, "Turkish Women in the Ottoman Em-
pire: The Classical Age," in Beck and Keddie, Women, p. 233.
    23. N.H. Youssef, "The Status and Fertility Patterns
of Muslim Women," in Beck and Keddie, Women, pp. 69-100.
    24. Abu Abd-Allah Muhammad Ibn Battuta, Rihlat Ibn
Battuta [Travels of Ibn Battuta], Ali A. al-Kattani, ed.
(Beirut: 1395H/1977], Vol. 1, p. 365; Vol. II, p. 777.
    25. Shirin Bayani, Zan dar Asr-i Mughul [Women in the

Mongol Period] (Tehran: Tehran University Press, 1352/
1973), p. 78; Rashīd ud-Dīn Fazullāh, Jāmi[c] ul-Tavārīkh
[The Collection of Histories](Tehran: Iqbāl Co., 1338/
1959), p. I, 133.

26. For the developments of Shi[c]i Islam in the Safavid period, and incorporation of popular belief, see Said
Amir Arjomand, "Shi[c]ism, Political Organization and Societal Change in Pre-Modern Iran: 1338-1850," Ph.D. dissertation, University of Chicago, 1980, pp. 141-44.

27. Iskandar Munshī, Alam Arā-yi Abbāsī [Universal
History of Abbas] (Tehran: Amir Kabir Press, 1334/1955),
p. 135.

28. Munshī, Alam Arā, pp. 226-27.

29. Munshi, Alam Arā, pp. 226-250.

30. For an account of these reforms, see Hafiz Far-
mayan, "The Forces of Modernization in Nineteenth Century
Iran," in W.R. Pork and R. Chambers, eds., Beginnings of
Modernization in the Middle East (Chicago: University of
Chicago Press, 1968).

31. Lady Sheil, Glimpses of Life and Manners in
Persia (London: John Murray, 1856), pp. 130-33, 204.

32. Dust[c]ali Mu[c]ayyir ul-Mamalik, Yāddāshthā'i az
Zindigānī-yi Khusūsī-yi Nasir ud-Dīn Shāh [Notes on Nasir
ud-Dīn Shah's Private Life] (Tehran: Ilmi Co., n.d.) p. 44.

33. For different interpretations of the impact of
the integration of Iran into the world market in the
nineteenth century, see A. Ashraf and H. Hekmat, "Mer-
chants and Artisans and the Developmental Process of
Nineteenth Century Iran," and V. Nowshirrvani, "The
Beginnings of Commercial Agriculture in Iran," in A.L.
Udovitch, ed., The Islamic Middle East, 1700-1900 (Princeton: The Darwin Press, 1981); Guity Nashat, "From Bazaar
to Market: Foreign Trade and Economic Development in
Nineteenth Century Iran," in Iranian Studies XIV (nos.
1-2, 1981):

34. Ahmad Mīrzā Azd ud-Dowleh, Tārīkh-ī Azudī [The
Azudi History] (Tehran: n.d.), p. 12.

35. M. Bāmdād, Sharh-i Hal-i Rijāl Irān dar Qarn-i
Davāzdah, Sīzdah, va Chahārdah-i Hijrī [Biographies of
Iranian Statesmen in the Twelvth, Thirteenth, and Fourteenth Centuries of the Hijra (Tehran: Zavvār Co., 1347/
1968), pp. IV, 51-77.

36. F. Adamīyat, Amīr Kabīr va Irān [Amir Kabir and
Iran] (Tehran: Khawārazmī Publishing Co., 1348/1957), pp.
658-65; Bāmdād, Sharh-i Hāl, IV, 326-28; Mu[c]ayyir ul-
Mamalik, Nāsir ud-Dīn Shah, pp. 172-76.

37. Muhammad Hasan Khan I[c]timād us-Saltaneh, Rūznāmeh-
yi Khātirāt-i I[c]timād us-Saltaneh [Memoirs of I[c]timād us-
Saltaneh] (Tehran: Amīr Kabīr Co., 1345/1966), pp. 123-26.

38. Guity Nashat, The Beginnings of Modern Reform in
Iran, 1870-1880 (Urbana: University of Illinois Press,
1982), pp. 91-93.

39. Bāmdād, Sharh-i Hāl, p. III, 315.

34

40. Bāmdād, Sharh-i Hāl, pp. III, 315.
41. For a detailed and vivid account of life behind the harem walls, see Muᶜayyir ul-Mamālik, Nāsir ud-Dīn Shāh, especially pages 10-51.
42. Rev. S.G. Wilson, Persian Life and Customs (Chicago: Student Missionary Campaign, 1895), p. 259.
43. Sheil, Glimpses of Life, p. 146.
44. Wilson, Persian Life, pp. 257-61.
45. Muᶜayyir ul-Mamālik, Nasir ud-Din Shah, pp. 32-36.
46. Mangol Bayat, Mysticism and Dissent: Socio-religious Thought in Qajar Iran (Syracuse: University of Syracuse Press, 1902), pp. 90-91, 113-16.
47. Wilson, Persian Life, p. 257.
48. Sheil, Glimpses of Life, p. 144.
49. F. Adamīyat and H. Nātiq, Afkār-i Ijtimāᶜī va Sīyāsī va Iqtisādī dar Asār-i Muntashir Nashudeh-yi Dowrān-i Qājār [Unpublished Social, Political, and Economic Thought of the Qajar Period] (Tehran: Agāh Press, 1356/1977), pp. 156-57.
50. Adamīyat, Afkar, pp. 162-63.
51. Bamdad, From Darkness, p. 36.
52. For the most recent account of the Constitutional Revolution including the role of Russia, see Ervand Abrahamian, Iran Between Two Revolutions (Princeton: Princeton University Press, 1982).
53. Bāmdād, Sharh-i Hāl, p. III, 325.
54. Hājjī Mīrza Yahya Dowlatabadi, "Maqām-i Zan," cited in Shams ul-Muluk Javāhirkalām, Zanān-i Nami-yi Islām va Iran [Famous Women in Islam and Iran] (Tehran: 1346/1967), pp. 439-43.
55. Bamdad, From Darkness, pp. 45-46.
56. Parī Shaikhulislāmī, Zanān-i Rūznāmehnigār va Andīshmand-i Iran [Women Journalists and Intellectuals in Iran] (Tehran: 1351/1972), pp. 65-66.
57. Shaikhulislāmī, Zanān, p. 97.
58. Bamdad, From Darkness, p. 46.
59. Shaikhulislāmī, Zanān, pp. 84-85.
60. There are many accounts of Mrs. Dowlatābādī's life. For an English version, see Bamdad, From Darkness, pp. 78-80; for the most comprehensive account in Persian, see Shaikhulislami, Zanan, pp. 88-99.
61. Abrahamian, Iran, p. 140.
62. Bamdad, From Darkness, pp. 92-95.
63. Bamdad, From Darkness, p. 134.
64. Abrahamian, Iran, pp. 153-55.
65. Bamdad, From Darkness, pp. 63-64.
66. Shahrough Akhavi, Religion and Politics in Contemporary Iran (Albany: State of University of New York Press, 1980), pp. 23-61.
67. Bamdad, From Darkness, p. 106.
68. Abrahamian, Iran, p. 336.
69. Abrahamian, Iran, pp. 335-36.
70. Akhavi, Religion, p. 63; Abrahamian, Iran, p. 336.

71. See the chapter by Erika Friedel in this volume.
72. For a discussion of the social and economic changes in Iran during the 1950s, 1960s, and 1970s, see Ervand Abrahamian, "Structural Causes of the Iranian Revolution," MERIP Reports, No. 87, May, 1980; for a limited discussion of the impact of these changes on women, see Mamideh Sedghi and Ahmad Ashraf, "The Role of Women in Iranian Development," in J. W. Jacqz, ed., Iran: Past, Present, and Future (Aspen: Aspen Institute for Humanistic Studies, 1976), pp. 201-13, and the chapter by S. Kaveh Mirani in this volume.

2
Status of Women in the Qur'an

Fazlur Rahman

The inferior status to which Muslim women have traditionally been relegated in Islamic society has changed
very little over the centuries. This status is primarily
due to the social milieu that developed in Muslim societies, a result of the interpenetration of many diverse
cultural traditions. Although women's inferior status
has been written into Islamic law, this analysis will
attempt to show that it is by and large the result of
prevailing social conditions rather than of the moral
teaching of the Qur'an. Furthermore, this chapter will
demonstrate that the primary intent of the Qur'an is to
ameliorate the position of women. Although new legislative measures do, to an extent, function as agents of
reform, to a much larger extent their efficacy is limited
by settled social attitudes. Basically, legal reform of
the status of women has to be a function of a much larger
and broader social change.

The teaching of the Qur'an on the subject of women is
a part of its effort to improve the condition of, and
strengthen the weaker segments of society in pre-Islamic
Arabia--orphans, slaves, the poor, women, etc.--segments
which had been abused by the stronger elements in the
society. In many instances a woman began life in dire
jeopardy. Among many Arab tribes, girls were buried alive
for reasons of poverty and honor (as the Qur'an makes
clear in VI, 138); many pagans believed that infanticide
was sanctioned by their gods. On the whole, the infant
girl was an unwelcome intrusion into the family:

> When one of them is given the glad tidings of
> [the birth of] a female, his face darkens as he
> tries to suppress his chagrin. He hides from
> people out of a sense of disgrace of the news
> he has been given and he ponders whether to
> keep her in disgrace or shove her under the
> earth. Evil is, indeed, what they judge (Qur'an
> XVI, 58-59).

The Qur'an put an end to this practice.

38

We must not judge from this, however, that the
women's position in pre-Islamic Arabia was necessarily
very low; even a slave woman could earn and own wealth.
Khadija, the first wife of the Prophet, owned a considerable business which the Prophet managed for her for some-
time before their marriage; after their marriage she helped him financially. Hers was not an isolated case; other
women also controlled wealth.

Women were central to the "honor" [ird] of men; "man-
liness" [muruwwa] demanded that that honor remain invio-
late. This also meant that women were among the "weak
spots" in a man's life and had to be protected. It was
this excessive preoccupation with honor and its defense
that ironically led to infant girls being considered a
form of disgrace whose removal was sanctioned by pre-
Islamic gods. A strange mutation indeed, but not rare in
human affairs!

The principal aim of the Qur'an was the removal of
certain abuses to which woman was subjected. At birth she
was liable to be killed; it was not uncommon for her
father to consider her a shameful burden to be tolerated
until she was married. There is no material evidence that
suggests that once she was married, however, she was considered shameful by her husband. Rather she was someone
to be protected and even loved. Although there was a
"division of labor" in the sense that men worked outside
while women worked at home (whether in the house or in the
tent), there is no evidence that a woman was regarded as
below a man in any essential human sense. At the pilgrim-
age--the most sacred rite for a pre-Islamic Arab--men and
women performed equally with individual responsibility.
Many Arabs believed the goddesses they worshipped (and
there seem to have been many more goddesses than gods) to
be Allah's daughters; they thought these goddesses could
intercede on behalf of humans. The Qur'an frequently
reprimands them for attributing to Allah what they would
rather not have for themselves!

Two pre-Islamic institutions affecting family relations were prohibited in the Qur'an because they were felt
to create false and abusive relations--zihar and adoption:
"God has not put two hearts in any man's breast: He has
not made your wives with whom you do zihar your mothers,
nor has He made your so-called [i.e., adopted] sons your
real sons" (XXXIII, 4). Zihar was a formula whereby a
man declared his wife to be as unlawful to him "as my
mother's back" (meaning front, as the commentators tell
us). This public condemnation of these institutions was
occasioned by the following situation, explained in
XXXIII, 37: Zainab, the Prophet's cousin, was married to
Zaid ibn Thabit, the Prophet's adopted son. She fell in
love with the Prophet and refused to live with Zaid as
his wife. Zaid eventually divorced her, and she married
the Prophet. The Qur'an scolds Muhammad for hesitating to

marry Zainab for fear of public scandal, "for God alone
[not people] is deserving of being feared," and adoption
is a meaningless word.

The Qur'an also prohibited (IV, 19) a pagan custom
whereby a son inherited his stepmother as part of his
father's legacy and could force her to marry him or,
coveting her property, could debar her from marrying anyone else throughout her life. In the absence of a son,
the next male kin of the deceased had the same power over
her. The same verse also prohibited the practice of forcing one's wife to make a will in one's favor that remitted
the dower or any other gifts one had already given her.
Men were strongly advised to keep their wives "even if
you may not like them."

> But if you do want to take another wife in her
> place [i.e., by divorcing her] and if you have
> gifted to her a heap of gold, do not take any-
> thing back from it: Will you take it back as a
> stunning lie and a clear sin? And how will you
> take it back when you have been intimate with
> each other and they have had solemn promises
> from you?" (IV, 20).

Although this is not the place to discuss slavery, a
word must be said about the status of slave women. It was
not uncommon for the owners of slave women to make prostitutes of them. This is explicitly stated in XXIV, 33 and
assumed elsewhere. In XXIV, 33 the Qur'an gives a general
command to slave owners to free slaves against earned payments by the latter and, if they do not have wealth, to
give them wealth; it also prohibits prostitution of slave
girls. Instead, they should be given in marriage. In IV,
25 it is stated that if a man cannot afford to marry a
free woman, he may marry a slave woman. If she then com-
mits adultery, she should be given half the punishment of
a free married woman. Incidentally, this verse also
proves that punishment of a married free woman by stoning
to death has no basis in the Qur'anic teaching since this
punishment cannot be halved for a married slave woman!
The same verse also emphasizes that slave women must not
indulge in whoredom or concubinage, implying that this
was fairly common among them. IV, 25 says that if a free
man cannot afford a free wife and fears that otherwise he
would go wrong, he should marry a slave woman; XXIV, 33
cautions a destitute man, whether free or slave, against
marriage "until God gives him wealth," while the immediately preceding verse enunciates a general law that all
Muslims, including free men, free women, and slaves,
should marry. The hope is expressed there that if they
are destitute God will give them wealth. While there is
an obvious tension between this caution and this universal
law, it is strange that most Muslim authorities reported
by al-Tabari (including himself) should regard the marri-

age of a free man with a slave woman as "unlawful" unless
he cannot afford a free woman and fears to fall into evil.
Only a few allow it unconditionally and Rabi^{c}a, one of the
very early Medinese authorities, even prefers it "if the
man falls in love with the slave woman." The Qur'an does
not talk about the impermissibility of such a marriage but
only cautions against it because, as al-Tabari says, the
children of a slave girl will be slaves. There is no way
to test this reasoning historically, although it is inconsistent with the Qur'an, where the marriage caution in
XXIV, 33 covers both freemen and slaves. But we know that
after a slave girl bore a child to her own master (and
became "Mother of the Child") she could not be sold or
given as gift by him; after his death she, along with her
children, was automatically freed. The case under consideration is more complex since the woman, while she is the
wife of one man, is slave to another person; yet it would
not have been difficult to work out a solution about her
fate or that of her children, especially since she is not
a concubine but is married to a free man. This is a good
example of how much Islamic history deviated from Islamic
norms.

The Qur'an advocates neither the veil nor segregation
of the sexes; rather it insists on sexual modesty. It is
also certain on historical grounds that there was no veil
in the Prophet's time, nor was there segregation of the
sexes in the sense Muslim societies later developed it.
In fact, the Qur'anic statements on modesty imply that
neither veil nor segregation of the sexes existed. If
there had been segregation of the sexes, there would have
been no point in asking the sexes to behave with modesty.
Here is the classic passage of the Qur'an:

> Say [O Muhammad!] to believing men that they
> should observe modesty of the eyes and guard
> their sexual parts--this is purer for them, but
> God knows well what they do. And say to believ-
> ing women that they should observe modesty of
> the eyes and guard their sexual parts and let
> them not display their attractions except those
> naturally exposed--and let them cast down their
> head-scarves onto their bosoms . . . (XXIV, 31).

"Modesty of the eye" spoken of here in connection
with both sexes would have no meaning at all if the sexes
were segregated or if hijab [veiling] as we know it today
were observed. On the subject of "not displaying their
attractions [zina] except those that are naturally exposed," the vast majority of the authorities hold that such
attractions as are commonly exposed include the face, half
the forearm, and any cosmetic or jewelry decorations they
might have, such as rings, bangles, rouge [khidab, which
colors fingers red], etc. Again, the words "and let them
cast their head-scarves down upon their bosoms" are also

clear proof that covering the face is not required. In
XXXIII, 59-60, Muslim women, including women of the Prophet's household, are asked to "draw tight their outer
garments" when they go out at night "so that they can be
recognized as Muslim women and not molested" and the
"Hypocrites" who are said to have molested women are
threatened with exile if they do not stop such practice.
There is nothing in these verses, however, that calls for
the veil as such. In XXXIII, 30ff., the Prophet's wives
are specially warned against any suggestion of immodesty
and are threatened with a "double punishment" if they are
immodest; XXXIII, 32 makes it clear that the "Hypocrites"
were eager to spread rumors about the Prophet's women
who are, therefore, advised "not to speak in an inaudible
voice to any male--if you are God-fearing--lest he in
whose heart there is sickness covets to exploit the
opportunity."[1] But this verse is a special case addressed
to the Prophet's wives, whom the Qur'an had already declared to be "Mothers of the Faithful" (XXXIII, 6).

In the face of this evidence, it would not serve any
essential purpose to pursue the question of whence the
practice of veiling women and the utter segregation of the
sexes comes or how it developed, interesting and important though this question is in itself. (The purpose of
the veil has not only been to segregate sexes but also to
act as a symbol of honor or status.) Already in the
Hadith literature we find major changes or deviations
from the Qur'anic norms. The Qur'an, for example, mentions both men and women separately as being absolutely
equal in virtue and piety and their opposites with such
regularity that it would be superfluous to give any
particular documentation. Yet, according to a very
famous and historically important Hadith, contained in
the most authoritative Hadith collections, the Prophet
once said to some women that womenfolk were inherently
inferior to men both in matters of religion and intelligence. Asked how they were weak in religion, he allegedly replied, "Because when you menstruate, you are required
neither to pray nor fast." It is absolutely clear that
this is contradictory to whatever the Qur'an has stated
on the equality of males and females in matters of piety
and religious merit. The women went on to ask the Prophet how they were inferior to men in intelligence, upon
which the Prophet said, "Is not your evidence [in a court]
half of the value of men's evidence?" The women replied,
"Yes."

This latter half of the Hadith is still more interesting. It presupposes the development of the law of
evidence in early Islam. According to this law, in order
to prove a case in court, two male witnesses or one male
and two female witnesses are required. The law is supposed to be based on Qur'an II, 282, which states that if
a person borrows money from another, then it should be put

in writing and either two males should witness it or one
male and two females "so that if one [of the women] should
make an error [in evidence], the other should remind her."
First of all, the Qur'an is not stating any general law
of the evidentiary value of male and female statements
as the law based upon this verse claims. Secondly, if the
Qur'an did really regard a woman's evidence to be half
that of a man, why should it not allow the evidence of
four females to be equivalent to that of two males and why
should it say that only one of the two males may be replaced by two females? The intention of the Qur'an
apparently was that since it is a question of financial
transaction and since women usually do not deal with such
matters or with business affairs in general, it would be
better to have two women rather than one--if one had to
have women--and that, if possible at all, one must have at
least one male. This point is not difficult to see. But
how can one deduce from this a general law to the effect
that under all circumstances and for all purposes, a
woman's evidence is inferior to a man's? If, however,
such a generalization were permissible in the past, then
why not change the law when social circumstances so change
that women not only are educated equally with men but also
become conversant with business and financial transac-
tions? The classical Muslim law itself regarded women
with knowledge of gynecology as the most competent witnesses concerning cases involving gynecological issues.
This verse, therefore, has not the slightest intention of
proving any rational deficiency in women vis a vis men,
and there is no doubt that the Hadith in question assumes
post-Prophetic legal developments.

According to another Hadith, the Prophet is reported
to have said, "No one may prostrate himself or herself
before anyone except God but if it had been permissible
at all for a creature to worship another creature, I would
have required a wife to worship her husband." The latter
part of this Hadith so obviously contradicts what we know
of the relationship of the Prophet with his wives that it
has to be discredited forthwith. The Prophet's wives, far
from worshipping him--despite all his religious authority
--demanded the good things of life from him so that the
Qur'an had to say, "O Messenger! Say to your wives: 'If
you want to pursue this worldly life and its good things,
then come, I will give you wealth but let you go in
gentleness [i.e., divorce you]" (XXXIII, 29). What the
Qur'an requires from a woman is to be a good wife, adding, "Good women are those who are faithful and who guard
what is their husband's in his absence as God wants them
to guard" (IV, 34).

In general, the Qur'an speaks of the husband-wife
relationship as that of "love and mercy" adding that the
wife is a "moral support" for the husband (XXX, 21). It
describes their support for each other by saying, "They

[i.e., your wives] are garments unto you and you are garments unto them" (II, 187). The term "garments" here
means that which covers up one's weaknesses: thus in
VII, 126, piety [taqwa] is described as the "best garment," and in LXXVII, 10, it is said, "We have made the
night a garment for you while the day We have made for
you to toil for livelihood." The natural thinking of the
Qur'an is in monogamous terms. We have already quoted
IV, 19-20 to the effect that a husband should, so far as
possible, keep his wife even if he may have developed
some dislike for her and that in case he cannot do so and
wants "to have another wife in her place" [i.e., not in
addition to her] then he must not take back from the
first wife any gift he may have given her--not even if
he had given her "a heap of gold."

We have disposed of arguments from the legal and
Hadith literature of Islam which were aimed at proving
the inherent inequality of sexes. There are, however,
certain factors or functions which, while they do not
make for any essential or inherent inequality of women
with men, certainly appear to point to a certain socio-
economic inequality in some areas. In II, 228, we are
told, "For them [women] there are rights [against men]
that are exactly commensurate with their obligations
[towards men], but men are one degree higher than women."
That is to say, in the social sphere [as opposed to the
religious], while the rights and obligations of both
spouses towards each other are exactly commensurate, men
are, nevertheless, a degree higher. The rationale is not
given in this verse which simply adds, "And God is Mighty
and Wise." This rationale is given later in IV, 34, the
middle part of which has been quoted above, but the whole
of which reads, "Men are managers over [i.e., are superi-
or to] women because some of the humankind excel others
[in certain respects] and because men expend of their
wealth [for women]; hence good women are those that are
faithful [obedient] and who guard what is their husband's
in his absences--as God wants them to guard. and such
women whose waywardness you fear, [first] admonish them,
[then] leave them alone in their beds and [finally] beat
them; if they obey you, do not transgress against them--
God, indeed is High and Great." The Qur'an, then, gives
two rationales for male superiority in socio-economic
affairs: (1) that man is "more excellent" and (2) that
man is charged entirely with household expenditures.
Since these two factors are apparently related, one must
fix the meaning of the phrase "more excellent." Now, the
Qur'an has used this phrase fairly frequently (II, 32;
II, 53; IV, 95; XVI, 71; XVII, 21; XVII, 55; etc.) to
denote the better performance of some humans over others
--not just of one sex over the other--either in earning
wealth or in some other way. Even among Prophets, the
performance of some has been better than others, despite
their equal status as Prophets (II, 253). This phrase,

therefore, does not and cannot refer to any <u>inherent</u>
inequality among persons. What the Qur'an appears to be
saying, therefore, is that since men are the primary
socially operative factors and bread-winners, they have
been wholly charged with the responsibility of defraying
household expenditure and upkeep of their womenfolk. For
this reason men, having gained more life-experience and
practical wisdom by their economic struggles, have become
entitled to "manage women's affairs" and, in the the
case of recalcitrance on the part of women, to admonish
them, to leave them alone in their beds, and, as a last
resort, to beat them.

The two allied questions to be asked here are
whether these socio-economic functions upon which this
inequality has been made dependent are unchangeable even
if women want to change them, and, if they are not unchangeable, whether overall human welfare requires them
to be changed, and, if so, how far. We have already
answered the first question by saying that since these
are basically socio-economic functions and not inherent
in the nature of the sexes there is nothing unchangeable
about them. If they are changed, then, given the necessary time, women will acquire the same experiences and
wisdom that men have accumulated over the ages. The
Qur'anic pronouncements have not the slightest tendency
to suggest otherwise.

The answer to the second question is not as easy.
It seems certain to this writer that traditional customs,
usages, and attitudes in Muslim societies have to change.
In fact, the need for change is urgent. In the first
place, women's dependence upon men has often been grossly
abused, and it is the most fundamental requirement of the
Qur'an that abuses and injustices in the social sector be
removed. Secondly, women must be allowed to work outside
the home and to become effective economic entities; this
is a necessity, because increasingly, families find that
they cannot live on the husband's earnings alone. But
whether women should ask for or be allowed to do any job
that men are doing, I am not at all sure. Of course, if
women insist on this and persist, they can and eventually will do so.

Educated women in Muslim societies are slow both in
wanting jobs and in getting them, the latter because of
high male unemployment. The pattern is, however, steadily changing, particularly among the middle-middle and
lower-middle classes, not only because of increasing
economic hardship in coping with inflation, but also
because of the availability and desirability of a greater
variety of consumer goods and comfort-affording commodi-
ties. So far as the normative teaching of the Qur'an is
concerned, there is no question but that equal work deserves equal reward. Since most jobs available to educated women are in the public sector where wage discrimination is not possible, equal pay is not presently a

factor in Muslim countries. Whether this equality of pay
will persist when women begin to be employed on a large
scale is difficult to say, but the basic pattern has been
set.

The other issue bearing on economic inequality is
that of the female inheritance-share, which is half of
the male's. The Qur'an states, "God admonishes you with
regard to your children: a male [child] shall have the
equivalent of two females" (IV, 11). Some Muslim modernists have contended that it would be more just to give
all children equal shares irrespective of their sex.
Other, socially more conservative modernists (for example,
Muhammad Iqbal) have argued that since the girl also gets
mahr [dower] from her husband, the apparent inequality of
inheritance-shares amounts to a real equality. However,
the mahr-benefit of an average bride is normally less
than her inheritance-share and, therefore, this argument
does not hold. But inheritance-shares, like other
economic values and obligations assigned to the sexes,
are a function of actual roles in traditional society.
We have argued above that there is nothing inherently
unchangeable about these roles--indeed, when justice so
demands, change is Islamically imperative. This is even
more apparent in the case of the widow whom the Qur'an
(IV, 13) assigns one-eighth of her husband's legacy if
he has children; if not, she gets one-fourth. In the
same verse the share assigned to a husband from his wife
is twice as much. It is evident that in a tribal society
members in pecuniary want are supported by other members
of the tribe. With social change, however, changes in
shares must follow, since in a de-tribalized society
social functions undergo radical changes. If some
Muslims do not like the share rules, arrangements can be
made during the individual's lifetime to dispose of his
property. But even though in theory Muslims do not like
to "change any rule in the Qur'an," they have, in practice, made radical and even devastating changes in
inheritance: witness the usually utter deprivation of
daughters of their shares in their father's inheritance
in the interests of keeping the patrimony intact--
despite not only the Qur'anic laws but the enacted laws
of the land!

Another important concept that has deviated from its
early Qur'anic position is that of polygamy. The Qur'an
states, "Give back to orphans [who were your wards and
who have now come of age] their properties and do not
exchange [their] good properties with [your] bad ones,
nor consume their properties by mixing them with yours;
it is, indeed, a great sin. But if you fear that you
cannot do justice to orphans, then you may marry from
among [adult orphan] women such as please you--one, two,
three, or four. But if you fear that you cannot do justice [among them], then marry only one, or [marry] your
women--slaves; this would be nearest to avoiding injus-

tice" (IV, 2-3). It is astonishing that such an important ordinance as this one, affecting as it does the regulation of marriage, should have been so variously interpreted in view of the fact that Qur'anic ordinances
are rooted in socio-historical facts. This is not the
place to go into detail, but al-Tabari, in his commentary,
gives five different interpretations, all of which are
obviously speculative, and none of which fits the Qur'anic
passage. If such a practical ordinance is so specula-
tively interpreted by the 3rd/9th century, this should
warn us that there is something wrong, or rather that
there is some fundamental dislocation between what the
Qur'an is saying and the practice of the community.
There is no other obvious explanation. What is equally
astonishing is that another passage of the same Sura
(IV, 127-29) which undoubtedly speaks to the same issue
but which obviously antedates the one quoted was never
brought to bear upon its interpretation at the formative
stage of the doctrine on polygamy. This second passage
reads, "They ask you concerning women. Say, 'God is
giving you His answer concerning them in what is being
recited to you in the Book about orphan women to whom
you do not give back what is due to them (i.e., their
properties) but you would rather marry them, and also
weak (i.e., minor) male children . . . . And you shall
never be able to do justice among women, no matter how
much you desire, so do not incline away completely from
one leaving her suspended."

It is clear from these passages that the Qur'an is
talking of polygamy in the context of orphaned girls who
had come of age but to whom their guardians were unwilling to give back their properties. Rather, the guardians
preferred to marry them so that they could continue to
use the properties, or else they would resort to "eating
up" their properties either by exchanging their good ones
for the guardians' bad ones or by "mixing up" properties.
The practices of guardians concerning their wards'
properties (both male and female wards) is a theme the
Qur'an has addressed recurrently both in Mecca and Medina.
It is clear that the second passage broached a problem
to which the earlier quoted passage first provided
definite answers. Guardians were allowed to marry up to
four female wards as a lesser evil to unlawfully consum-
ing wards' properties, if the guardians were unwilling to
do justice to the wards' properties. The Qur'an, of
course, puts a rider to such permission for polygamy by
making it conditional upon the guardians doing justice
among the female wards they marry and by requiring that
they marry only one "if you fear you cannot do justice."
In a passage adjacent to the second passage quoted above,
after a general admonition to do justice to orphans, the
Qur'an says, "And you shall never be able to do justice
among women, no matter how much you desire this; so [if
you cannot do full justice], at least do not incline away

totally from one, leaving her suspended" (IV, 129).
   The dislocation we have alluded to between the
statements in the Qur'an and the practice of the community is then, not the one emphasized by so many Muslim
Modernists, viz., that by its statement that it is impossible to do justice among co-wives while at the same time
requiring justice, the Qur'an undercuts the general permission granted to Muslim males to marry up to four wives
by classical Islamic law. This question is certainly important, and we shall deal with it presently; but what is
germane is that in the polygamy clause the Qur'an refers
specifically to orphan girl-wards whose properties their
custodians were abusing. Apparently at some early point
in Islamic history Qur'anic permission for polygamy up to
four must have been made unconditionally general. It is
possible this occurred in Umar I's time, when due to
quick conquests and consequent enslavement of conquered
peoples, women were cheap and numerous. A final solution
of this problem would depend upon a detailed historical
study of the marital practices of the Companions of the
Prophet and of the next generation, the "Successors." In
pre-Islamic times, we are told, polygamy was quite widespread in Arabia because of the abundance of widows left
by frequent wars.
   Let us now turn to the Modernists' treatment of
the treatment of polygamy in the Qur'anic statements.
The Modernists have essentially contended that since the
Qur'an requires justice to be done among co-wives, and
since the Qur'an itself states categorically that this
justice is humanly unattainable, the Qur'anic demand
amounts to monogamy rather than polygamy. This is in
essence correct, but the formulation as it stands is not
very convincing for it accepts a contradiction in the
Qur'an because the Qur'an does give express permission
for up to four wives. The traditionalist solution of
the contradiction was that the clause giving permission
for four wives has legal force while the clause about
justice is only a private "recommendation" to individual
polygamous husbands to see for themselves that they do
not do injustice. They also construe the warning in
verse 129, "You shall never be able to do justice . . . ."
as a private though strong recommendation or advice for
justice to individuals, and they contend that if these
words had legal force then the Qur'an would not go on to
plead in the same verse, "So [if you cannot do full jus-
tice] at least do not incline away totally from one,
leaving her suspended," for in such a case of injustice
it would simply prohibit polygamy.
   The Modernist, who wants to give legal force to the
justice clause plus the warning that men will never be
able to do justice among co-wives, when faced with the
contradiction, seeks to relieve it by saying that the
permission for polygamy must be considered to have been
temporary and that the real intention of the Qur'an is

to abolish polygamy. This position is certainly in keeping with the purposes of the Qur'an concerning social
justice in general and women's justice in particular.
But in order to arrive at this position, the matter needs
restatement. One must completely accept the general contention that the specific legal rules of the Qur'an are
conditioned by the social-historical background of their
enactment; what are eternal therein are the social objectives or moral principles explicitly stated or strongly
implied in that legislation. This would clear the way
for further legislation in the light of those social
objectives or moral principles. This argument has not
been explicitly or forcefully developed by the Modernists,
who have used it in an ad hoc manner only for the issue
of polygamy, and have not formulated it as a general
principal. Otherwise, it is not at all clear why the
permission for polygamy should be regarded as being only
temporary. (And, indeed, the Qur'an specifies only
orphan women, not women in general.)

The early political and military developments in
Islam, the rapid conquests of vast territories, the
influx of large numbers of slave women tended to thwart
the general moral objectives of justice repeatedly
enunciated by the Qur'an for women. One has only to look
at the social legislation of Umar I contained in the
Kitab al-Muwatta' of Malik (d. 179/795) to see the dimensions of social problems these conquests created. Under
the circumstances, it is not surprising that Muslim
jurists regarded the polygamy permission clause as having
legal force and the strong words of the Qur'an about
justice as being only recommendations. They did pay
attention to the commandments of justice so far as to
allow a woman who was the victim of gross injustice to
get a divorce. They even legislated that a woman could
include a clause in her marriage contract to the effect
that if her husband took another wife she would stand
divorced. But solutions through divorce are hardly the
best solutions for marital problems.

The question of polygamy seems to be parallel to the
question of slavery. The Qur'an (XXIV, 33) commands the
freeing of slaves on the basis of a purchase-of-freedom
contract [mukataba], and in the same verse commands
slave owners to give their slaves the wealth that God
had endowed them with; however, most jurists regarded
this only as a recommendation and not mandatory.

In recent decades, the major Muslim countries with
the exception of Egypt have passed laws either restrict-
ing or banning polygamy altogether. Turkey and Tunisia
banned polygamy, Turkey on a secular basis by adopting
the Swiss Civil Code in 1926, Tunisia on an Islamic
basis, arguing from the Qur'an, in 1956. Most Muslim
countries have discouraged and restricted polygamy by
laying down a legal procedure that makes it difficult
to contract a second marriage during existence of the

first marriage, providing penalties for violating the
procedure. Whatever evidence is available suggests that
these limitations have had an effect which has been further strengthened by increasing economic hardship in
maintaining more than one wife.

Far more injurious to Muslim society has been the
practice of an extremely abusive form of divorce by the
husband, known as the "triple divorce," which merely
consists of the husband pronouncing "I divorce you" to
his wife three times in one sitting. This formula is
sufficient to divorce a couple forever; they cannot
remarry each other unless the wife is first married to
another man who subsequently divorces her or dies. This
kind of repudiation is usually done by a husband in
intense anger and if, as is common, he repents afterward,
frequently nothing can be done.

The most unreasonable stand on divorce is that of
the Hanafi school, which, although more liberal on many
other legal issues, holds that divorce becomes effective
even when a man divorces his wife under the influence of
a drug or alcohol, or when he is under dire and immediate
threat to his life, or even if he does it as a joke.
While other schools of law allow the husband to be
questioned after the pronouncement of divorce as to
whether or not he really intended to divorce his wife,
the Hanafi school assumes a penalizing stance because
marriage is so sacred that it must not be trifled with in
anger, or under the influence of a drug, or even under
threat. It is, however, a penalty that defeats its
purpose.

It is abundantly clear that the Qur'ran insists upon
the continuance of family and home, favors remarriage
between divorced couples, and emphasizes reconciliation.
Here is the locus classicus on divorce

> . . . and [in the case of divorced women], their
> husbands are more entitled to take them back if
> they want reconciliation . . . . Divorce is [law-
> ful] twice; then either keep them [i.e., women]
> in goodness or set them free with kindness; and
> it is not permissible for you to take back [from
> them] anything you had gifted them -- except
> when they fear that they will not be able to
> observe God's limits [i.e., they fear that trouble
> between themselves will continue] -- so, if they
> fear that they will not be able to observe God's
> limits then there is no harm if she sacrifices
> something [i.e., gives back a little of the gifts
> he gave her]. These are the limits of God, do
> not transgress them for whoever transgresses the
> limits of God, they are the unjust ones. Then,
> if he divorces her [for the third time], she is
> lawful for him afterwards [in marriage] until she
> marries another man; then, if the latter divorces
> her, there is no harm if they return together in

remarriage [for the fourth time], if they think
they can observe God's limits. These, then, are
God's limits for a people who know. When you
divorce women [i.e., for the first two times]
and they have reached the end of their waiting
period, then either keep them in goodness or let
them go in goodness; do not keep them harmfully
in order to commit transgression against them
[i.e., do not keep them in order to divorce
them again and again and thus torture them],
for whoever does this, he shall have been a
tyrant over his self. Do not take God's Commands in frivolity. . . . When you divorce
women and they have reached the end of their
waiting period, do not prevent them from
[remarrying] their husbands if they reconcile
between themselves in goodness. Even so are
being admonished those of you who really
believe in God and the Last Day -- this is
more virtuous and more pure for you, for God
knows and you do not know (II, 228ff).

The passage makes the following points:

i.   A wife can be divorced twice and the divorced
spouses can remarry each other.
ii. Women must not, under any circumstances, be
prevented from or pressured against remarrying their
husbands if the two are prepared to live with each other
amicably.
iii. If the marriage has proven unsuccessful three
times (including the original marriage), then husband
and wife are prohibited from remarrying one another
unless the woman marries another husbands who either dies
or divorces her. Otherwise, after three consecutive
chances, remarriage would threaten to become a farce.
iv. Men may not take away any gifts, including the
dower, that they have given their wives unless they
fear they would violate "God's limits" in which case the
wife might part with some of what her husband had given
her. However, earlier we quoted Qur'an IV, 20 which
prohibited in strong terms the taking back of any such
gifts even though they were a "heap of gold." Since
IV, 20 is later than II, 229, the Qur'an seems to pro-
prohibit any return of gifts. The Muslim jurists, however, recognize the validity of return of at least a
part of these gifts, especially the dower, in case the
wife sues for divorce (see below), but not if the husband divorces his wife.
Muslim jurists speak of five categories of dissolution of a Muslim marriage (apart from the form when both
take action for divorce. This requires a simultaneous
action from both sides; each declares that he/she is
quit of the other):

i. The husband pronounces the formula of divorce once and either is reconciled with his wife during three following months, or, at the end of that period, the wife is divorced. This is called "the best form of divorce" and the couple may remarry twice after this kind of divorce.

ii. The husband pronounces the formula of divorce once every month, and, unless he stops and reconciles himself with the wife during three months, after the third pronouncement the wife shall be divorced irrevocably, according to most authorities, unless she marries another man who divorces her or dies. This is called "good divorce."

iii. A husband pronounces the formula of divorce three times in one sitting; the divorce becomes effective instantaneously and irrevocably. This is called "irrevocable divorce" or "innovative divorce." Jurists do not like it, but it has nevertheless been held to be effective almost universally. The fourteenth century theologian and jurist Ibn Taimiya (d. 1328) is the only voice against this form of divorce; he declared it to be without any basis in the Shari^{c}a. This form of divorce, he tells us, was introduced by Umar I as a penalty when it was reported to him that since women were so abundant in Medina and Mecca due to conquests, many men divorced their wives a number of times, each time retracting the divorce, and thereby torturing their wives. However, it was universally accepted by Muslim schools of law, so that something that was intended as a penalty became a major crime against society--particularly in the lower strata of the society where men, until the recent family reform laws were enacted in most Muslim countries, would very often resort to this form of divorce in a fit of temper.

iv. The wife, under certain circumstances (such as a husband's prolonged imprisonment or insanity, his refusal to support his wife or to perform his marital obligations for a period of two to three years), can petition a court for divorce. This form of divorce allows a woman to "get rid" of a cruel or undesirable husband, but she has to return to him at least a part of the dower money and other gifts she received from him.

v. A woman can also sue for divorce in case a husband deserts her. The Hanafi law in this case asks the wife to wait for a period of over ninety years (the idea being that as long as the husband can be presumed to be alive, she cannot remarry) while the Maliki law stipulates a four-year period on the basis that a woman's maximum period of gestation is four years! All modern Muslim family laws have adopted a four-year period without using the Maliki rationale for it.

The fourth and fifth forms of divorce appear quite reasonable, and it must be granted that, in giving the wife the right of divorce (which she exercised "by dele-

gation" from her husband if she stipulated it in her
marriage contract), Islam was far ahead of other world
civilizations, although the return of the gifted property
in the fifth form is in express conflict with the later
teaching of the Qur'an. However, the question is whether
the exercise of unilateral repudiation by the husband--
and particularly in the most common form of triple di-
vorce--is in conformity with the intentions of Islam.
We invite the reader to compare the divorce passage
quoted from the Qur'an in extenso with the divorce forms
and their procedures worked out by lawyers and frankly
judge whether the latter conform both in letter and
spirit with the former. It is true that the Qur'an does
not speak about the matter being taken to a court (though
the word "you" so often used by the Qur'an in such contexts is often taken by the classical jurists themselves
to refer to the community or the society as a whole,
which means social institutions), but in view of the
Qur'an's heavy emphasis on justice and its going to such
great lengths in a strenuous effort to enforce it, why
was family life allowed to deteriorate and, since abuses
were quite frequent, why were men not required to go to
court, when women were? There were, no doubt, socio-
economic causes for these developments--the main cause,
of course, being the male social and economic hegemony
itself--but the extent of deviation from Qur'anic norms
is appalling. The Qur'an, in fact (II, 236) asks the
husband to give some gift to the wife in accordance with
his financial status even if neither consummation took
place before separation, or indeed, before the amount of
the dower was named (which means that marriage did not
actually take place, since dower is an inalienable condition for the validity of a marriage)--which is tantamount
to saying that a would-be wife should be paid for a
broken promise of marriage. In II, 237, Muslims are
asked "not to forget to do good to each other" even when
marriage breaks up before consummation, and, in fact,
husbands must pay half the dower-money unless the wife or
her representative forgoes the sum.

  Marriage of minors was allowed in classical Islamic
law. The idea behind it was that in a case where parents
were old and children young, parents (or in case they
were ill or dead, the next of kin) should be allowed to
make the best marital arrangements for the young children.
Or, if two families happened to live in proximity to each
other and have come to like and trust each other, then in
order to avoid insecurity for their children who might be
of comparable ages, the parents of both sides might make
a marital arrangement that seemed to be in the interests
of both. Children of either sex, on coming of age, were
free to annul such marriages by the exercise of "the
right of puberty [khiyar ul-bulugh]" but only before
consummation of the marriage took place. By recent
legislation the minimum ages for marriage of male and

female minors in most Muslim countries have been fixed.
These are usually 18 and 16 respectively; in come countries they are higher on the ground that 18 and 16 is
too young for couples to make up their own minds.

However, modernizing legislation without a basis in
adequate social change can succeed only to a limited
extent in producing that social change. This is confirm-
ed by the limited success of the efforts of Kemal Ataturk
to abolish polygamy and to liberate women in Turkey. Not
much of a result seems to have been produced beyond the
three cities of Izmir, Istanbul, and Ankara. Even in
the big cities a reaction is visible, for with the current renaissance of Islam, there has also been a resur-
gence of conservative Islam. This is not to say that
legislation should stop, particularly for the eradication
of heinous abuses of women, but it is certain that for
such legislation to be really bona fide and effective,
rather than being a mere fiat of a Westernized ruling
elite that seems to move like quicksand as the recent
reversal in women's status in Iran indicates, it is far
more important to strengthen more basic forces of social
change. The most basic of these forces are education and
employment opportunities for women.

The same is true of the problem of family planning
and bringing some kind of control to the runaway rise in
population, not only for prosperity but for the mere survival of the societies of the Third World. One big
barrier to the solution to these problems has been that
the reformers have all too often been seen as and have
behaved as instruments of Westernization, not of Islamic
modernization. In the frontierless world of today, it
is, of course, not possible to make sharp distinctions
and to compartmentalize different forces; nor is it
desirable to do so, for eventually the West and the East
have to solve all human problems together. But it must
be admitted that for most Muslims the West, with its increasing number of broken homes, abused children, and
general socio-moral lawlessness of which sexual chaos
is a component, hardly offers a model to be followed.
In Muslim societies, education of women and removal of
the veil are hardly questioned today, even though their
pace can be questioned. And yet only a few decades ago
both were issues worthy of being battled against and
their advocates worthy of being dubbed kafirs [unbeliev-
ers]. What has happened? The changes constitute real
needs of the Muslim society without which the society
would have faced grave danger. Muslim law, despite its
many deviations from the Qur'anic norms, particularly
under the influence of customs, has, from the beginning
of its formulation, recognized the principles of necessity [darura] and of Public Interest [maslaha] as being
of overriding importance for the community. The community itself, though it makes confused and contradictory
movements at critical and acutely demanding times such

as this one, has, through past experience, learned how to
adjust itself finally to new situations. But there is no
denying the fact that this present juncture is uniquely
acute and unprecedentedly demanding, and the question
awaiting answer is: will the Islamic Community be able
to rise to this occasion without undue waste of human
resources (and females are about 50 percent of the total
population in the Muslim world) which might prove overly
costly for its future but also without undue corrosion of
the moral fiber which might destroy its very future as
Muslim Community?

NOTE

This is a revised version of my paper entitled
"The Status of Women in Islam: A Modernist Interpreta-
tion," in Hanna Papanek and Gail Minault, eds., Separate
Worlds: Studies of Purdah in Southeast Asia (Columbia, MO:
South Asia Books, 1982), pp. 285-310. For more discus-
sion of the points I have raised here, also see my
"Islamic Modernism: Its Scope, Method, and Alternatives,"
International Journal of Middle Eastern Studies 1 (no. 4):
317-33 and "A Survey of Modernization of Muslim Family
Law," in International Journal of Middle Eastern Studies
11 (no. 4): 451-65.

3
Women in Shi'i Fiqh: Images Through the Hadith

Adele K. Ferdows and
Amir H. Ferdows

The status of women in Iran has been deeply influenced by the writings and attitudes of Shi^{c}ite ulama
toward women and their role in society. The Shi^{c}i ulama
based their pronouncements on the hadith collections compiled by early hadith scholars. These collections include
the purported sayings of Prophet Muhammad and those of the
twelve Imams and are considered second only to the Qur'an.
The study and analysis of these works is a valuable aid in
understanding the origins of contemporary practices,
values, and rules regarding women in the Islamic Republic
of Iran. If we are to grasp the force of these beliefs
and practices, we must understand how the "natural" gender
roles are constructed and where they originated. Here we
will examine the image of women that emerges from the
hadith collection Hilyat ul-Muttaqin [The Ornament of the
Pious] compiled and written by 'Allameh Muhammad Baqir
Majlisi (d. 1699), the best-known and frequently quoted
Shi^c theologian.

Majlisi represents the traditional religious leader.
He was educated in the madrasa system and became the most
acclaimed teacher and scholar of his time. He is one of
the most widely acknowledged hadith scholars, best known
for his monumental compendium of the Ithna-Ashari hadith
in Arabic, the Bihar ul-Anwar [The Ocean of Light]. This
work has been referred to in the most recent study of
Shi^{c}i jurisprudence as a "standard work for all Shi^{c}ite
studies."[1] Some scholars have referred to Majlisi as
"the greatest theologian of the Safavid period," and a
"diligent scholar", "one of the greatest, most powerful
and fanatical mujtahids."[2] Ayatullah Khomeini makes
several references to Majlisi as a "great scholar" and
calls him "Allameh-yi Muhaddithin" (hadith expert). In
addition, Khomeini advises the people of Iran, particularly the youth, to read the books of Majlisi in order to
become enlightened and informed about Islam instead of
remaining ignorant and in an abyss.[3] In fact, Khomeini
relies on Majlisi's book Haqq ul-Yaqin [The Real Truth]
for his long discussion of the doctrines of imamate and

55

and sinlessness of the imams. He also devotes many pages
specifically to the defense of Majlisi's best known work,
the Bihar, which he states is composed of four hundred
volumes. A recent anthology on Shi^{c}i Islam bases one-
third of the book on Majlisi's commentaries, discussion,
and explanation of the concept of Unity.[4] It is significant to note, also, that the selection of the Shi^{c}i
sources for the anthology is made by one of the best-
known Iranian Shi^{c}i scholars, the late Allameh Muhammad
Tabataba'i (d. Nov. 15, 1981). Professor S. H. Nasr has
written the introduction to the work emphasizing that
these hadith collections were "extremely important for
the development of Shi^{c}i law and theology as well as the
very vital role that they played in the development of
distinctively Shi^{c}i religious writings and way of life."[5]
Allameh Tabataba'i's own writings on Shi^{c}ism also rely
very heavily on Majlisi as the source of hadith.

In his Towzih ul-Masa'il [Explanation of Problems],
Khomeini discusses a very wide range of issues related to
women, including marriage (both permanent and temporary),
divorce, adultery, homosexuality, inheritance, and guardianship, as well as women's rights and obligations. Although he does not support each ruling by any specific
hadiths, his rulings, like those of other Ayatullahs
(Milani, Mutahhari, Khu'i, Tabataba'i) are almost identical to those presented by Majlisi. However in
Majlisi's work, Hilyat ul-Muttaqin, each ruling is supported by one or more hadiths attributed to the Prophet
or to the Imams. Majlisi's success in making the sources
of Shi^{c}i faith available to the ordinary population of
Iran seems remarkable. One of the reasons given for his
prominence in Shi^{c}i Iran is that he managed to put the
bulk of the vast amount of hadith literature into a
series of books in Persian, making it comprehensible and
accessible to the ordinary Iranian who could not read
Arabic. He published nine books in Persian, of which
the most famous is Haqq ul-Yaqin.

Hilyat ul-Muttaqin, the hadith collection in Persian
that was reprinted over a year ago in Tehran, contains
167 hadiths dealing with topics ranging from rules on
property ownership to the treatment of dogs and the
rights of women. The book is divided into fourteen
chapters, each chapter containing twelve sections in
addition to a lengthy concluding chapter covering miscellaneous issues. In the introduction to the book,
Majlisi alleges that all the hadiths quoted there are
sahih [sound], indicating that they can be traced
directly to the holy Imams and the Prophet, and that they
have been verified by detailed documentation. This is an
important claim since the statements and rulings of the
Prophet and the Imams are second only to the word of God
as revealed in the Qur'an as the source of all Shi^{c}i law.
Ayatullah Khomeini refers to them as "the God-ordained,
everlasting, unchangeable rules."[6]

II

In one hadith, according to Majlisi, the Prophet
suggests that the choice of a wife must be very carefully
considered because the woman's womb should be worth
carrying the husband's sperm. Women are thus assigned
the position of fertile fields where men can sow seeds
and watch them grow. A woman's own sexuality and personality are considered to be in conflict with the common
good of the society and so must be kept in strict confinement. Women tempt men to bestial passion, lead them
away from the straight path, and undermine their whole-
someness.[7] Thus the attempt is made to downgrade women
to negligible and insignificant roles. The overemphasis
on women's childbearing function is based on the widely
held notion that biological differences determine the
psychological, intellectual, and legal status of women.
This view of the biological differences of women has been
used as an argument for women's vulnerability and
inferiority, and it has also supplied an alternative
basis for self-esteem for women who share this belief.
In this identity, child-bearing capacity gains an over-
riding importance, becoming the major focus in a woman's
life and hence is the prime determinant of her position,
personality, desires, and responsibilities.

On the importance of having many children, a hadith
is related in which the Prophet supposedly recommends
that men marry virgins because, according to him, virgins
produce numerous children, their wombs are drier, their
breasts have more milk, and their breath smells fresher.
At the same time, he warns against seeking barren women
merely because they are beautiful. This preoccupation
with children is reflected in yet another hadith in which
the Prophet declares that barrenness is a curse of God.[8]
Therefore, child-bearing and child-rearing become the
woman's unique and all-important contribution to society
and the chief avenue for her fulfillment as a viable
being. This is seen as an "obvious" and "natural" answer
to the woman in search of identity, offering her ease,
comfort, and relief from the daily struggles and responsibilities of adult humans. Thus it is the woman's role
as a carrier of man's children that primarily determines
her chances of being selected as a wife and her position
after marriage within the household. She obviously gains
status by giving birth to children; the greater the number of children, the higher the status. However, it is
only giving birth to sons that raises a woman's esteem in
her husband's eyes; if she produces daughters, she adds
to the burden, shame, and hardships of her husband. The
following hadith attributed to the Prophet clarifies this
point: "If a man has one daughter he has a very heavy
burden to carry; if he has two, rescue him; if he has
three, [jihad] holy war and other religious hardships
should be waived for him. If he has four daughters, O

Believers, assist him, loan him money, pity him."[9] In a
similar vein the Prophet declares that if a man provides
financial subsistance for three daughters, his place is
in paradise [10]

Majlisi attributes another tradition, which seems to
be popular with Christians as well as with Muslims, to
the Prophet; he likens a woman to a crooked rib: "If you
try to straighten it, it will break." A man is advised
to have patience with her and her wrongdoings: she is
expected to act childish and do wrong because it is in
her nature to do so. Having been so created, she must be
tolerated and a man must accept her deficient mind. It
is in light of her inborn limited intellectual capacity
that her acts and thoughts are to be valued and weighed.
Perhaps nothing can better indicate a woman's position
in the family and in society than the amount of respect
accorded to her views and opinions. The following hadith
helps illustrate the position of Shi[c]i ulama on this
point: "The Prophet said that if a man obeys his wife,
God will condemn him to hell."[11] One is surprised, however, to find that the Prophet always consulted his own
wives before embarking upon a battle. Of course, we are
reminded immediately that he would then do exactly the
opposite of their advice.[12] Clearly Imàm Ali reinforces
the Prophet's tradition by declaring that: "A man whose
consultant is a woman is cursed by God."[13] In addition,
he advises his son Imam Hasan "not to consult women
because they are feebleminded and their will is weak.
Always to keep them veiled, not allow them outside the
house, and try hard to prevent them from ever meeting
other men. Not to serve them except with what is their
right. Respect them but not to put oneself at their
service and not to listen to what they tell about
others."[14] Imam Sadiq defines a wife as a leash around
the husband's neck. He advises men to be extremely careful in the selection of the leash that they choose to
put around their own necks.[15] Another imam, Imam Musa,
regards wives as hostages and slaves of the husband, and
suggests that God loves men who treat their slaves with
kindness.[16]

Imam Sadiq quotes a statement from the Prophet to
the effect that upon the birth of a boy he should be
given a good name, be taught the Qur'an, be circumcised,
and be taught to swim. Upon the birth of a girl, however,
she should be given a good name, be taught sura al-Nur of
the Qur'an (sura 24), be prevented from reading sura
al-Yusuf (sura 12), and be married off at an early age
(i.e., before puberty).[17] Upon the examination of the
above suras, the following emerges: sura al-Nur deals
with punishment prescribed for women sex offenders and
deals with chastity and piety and the Qur'anic rules
on them. Sura al-Yusuf, however, is the story of the
burning passion and love of the wife (Zulaikha) of the

Pharaoh for Yusuf, a slave that her husband had bought. One may draw one's own conclusions as to the reasoning behind this hadith. Suffice it to say that from the moment of birth girls and boys are to be raised and treated differently. The question of equality of girls' rights with boys' is irrelevant since women have different aims in life, different modes of thinking and feeling, and different conceptions of what is important. This moral system penetrates the conscience of every woman, religious or not-so-religious, educated or illiterate. It is a vividly binding force that can effectively squash any attempt at sexual equality. The woman is to be protected, looked after, and controlled. In this relationship, she has few rights but many obligations toward her male kin.

Some of Majlisi's hadiths deal with woman's rights, or rather with man's obligations toward his wife. Among the most important obligations are the provision of food, shelter, and clothing for her (e.g., four dresses a year is suggested as the proper number).[18] A hadith attributed to the Prophet provides us with the rights of women relative to their husbands: "A husband has most rights over his wife while only his father has most rights over him. A woman does not have one-hundredth of the rights that a husband has over his wife."[19] The Prophet declares: "If I could order any person to prostrate [sujdah] before anyone except God, I would command that women prostrate before their husbands."[20] Not only is the woman commanded to fully submit to God's will but also to that of her husband. A hadith attributed to Imam Ja^{c}far al-Sadiq declares that the rewards for a woman's lifetime of prayers and good deeds will be completely wiped out in the eyes of God if she ever states that she has never seen kindness from her husband.[21] The sense of guilt and low self-esteem which this tradition can engender is clear. The woman not only has the burden of living up to man's expectations but also has the added burden of justifying his questionable treatment of her. Another hadith attributed to the Prophet states that if a woman offends her husband, none of her good deeds and prayers will be accepted by God until she makes him happy again.[22] There is some concern for women's happiness, particularly in sexual relations, where a husband's failure (usually due to impotence) to meet her rights in this area gives her the right to divorce him. The Prophet warns men to observe this requirement by exhorting them to "copulate with her at least once every four months."[23] This obligation, however, does not apply to concubines and temporary wives.

There are many hadiths on the rights of men over their wives, among which is one by Imam Ja^{c}far on polygamy and concubinage. It is stated that God has bestowed a sense of honor [ghayrat] on men only. This is

justification for men to marry four wives and to have an
unlimited number of concubines and temporary wives while
women are limited to only one husband. It is reasoned
that since women lack a sense of honor, they do not feel
jealous when their husbands share their love and property
with other women, whereas men are very jealous and have a
monopoly over honor as a trait. Furthermore, a woman who
desires or wishes men other than her husband becomes
guilty of adultery before God.[24] Women are in general
discouraged from having any contact with men to whom they
are not related. A hadith attributed to the Prophet forbids women from uttering more than five words to
nunmahrams [male strangers] lest they violate their obligations to their husbands.
     While a woman may not have sexual relations with
anyone other than her husband, he is free, except in
regard to another man's wife. It is further argued that
since the wife is the property of the husband, not only
are polygamy and concubinage permitted for men while
being denied to women, but woman's religious duty is submission to all of her husband's sexual demands. This
brings up the question of whether it is morality or
merely the violation of the property right of another man
that leads to this ban and makes it punishable by death
to have sexual relations with another man's wife. This
punishment is meted out to both parties of the sexual act
and takes the form of stoning.
     Khomeini makes the ruling that a married woman must
yield to any of her husband's sexual desires at all times
and must never refuse such demands (except during the
menstrual period, as permitted by the Shari^ca.[25] This
ruling seems almost identical with a hadith attributed to
the Prophet by Majlisi: "A woman must obey her husband's
orders and willingly submit to his sexual demands. She
must never demand sex from him . . . the worse women are
those who disobey their husbands and refuse (like a
camel) to submit to his sexual demands and whatever else
he desires from them."[26] Khomeini further states that it
is a sin for a woman to disobey her husband, and in consequence of her transgression she loses her right to
food, shelter, and sex.[27] In another place, Khomeini and
others issue the ruling that a wife must not leave home
without the permission [ijazeh] of her husband.[28] The
hadith offered by Majlisi likewise reads: "The Prophet
said that a wife must obey her husband, never disobey his
commands, never leave house without his permission, if
she does, the angels in the sky will curse her until she
returns."[29] In fact, most of the hadiths dealing with
women are concerned with the woman's extensive duties and
obligations to her husband.
     The one area in which Islam grants equality and in-
dependence to women is the economic sector, namely,
women's right to own personal property and possess in-

come. Even this right, however, has been circumvented by
a hadith ascribed to the Prophet stating that a woman may
not give to charity without her husband's consent. Such
an act of charity without his consent would be tantamount
to committing a sin by the woman, and the reward for the
act of charity will belong to him.[30] This does not apply
solely to her husband's property, as exemplified in the
hadith which states: "A woman may not give to charity
even of her own personal property without her husband's
permission except for that which she contributes to her
religious tax [zakat] or to her parents."[31]
  The rights and position granted women discussed
above seem universally supported by the Iranian ulama,
past and present. One scholar has observed that although
there were differences of opinion on various questions
among the ulama of the 1950's, the one area in which a
uniformity of interpretation existed was on the issues
relating to women.[32] Our study would appear to strongly
confirm this observation.

III

  As mentioned before, marriage and child-rearing are
among the most important values in Islam. Muslim
societies assign first priority to maternal rearing of
children. Celibacy is forbidden outright, and marriage
for the purpose of having children is encouraged. Highest priority in the social fabric of Islam is given to
the cohesion of the family. It is in this light that the
role of sex and women's place in the sexual relation is
determined. However, in the view advocated by the Shiᶜi
ulama the role of woman is that of an object solely for
the pleasure and sexual use (or abuse) of her husband.
She is not only instructed to be submissive at all times
and to all forms of his sexual pleasures but also to be
enthusiastic and willing. Her own sexual expectations
and demands are to be stifled. There are many hadiths
which allege to reveal the attitude of the Prophet and
the Imams toward sexuality in women. According to
Majlisi, the Prophet termed the following three traits
desirable in men: "1. to smell good, 2. to clear
(shave) their pubic hair, and 3. to have many women and
copulate with them a lot." Majlisi also claims that Imam
Muhammad al-Baqir stated that he would not want the world
or anything in the world if he had to sleep one night
without a woman.[33] Such preoccupation with women and
sexual relations naturally leads to a large volume of
detailed rules dealing with marital and polygamous
relationships and the rights and obligation of co-wives.
One such ruling deals with the minimum number of times
that a husband must have sexual intercourse with each of
his wives. For example, Majlisi comments that there is
agreement among the ulama that a man must sleep in turn
with each of his wives once every four nights (when there

are four wives) except when he marries a new wife and is
allowed to spend the entire first week of marriage with
her (but only if she is a virgin).[34] This exception does
not apply to widows or divorcees, demonstrating again the
emphasis put on female virginity. The strict demand for
female virginity prior to marriage as well as other
practices such as female circumcision and enfibulation
are variously interpreted as means for sexual control of
women through religious rituals. Unmarried women who are
found to have lost their virginity are punished harshly
in most instances, sometimes even being put to death by
the male kin. The emphasis on virginity may be because
women are seen as objects of male sexuality and virility.
Therefore, if women deviate from society's rules, men
feel it as a betrayal. In fact, the word "betrayal"
[khiyanat] is used to denote extramarital affairs.

In addition to the hadiths on the position and
rights of women, a few hadiths deal with the rules of
female circumcision. Although female circumcisions are
not practiced in Iran (except perhaps among the Kurds
in Kirmanshah and in the Khuzistan province), its discussion in Majlisi's work is significant and indicates that
it may have been more widely practiced in Iran in the
past. A hadith is related in which the Prophet, upon
meeting a woman whose profession had been circumcising
women, inquires whether she still does circumcision. The
woman responds in the affirmative, adding that if the
Prophet would order her not to, she would obey his command and quit immediately. The Prophet, however, not
only persuades her to continue her profession but in
fact instructs her and gives her advice on the proper
manner of female circumcision, emphasizing a very light
cut rather than a deep cut. He states, in addition, that
a woman who is circumcised will have a charming face with
a halo, will get fairer skin color, and will be dearer to
her husband.[35] Imam Ali is said to have ordered the
prohibition of circumcision of women before the age of
seven. He also declared that although male circumcision
is a sunna [religious rule], in females it is not,
although its execution will endear women to their husbands.[36] Majlisi presents the opinion that the circumcision of boys preferably should be done no later than
the seventh day of birth. He indicates also that the
girls' circumcision is not a sunna and that only a very
little must be clipped. The extent of the practice in
Iran is still unknown although recent studies indicate
its presence in many Muslim as well as Christian communities in the Middle East and Africa.[37]

A hadith related to the Prophet is among the first
ones quoted in the section dealing with women in the
Hilyat. It relates the Prophet's advice to Imam Ali:
"Remember this advice from me, as I learned it from
Gabriel." The Prophet then sets very detailed rules

governing the days, times, places, and manners of sexual
intercourse. Similarly, the specific times or periods
during the day, the week, or the month when sexual intercourse is prohibited are also stated. Tragic consequences in the form of various diseases or handicaps such
as blindness, mental retardation, leprosy, cowardice,
etc. would afflict the woman who had sexual intercourse
during these proscribed periods, or would afflict her
baby conceived during them. But there is no mention of
any harm that would afflict the man violating this ban.
In addition, specific prayers are suggested to be offered
(in Arabic) at different stages prior to, during, and
after intercourse in order to prevent Satan's presence or
participation.[38]

Many hadiths are reported that deal with the nature
and characteristics of women, among which is one attributed to the Prophet where he lists mild temper, low dowry
[mahr], and descent from the Prophet through Fatimeh's
line as the characteristics of the best women.[39] It must
be pointed out that this concept of kinship and blood tie
as the basis of distinction seems in contradiction to
the Qur'anic teaching, which considers piety the sole
basis for distinction. There are also those hadiths
that describe the most desirable features of women, such
as the color of her skin (in one instance there seems to
be a difference of opinion and taste between the Prophet,
who prefers an olive complexion and Imam Riza, who
considers a man with a fair-skinned woman a lucky one).
One hadith is quoted in which the Prophet states willingness to marry any woman about to be divorced by her husband, provided that she is tall, has large black eyes,
and an olive complexion. The Prophet offers to pay her
dowry [mahr] any time. He also expresses his preference
for women with plump ankles and sweet-smelling necks.[40]
Among the characteristics stated by the Prophet as being
"best" for a woman are giving birth to numerous children,
being virtuous, being loved by her family, and being
zalil [servile] to her husband. Along the same lines,
she must be obedient to her husband by being willing to
comply with and submit to his sexual demands with a happy
and loving attitude. At the same time the Prophet forbids the woman from making sexual demands upon her husband or forcing him into intercourse against his wishes.
He is alleged to have stated that sexual agressiveness
would make her a domineering wife, and domination over
her husband, along with barrenness and disobedience to
him, are the qualities of the "worst" kind of woman.[41]
The woman is told to wear perfume, her best clothes, and
jewelry for her husband, and to offer herself every
night and every morning to him, so that if he has sexual
desire, he is not inhibited but is encouraged and
enticed. She is told that she must never allow her husband to go to sleep while angry at her even if he has

done an injustice to her. A woman should not intention-
ally lengthen her prayer in order to avoid sexual intercourse, for if her husband falls asleep due to delaying
tactics, angels will curse her until he wakes up.[42]
This obviously implies that women, being devious and cun-
ning by nature, will try to avoid intercourse they themselves don't desire. To prevent such trickery, God's
anger is used as an inhibitor. Also, because women by
nature are sexually uninhibited, they must be controlled
from an early age in order to prevent deviation and
corruption. One such means is to forbid women to sleep
naked beside another woman or even next to her own
daughter. Once a girl reaches age six she may not kiss
boys. Imam Riza states that violation of these rulings
is tantamount to adultery.

IV

In general, the image of the position of woman and
her role in relation to her male kin as revealed from
these hadiths reinforce all the traditional practices
and beliefs of degradation, subservience, and segregation
that the Iranian women have been subjected to for centuries. Whether these hadiths propogated by the ulama
have been the basic reason for such mistreatment and
humiliation or have only reinforced the dominant cultural
patterns of thought and behavior is a separate area of
research which goes beyond the scope of this work.
It is clear, however, that these rules and regulations are made in the name of Islam and based on the
Islamic standards exemplified by the type of hadiths
presented in Majlisi's works. What has been presented
here from the hadiths is only a glimpse of the vast
amount of religious literature from which the Ithna-
Ashari Shi^{C}i laws and rules regarding women have
originated. In addition, the day to day practices,
general attitudes, and beliefs of the Iranians as regards
women's position emerge remarkably similar to that presented by Majlisi. Thus we can conclude that perhaps
the position to which Iranian women have been relegated
has come about because of the particular clergy-dominated
interpretations. It is very likely that these clerical
interpretations are probably fabrications and misrepre-
sentations of the Prophet's and Imams' statements on
these matters. As we have seen, they emphasize woman's
biological differences from man, concentrating on the
privileges of femininity which gives her status men can
never attain. They further state that it would be demeaning to suggest that she is equal to men. This "true
Muslim woman" image presents an elusive and closed world
of feminity where a woman would have to be crazy to
choose to be anything but a "true Muslim woman".
Ignorance breeds fanaticism, dogmatism, and superstition. Fanaticism leads to blind obedience to those

65

who claim authority, particularly religious authority.
Clergy-made and fabricated rulings form the basis of many
of the hadiths on women that have helped keep the Iranian
women subservient, ignorant, and exploited. This ignorance and superstition has resulted in women being the
most downtrodden and suppressed group in Islam. Their
enslavement and degradation has been imposed on them with
the help of religious traditions supposedly handed down
directly from the Prophet and Imams. The clergy, including Majlisi, Khomeini, Milani, and Mutahhari have been
instrumental in this process since these allegedly God-
ordained rules have had to be followed, as relayed by
them, absoultely and unquestioningly. As Keddie put it
so aptly, although we cannot overemphasize the Qur'an's
certain role in the position of women, what we should
look to as perhaps more important is what the Muslims
believe the Qur'an and the traditions teach; in other
words, what is transmitted to the people by the clergy
as their interpretations of what the law says.[44] The
strength of the traditional Islamic forces of the kind
presented through the hadiths lead many observers to
look askance at the future of women in Iran, particularly
because women themselves have come to believe in and submit to the degrading and humiliating treatment by males,
meted out under the guise of religious belief and
devotion.

As reflected in these hadiths and more recent rulings on women in Iran, it seems that to call the laws of
Shi^ci Islam (the only Islam recognized in Iran today)
sexist is an understatement. These rules do not recognize women as full human beings. To say that they promote a double-standard is not correct; they promote only
one standard, the male one. Perhaps the most serious
tragedy is that even educated women of Iran have been
influenced to a large degree by this pseudo-Islamic
cultural outlook. Although many women may intellectually
reject the letter of these rules and precepts, its
emotional impact is so internalized that it cannot help
but affect their self-image.

NOTES

1. William Chittick, ed. and trans., A Shi^cite
Anthology (Albany, N.Y.: SUNY Press, 1981), p. 17.
2. E. G. Brown, A Literary History of Persia, vol.
4 (London: Cambridge University Press, 1953), pp. 417-18;
and Dwight M. Donaldson, The Shi^cite Religion (London:
Luzac and Company, 1953), pp. 303-04.
3. Ruhullah Khomeini, Towzih ul-Masa'il [Explana-
tion of Problems], (Tehran: Piruz, 1979), p. 121.
4. Chittick, Anthology, pp. 23-51.
5. Ibid., p. 5.

6. Rūhullāh Khomeinī, Kashf ul-Asrār [Discovery of Secrets] (Tehran: Zafar, 1979), p. 107.

7. Muhammad Bāqir Majlisī, Hilyat ul-Muttaqīn [The Ornament of the Pious] (Tehran: Qā'im, 1979), p. 69.

8. Ibid., p. 69.
9. Ibid., p. 83.
10. Ibid., p. 83.
11. Ibid., p. 81.
12. Ibid., p. 81.
13. Ibid., p. 81.
14. Ibid., p. 81.
15. Ibid., p. 69.
16. Ibid., p. 97.
17. Ibid., p. 95.
18. Ibid., p. 80.
19. Ibid., p. 68.
20. Ibid., p. 68.
21. Ibid., p. 80.
22. Ibid., p. 336.
23. Ibid., p. 82.
24. Ibid., p. 79.
25. Khomeinī, Tɵwzīh, p. 386.
26. Majlisī, Hilyat, p. 70.
27. Khomeinī, Towzīh, p. 386.
28. Ibid., p. 80.
29. Majlisī, Hilyat, p. 79, 333.
30. Ibid., p. 80.
31. Ibid., p. 80.

32. Shahrough Akhavi, Religion and Politics in Contemporary Iran (Albany: State University of New York, 1980), p. 63.

33. Ibid., p. 68.
34. Ibid., p. 82.
35. Ibid., p. 93.
36. Ibid., p. 92.

37. Nawal Saadawi, Hidden Face of Eve, ed. and trans., Sherif Hetati (London: Zed Press, 1980); and Lilian Passmore Sanderson, Against the Mutilation of Women (London: Ithaca Press, 1981).

38. Majlisī, Hilyat, pp. 72-79.
39. Ibid., p. 70.
40. Ibid., p. 70.
41. Ibid., p. 70.
42. Ibid., p. 80.
43. Ibid., p. 97.

44. Nikki Keddie, "Iran: Change in Islam; Islam and Change," IJMES 11 (no. 4): 538.

BIBLIOGRAPHY

Abd al-Ati, Hammudah. Family Structure in Islam.
    (Indianapolis IN: American Trust Publication, 1977).
Akhavi, Shahrough. Religion and Politics in Contemporary
    Iran. (Albany: State University of New York, 1980).
Ali, (Imam). Nahj ul-Balagheh. S.M. Askari Jafery,
    trans. (Elmhurst: 1977).
Beck, Lois and Nikki Keddie, eds., Women in the Muslim
    World (Cambridge, MA: Harvard University Press, 1978).
Brohi, A.K. Islam in the Modern World. Khurshid Ahman,
    ed. and trans. (Lahore: Publishers United, Ltd.,
    1975)
Browne, E.G. A Literary History of Persia, vol. 4.
    (London: Cambridge University Press, 1953).
Chittick, William C., ed. and trans. A Shi^{c}ite Anthology.
    (Albany: State University of New York Press, 1981).
Coulson, Noel J. A History of Islamic Law. (London:
    University of Edinburgh, 1964).
Donaldson, Dwight M. The Shi^{c}ite Religion. (London:
    Luzac and Co., 1953).
Esposito, John L., Women in Muslim Family Law. (Syracuse,
    NY: Syracuse University Press, 1982).
Fernea, E. and Basima Bezirgan, eds. Middle Eastern
    Muslim Women Speak. (Austin: University of Texas,
    1977).
Fyzee, Asaf A.A. A Shi^{c}ite Creed, Islamic Research
    Associates Series, No. 9. (London: Oxford Univer-
    sity Press, 1942).
Ghaffari, Salman. Shi^{c}ism. (Tehran, 1967).
Keddie, Nikki. "Iran: Change in Islam; Islam and
    Change," in IJMES 11, no. 4 (1980): 527-42.
Khomeini, Ayatullah Ruhullah. Towzih ul-Masa'il
    [Explanation of Problems]. (Tehran: Piruz, 1979).
_____. Kashf ul-Asrar [Discovery of Secrets]. (Tehran:
    Zafar, 1979).
Lari, Siyyid Mujtaba Rukni-Musawi, Western Civilization
    Through Muslim Eyes. F. J. Goulding, trans.
    (Houston: Free Islamic Literature, 1979).
Madelung, Wilfred. "Shi^{c}i Attitudes Toward Women as
    Reflected in Fiqh," in Afaf L. Marsot, ed., Society
    and the Sexes in Medieval Islam. (Mailbu, CA: Undena,
    1979).
Majlisi, Allamah Muhammad Baqir. Hilyat ul-Muttaqin
    The Ornament of the Pious . (Tehran, n.d.).
Milani, Ayatullah Siyyid Muhammad Hadi. Towzih ul-
    Masa'il [Explanation of Problems]. (Tehran: Ilmi,
    1964).
Mina'i, Naila. Women in Islam. (New York: Seaview Books,
    1981).
Mutahhari, Ayatullah Murtiza, Nizam-i Huquq-i Zan dar
    Islam [Women's Rights in Islam]. (Tehran: Islami,
    1974).

Nasr, Siyyid Husayn Nasr, Islamic Life and Thought.
     (Albany: State University of New York Press, 1981).
Rahman, Fazlur. Islam. (Garden City, NJ: Anchor, 1966).
_____, "A Survey of Modernization of Muslim Family
     Law," IJMES 11, no. 4 (1980): 451-65.
Saadawi, Nawal. Hidden Face of Eve, 2nd ed., Sherif
     Hetati, ed. and trans. (London: Press, 1981).
Sanderson, Lilian P. Against the Mutilation of Women.
     (London: Ithaca Press, 1981).
Savory, Roger. Iran under the Safavids. (London:
     Cambridge University Press, 1980).
Tabātabā'ī, Allāmeh Siyyid Muhammad Husain. Shi^cite
     Islam. S. H. Nasr, trans. (Houston: Free Islamic
     Literature, 1979).

4
Social and Economic Change in the Role of Women, 1956–1978

S. Kaveh Mirani

A study of the social and economic positions of women in Iran requires some knowledge of the major economic characteristics of the country and the changes which took place in that society between 1956 and 1978. While a detailed account is beyond the scope of this chapter, a brief summary of Iranian economic development during that period is in order.

To a large extent the structural changes that characterized the economic growth of Iran did not differ greatly from standard cases of development. More capital intensive methods of production, movement of labor from low to high productivity sectors, and diminishing importance of the agricultural sector are the common changes which take place in the early stages of economic development. An additional component of Iranian economic growth, however, was that large shares of the capital formation in the economy were initiated by the public sector or influenced by its policies.

Under the guidelines set forth by the Plan and Budget Organization, a public sector agency, the first national development plan in Iran was launched in 1949. The public sector's priorities for economic growth were carried out through five medium-term development programs, ending in 1978. Due to increasing political and economic problems, the sixth plan, expected to begin in 1978, was postponed; it was scrapped after the revolution of 1978-79.

Over time, the direct and indirect investments in the economy made by the government became progressively larger relative to national income. The increasing role of the government, made possible primarily through oil revenues, was a crucial factor in shaping the level of income and in determining the sectoral and personal distribution of wealth throughout the period.

During the twelve years between 1960 and 1972, national income in real terms grew at an average annual compound rate of 8.7 percent. Consequently, per capita income rose at an average of 5.8 percent in the same period. The quadrupling of oil prices in 1973-74 resulted in an

69

70

increase of 34 percent in real Gross National Product [GNP]
over 1972 followed by a further increase of 42 percent in
1974. After 1974, until 1978, the rate of growth was substantially lower, although real income continued to grow.

TABLE 1

Gross National Product (in 1971 Prices)

Year	Total GNP millions of $	Per capita GNP	Compound growth rate of per capita income (%)
1960	5040	234	--
1965	6970	281	3.7
1966	7510	294	4.5
1967	8390	319	8.2
1968	9200	340	6.4
1969	10020	359	5.4
1970	11150	389	8.0
1971	12750	428	9.5
1972	14400	470	9.4

Source: H. Askari & S. Majin, "Recent Economic Growth
in Iran," Middle Eastern Studies 12 (no. 3, 1976): 106.

Along with the growth in GNP, the sectoral distribution of income changed. Table 2 shows the sectoral distribution of Gross Domestic Product [GDP] over the 1959-
1974 period.

TABLE 2

Sectoral Distribution of Income in Iran: Percentage
Contribution to GDP (selected years)

Year	Agriculture	Industry	Services	Oil
1959	32	17	41	10
1962	30	18	40	12
1968	23	22	41	14
1971	18	22	40	19
1974	9	14	26	51

Source: C. Issawi, "The Iranian Economy 1925-1975:
Fifty Years of Economic Development," in G. Lenczow-
ski (ed.), Iran Under the Pahlavis (Stanford: Hoover
Institution Press, 1978), p. 142.

The agricultural sector, which produced almost one-
third of the national product in 1959, steadily lost its

importance; its contribution fell to 18 percent of GDP by 1971 and stayed in the vicinity of 10 percent between 1974 and 1978. The falling share of the agricultural sector was offset by the growing shares of the oil and industrial sectors so that together these latter sectors produced some two-thirds of the GDP. Later, however, due both to a worldwide reduction in the demand for oil and a continued rise in the level of production of other sectors, the share of oil in the gross domestic product declined.

The personal distribution of income also changed during the period. Despite substantial rises in the income received by virtually all strata of society, the gap between the rich and the poor widened, as demonstrated by the expenditure shares of the top and bottom 20 percent of the population.[1] The Gini coefficient, an indicator of overall inequality of income, also increased between 1959 and 1973.

TABLE 3

Four Measures of Inequality of Consumption Expenditure in Urban Areas

Year	Gini Coefficient	Share of Top 20 Percent	Share of Middle 20 Percent	Share of Bottom 20 Percent
1959	0.4552	51.79	13.54	4.73
1969	0.4710	52.91	13.90	4.45
1970	0.4849	54.30	13.28	4.10
1971	0.5051	55.48	12.60	3.73
1972	0.4916	55.33	12.14	3.88
1973	0.4946	55.56	11.93	3.77

Source: J.H. Pesaran, "Income Distribution and Its Major Determinants in Iran," in J.W. Jacqz, Iran: Past, Present and Future (Aspen, Colo.: Aspen Institute for Humanistic Studies, 1976)

It is also important to note that the fast reduction in the share of the agricultural sector in the GDP did not accompany a corresponding reduction in the labor force in that sector. Although the overall income received in the rural sector presumably increased over time and seasonal migration to cities resulted in improved earnings for rural families, the gap between income received by the urban population and the rural population enlarged. During the fourteen-year period between 1959 and 1973, the per capita consumption expenditure of the urban population relative to that of the rural population rose from 2.13 to 3.16.[2]

The rapid changes in the economy naturally affected the economic and social positions of women. The increase in income and in the stock of capital increased the demand for labor of all kinds, including the demand for female workers. The gradual upward trend in the participation of women in market activities, together with improved facilities for female education, generated a greater incentive for families to invest in the education of their female children. The indicators pertaining to family structure-- marriage, divorce, fertility, etc.--exhibited noticeable if not profound changes. Finally, the government introduced certain measures to enhance the position of women in society. While some of these measures, particularly in relation to a rather small stratum of the society, did elevate the opportunities open to women, for the most part they had little effect on the status of the majority of women in Iran.

Demographic and Family Characteristics

The first national census of housing and population, in 1956, estimated the total number of women in Iran to be approximately 9.3 million. Of these, over two-thirds resided in rural areas or belonged to nomadic tribes; the rest were scattered in some 186 urban centers. By 1976, the female population had increased to roughly 16.4 million, a growth of 76 percent at an average annual compound rate of 2.8 percent.

TABLE 4

Population of Women in Iran
(in thousands)

Year	Urban	Rural	Total	Urban Share %
1956	2883	6426	9310	31
1966	4698	7735	12433	38
1968[a]	5276	8027	13303	40
1971[a]	5806	8036	13842	42
1976[b]	7964	8422	16386	49

Source: Markaz-i Amar-i Iran [Iran Center for Statistics], Statistical Abstracts of Iran (Tehran: Government Printing Office, 2535/1976)

[a]Sample surveys
[b]Population of women has been calculated from total population, assuming a sex ratio of 105 for both urban and rural areas.

One of the demographic consequences of the industrialization of the country between 1956 and 1978 was a steady flow of population from rural into urban areas. By 1978, the urban population had increased from less than one-third to approximately one-half of the nation's population. In the absence of direct data on the inter-

nal movement of the population, the exact magnitude of
the migration is difficult to assess. However, judging
by Table 4, it can be seen that the female population of
urban areas grew at an average compound rate of 4.9 percent between 1956 and 1966 and at 5.3 percent between
1966 and 1976. The corresponding figures for the rural
sector are 1.8 and 0.8 percent respectively. Thus, it
is clear that the magnitude of migration into cities
intensified during the years between 1966 and 1976.

According to a survey conducted in 1964, two-thirds
of the female migrants who moved into the cities were
following either their husbands or their parents. Among
the one-third who migrated independently, almost 90 percent moved for work-related purposes; the remainder moved
for marriage, for study, or for miscellaneous or unspecified reasons.

The rate of growth of population from 1956 to 1968
was relatively high compared both to the experience of
the country in the past and of other countries in the
same period. This high rate was achieved in part as a
result of improvements in medical care, knowledge of
hygiene, and a higher standard of nutrition, resulting
in reduced mortality rates among both adults and infants.
For example, the child mortality rate decreased by 40
percent between 1960 and 1977. The crude death rate
declined by about one-third in the same period, as shown
in Table 5.

TABLE 5

Vital Statistics: Iran

Year	Crude death rate (a)	Child mortality rate (b)	Life expectancy at birth (yrs)
1960	21	24	46
1970	16	18	50
1977	14	14	52

Source: World Bank, World Tables (Washington, D.C.:
The World Bank, 1980)
(a) Per thousand population
(b) Children aged 1-4 years per 1000 of the population.

The rate of fertility in Iran did not follow a
steadily declining trend during the ongoing economic
growth, contrary to the experience of many countries in
a similar stage of development. Rather, the average
crude birth rate, taken here as the representative measure of fertility, dropped for the most part in the fifties and sixties, and then rose slightly in the first six
years of the seventies.

74

TABLE 6

Crude Live Birth Rate, 1950-1976 (per 1000 population)

Year	Urban	Rural	Total	Rate of Change %
1950-54	--	--	48	--
1955-59	--	--	45	- 6.0
1960-64	--	--	38.4	-14.7
1965	--	--	42.3	+10.1
1966	--	--	42.5	+ 0.7
1967	34.7	40.9	38.4	- 9.6
1968	35.5	40.1	38.1	- 0.8
1969	33.2	43.2	39.1	+ 2.6
1970	35.2	46.1	41.6	+ 6.4
1971	36.3	46.3	42.0	+ 1.0
1972	32.6	41.8	37.8	-10.0
1973	33.3	44.2	39.4	+ 4.2
1974	33.1	45.0	39.7	+ 0.8
1975	35.5	46.5	41.5	+ 4.5
1976	35.4	47.3	41.7	+ 0.5

Source: United Nations, Demographic Yearbook,
New York: United Nations, 1950-1966), for 1950-
1966; Markaz-i Amar-i Iran [Iran Center for
Statistics], Statistical Abstracts of Iran
(Tehran: Government Printing Office, 2535/
1976), for 1967-1976. [There are slight
differences between the UN and SAI rates.]

To calculate the rates, population figures
for 1967-75 have been estimated on the basis
of an average growth rate of population.

As may be inferred from Table 6, fertility rates
were consistently higher in rural areas. Some of the
reasons for this will be discussed later in this chapter.
On an international basis, Iran's average fertility rate
was rather high, even when allowances for certain dis-
similarities in economic and social factors are made.[3]
The government encouraged the passage of various
measures by Parliament to improve the condition of women
in the family. The first of these was the Family Protection Law, enacted in 1967. The second was the amendment to that law in 1975. The Family Protection Law was
designed to ease the dominance of men in such matters as
divorce, child custody and polygamy. Under this law,
men who wished to divorce their wives had to obtain court
permission; until this time, men had been permitted to
divorce their wives at will and with no judicial proceed-
ing. The new law facilitated the process of divorce for
women by allowing wider grounds for divorce; further, the
law made it possible for women to be granted custody of

their children in the event of divorce. Under the new
law, men desiring additional wives were required to obtain
the consent of their existing wives or of the courts.[4]
    Many individuals and groups resented the Family
Protection Law, believing that the legislation would
damage the structure of the family. Supporters of the law
felt that it would enable those women who could not get a
divorce under the existing code to break their marriage
contracts. Furthermore, since polygamy and rules pertaining to child custody were unfavorable to women, enactment
of the law was felt by its proponents to be a decisive
step in improving women's welfare.
    Neither the fears of the critics nor the hopes of
the advocates were realized during the Law's ten-year life.
Indeed, contrary to the apprehension of many who believed
that divorce, an indicator of deterioration of the family
structure, would increase, the trend in the divorce rate
was downward after 1967 and into the seventies, as indicated in Table 7.

TABLE 7

Crude Divorce Rates: 1953-1976
(Number of divorces per 1000 population)

Year	Urban	Rural	Total	Rate of Change (%)
1953-1957	--	--	1.39	--
1958-1962	--	--	1.17	-16
1963	--	--	1.09	- 7
1964	--	--	1.07	- 2
1965	--	--	1.00	- 7
1966	--	--	0.97	- 3
1967	--	--	0.77	-20
1968	--	--··	0.57	-26
1969	1.1	0.2	0.57	0
1970	1.1	0.2	0.58	+ 2
1971	1.0	0.2	0.55	- 5
1972	1.2	0.2	0.60	+ 9
1973	1.2	0.2	0.63	+ 5
1974	1.2	0.2	0.64	+ 2
1975	0.9	0.2	0.55	-14
1976	0.9	0.2	0.54	-16

Source: Demographic Yearbooks, 1950-1965 (New York:
United Nations, 1950-1965) for nationwide figures;
Markaz-i Amar-i Iran [Iran Center for Statistics]
Statistical Abstracts of Iran (Tehran: Government
Printing Office, 2536/1977) for urban/rural breakdown.
Rural/urban rates calculated from number of divorces
in each sector assuming average annual rate of popula-
tion growth between 1966-1976.

The impact of the Law on polygamy also seemed to be negligible. Although there are no reliable statistics on the extent of polygamy in Iran, an estimate made in 1964 revealed that no more than 1.5 percent of all households were polygynous.[5] Polygamy was an uncommon phenomenon in 1964, and presumably it was even more uncommon in the later years. Given that the Family Protection Law did not totally forbid polygamy and merely required the consent of the existing wife, it would be safe to say that the impact of the Law on the incidence of polygamy was minimal. Nevertheless, despite the fact that fundamental aspects of the family were unaltered, the well-being of women, whether married or divorced, was marginally enhanced by the Law. An obvious example of such gain was that under the new law some women could obtain custody of their children by court order after divorce.

Participation in Market Activities

The increase over time in the capital stock and the demand for goods and services generated an increased demand for labor of all kinds, including female workers. The initial response of women to the more attractive opportunities in the market place was an increased participation in the work force; during 1955-66 the participation rate among women aged ten years and older increased from 9.2 percent to 12.5 percent. After 1966, however, the participation rate in the urban centers declined considerably while that in the rural sector continued to increase until 1971.

TABLE 8

Women's Economic Activity
(in thousands)

Year	Population (10 yrs & over)			Economically Active			Activity Rate (%)		
	Urban (a)	Rural (b)	Total (c)	Urban (d)	Rural (e)	Total (f)	Urban (d/a)	Rural (e/b)	Total (f/c)
1956	2014	4227	6242	187	388	576	9.3	9.2	9.2
1966	3209	4780	7990	319	681	1000	9.9	14.2	12.5
1968	3677	5234	8911	284	777	1061	7.7	14.9	12.0
1971	4039	5200	9239	302	819	1121	7.5	15.7	12.1

Source: Digarguniha-yi Ijtima^{c}i va Iqtisadi-yi Zanan-i Iran [Social and Economic Developments in the Positions of Women in Iran (Tehran: Plan and Budget Organization, 1352/1973)

A breakdown of the female participation rates in the work force indicates that while the rate of participation of all ages except 10-14 year-olds increased between 1966 and 1971 in the rural sector, it declined for all ages in the urban areas.[6]

TABLE 9

Labor Force Participation Rates for Urban and
Rural Women of Various Age Groups

Age group years	Urban		Rural	
	1966	1971	1966	1971
10-14	8.9	5.1	18.1	16.9
15-19	9.8	6.7	19.8	22.0
20-24	12.1	12.0	15.6	18.1
25-34	10.2	9.1	13.7	15.7
35-44	10.7	6.4	13.5	15.5
45-54	11.0	7.6	11.7	12.7
55-64	8.9	5.8	7.8	8.0
65 and over	5.7	7.6	3.9	4.0

Source: Digarguniha-yi Ijtima^{c}i va Iqtisadi-yi
Zanan-i Iran [Social and Economic Developments
in the Positions of Women in Iran](Tehran: Plan
and Budget Organization, 1352/1973)

The rate of decline of female participation in the
labor force in urban areas was higher in the 10-19 and
35-54 age groups. While the decline in the younger group
was possibly due to a higher rate of school attendance,
the reason for the reduction in the participation rate of
the older age group is not clear. The increase in the
employment rate of women over 15 years of age in the
rural sector could be attributed to several factors. The
most important were the higher wages paid in cottage
industries due to increased prices of handicrafts and the
migration of many male workers to cities, resulting in a
shortage of farmworkers.

TABLE 10

Distribution of Women in the Work Force:
Major Industries, 1971 (% of total)

Activities	Urban	Rural	Total
Agriculture	1.7	41.1	29.8
Mining	--	--	--
Manufacturing	39.6	55.8	51.1
Construction	0.5	0.1	0.2
Energy & Health	0.7	--	0.2
Commercial	2.9	0.1	0.9
Communication/Trans- portation	1.6	--	0.4
Services	53.0	2.5	16.4

Source: Digarguniha-yi Ijtima^{c}i va Iqtisadi-yi
Zanan-i Iran, pp. 76-78.

The distribution of women in different industries is given in Table 10. The majority of active women were employed in manufacturing; agriculture and services accounted for an additional 46.2 percent of female employment. The high rate of female employment in manufacturing is primarily caused by the inclusion of cottage industries in this sector. In fact, in 1971 more than half of the economically active women in rural areas worked in small textile workshops.[7] More than 88 percent of these were carpet-weaving workshops; the rest comprised such crafts as spinning, knitting, and rug weaving.

Over time, the ratio of female to total employment in various industries changed. These changes were more pronounced in the commerical and agricultural sectors. The particularly large increase in the former was presumably due to the many white collar positions filled by women in both public and private sectors.

TABLE 11

Ratio of Women to Total Persons Employed
in Major Industries (%)

Sector	1956	1͜
Agriculture	4.3	8.8
Manufacturing/Mining	33.1	37.2
Construction	0.4	0.4
Energy & Health	2.6	2.1
Commercial	1.0	20.9
Communication/Transportation	0.6	1.6
Services	21.4	20.4

Source: Markaz-i Amar-i Iran [Iran Center for Statistics]. Statistical Abstracts of Iran (Tehran: Government Printing Office, 2530/1971; 2536/1977)

The majority of women in the workforce were unpaid workers. As suggested by Table 12, this was particularly true in the rural sector where fewer than a quarter of women workers received payments for the services performed. The comparable figure for urban areas shows that the percentage of unpaid workers in the rural sector is unusually high. This is most likely due to the prevalence of small workshops and of family farmworkers in this sector. If this is the case, however, perhaps the activities of these women should have been classified as "household" rather than "market" activities.

Information on wages or salaries paid to women is generally unavailable. Therefore, the relative earnings of women to men are hard to establish. The only exception to this is information on wages paid to female farmworkers. According to a survey conducted in 1971, the average daily wage paid to a female farmworker was Rls. 48 ($0.70) compared to Rls. 89 ($1.27) paid to male workers. The ratio of 52 percent implied by the above figures was fairly stable (with a standard deviation of 10 percent) across different provinces of the country.[8] However, the earnings differential among agricultural workers cannot be generalized to reflect the relative earnings of women nationwide and across various industries.

TABLE 12

Types of Employment of Women in the Workforce in 1971
(percentage of total employment in each sector)

Status	Urban	Rural	Total
Employer	0.9	0.7	0.7
Self employed	10.0	5.7	7.0
Civil servant	29.8	0.8	9.2
Wage earner	46.0	15.2	24.0
Unpaid	13.3	77.0	59.1

Source: Digarguniha-yi Ijtima^{c}i va Iqhtisadi-yi Zanan-i Iran [Social and Economic Developments in the Position of Women in Iran] (Tehran: Plan and Budget Organization, 1352/1973), pp. 82-84.

Education

One of the most important causes of the low earnings of women in the workforce was their inferior level of education. The proportion of literate women in the labor force in 1966 was only 11.6 percent, a figure substantially below the literacy rate for men. The difference was even more pronounced in the rural sector.

TABLE 13

Literacy Rates Among Men and Women (Rural/Urban)

Year	Urban		Rural		Total	
	Women	Men	Women	Men	Women	Men
1956	22.4	45.9	1.2	10.9	8.0	22.4
1966	38.9	61.9	4.3	25.4	17.9	40.1
1971	48.1	68.7	8.3	31.9	25.5	47.7

Source: Population Census of 1956; Population Census of 1966; Sample Survey of 1971.
Figures for 1956 and 1966 refer to persons seven years and older while those for 1971 refer to persons six years and older.

On a nationwide basis and among persons six years and older, females were 1.4 times more likely to be illiterate than males in 1971. This probability was lower in the rural areas (1.3) and higher in the urban sector (1.7). The rate of illiteracy for women in the rural sector in 1971 was 92 percent compared to 52 percent for urban women.

Despite the enactment of "cumpulsory education" in 1944 (not effectively enforced until 1955), the establishment of the Literacy Corps in 1963 (to which women were admitted in 1968) and certain other measures to combat illiteracy,[9] the importance attached to public education in Iran was low. While income and the absolute expenditure on education grew considerably from 1956 to 1978, the proportion of GNP spent on public education remained roughly the same. Moreover, as the share of government expenditure in the national income rose over time, the implication is that the share of education in public sector spending declined. The table below shows the expenditure on public education proportional to GNP for selected years and groups of countries.

TABLE 14

Expenditure on Public Education as Percentage of GNP
(Selected Years and Groups of Countries)

Year	Iran	World	Developed Countries	Developing Countries	Arab States
1960	3.2[a]	3.9	4.2	2.4	4.5
1965	3.2	4.8	5.1	2.9	4.0
1970	2.5	5.4	5.7	3.2	4.9
1973	3.1	5.6	5.8	3.8	5.4
1975	4.6	5.7	6.0	4.1	6.8
1978	5.7[b]	5.6	5.9	4.1	5.6

Source: Statistical Yearbook (New York: UNESCO, various issues, 1969-1980).
(a) Figure is for 1963.
(b) Figure is for 1977.

Whether the increase in expenditure on public education facilitated the opportunities for schooling of women relative to men cannot be deduced from Table 14. However, both the nationwide rate of school attendance of women and their school enrollment relative to men increased in all levels of formal education over time (see Table 15).

The breakdown of school attendance figures for the first level for 1966 into rural and urban suggests a large difference between the two areas. In the 7-14 years age group, only 11.6 attended school in the rural sector,

compared to 68.1 percent for the urban areas. The rates
for the male population in this same age group were 45.2
percent and 82.8 percent for the rural and urban centers
respectively.

TABLE 15

Gross School Enrollment Ratios*
F = Females; M = Males

Year	Sex	First Level	Age Group (yrs)	Second Level	Age Group (yrs)	Third Level	Age Group (yrs)
1960	F	27	(7-12)	7	(13-18)	0.42	(20-24)
	M	56		16		1.98	
1965	F	31	(7-14)	18	(15-18)	0.75	(20-24)
	M	66		39		2.34	
1970	F	60	(6-10)	17	(11-16)	1.59	(20-24)
	M	107		34		4.53	
1974	F	67	(6-10)	27	(11-17)	2.69	(20-24)
	M	112		48		6.55	

Source: Statistical Yearbook, 1976 (New York: UNESCO, 1976).
*percent of total enrollment in each level as a proportion of the
corresponding population in that age group. Some ratios in the first
level exceed 100 because of the enrollment of older students in that
level.

An Economic Explanation

Although selective aspects of women's life in Iran--
demographic characteristics, labor force participation,
earnings, education--have been considered separately in
this chapter, they are very closely interrelated. Education directly affects women's earnings in the marketplace,
but the amount of education acquired is also influenced by
potential future earnings. Fertility, an important
determinant of population growth, depends on the age at
marriage, likelihood of divorce, income of the family,
and the time spent working outside the household. The
government can change many of these variables through
specific policies or through altering the level and distribution of income. Cultural peculiarities of a society,
such is its religion and traditions, also play their role
in determining the forces that affect the welfare of women
and their role in the society.

To a large degree both the path of economic growth
and the way it affected women in Iran were similar to the
process of economic development and its impact on the role
of women in the family and in the marketplace throughout
the world. This fact has unfortunately been overlooked
by many students of Iranian culture, who have commonly
endeavored to portray the social and economic experience
of Iran and the changing relationships between different
groups and strata of her society, within a culture-bound

framework, as a special and isolated case.

One of the major factors that confront the family over the course of economic growth of the type experienced in Iran is the increased opportunity to work and to earn higher wages for virtually all members of the family. The father may decide to work longer hours; the mother may turn partly away from time-intensive household activities and decide to join the labor force full- or part-time. At the same time, the higher income of the family will generally tend to increase the demand for the "quality" of children, which usually results in fewer children per family (lower fertility rates).[10]

Since education of children entails both direct and indirect costs--school expenses as well as the income children do not earn if they go to school--the decision about the duration and quality of education must be viewed as an investment decision, with consideration given to the returns from the investment. Without any discrimination on the part of parents between daughters and sons, social and economic factors may dictate a lower investment in the formal education of female children because, among other things, the costs of the formal schooling of female children in a society like Iran's tend to be higher.[11] This would divert parents' investment in formal schooling to some other forms of investment to improve the "quality" and thereby the welfare of female children. Money spent on a dowry and time foregone in teaching household skills to daughters are among the more common examples of alternate investments in female children.

Forms of alternate investment also explain the difference that exists in Iran with regard to the rates of school attendance and literacy on the one hand and labor force participation on the other between rural and urban sectors. Since most of the occupations for women in the rural areas are unskilled or do not require formal education, the return on any given level of schooling is lower compared to the cities, where education plays a more important role in determination of women's earnings. Also, women in rural areas can obtain work more easily than their counterparts in the urban sector. The prevalence of cottage industry and farm-related jobs within the community provides many possibilities for women to work outside of the household in rural areas. Furthermore, since demand for quality of children is positively related to the level of income, urban families, who command a far higher level of prosperity in Iran, spend more on the education of their children.

As indicated by the figures on labor force participation and school attendance of women, the nationwide decline in the former was accompanied by an increase in the latter. In the rural sector the overall increase in work force participation of women, which continued unabated despite a reduction in the activity rate of the 10-14-year-old age group, was made possible through in-

creases in the activity rates of other age groups. Later
age of marriage (from 1966 onward) and a reduction in the
supply of male workers due to school attendance and the
seasonal migration of men to cities were among the reasons for the steadily rising rate of economic activity
among rural women. In urban areas, the steadily rising
rate of school attendance from 1956 onward was accompanied by both a decline in the rate of labor force participation of women and, as indicated by the decline in
the percentage of married women in the 15-19-year-old age
group, a rise in the age at first marriage.12 This was
due to the growing importance attached to the education
of women, both because of better opportunities for educated women in the workforce and because of higher investments in the "quality" of children associated with the
higher income of the family.

Analogous to the experience of many developing
nations, Iran experienced noticeable impacts on the
decisions for marriage and divorce, and on fertility as
a result of urbanization, the gradual increase in the
literacy rate among the population, and the overall increase in the incomes of families. For instance, the
decision to marry is subject to different, often opposing
considerations. On the one hand, urbanization, improvements in pre-marital contacts between men and women,
particularly in cities, and weakening of social taboos
against divorce are among the forces that would tend to
increase the frequency of marriage. However, there are
opposing forces that tend to reduce the rate of marriage:
increased opportunities for women to work outside of the
home resulting in financial independence, increased value
of education resulting in a higher rate of school attendance, etc. In Iran, these latter forces more than offset
the former, so that the crude marriage rate (the frequency of marriage as a proportion of the total population)
declined from the fifties into the sixties and stayed
roughly the same through the sixties and most of the
seventies.13

Contrary to the popular belief that women's emancipation in society (financial independence, higher level of
education, increased opportunities for remarriage after
divorce) will result in higher divorce rates, the frequency of divorce in the population declined over time.
Indeed, while the factors mentioned above do tend to increase the frequency of divorce, the improved efficiency
of new marriages, reflecting a better sorting of mates
or more suitable matches, apparently overrode the tendency of the changed variables to increase the divorce
rate.14 Furthermore, the Family Protection Law, which
had given rise to fears that the stability of the family
would be destroyed, actually exerted little or no influence on the various indicators of the family, as witnessed by the existing aggregate data.

The earlier (1956-66) decline in the rate of fertil-

ity, in common with other indicators of the family, is
dependent upon several social and economic variables
confronting the family. A major variable which tends to
reduce the rate of fertility during periods of economic
growth is the increased value of time, resulting in a
shift from the "quantity" of children to fewer children of
higher "quality." Given the economic and social conditions of Iran during the period under study and the introduction of contraceptives in the sixties, one would have
expected the rate of fertility to have continued its decline into the seventies. Iran is not the only developing country to have demonstrated an increased rate of
fertility in the seventies, and a closer examination of
the factors influencing fertility is needed to shed some
light on this subject.

Summary and Conclusions

The foregoing analysis has relied heavily upon published statistics whose accuracy may rightly be questioned
by those who are aware of the many possible flaws in data
published in developing countries. There are, however, at
least two major reasons to justify such heavy use of these
statistics: they constitute the best available source of
information, and they do tend to reflect a picture of
reality which is by and large within theoretical and in-
tuitive expectations. But any statement about the overall status and welfare of women in society is inevitably a
relative proposition with several possible dimensions:
the differences that existed between men and women, those
that remained between the rural and urban sectors, and the
changes which were made over time.

At least three major conclusions emerge from this
analysis: 1) the overall position and welfare of women
did improve over time; 2) these improvements were primarily due to the changing economic environment rather than to
the specific measures taken by the government to improve
the status of women; and 3) despite cultural differences
as well as certain peculiarities of Iranian economic
development, the observed changes in the positions of
women followed a pattern similar to those experienced by
other countries in the course of economic growth. However, many important questions regarding women in Iranian
society remain unanswered; these questions deserve careful
scrutiny and further research.

NOTES

I am grateful to Gary S. Becker, Behrooz Hadavi, Mary
T. Jones, and Robert T. Michael for many helpful comments
and suggestions.
1. Comparison of Gini coefficients for the rural
sector for 1969 and 1972 points to a lower degree of inequality relative to the urban sector.
2. F. Vakil, "Iran's Basic Macroeconomic Problems:

A 20-Year Horizon," in J.W. Jacqz, ed., Iran: Past, Present and Future (Aspen, Colo.: Aspen Institute for Humanistic Studies, 1976), p. 101.

3. Some have connected this relatively high level of fertility to Islam; see Nadia H. Youssef, "The Status and Fertility Patterns of Muslim Women," in L. Beck and N. Keddie, eds., Women in the Muslim World (Cambridge: Harvard University Press, 1978), pp. 69-99.

4. For more detail see F.R.C. Bagley, "The Iranian Protection Law of 1967: A Milestone in the Advance of Women's Rights," in C.E. Bosworth, ed., Iran and Islam (Edinburgh: Edinburgh University Press, 1971), pp. 47-64.

5. There were 74,000 co-wives in 1964 compared to roughly 4.9 million married women. The figure is from Bagley, "The Iranian Protection Law." See also B. Pakizegi, "Legal and Social Positions of Iranian Women," in Beck and Keddie, Women in the Muslim World, pp. 216-26.

6. The exception is 65 years and older.

7. A small workshop is one employing a total of ten people or less. The majority of these "workshops" did not have more than a single worker; the average labor per workshop was only 1.24 in 1971.

8. The same survey found that although the wages paid to both men and women had risen in 1972, the ratio of 52 percent had not changed.

9. See Issa Sadiq, History of Education in Iran, 7th ed. (Tehran: Tehran University Press, 1975).

10. "More children" is contrary to the recent experience of most Western countries, where economic growth has resulted in lower fertility rates. Nonetheless, some countries have exhibited exceptions to this trend; see M. Gomez, "An Analysis of Fertility in Mexico," Ph.D. dissertation, University of Chicago, 1980.

11. Formal education may even have a negative return for girls in the sense that an "enlightened woman" is not considered to be a suitable wife in some traditional circles.

12. An initially small increase in the rate of labor force participation from 1956 to 1966 was followed by a sharp decline from 1966 to 1971. See Table 8.

13. The average rates per thousand population are 7.5, 6.0, and 5.9 for 1953-59, 1960-69, and 1970-77, respectively.

14. For a theoretical discussion, see G.S. Becker, A Treatise on the Family (Cambridge: Harvard University Press, 1981), chapter 10.

BIBLIOGRAPHY

Askari, H. and Majin, S. "Recent Economic Growth in Iran," Middle Eastern Studies 12 (No. 3, October 1976): pp. 105-23.
Bagley, F.R.C. "The Iranian Protection Law of 1967: A

Milestone in the Advance of Women's Rights," in
Bosworth, C.E., ed. Iran and Islam (Edinburgh:
Edinburgh University Press, 1971), pp. 47-64.

Becker, G.S. A Treatise on the Family (Cambridge: Harvard University Press, 1981)

Demographic Year Book (New York: United Nations, 1969-
1980).

Gomez, M. "An Analysis of Fertility in Mexico." Ph.D.
dissertation, University of Chicago, 1980.

Issawi, C. "The Iranian Economy, 1925-1975: Fifty Years
of Economic Development," in Lenczowski, G., ed.
Iran under the Pahlavis (Stanford, CA: Hoover Institution, 1978), pp. 129-66.

Markaz-i Amār-i Irān [Iran Center for Statistics].
Statistical Abstracts of Iran (Tehran: Government
Printing Office, 2530/1971, 2535/1976, 2536/1977).

Pakizegi, B. "Legal and Social Positions of Iranian
Women," in Keddie, N. and Beck, L., eds., Women
the Muslim World (Cambridge: Harvard University
Press, 1978), pp. 216-26.

Pesaran, J.H. "Income Distribution and Its Major Determinants in Iran," in Jacqz, J.W., ed. Iran: Past,
Present and Future (Aspen, Colo.: Aspen Institute
for Humanistic Studies, 1976), pp.___.

Plan and Budget Organization. Digargunīhā-yi Ijtimā^{c}ī
va Iqtisādī-yi Zanān-i Irān [Social and Economic
Developments in the Positions of Women in Iran]
(Tehran: Government Printing Office, 1352/1973)

Sadiq, I. History of Education in Iran, 7th ed.
(Tehran: Tehran University Press, 1975).

Savory, R.M. "Social Development in Iran During the
Pahlavi Era," in Lenczowski, G., ed. Iran Under the
Pahlavis (Stanford, CA: Hoover Institution Press,
1978), pp. 85-127.

Statistical Yearbook (New York: UNESCO, 1969-1980).

Vakil, F. "Iran's Basic Macroeconomic Problems: A 20-
Year Horizon," in Jacqz, J.W. ed. Iran: Past, Pres-
ent and Future (Aspen, Colo.: Aspen Institute for
Humanistic Studies, 1976), pp. 83-104.

World Tables (Washington, D.C.: World Bank, 1980)

Youssef, N.H. "The Status and Fertility Patterns of
Muslim Women," in Beck, L. and Keddie, N., eds.
Women in the Muslim World (Cambridge: Harvard Uni-
versity, 1978), pp. 69-99.

5
Fatimeh as a Role Model in the Works of Ali Shari'ati

Marcia K. Hermansen

The position of women in contemporary Iran is a subject of interest and controversy. The call for a return to traditional dress has evoked concern and sparked protest, but the analysis of the pre- and post-revolutionary situation in Iran is much more complex than a dichotomy between 'modernized' and 'reactionary'. Although other dimensions and options have been obscured by recent extreme events, they exist. In this chapter I present an example of Islamic modernist thought in Iran-- ideas about the role and identity of women--as found in two works of Ali Shari^{c}ati (1933-1977), an Iranian sociologist and Islamic scholar. These are Fatimeh Fatimeh Ast [Fatimeh Is Fatimeh] and Zan-i-Musalman [The Muslim Woman].

Shari^{c}ati was born near Sabzivar in Khurasan province in 1933, the son of an expert in Qur'an interpretation. From a politically active family, Shari^{c}ati was imprisoned from 1957 until 1960 for his political activities. Following his release from prison he studied sociology and religion at the Sorbonne, receiving a doctorate in Sociology in 1964. He returned to Iran and taught for a time at Firdowsi University in Mashhad, but left that post to become active in the Husainiyyeh-yi Irshad, an educational institution organized by prominent scholars and Islamic clergy to introduce Islamic ideology to contemporary youth. It opened in 1965, and Shari^{c}ati was prominent in its activities from 1967 until 1973, when it was closed by the government.[1] Shari^{c}ati was imprisoned for a year-and-a-half and then released under surveillance for two years. In June, 1977, he was permitted to travel to Europe; on June 19, 1977 he died in Southern England.

According to the categories proposed by Gibb, Shari^{c}ati can most appropriately be termed an Islamic modernist: one who wished to reaffirm the basic principals of Islam but who recognized the need for change and adaptation within that framework. In his modernism Shari^{c}ati was influenced by Muhammad Abduh (d. 1905),

87

Muhammad Iqbal (d. 1938), and Jamaluddin Afghani
(d. 1897). He was particularly influenced by Jamaluddin
Afghani's campaign against imperialism. Shari^{c}ati was
unpopular with many of the Shi^{c}ite ulama of Iran; they
tended to question his competence in the Islamic disci-
plines, since he had not gone through their traditional
course of instruction nor obtained a diploma of ijtihad
[the right to use individual independent reasoning in
deciding questions of fiqh (Islamic law)]. In turn,
Shari^{c}ati attacked the rigidity of most of the clergy;
he felt that their attitude aided the penetration of
Western ways and materialism, particularly among younger
people. In The Muslim Woman he describes the effect
of the conservative approach to these new challenges:
"[It is] as if gas is spilled in a house and somebody,
impulsive, inexperienced, and illogical, tries to ex-
tinguish the fire but ends up spreading it and helping
it all the more."[2]
      Shari^{c}ati's Western training appears in his writing
in references to Durkheim, Freud, and Marx, although he
finds their conceptions superceded by the teachings of
Islam. Although Shar^{c}ati has been criticized as fuzzy
and not objective in methodology, he must be credited
for an original attempt to synthesize some of the more
recent concepts of Western philosophy and social science
with his tradition in a manner which is often intense,
insightful, and stimulating, if at times polemical or
extreme. His popularity in Iran, especially among young
people, was great. After the ban on his work was lifted
in the year preceding the revolution, stalls selling
primarily his works sprang up on many street corners in
Iranian cities.
      One of Shari^{c}ati's main concerns was to promote
knowledge and understanding of Islam through research.
He advocated the use of historical and analytical methodology in the study of religion. Again and again in his
writings he deplored the lack of knowledge which Iranians
have about the great personalities and classical texts of
Islam despite their love, reverence, and praise for them.
He wrote, "We don't lack faith, just knowledge, . . .;
love without knowledge has no value, it is idolatry."[3]
In order to remedy this lack Shari^{c}ati prepared studies
of the lives of Ali, Husain, Zainab, and other great
Shi^{c}ite religious figures; the works with which this
paper are concerned are those about Fatimeh, daughter of
Prophet Muhammad and wife of Ali, the first Shi^{c}ite imam.
      Fatimeh Is Fatimeh is a lecture delivered at the
Husainiyyeh Irshad, directed primarily at the young women
of Iran who are facing a choice among several alternative
roles and attempting to decide what kind of a person one
should be. Shari^{c}ati perceives that "they want to choose
themselves, to make themselves--they want a pattern, an
ideal type."[4] He sees available to them three principle

alternatives: the traditional way, the modernized,
European way, and the way of Fatimeh.[5]

His expression for the first way is chihreh-yi
sunnati [the traditional countenance]. He points out
that his use of 'sunnat' does not refer to Islam or the
way of Muhammad, but rather is opposed to madhhab [reli-
gion]. 'Sunnat' for Shari[c]ati is the national and historical accretions which people tend to confuse with the
essence of the faith. He sees this category as that of
the most conservative, who "confuse being old-fashioned
with being religious."[6] He condemns the place allotted
to woman in Islam as it has evolved in the Iranian context, indicating that her participation in religious activities is generally limited to such folk practices as
the rowzeh and the sufreh. The first is a ceremony in
which women gather to hear a sermon and to mourn for the
martyrs of the Prophet's family. Although mixed rowzehs
do take place, they are usually exclusively female
functions at which the reciter is also a woman. The
mourning often becomes very demonstrative, with the
women "sobbing and beating their thighs, heads and
chests."[7] The sufreh is a ritual dinner given in the
name of Abbas, another son of Ali. Shari[c]ati objects
to these rituals "due to the mercantile attitudes reflected in making rowzeh-connected vows and the tendency
to emphasize the social aspects of the ceremony rather
than sincerely expressing devotion to God."[8]

Shari[c]ati further criticizes the distinction between
men's and women's levels of participation in religion:
"It [religion] has become zananeh [for women only] and
mardaneh [for men only]: saying proverbs and mourning and
rowzeh and sufreh is the religion of women; religious
colleges, the pulpit, religious schools, libraries, study
and research and lectures is the religion of men."[8]
After discussing historical aspects of the evolution of
such a role for women, Shari[c]ati concludes that it is not
Islamic. "In the name of Islam they took away from her
the rights and possibilities which Islam itself had given
to her, and they ranked her social standing at the level
of a washing machine, and brought down her human worth
in the form of [calling her] 'mother of children', and
they were ashamed to mention her name, and called her by
the name of her child [as long as that child was a
boy].[10]

On the subject of the education of women, Shari[c]ati
cites the hadith, "Educate the Muslims, men and women,"[11]
and protests that the conservative husbands and fathers

> only for the sin of being a woman, and some-
> times in the name of being religious and loyal
> to the faith, kept her from acquiring an edu-
> cation and obtaining fulfillment--despite the
> fact that in the history of Islam many women

reached the level of ijtihad, and gave
lessons in the religious schools, and wrote
very useful moral and intellectual books.[12]

In his portrayal of the second alternative open to
the Iranian woman, Shari^c ati goes into some detail in
describing the contemporary Iranian social situation and
historical and cultural developments in East and West
leading up to it. This modernized European woman is
represented by the newly-Westernized woman of upper-class
urban society, but she in turn is imitating a false image
of the Western woman projected by the mass media.
Shari^c ati, who lived for years in the West, wants Iranians to know that the European women depicted by such
mass-consumption magazines as Zan-i-Ruz and Ittila^c at-i-
Banuvan, is a false one, depicting only a minority of
jet-setters and movie-magazine favorites. To correct
the unfortunate misimpression that clothes rather than
achievement are the important criterion of woman's
personhood in the West, Shari^c ati cites positive
examples of Western women of whom Iranians never or rarely hear, mainly scientists and social and political activists. He gives as examples a mother and daughter who
study the communication systems of ants in remote desert
areas; Madame Goichin, who spent her life researching
Islamic philosophy and correcting translations based on
her knowledge of the Greek sources; Mme. Della Vida
an Italian Islamist, who worked on Ibn Sina; Mme. Curie;
Mme. de la Chapelle, a Swede, who studied extensively
the life of Ali and compiled an edition of the Nahj ul-
Balagheh; Mlle. Maishan, a French resistance fighter, who
supports the Palestinian cause although she is Jewish;
the Parisiennes who worked for the liberation of Algeria;
Angela Davis; and an Irish woman activist.[13] He says,

Not once have we seen them hold up a picture
from the University of Cambridge, or the Sorbonne, or Harvard; saying how the female students come and go, how they sit from morning
until night in the libraries, bent over European manuscripts from the fourteenth and fif-
teenth centuries, and tablets from 2500 and
3000 years ago found in China, or over a manuscript of the Qur'an, or a handwritten text in
Latin, Greek, Cuneiform, or Sanskrit.[14]

In contrast, Shari^c ati cites the negative models familiar
to Iranian women from the magazines, such as Miss World,
Princess Grace, Twiggy, and Brigette Bardot.
Shari^c ati describes the superficially modernized
women in Iran in several sections of Fatimeh Is Fatimeh.
He calls them hich va puch [null and void], staying at
home to do nothing except to beautify themselves, full of

hatred, envy and pride, flirting and lying.[15] He is
sympathetic to the situation of the daughters of such
women because the daughters cannot find anything worth
emulating in their mothers' relgious observances, con-
sisting as they do of

> holding quasi-religious parties or ones resem-
> bling the old religion for one another; sufrehs
> to make vows and seasonal rowzehs and aqiqeh
> meetings [for the baby's first haircut] and
> sacrifices and childbirth parties and farewell
> parties and activities to get daughters-in-law
> and trap sons-in-law and so on and so on, so
> that she can hide her lonliness and uselessness
> under her cloak of religion and tradition or
> custom; and which bestow on her a sense of
> doing something right, and of activity, respon-
> sibility, coming and going, struggle, making a
> fuss, sensation, planning, and designing and
> false goals--and which provide her a place to
> display attractiveness, fashion, gowns, jewels,
> and the glory of her family.[16]

The daughter sees that her mother "lives in a kind of
inanity and tranquil futility, with neither purpose nor
responsibility, neither a philosophy of life nor a meaning of existence."[17] The young daughter of a woman of
this type breathes a different air and is torn apart by
her exposure to the intellectual and emotional excitement
of a new world opening before her; however, she is en-
trapped "in the prohibitions of her parents who want her
to sit in a concealed corner of the house until a husband
comes along, after which she will be subjugated to satisfying his physical desires while he will allow her no
share in religious sentiments and assemblies."[18]
    Shari^cati thus finds neither the traditional nor the
Westernized model of woman appropriate, rejecting the
facile solution of some modernizers who say, "Cut short
the chadur! Woman will be instantly enlightened!"[19] He
feels that these two approaches combine to make "our
girls plaster mannikins in the shop window who are
neither Eastern nor Western, 'foreign dolls' empty inside, artificially decorated and painted-up, who have
neither the feelings of the women of our yesterday, nor
the knowledge of the women of their [the Western]
today."[20]
    Having rejected these models, Shari^cati holds up
Fatimeh as the exemplar and ideal type. In his study of
Fatimeh he mentions the efforts of Louis Massignon in
collecting information about the Prophet's daughter, and
he also cites the work of Bint al-Shati' (Aisha Abd-ul
Rahman), a contemporary Arab scholar teaching in Egypt,
while avoiding the body of legendary and miracle litera-

ture. Although material about Fatimeh which is of the
factual rather than the legendary genre is somewhat
scanty (see Lammens [1912], Vaĺieri [1954]), Shariᶜati
finds several themes on which to elaborate in this biography. Elsewhere he stated that it is sufficient to re-
call the worthy personages of the Islamic tradition in
order to be inspired; this is consistent with his attitude toward the dynamic nature of religious motifs. In
Fatimeh Is Fatimeh he evokes Fatimeh's close relationship
with her father, for which she was known as Umm Abĭha
[mother of her father], as well as her unique role in
being so honored in a society in which being female was a
disgrace and in which female infanticide had been a prevalent practice. Shariᶜati sees this special status of
Fatimeh as a prelude to the theme of the improvement of
the role of women in Islam. At the same time he notes
that while such a positive attitude toward a female was
revolutionary in pagan Arab society, it was prefigured
in the Abrahamic tradition, for Hagar, a woman, was the
only person granted the honor of burial in the Kaᶜaba.[21]
    Later in the study Fatimeh's strength in enduring
adversity is illustrated by the hardships she experienced
with her family during the boycott of the Bani Hashim by
the Quraish. Other aspects of Fatimeh's character are
revealed through incidents in her life: her courage in
confronting the then-ruling Abu Bakr and Umar, her
knowledge of politics and skill in interpreting the
Qur'an, her sense of social responsibility, and her protest against the increasingly materialistic trend which
the Islamic society was following. All of these can be
seen as relevant traits in the context of Iran in the
1970s without the specific connection having to be made
by the author. Rather, Shariᶜati uses such suggestive
language as "Muhammad had to bear the heavy burden, and
Fatimeh had to demonstrate in herself the character of
the new, revolutionary values."[22]
    The other dimension of Fatimeh brought out in
Shariᶜati's biographical study is more subtle and inter-
pretive and is best illustrated by his treatment of two
incidents. In one, the newly married Fatimeh and Ali
are living in poverty on the outskirts of Medina.
Fatimeh is having difficulty handling the heavy housework, so she and Ali decide to ask the Prophet for one
of the women captives to assist her. Prophet Muhammed
refuses, preferring to employ all resources for the
benefit of the poor people among the Muslims. That night
the Prophet comes to the house of Ali and Fatimeh and
presents them with a greater gift, a special litany to
recite which was given to him by the angel Gabriel.
Shariᶜati comments, "Once again, Fatimeh learned such a
lesson, once again, with a soft blow that informed her to
the depths of her being, Fatimeh learned that, 'She was
Fatimeh.' . . . This is not a lesson of 'knowing' but a
lesson of 'becoming'. Becoming Fatimeh is not easy."[23]

The other passage in this vein focuses on Fatimeh's
independent personhood. The Prophet once admonished her,
"Fatimeh, do your work, for I won't always be here to
help you."[24] At this point Shari^{c}ati interjects, "See
what a difference there is between this Islam and an
Islam where they say 'One tear drop for Husain extin-
guishes the fires of hell.'" He further comments,
"Fatimeh had to become Fatimeh on her own, being the
daughter of Muhammad would not do it for her." This
introduces Shari^{c}ati's reinterpretation of shifa^{c}at
[intercession].[25]

> Fatimeh through the shifa^{c}at of Muhammad be-
> came Fatimeh, for shifa^{c}at in Islam is the
> cause of acquiring 'being worthy of salvation'
> not a means for 'the salvation of the unworthy'.
> It is the individual who must seize shifa^{c}at
> from the intercessor and through it change his
> [or her] own destiny. . . .He must seize it,
> Shafi^c [the intercessor] does not bestow it
> [automatically] on the individual.[26]

In other words one has to be affected, emotionally, intellectually, and in his or her whole nature by this
exemplar, in order to make oneself. The conclusion of
the book echoes this Existentialist refrain:

> I wanted to say, Fatimeh is the daughter of
>   noble Khadijeh.
> I saw, this is not Fatimeh.
> I wanted to say, Fatimeh is the daughter of
>   Muhammad.
> I saw, this is not Fatimeh.
> I wanted to say, Fatimeh is the wife of Ali.
> I saw, this is not Fatimeh.
> I wanted to say, Fatimeh is the mother of
>   Hasan and Husain.
> I saw, this is not Fatimeh.
> I wanted to say, Fatimeh is the mother of
>   Zainab.
> Still, I saw that this is not Fatimeh.
> No, she is all of these but all of these are
>   not Fatimeh.
> Fatimeh is Fatimeh.[27]

Thus concludes Shari^{c}ati's lecture, a message for
the young women of Iran. At times the connection of the
biography of the historical Fatimeh with the situation
of the modern woman seems vague, as if by merely
invoking the name and some events Shari^{c}ati can make
available a sufficiently coherent identity without offering a concrete plan of action for women. Shari^{c}ati has
argued elsewhere for the vitality of the symbol, but one

94

wonders whether this type of inspirational biography can
be effective since it relies so heavily on an inner
attitude rather than a specific program for education.

As he presents Faṭimeh and the positive traits for
women in general, Shir^cati's third alternative consists
of being religious, strong, patient, committed, socially
aware, intellectually developed, and most of all, of
being a woman who has a personhood and identity to grow
into and fulfill.

It is, however, possible to criticize Shari^cati's
view as being alienated from aspects of women's religious
and social lives which arise from social, cultural, and
religious needs. For example, the rowzeh, the hammam
[bathhouse] as a place for socializing with other women,
and the women's societies are all rejected by Shari^cati
without mention of the need for women's networks and
their value in the existing social milieu. How could the
society be expected to make such a transition from a
'popular' Islam, integrated into daily life, to a more
severe, intellectually 'pure' Islam? One may also
speculate that in living this intellectually 'pure'
Islam there is little scope for emotional expression
aside from anger and determination.

Having deprecated popular practices, Shari^cati cannot turn to legal reform since he is not a mujtahid or
faqih. Like Afghani, he is a philosopher-reformer,
embroiled in a political struggle, himself becoming a
symbol and inspiration, but somehow removed from his own
society.

The continuing influence of Shari^cati in Iran and
the other Islamic countries can only be assessed after
more time has passed. His view of Islam as going beyond
both Marxism and Western ideologies in "working to
liberate the nature of man (and woman*), both spiritual
and realistic"^28 represents an alternative for young
Muslims, but the distance between popular tradition and
intellectual purity is perhaps no less difficult to
bridge than the gap between the conservative ulama and
the militant students in Iran.

*My addition. M.H.

NOTES

1. Shahrough Akhavi, Religion and Politics in
Contemporary Iran (Albany: State University of New York
Press, 1980), p. 144.
2. Ali Shari^cati, Zan-i-Musalmān (Teheran: n.d.),
p. 6.
3. Ali Shari^cati, Ali Tanhā Ast (Teheran: n.d.),
p. 6.

4. Ali Shari^{c}ati, <u>Fatimeh Fatimeh Ast</u> (Teheran: n.d.).
5. Ibid., p. 46.
6. Ibid.
7. Anne Betteridge, "Controversial Vows of Urban Muslim Women in Iran," in N.A. Falk and R. Gross, eds., <u>Unspoken Worlds, Women's Religious Lives in Non-Western Cultures</u> (San Francisco: Harper & Row, 1980).
8. Ibid.
9. Shari^{c}ati, <u>Fatimeh Fatimeh Ast</u>, p. 109.
10. Ibid., p. 99.
11. Ibid.
12. Ibid., p. 103.
13. Ibid., p. 75-77.
14. Ibid., p. 78.
15. Ibid., p. 106.
16. Ibid., p. 107.
17. Ibid., p. 109.
18. Ibid.
19. Ibid.
20. Ibid., p. 79-80.
21. Ibid., p. 125.
22. Ibid., p. 121.
23. Ibid., p. 149.
24. Ibid., p. 152.
25. Ibid., p. 152-53.
26. Ibid., p. 154.
27. Ibid., p. 216.

BIBLIOGRAPHY

Akhavi, Shahrough. <u>Religion and Politics in Contemporary Iran</u>. Albany: State University of New York Press, 1980.
Beck, L. and Keddie, N., eds. <u>Women in the Muslim World</u>. Cambridge: Harvard University Press, 1978.
Bellah, R., ed. <u>Religion and Progress in Modern Asia</u>. New York: Free Press, 1965.
Betteridge, Anne. "Controversial Vows of Urban Muslim Women in Iran," in Falk, N.A. and Gross, R., eds. <u>Unspoken Worlds, Women's Religious Lives in Non-Western Cultures</u>. San Francisco, Harper & Row, 1980.
Falk, N.A. and Gross, R., eds. <u>Unspoken Worlds, Women's Religious Lives in Non-Western Cultures</u>. San Francisco: Harper & Row, 1980.
Fisher, Michael M.J. "On Changing the Concept and Position of Persian Women," in Beck, L. and Keddie, N., eds. <u>Women in the Muslim World</u>. Cambridge, Harvard University Press, 1978.
Lammens, H. <u>Fatima et les Filles de Mohammet</u>. Rome: Samptibus Ponificii instituti biblici, 1912.
Mernissi, F. Beyond the <u>Veil</u>. Cambridge: Schenkman Publishing Co., 1975.

96

Rowbotham, Sheila. Women, Resistance and Revolution.
    New York: Vintage Books, 1974.
Shariᶜatī, Alī. Alī Tanhā Ast. Teheran: n.d.
_____. Fātmieh Fatimeh Ast. Teheran: n.d.
_____. Zan-i Musalmān. Teheran: n.d.
_____. On the Sociology of Islam. H. Algar, trans.
    Berkeley: Mizan Press, 1979.
_____. Marxism and Other Western Fallacies. R. Camp-
    bell, trans. Berkeley: Mizan Press, 1980.
Vaglieri, L.V. "Fātima" in Encyclopedia of Islam.

6
An Analysis of Fida'i and Mujahidin Positions on Women's Rights

Eliz Sanasarian

> Women have come to revolutionary consciousness
> by means of ideas, actions, and organizations which
> have been made predominantly by men. We only know
> ourselves in societies in which masculine power
> and masculine culture dominate, and can only as-
> pire to an alternative in a revolutionary move-
> ment which is male defined. We are obscured in
> "brotherhood" and the liberation of "mankind."[1]

In almost every national context and at different
historical periods women have been recruited either as
an auxiliary workforce or for direct combat during wars,
civil strifes, national liberation movements, and revolutions. These events oftentimes have highlighted the
significance of the female population as a national
resource. Still, women were followers even when they
undertook nondomestic tasks and responsibilities.
In any study of the women's role in major national
upheavals a clear conceptual separation should be made
between the ideals of the movement and the rights of
women. There is an erroneous tendency to combine the
two, the result of which is the dissolution of the latter.
The victory of a movement and the liberation of women are
two different ideas. The issue of women's rights may be
present or absent, depending on the specific nature of a
movement. For instance, this issue coexisted (somewhat
uncomfortably) with the leftist ideology during the 1917
Bolshevik Revolution in Russia.[2] However, despite the
use of women in combat in the Algerian national liberation
movement, there was no mention of the future role and
rights of the female participants.[3] In Iran, as in other
countries, women have been encouraged to take part in
major national upheavals. Various political groups, at
different periods, have consistently sought female
membership. Some have addressed the women's rights issue
while others have ignored it.
This paper focuses on the women's rights issue as
defined by two active political groups in Iran: the

Fida'i and the Mujahidin organizations. Both were
functioning as guerrilla units in the 1970s in opposition
to the Shah Muhammad Riza's regime. They also had (and
continue to have) many active female members. However,
as the authority of the Islamic Government was strengthened these groups adopted opposing views. While the Fida'i
organization today tacitly supports (along with the Tudeh
Party) the actions of the theocratic regime, the Mujahidi
organization has become its most active and ardent oppo-
nent. More specifically, this chapter will address a
number of questions: What is the ideological position of
each group on the rights of women? How have each treated
the women's rights issue in practice? What are the
similarities and differences of these organizations on
this issue? And what are the implications for women if
one or the other group gains control of the government?
This study uses the publications of both organizations
plus a number of informal and formal interviews with the
women of the Fida'i as well as the Mujahidin organizations. A more detailed analysis of the evolution of the
women's rights issue in Iran is presented in another
work.[4]

The Fida'i Organization

The Sazman-i Chirikha-yi Fida'i-yi Khalq-i Iran [The
Organization of Iranian Peoples Fida'i Guerrillas], known
as the Fida'i, was the end result of the merger of three
separate groups in 1971. It operated as a guerrilla unit
for many years. A few splits in its leadership ranks
resulted in the formation of other organizations.[5] After
the 1979 Revolution, the Fida'i organization continued to
support the Islamic Republic. In the summer of 1980,
disagreements in the leadership ranks primarily over this
issue split the organization. The group which broke away
was identified as the Fida'i (the minority), and the
original group became known as the Fida'i (the majority).
These labels were not a reflection of their membership
size but rather the political divisions in the leadership
cadre. Whenever referring to the present, this chapter
concerns the Fida'i (the majority) group.
The Fida'i organization, from the time of its in-
ception in 1971, did not take a strong position on women's
rights. Like the majority of the leftist organizations in
other nations, the Fida'is have never acknowledged women's
oppression to be separate from the overall oppression of
the masses. Women's oppression is identified in class
terms only and is to be overcome by the destruction of the
class system. The specifics of their stand on women were
never spelled out either before or after the 1979 Iranian
Revolution. They simply argued that the process of
socialism would automatically take care of the rights of
women.

The Fida'i contend that the rights of women are not distinct from the rights of men. This contention is partially correct because political and economic conditions affect both sexes. For instance, male as well as female anti-Shah activists were captured and tortured with no show of discrimination or mercy with respect to their sex. Also, it is correct that the variable of class affects certain rights of women. While issues such as hygiene and disease primarily affect lower class women, other issues such as early and forced marriages of young girls affect all classes of women. Upper-class women are better sheltered, fed, and dressed than lower class women. They do not have to struggle for meager wages and work in the worst possible conditions to survive. These are simple facts which strengthen the relationship between sex and class, relating the two on the generalities of human existence.

The Fida'i stand on this issue is not unique. A majority of the leftist organizations in the world, including established communist regimes, have viewed sexual discrimination only in the context of class relations. Neither the Fida'is nor other leftist groups in Iran has ever tolerated a continuous independent and outspoken feminist voice within its organization. This traditional stand has been challenged in the Western world by leftist women much more rigorously than in the third world nations. Despite the conceptual ties between socialism and feminism they are not one and the same. Socialist feminists say that to argue that the rise of the working class populace will bring about the rise of women is to ignore the elements of cultural patriarchy and the historically rigid socialization process. These elements give a special dimension to the status of women. They demonstrate that women are discriminated against not only on the basis of class, but also on the basis of sex. A working class woman is exploited not only as a worker but also as a female by the male workers of her own class. Socialist feminists have argued that a socialist stand without a feminist component is not Marxism.

> The prevalent notion that the struggle for
> women's liberation is "secondary" to that
> for proletarian revolution, meaning not
> only dependent but also comparatively un-
> important, is not Marxism but mechanical
> materialism.[6]

In the months following the Revolution, the Fida'i organization refused to back any endeavor for women's rights. Ayatullah Khomeini's statement in March 1979 that women employees of government agencies should wear the Islamic hijab [head covering] drove thousands of women to protest.[7] During a five day demonstration, women demanded a greater voice in the government, equal

wages for equal work, the right to choose what to wear,
and the preservation of Family Protection Laws.[8] Even
though none of these demands were class-based, the Fida'i
organization accused the demonstrators of being pro-Shah
and upper-class oriented. The second collective attempt
by pro-women's rights groups was the Conference of the
Unity of Women in December 1979 in Teheran. Despite the
plea of women's groups not to do so, the Fida'i organiz-
tion arranged a demonstration on the same day and at the
same time as the conference, therefore diverting attention of many (including their female members) away from
the women's conference. Their reaction was in tune with
the Islamic fundamentalists who cut off the electricity
of the building in order to stop the conference. In spite
of such efforts, the conference was convened by candle-
light.[9]

It is imperative to point out that the Fida'is have
never endorsed the repressive policy of the Islamic
Republic regarding women. In fact, they have mildly
acknowledged that the status of women is in a dismal
state and that the government is inattentive to women's
rights. The Fida'is, however, have proposed a remedy:
as the revolutionary process continues the role of
imperialism will decrease, resulting in a better condition
for the masses. This will in turn elevate the status of
women.[10]

The leadership of the Fida'i organization has
encouraged its female members to dress moderately, and to
wear a scarf as a sign of respect to the masses and for
their own protection.[11] As the Iran-Iraq war broke out
in late 1980, their publications continued to glorify
women's heroism and sacrifice. Mothers who had lost sons
in the war were referred to as great female heroines.
The sewing of clothes for the soldiers and encouraging
them to fight against the Iraqis were also identified as
acts of heroism by women.[12]

The stereotypes and contradictions inherent in the
Fida'i organization's position on women's rights stem
from a male-dominated, upper-class leadership cadre
(typical of leftist groups worldwide), who have certainly
read Marx but have failed to shake off their paternalistic
sense of superiority towards the female sex. Women who
joined the organization naturally adopted the same outlook
as the men, even though at times some have sensed a conflict between their inner desires and those of the
organization. Acknowledging that the female populace has
been denied many rights and repressed by Khomeini's rule,
one Fida'i woman in a 1981 interview with this author
stressed that none of the rights lost were important
because of more serious "threats to our country."

The Fida'i women who were interviewed identified
themselves as atheists, stating that women's liberation
was not inherent in Islam. They saw Islam as a repressive rather than a liberating force. Despite this belief,

the Fida'i women opposed any organized activity to liberate women. Echoing the ideas of their male comrades,
they argued that to pursue the women's rights issue would
hurt the cause of the revolution. They were unable, however, to elaborate why such a struggle would damage the
long-range goals of a socialist movement. The Fida'i
women interviewed also admitted that men dominated most
of their group meetings. They confessed feeling inferior
to their male partners in terms of knowledge and ability.
It was striking to witness the ease with which the idea
of inferiority was internalized by these educated women
and to realize that the Fida'i organization had done
nothing to alter it. If anything, by projecting a cultural stereotype of women as second-class citizens under
the guise of leftist rhetoric, the organization may have
further reenforced female insecurities about the role of
women in society.

The Mujahidin Organization

The Sazman-i Mujahidin Khalq-i Iran [The Organization of Iranian People Fighters] differs radically from
the Fida'i. Founded in the 1960s, it did not operate as
a guerrilla unit until 1971. The Mujahidin's ideology
is based on a leftist interpretation of the Qur'an,
advocating a progressive Islam. As one scholar has
observed:

> They intended to break the clerical monopoly
> over religion and develop a new Islam that
> would synthesize the mild features of European
> socialism with the progressive ideas of early
> Iranian Shi^{c}ism, and the advantages of indus-
> trial technology with the cultural values of
> their own traditional society.[13]

The Mujahidin were at odds with the Islamic authorities from the early months of 1979. As the new constitution was being discussed, the Mujahidin suggested the
addition of fourteen points. One of them was the acknow-
ledgment of full Islamic equality of men and women. None
of their points was accepted, and the Mujahidin refused
to support the constitution.
An interesting aspect of the Mujahidin organization
is the consistency with which they address the issue of
women's rights. This is demonstrated in their numerous
pronouncements and publications. Women are clearly
recognized as a revolutionary force. Since they constitute half of the population of every society, no revolution will be complete without their participation. The
Mujahidin argue that the status of women as second class
citizens will not change with a few legislative measures
such as divorce rights. What needs to change is the
whole social, economic, political, and cultural make-up

of Iran. In all these spheres women have been judged by
their sexuality rather than by their humanity. This false
approach has created stereotypes of women as wives and
mothers, and therefore eliminated them from social and
political activism. The liberation of women requires
the restructuring of many traditional relations, and even
men's thoughts should undergo a major change. Confining
women to the family sphere is viewed by the Mujahidin as
enslavement to the husband. They argue that the capital-
ist system allows women to enter the marketplace for
further exploitation and prevents them from entering the
society.[14]

These views are probably very impressive to Western
feminists. However, there is more to the Mujahidin's
position on women. They have favored the use of an
Islamic hijab in the form of rusari [scarf] for their
female members without imposing an equivalent restriction
on male members. The use of the hijab is considered
essential for the "preservation of the moral health of
the society." In spite of this, they oppose forced veiling of women under the Islamic Republic, calling it
"illogical."[15] A Mujahid woman in a personal interview
with me described the rationale behind the use of the
hijab:

> We believe in evolutionary change. Since class
> relations persist and humans are judged based
> on their sexuality, women have been exploited
> as sex objects. In order to remove this type
> of outlook and restore the health of the
> society, women should wear modest clothing
> and wear the rusari.

When asked why men were not subjected to the same restriction, she simply replied, "Women have been viewed more as
sex objects than men."

Another feature of the Mujahidin which raises doubts
among many secular elements is their heavy reliance on the
Qur'an and Islam. How they compromise between socialism
(a secular ideology) and Islamic thought remains a puzzle
to many. This uneasy ideological compromise was first
initiated by Ali Shari^{c}ati, an Iranian sociologist who
wrote extensively about the need to reform and modernize
Islam by incorporating ideas about the new socio-political
phenomena of the twentieth century, including the women's
liberation movement.[16] The Mujahidin's organizational
ideology was deeply influenced by Shari^{c}ati's work. However, his arguments concerning the woman's role in society
were plagued with contradictions and inconsistencies which
the Mujahidin have inherited. These contradictions are
reflected specifically in the Mujahidin's interpretation
of the Qur'an regarding women's rights.[17] They rely
heavily on those verses which are addressed to the
"masses" and seem favorable to women and leave out those

which explicitly deny specific rights to women (e.g., the
inheritance of daughters is half that of sons; two female
legal witnesses are equal to one male). Like the Fida'is,
they refused to back the March 1979 demonstrations and
December 1979 women's conference. As a male member of the
group put it, "although it becomes a major issue at times,
the question of women is not the main one, which is the
need to sweep away the traces of imperialism."[18]

It is important to point out that despite the uneasy
encounter of the educated, pro-secular, and non-Islamic
Iranians with the Mujahidin, they have always been popular
among the traditional middle class and the progressive
bazaar people. They were the first major pro-Revolution
group to publicly deny Khomeini's concept of an Islamic
Republic. Hundreds of their members have been killed by
the officials of the Republic in different cities.
Numerous female sympathizers and members as young as nine
years old have been tortured, executed, or gunned down in
the streets.[19] As has been the case in other countries
(and as was the case during the Pahlavi era), women
revolutionaries have received no special treatment in
punishment from the authorities.

A striking feature of the Mujahidin is the glorification of martyrdom. The endorsement of martyrdom has
been the feature of many religious and secular movements
in the West as well as in other parts of the world. The
concept of martyrdom is also very much in tune with
Iranian Islamic culture. This unusual aggrandizement of
self-sacrifice apparently binds members of a group
together. It seems, however, to appear with great intensity among the Mujahid women. Their writings demonstrate
a burning desire for death. The intensity of this desire
is so overwhelming that at times it seems to take over
everything else. The means (death) is more important
than the end (victory), and in a symbolic realm the means
become the end. Excerpts from the inheritance letters
(wills) of two Mujahid women exemplify this point.

Sima Sabaq was killed in the street in the city of
Lahijan by a group of militiamen loyal to the Islamic
Republic. In her inheritance letter she had written,
"I know that I have to sacrifice myself for God and for
the masses. . . . If by shedding my blood we will achieve
freedom, let there be more shedding of blood of the children of the masses in this land."[20] She was only fifteen
years old at the time of her death. Gawhar Adab-Avaz,
another Mujahid woman, was killed while carrying out the
assassination of Ayatullah Dastghaib (the personal representative of Ayatullah Khomeini in Shiraz) and a reported
seven to twelve of his compatriots. In her will she had
written, "I have always wished to become a martyr en route
to my goal. . . . My soul belongs to God and to the masses
and whenever it is necessary it will fly out to them
. . . . I hope God will accept this martyr [herself] from
the masses."[21] She was twenty-one years old when she died.

Indeed, there is a need for a comprehensive study of why these women long for death. Is it a way to express their personal discontent with life? Is the glorification of death merely a cultural trait? Does it stem from the teachings and socialization of Islam reenforced by the political ideology of the Mujahidin? Does the women's youth make them vulnerable to martrydom? It is, of course, outside the scope of this study to search for answers to these questions (if there are any). The important point, here, is that there is much fantasizing about martrydom which might be related to the political role of women. As females they are denied major leadership positions in the organization. This, in addition to their subjugated upbringing, turns women into loyal and dedicated followers. As leaders they would have been taught to maintain the cause, but as followers they are conditioned to give for the cause. Dissolving themselves in the idea of service to God and to the masses (which is in accordance with their traditional socialization), they begin to fantasize about death. They seem to internalize the belief that their death will enhance the cause of the organization. The Mujahidin have done nothing to alleviate this tendency. In fact, a common practice is to congratulate the close relatives and friends of a Mujahid martyr.

A Dismal Picture

A direct comparison between the Fida'i and the Mujahidin organizations shows both similarities and differences in relation to women. Both are run by an all male leadership, with no females in commanding positions. The Mujahidin, however, regard women as a revolutionary force and encourage their participation in armed struggle against the Islamic Republic. Before the Revolution the Feda'i also allowed an active role for their women, but after the Revolution and their subsequent pro-Khomeini stand, the role of women has deteriorated to the distribution of leaflets and the performance of nonessential services.

Neither group believes in a separate movement for women's rights. Both perceive these rights to be inseparable from the overall rights of the people. The Mujahidin, however, have taken time to address the question in more detail. They should be credited for acknowledging the women's question. Their publications are always addressed to both sexes, treating women's rights as a viable issue in need of close attention. Mas^{c}ud Rajavi, the leader of the Mujahidin, consistently refers to "women's rights" in his interviews. However, his recommendations for improving the condition of women in Iranian society are neither female-based nor female-initiated. The Fida'i organization, on the other hand, does not bother itself with such delicacies. It simply proclaims Marx's view on the issue without elaboration. The Mujahidin more accurately reflect the traditional populace and are more in tune with the Islamic cultural heritage of Iran. The Fida'i stand on women's rights is more pretentious and highly hypocritical. Admitting that the Khomeini reign has repressed women's rights, they have never taken a strong public stand against it.

Interestingly, the Mujahidin women interviewed demonstrated much more self-respect, confidence, and knowledge about their organization than the Feda'i women. Although more rigorous study is needed, these unusual differences might be related to each group's stand on women's rights. The Mujahidin women are taken seriously as a revolutionary force. This revolutionary zeal allows them to operate separately from their loved ones (even their husbands), giving them a separate identity and a certain degree of freedom.[22] The Fida'i (majority) women realize that their rights have been repressed but, while resenting Islam, feel obligated to follow the organizational line of support for the Islamic Republic, a contradiction which may be suppressed in the subconscious but surfaces in attitudes and behavior. The Mujahid women seek to remedy social ills in general through anti-establishment activities. Also, the endorsement of Islam, a traditional ideology, along socialist lines, a modern ideology, provides a psychological compromise for many young Iranian women. Although to many people this might appear to be a contradiction, to a traditional-minded (even though educated) woman with an awareness of the requirements of modern times, it could be a salvation from contradiction. This might partially explain the ease and confidence of many Mujahid women.

At the core, however, both groups are led by males and are defined in masculine terms. They represent a culture dominated by masculine power and supremacy. Female members ardently define their status in terms dictated by males. Neither group has a feminist-oriented clientele to keep a watchful eye on future developments. In spite of this, no matter which group wins power, the status of women will improve. This is primarily because women's rights have been severely repressed under the Islamic Republic. Both groups will certainly support a number of legal changes such as increasing the age of marriage for young girls and establishing women's rights to divorce. However, given the male-dominated political leadership and the culturally reenforced socialization of the women, it is unlikely that the status of women will change profoundly. The liberation of women, like the concept of the liberation of workers, is a cause in its own right, requiring consciousness-raising and a movement of its own, neither of which exist today.

106

NOTES

1. Sheila Rowbotham, Women, Resistance, and Revolution (New York: Vintage Books, 1974).
2. For an excellent analysis of the women's movement in Russia refer to: Richard Stites, The Women's Liberation Movement in Russia: Feminism, Nihilism, and Bolshevism, 1860-1930 (Princeton, NJ: Princeton University Press, 1978).
3. For a detailed study see: Juliette Minces, "Women in Algeria," In Lois Beck and Nikki Keddie, eds., Women in the Muslim World (Cambridge, MA: Harvard University Press, 1978), pp. 159-71.
4. For a comprehensive analysis of the women's rights issue in Iran see: Eliz Sanasarian, The Women's Rights Movement in Iran: Mutiny, Appeasement, and Repression from 1900 to Khomeini (New York: Praeger, 1982).
5. For more specific information about the Feda'i organization see: Bizhan Jazani, Capitalism and Revolution in Iran, The Iran Committee, trans. (London: Zed Press, 1980) and Ervand Abrahamian, "The Guerrilla Movement in Iran, 1963-1977," MERIP Reports (no. 86, March/April 1980): 3-15.
6. Meredith Tax, "The United Front of Women," Monthly Review 32 (October 1980): 31.
7. Los Angeles Times, March 9, 1979, p. 1; and Wall Street Journal, March 12, 1979, p. 1.
8. Family Protection Laws were promulgated in 1967 and 1975. They covered marriage, divorce, and family relations in general. Legally, they improved women's rights slightly; however, these laws were revoked shortly after the 1979 revolution.
9. Hafteh Nameh-yi Rahā'i, 1st year, no. 14, Azar 13, 1358, p. 7.
10. Kār, 2nd year, no. 100, Isfand 13, 1359, p. 26.
11. This information was provided by a Fida'i woman in an interview with the author.
12. Kār, Isfand 13, 1359, pp. 25-27.
13. Abrahamian, "Guerrilla Movement," p. 9.
14. For the Mujahidin view on women's rights see: Zan dar Masīr Rahā'i (Woman on Her Way to Freedom), Sazmān-i Mujāhidīn-i Khalq, 2nd ed., Tir 1359.
15. Majmūᶜeh-yi Iᶜlāmīyeh-hā va Mowziᶜgirīhā-yi Sīyāsī-yi Mujāhidīn-i Khalq-i Irān (1) az 21 Day 1357 ta 18 Tir 1358 [A collection of political pronouncements of the Mujāhidin], 1st ed. Sāzmān-i Mujāhidīn-i Khalq Irān, Bahman 1358, pp. 53-54.
16. See the chapter by Marcia K. Hermanson in this volume.
17. Zan dar Masir Rahā'i, pp. 14-16.
18. Fred Halliday, "Interviews," MERIP Reports (no. 86, March/April 1980), p. 19.

19. Iran Times, July 10, 1981, p. 11 and April 2, 1982, p. 1.
20. Mujahid, 2nd year, no. 113, Isfand 21, 1359, p. 19.
21. Nashrīyeh-yi Anjumanhā-yi Dānishjūyān-i Musalmān--Ūrūpā va Imrīkā (Havādārān-i Sāzmān-i Mujāhidīn Khalq-i Irān), no. 31, Isfand 28, 1360, March 19, 1982, pp. 20-21. Also see: Iran Times, December 18, 1981, p. 1.
22. This was clearly demonstrated in the case of Ashraf Rabīᶜī, the wife of Masᶜūd Rajavī, leader of the Mujahidin organization. She had been active in the group since the early 1970s and was captured and tortured a number of times by the Shah's secret police. She remained in prison until the Shah's downfall. She was active in Teheran while her husband was in Paris; Ashraf Rabīᶜī played a crucial role in arranging ex-President Bani Sadr's removal from Iran. She was killed in an ambush by government forces in February, 1982.

BIBLIOGRAPHY

Abrahamian, Ervand. "The Guerilla Movement in Iran, 1963-1977. MERIP Reports, no. 86 (March/April 1980): 3-15.
Hafteh Nāmeh-yi Rahā'ī. 1st year, no. 14, Azar 13, 1358, p. 7.
Halliday, Fred. "Interviews." MERIP Reports, no. 86 (March/April 1980): 16-21.
Iran Times, 10 July 1981, p. 11; 18 December 1981, p. 1; 2 April 1982, p. 1.
Jazani, Bizhan. Capitalism and Revolution in Iran. The Iran Committee, trans. (London: Zed Press, 1980).
Kār, Isfand 13, 1359, pp. 25-27.
Los Angeles Times, 9 March 1979, p. 1.
Majmūᶜeh-yi Iᶜlāmiyeh-hā va Mowziᶜgīrīhā-yi Siyasī-yi Mujāhidīn-i Khalq-i Irān (1) az 21 Day 1357 ta 18 Tīr 1358 [A collection of political pronouncements of the Mujāhidin]. 1st ed. Sāzmān-i Mujāhidīn-i Khalq Irān, Bahman 1358, pp. 53-54.
Minces, Juliette. "Women in Algeria," Nikki Keddie, trans., in L. Beck and N. Keddie, eds. Women in the Muslim World (Cambridge, MA: Harvard University Press, 1978), pp. 159-71.
Mujāhid. 2nd year, no. 113, 21 Isfand 1359, p. 19.
Nashrīyeh-yi Anjumanhā-yi Dānishjūyān-i Musalmān--Ūrūpā va Imrikā (Havādārān-i Sāzmān-i Mujāhidīn Khalq-i Irān), no. 31 (Isfand 28, 1360/March 19, 1982), pp. 20-21.
Rowbotham, Sheila. Women, Resistance and Revolution (New York: Vintage Books, 1974).
Sanasarian, Eliz. The Women's Rights Movement in Iran: Mutiny, Appeasement, and Repression from 1900 to

Khomeini (New York: Praeger, 1982).

Stites, Richard. The Women's Liberation Movement in Russia: Feminism, Nihilism, and Bolshevism 1860-1930 (Princeton, NJ: Princeton University Press, 1978).

Tax, Meredith. "The United Front of Women." Monthly Review 32 (October 1980): 30-48.

Wall Street Journal, 12 March 1979, p. 1

Zan dar Masīr Rahā'i [Woman on Her Way to Freedom]. Sāzmān-i Mujāhidīn-i Khalq, 2nd ed., Tir 1359.

7
To Veil or Not to Veil:
A Matter of Protest
or Policy

Anne H. Betteridge

A distinctive feature of the Iranian revolution was
the participation of large groups of women. Western
audiences were particularly impressed by the sight of so
many black-veiled women involved in the "referendum of the
streets," but subsequently they have been somewhat baffled
by the loss of freedom experienced by the very women who
helped bring the Islamic Republic to power. The question
naturally arises in retrospect, what were the women thinking in supporting the revolution and, for some of them,
donning the veil when they participated in it? Briefly,
it is my contention that women were participating primarily as Iranians who opposed the Pahlavi government and not
as women per se. There was, however, an understanding
that the goals of the Islamic revolution included respect
for women and appreciation of their position in society.
At the time of the revolution the specifics of what that
role was envisioned to be were not spelled out, so that
each woman could understand it as she chose, and women of
different backgrounds and political philsophies could all,
in good conscience, support and participate in revolutionary activity.

Much about women's feelings concerning themselves
and their environment--social and political--is revealed
in their understanding of the meaning of the veil. In
the course of this chapter I will deal with the issue of
the veil, or chadur, how women felt about wearing it, and
the intentions of veiled women who joined in the anti-
government demonstrations. The veil is a particularly
good focal point since it is both an obvious symbol of a
woman's position in the world around her and a matter of
some contention. To some it represents oppression; to
others it is an indication of spiritual independence and
self-worth.

This paper is based on my experience in Shiraz, a
city in southwestern Iran, in the mid to the late 1970s.
During that time the possibilities for women's religious
education at various levels increased; many women came to
feel that Islam offered them opportunities for self-reali-

zation and self-respect which they had found lacking in
the Western way of life as they understood and experienced
it.

In studying Islam rather than simply accepting their
religion as a fact of life, many women felt that they were
emerging from their traditional position as passive objects whose power was confined to behind-the-scenes maneu-
vering and whose prospects for the future were limited to
domestic existence in successive roles as daughter, wife,
mother, and mother-in-law. With increasing opportunities
for education in Iran, women were able to achieve a new
degree of independence and self-esteem; this was as true
in religion as it was in the workplace.

Some women who had previously gone bareheaded expressed their new appreciation of their role as Muslim
women by dressing in accordance with Islamic law. Other
women continued dressing as they had before--veiled or
unveiled--yet with a renewed commitment to their religion.
When the revolution got underway, women were prepared to
march wearing black veils as a means of expressing their
unity and opposition to the Pahlavi government. Wearing
the veil represented a particular moral stance--morality
defined positively by Islamic law or negatively by
opposition to the immorality of the Shah's regime and to
the West in general.

Once the revolution was accomplished, the situation
changed. Wearing Islamic forms of dress was first
encouraged by social pressure and later enforced by
official decree. Dress was no longer the matter of individual choice which it had been before and during the
revolution.

It should be noted that there were women who did
not support the revolution. There were those whose
station in life was in some way bound to the continuation
of the Pahlavi regime. This group included wives of high-
ranking government officials and military men and included
even village women whose families were allied with the
government.[1] Older women who had seen numerous political
storms come and go in their lifetimes were inclined to be
cynical about the prospects for the success of the revolution and genuine change, believing that, as one woman
commented, "The Shah has left before and come back; what
makes you think he won't return this time?" Those who
had suffered often in the past--both the very poor and
members of minority groups--feared that what little they
had gained might be lost under another government and
tended to adopt a wait-and-see attitude. These qualifica-
tions aside, support for the revolution was widespread
among women.

The Background: Urban Women and Religious Education

Before dealing with women's involvement in the
revolution itself, I would like to review the situation

of women in the mid and late 1970s as I came to know it
in Shiraz. I should emphasize that the women with whom I
associated tended to be sympathetic to religion. Not all
of them were veiled, but they did respect Islam and felt
that an Islamic government would respect them. I believe
their sentiments were representative of those of most
Iranian women. Women's legal position has been discussed
in detail elsewhere;[2] I am primarily interested in women's
conceptions of themselves and of their relation to Islam.
These attitudes formed the basis for many women's participation in the revolution of 1978-79 and the veiled form
it often took.

When I first arrived in Shiraz late in 1974, I was
unaware of the extent of religious activities open to
women. Generally speaking, these gatherings were relatively informal in character and not publicly announced
--knowledge of them spread by word-of-mouth. Unlike
members of the male religious establishment, women of
religious learning wore no identifying outfits. It was
not until I became acquainted with women involved in
religion and expressed my interest to them that I was
introduced to the wide array of religious activities in
Shiraz. These ran the gamut from traditional observances
such as the celebration of fulfilled vows, sponsorship of
ritual dinners, pilgrimages to local shrines and attendance at the mosque to participation in women's religious
classes. Ritual observances had long played a major role
in the social lives of traditional urban women, but the
emphasis on religious education for women was new. There
was a definite upsurge in activities related to women's
religious education in the mid and late 1970s. During
the time that I was in Shiraz numerous classes were
established, and I was told that girls and women had
previously had few opportunities to study religion with
any seriousness. Further, a woman in her seventies told
me that in years gone by working as a female preacher was
looked down upon to some extent.

The religious classes and gatherings themselves
varied a great deal. Some met at regular times and followed a definite course of study; others occurred on a
more irregular basis, usually coinciding with religious
holidays. The women conducting the lessons were of
assorted persuasions, ranging from the extremely conservative to liberals whose inclination was to make Islam
palatable to modernized young women and who advocated
forms of Islamic dress other than the veil.

Following a ceremony in the home of friends I talked to the wife of a government clerk about classes for
women in the town. She immediately reeled off the names
of eight women, their addresses, the times at which they
taught, and something of their backgrounds. I was aware
of a number of other regular gatherings and had attended
some of the ones she mentioned.

Religious lessons were also available for girls,

some taught at the conservative girls' parochial school
in town, others offered in homes on the weekends on on
afternoons during the week.[3]

One class which I attended was formed when a group
of professional women and university students asked a
clergyman whom they respected to give weekly lectures in
the home for them. Some of these women were veiled in
their daily lives, others were not. All wore veils when
attending the class and were aggressive in questioning
points of religious law. The women attending the sermons
or classes were involved in defining themselves and their
role in society in terms of religion. Some accepted the
basic premises of women's position and duties as outlined
in the Qur'an and were concerned with the fine points of
their own behavior. Others were more skeptical and were
trying to establish their own opinions about religion and
women's position vis-a-vis Islam.

During this time I saw some women who had previously
left their hair uncovered assume Islamic dress. Generally, the change corresponded to having gone on the hajj,
the pilgrimage to Mecca. Upon their return, the women,
moved by their religious experience, took on the Islamic
form of dress they had previously regarded as unnecessary
or even undesirable.

In the late 1970s, Dr. Ali Shari^cati's works on
Islam circulated widely, although clandestinely, and grew
in popularity.[4] Being religious was no longer regarded as
backward, but if anything, as a liberal attitude; it was
also rather fashionable in some circles and became increasingly so as the revolutionary movement gained momen-
tum. One woman, a physician, told me that she had been
encouraged by others to take on Islamic dress. They told
her that religious beliefs would be greatly furthered if
she, as an educated woman prominent in the city, would
demonstrate her religiosity in this way. It would serve
as an inspiration to other women and prove that there was
no contradiction between being an educated professional
woman and being devout. It appeared to me that the
social pressures active at the time played a large part
in her decision to change her style of dress.

Among the women with whom I associated, admittedly
people with a great deal of sympathy for and belief in
Islam, I encountered no sense that the position of women
in society would be downgraded under Islamic rule. If
anything, they felt that the position of women would be
exalted. They pointed to recent changes in the religious
establishment, such as the admission of girls to theological schools in Qum,[5] as evidence. Traditionally, women's religious education had been largely informal and
conducted at home, its depth determined by the resources
and inclinations of a girl and her family. It was in
this protected environment, taught at home by private
tutors, that Khanum-i Amin of Isfahan received the education which provided the basis for her numerous books on

religion and for her eventual attainment of the high
clerical degree of mujtahid.[6] The existence of a woman
mujtahid served as an example of the position women could
attain in Islam; she was an inspiration to many women in
their own religious studies.[7]

I was privileged to visit Khanum-i Amin in the fall
of 1976. She was an elderly woman in her eighties, dressed simply in a pale yellow suit and a blue-flowered white
veil. She wore thick glasses and had to be assisted in
walking, but the impression of her frailty was dispelled
as soon as she began to speak, forcefully and with conviction. Her view of women and their potential was very
positive; she saw no reason why other women could not
achieve the status of mujtahid and suggested that even I
might do so. Her servant woman, who was present during
the interview, commented that Khanum i-Amin told her the
same thing. At this time in Iran, many women were gaining
confidence in themselves and their futures, and this included their place in the religious establishment.

In attending sermons and religious classes I encountered two themes predominant among women. On the one
hand, studying Islam seriously was seen as the renuncia-
tion of traditional patterns of belief, time-honored
superstitions which women had played a major role in
preserving and continuing. One preacher was particularly
outspoken in condemning women who attended sufrehs
[religious dinners] and other ceremonies, chanting "Ya
Ali" while at the same time they had long, lacquered
fingernails and neglected their prayers. He counselled
the women to reject superstitions, such as refusing to
travel or to marry on inauspicious days, saying, "People,
does God have a watch? No, God has no time other than the
time of the Day of Judgement!" In general, women found
his exhortations persuasive, although they did not appreciate his condemnation of the ritual dinners to which they
were so attached.[8] Rather than fearing certains days of
the week or times of the month, women were told, "Fear
God, and if you fear God, you will fear nothing."

A second theme of interest to women was that in
turning to religion, they were turning away from the West
both culturally and materially. The movement toward
religion was neither traditional nor Western, the two
previous choices obvious for women, but Islamic. In
accepting this alternative, women saw themselves neither
as reactionary nor as compromising themselves culturally.
They were instead asserting their own identity and
strength by allying themselves with what they saw as an
enlightened interpretation of Islam; for some women this
assertion was expressed by wearing Islamic forms of dress.
In the climate in which religiosity and study of religion
were highly valued, urban women were likely to be recep-
tive to a revolution couched in Islamic terms and to join
such a revolution.

Support of the Revolution

An important point to keep in mind is that in supporting the revolution these urban women were acting
primarily as Iranians, sharing the same basic complaints
about the regime as men had. They too opposed the corruption and repression of the Pahlavi government and
experienced the economic hardship which accompanied increasing inflation. Women were as horrified as men by
the violent way in which peaceful demonstrations were
dealt with by the government. They also suffered: women
perished in the fire at the Rex movie theater in Abadan,
attributed to the regime; they died in great numbers in
Jaleh Square on Black Friday--September 8, 1978--along-
side men. Women were, in this sense, directly attacked,
and it is not surprising that they responded by expressing their outrage, not only as mothers and wives, sisters
and daughters, but as individuals.

Much has been said about the reforms brought about
for women under the Pahlavi regime: women had increased
opportunities for education; they gained the right to
vote, and family law was changed to their advantage,
allowing women greater rights to initiate divorce and
making it more difficult for a man to take more than one
wife. The effectiveness of these measures in changing
women's daily lives is another matter. There was the
question of how valuable voting rights were where
elections were viewed as rigged, and men often found ways
to get around the newly liberalized laws governing family
relationships by taking advantage of a wife's ignorance,
illiteracy, or economic dependence. The fact that some
women were educated and employed meant that they experienced the same dissatisfactions as men. It is also worth
noting that many women had never lived under any other
form of government in Iran than that headed by the Pahlavis, who had been in control since 1925, so they would
be unlikely to compare conditions favorably with pre-
existing circumstances.

The way in which many women had come to see themselves and to interpret the government's attitude toward
women is also significant. I am speaking not of specific
policies, but of the way in which some women perceived
the official point of view. Prior to the revolution,
women were presented with numerous, often conflicting,
possibilities: following a traditional lifestyle as a
married woman in her husband's home, obtaining an education and entering the job market, or following the path
indicated in the mass media--being beautiful objects,
fashionably dressed and made up. A large number of women
I encountered felt that the government was actively
involved in encouraging the third alternative--the image
of the mindless woman. This was not seen simply as an
unflattering attitude held about women and their role in
life, but as one which the government wished to foster.

As an example of this view, the then-popular magazine Zan-i Ruz [Today's Woman] deserves mention. It was a
ladies' magazine featuring pictures of movie stars and
popular singers, articles about fashion, romantic short
stories, and horoscopes. It even sponsored beauty con-
tests. I was told that the Shah's government was behind
the magazine, actively promoting the image of woman as a
painted plaything, in part to distract women from the
serious business of politics and religion and keep their
thought at a low, frivolous level, and in part to encourage dependence on such Western products as make-up and
fashions, thus binding Iran to Western markets. This view
was not exclusively held by women, it surfaced as a basic
element in revolutionary rhetoric.[7]
        Every now and then I was told stories which supported
the view that Iranian women and their position in society
were in trouble. A typical one concerned a young school
girl who was giving her favors to an older man in return
for a few blouses and a new pair of slacks--evidence that
material concerns far outweighed spiritual ones in the
minds of some young Iranian women. The teachers who were
worried about the girl's welfare had been forced to dis-
continue religion classes for the girls in the school.
According to the teachers, religion was seen as a powerful
force which could enlighten and strengthen young people,
and so was vigorously opposed by the government.
        The Shah's opinion of women, given in an interview
with Oriana Fallaci, did nothing to dispel the view
that the government was not sincerely concerned with
improving the position of women in Iranian society. In
the interview the Shah said:

        In a man's life, women count only if they are
        beautiful and graceful and know how to stay
        feminine . . . and this Women's Lib business,
        for instance. What do these feminists want?
        What do you want? Equality, you say? Indeed!
        I don't want to seem rude, but . . . . You
        may be equal in the eyes of the law, but not,
        I beg your pardon for saying so, in ability.[9]

The Shah's remarks did not go unnoticed by his
opponents. In reference to the Fallaci interview,
Khomeini later remarked:

        In an interview with an Italian journalist,
        the Shah declared that women should only be
        objects of sexual attraction. It is this con-
        cept which leads women to prostitution and
        reduces them to the status of sexual objects.
        Religion is opposed to this view of women, and
        not to their liberty and emancipation. The
        fact that women from all levels of society
        took part in the recent demonstrations, which

> we are calling the "referendum of the streets,"
> shows the falsity of these allegations. Women
> fought side by side with men in the struggle
> for their independence and their liberty.[10]

Many women saw concentration on religion as an alternative
to the behavior advocated by the Shah. The opposite of
flaunting their physical attractions would be to give
greater importance to religion in their own lives; this
might or might not include wearing proper Islamic forms of
dress.

Religious sermons and classes served as forums in
which an alternative to the 'modern' view of women was
communicated. The decent Muslim woman was opposed to the
Western floozy, and the comparison proved to be very
persuasive. At one religious gathering I attended in
Shiraz in January, 1976, a young woman had been invited
to speak in addition to the older woman who was conducting
the assembly in her own home. The young woman spoke of
the need for piety and the fear of God, stressing that
these include dressing properly. A woman ought to preserve
her hijab [veiling] and make sure that her hair is covered. She discussed behavior in the world outside the home,
chastising women who go out in thin chadur and laugh in
public in front of shopkeepers. The young woman, who had
recently moved to Shiraz from the more conservative city
of Mashhad, added that she had been in Shiraz for seven
months and was appalled at the behavior of most women in
the streets. In her opinion, if a woman would wear a
thick black veil for a ceremony in the name of God, she
should dress that way all the time. In the middle of one
of the young woman's more forceful tirades, the older
speaker interjected, "It is not really that hard to lead
a good life; in fact, one can derive real enjoyment from
it," apparently attempting to soften the blows of the
young woman's accusations. One woman in the audience
shouted out, "What about those women who use a lot of
make-up and wear alluring clothes?" The young speaker
appeared to think that subject not even worth discussing
--those women were beyond help.

In another instance a woman recommended an older
speaker to me, saying that she was very forward thinking
and advocated a modern form of hijab. Clearly there was
much discussion among the women as to what constituted
appropriate dress, and there was no single opinion on the
matter. Many urban women who themselves might go veiled
had daughters who would go out in the streets bareheaded.
One one occasion I was visiting a woman whose daughter
had recently returned from college in Florida. The
mother jokingly cursed women who, like her daughter, did
not wear chadur in the summer heat while she sweltered
under hers. In this family, as in many others, forms of
dress were increasingly a matter of individual choice,
and a woman's religious sentiments could not necessarily

be predicted by attention to her clothing.

Even among devout women the necessity for wearing
Islamic dress was variously understood. For some women
the absence of proper dress was seen as provoking a
deterioration of family structure. Men would be lured
away from their wives, attracted by "naked" women. One
woman told me this directly, stating that her husband,
whom she had supported through his university studies by
teaching school, had left her for a woman student who
went unveiled. She felt that had such temptations not
existed, her marriage would have remained intact.

In general, religious women accepted the view that
modest dress is necessary because its absence excites
men's attentions and leads to undesirable consequences.
Another interpretation was provided by Khanum-i Amin.
She believed that the use of hijab was necessitated by
the nature of women. According to her, the most important
thing for many women (at the time we spoke, November 1976)
was to struggle against their passion for jewelry,
ornamentation and the latest fashions. The veil, or any
other form of suitable covering, in obscuring these would
allow women to concentrate on other, more worthwhile
things. Instead of being inordinately concerned with
their appearance, women would devote more time to their
studies, religion, and families. In this view, the veil
serves more to check women's own shortcomings than to
control men's responses to women.

In Isfahan in 1976 I was able to visit a group of
young women who were involved in publishing a religious
magazine, Fursat dar Ghurub [Opportunity at Twilight or,
less poetically, The Last Chance]. Only a few issues had
been printed at the time of my visit. Young women wrote
the articles and poems in the magazine and conducted
interviews with major religious figures, among them
Khanum-i Amin, on subjects of interest to girls and women.
A university student active in the writing of Fursat
dar Ghurub was proud to tell me that she attended her
classes veiled and sat in the front row so that her
presence would be felt. In the mid-1970s there was a
concerted effort on the part of the authorities to discourage women from attending universities veiled; the
veiled woman's statement was political as well as
religious. Religion provided a mode of opposition to the
regime, which was equated with the West and all the
decadence that implied.

Although women were not thinking of what they in
particular would gain by participation in the revolution,
it is nonetheless true that women understood that they,
as a group, were specifically invited to join in the
revolution. Their participation was solicited and encouraged by religious leaders. Statements made by
Ayatullah Khomeini were widely distributed and addressed
to both the men and the women of Iran. For example, in a
statement issued from France concerning the strikes which

were so important in the success of the revolution,
Khomeini commented,

> I am grateful to all government employees and
> others who, by staging strikes, have declared
> support for their brothers and sisters. This
> is an Islamic duty and binding on all . . . .[11]

Men and women were seen as working side by side in making
the revolution. The image of the khwahar-i mujahid
[warrior sister] was prevalent throughout the revolution
and included in revolutionary slogans and chants. Speaking after the revolution, Zahra Rahnavard, outspoken
supporter of the Islamic Republic, noted that

> Khomeini sent a message from France saying,
> "Any nation that has women like the Iranian
> women will surely be victorious" and went on
> to explain that this comment served to en-
> courage women to be proud of themselves and
> even to become martyrs.[12]

Women felt that they were taken into account in the
statement of the aims of the revolution. Early on,
Khomeini said:

> As for women, Islam has never been against
> their freedom. It is, to the contrary,
> opposed to the idea of woman-as-object and
> it gives her back her dignity. A woman is
> a man's equal; she and he are both free to
> choose their lives and their occupations.
> But the Shah's regime is trying to prevent
> women from becoming free by plunging them
> into immorality. It is against this that
> Islam rears up. This regime has destroyed
> the freedom of women as well as men. Women
> as well as men swell the population of Iranian
> prisons, and this is where freedom is threat-
> ened. We want to free them from the corruption
> menacing them.[13]

At the conclusion of the massive demonstrations held on
Ashura, the tenth day of mourning for the death of Imam
Husain (d. 681), a manifesto was read declaring the goals
of the revolutionary struggle. Point Seven of this
Declaration of Independence read:

> True liberty, honor, integrity and the human
> dignity of women given by Islam; as well as
> social rights and the grounds for the develop-
> ment and realization of their potentialities
> must be guaranteed.[14]

Although specific programs were not outlined, women did
feel that they were importantly involved in the revolution and that they were respected by it. The fact that
the details of what was felt to be appropriate for women
were not spelled out allowed each woman to interpret
these general remarks in her own way. It was not until
March 1979 that the discrepancy between some women's
perceptions and that of the revolutionary leaders became
apparent.

In mid-March of 1979, International Woman's Day was
observed in Teheran. The observances included demonstrations protesting Khomeini's pronouncements on women's
dress. It was understood that he advocated a return to
the veil, and many women wished to register their objections. Some 15,000 unveiled women and girls marched in
Teheran. Khomeini's aides later qualified his remarks,
saying that he had simply meant that women should dress
modestly. Youssef Ibrahim quoted one young woman at the
time as saying,

> They are calling us American dolls because we
> don't want to wear the chadur. They say our
> moral character is flawed because we wear
> Western clothes. But we are getting tired of
> people who cannot tolerate another way of life
> or another point of view. Khomeini knows that
> this is why we got rid of the Shah and he is
> now talking a different tune from what he used
> to say in Paris. He has betrayed our trust.[15]

Role Models

The Imams--a series of descendants of the Prophet
Muhammad who are regarded by Shi[c]is as the rightful
leaders of the Islamic community--and their families play
a major role in the daily devotional life of Shi[c]i Muslims. Stories about their lives and their martyrdom
serve as examples for the Shi[c]is to emulate in their own
lives. This is as true for women as it is for men. The
religious establishment encouraged women in this outlook;
figures from Shi[c]i hagiography provided models for women's
support of the revolution and their involvement in it.

One of the unusual features of this revolution was
the use of Zainab, sister of Imam Husain, as a role model
for inspiring political opposition among women. Women
were encouraged to emulate her. In popular understanding
she is best known for her supporting role at the Battle
of Karbala, caring for the children while the men were
engaged in fighting. However, after her brother's death
she came to the fore, speaking out openly and effectively
against his enemies. Once her nephew, the fourth Imam,
recovered from an illness, he took over the primary role
in representing the Prophet's family. A close friend
of mine, particularly taken with Zainab, told me that

Zainab had divorced her husband in order to accompany her
brother to Karbala. My friend interpreted this as an
example of how independent women should be in their own
lives, even if it meant disobeying or leaving their husbands to accomplish higher aims.

In more peaceful times it is the Prophet's daughter
and Zainab's mother, Fatimeh, who serves as the primary
role model for women in her capacity as the ideal
daughter, wife and mother. She was self-sacrificing and
raised exceptional children--two Imams and Zainab; it is
these virtues for which she is best remembered and which
women are advised to imitate in their lives. The strength
of these models affected not only the traditionally
religious Shi^{c}ite women, but also, through the writings of
Ali Shari^{c}ati,[16] university students and educated women.

The two images of women are in no way regarded as
contradictory, but are seen as suited to different circumstances. It is regarded as perfectly reasonable that
a woman would, and should, become involved in revolutionary activity when necessary and should at other times
assume primary responsibility as wife and mother.

The Nature of Women's Participation

The involvement of large numbers of women in Iran's
revolution was facilitated by the character of the
revolution itself: it was essentially non-violent. The
violent acts that did occur, such as bank burnings and
destruction of private property, were usually blamed on
government agents attempting to discredit the revolutionary movement. Only at the very last stages of the revolution were government institutions--police stations, SAVAK
headquarters, etc.--under concerted attack. In general
the tactics which contributed to the success of the
opposition movement included demonstrations, strikes, work
slow-downs, and the establishment of an effective network
of literature, tapes, and discussions of the latest news.
Women's participation was generally in this non-violent
mode and regarded as appropriate for them. They were also
involved in caring for the wounded; women opened their
homes in the poorer sections of town to receive the
wounded, and female doctors were among those who responded
to the call for help, going to those homes and providing
medical assistance as needed. Women themselves were among
those arrested, wounded, tortured, and killed; some became
famous for their guerilla activities.[17] However, most
women contributed in non-violent ways, and their contributions were most welcome.

Many women who did not appear in the streets for
reasons of health, domestic responsibilities, or employment were in whole-hearted support of the revolution.
They took great pride in their sons' and daughters'
revolutionary activities and delighted in the nursery-
rhyme-like "revolutionary slogans" chanted by their young

children.[18] Women who could not join in the demonstrations were still able to prepare tea for demonstrators or lunch for family members back from the marches and to keep up with all the news.

The circumstances of life at the time of the revolution also served to involve women politically. The combination of martial law with its curfew hours and the closing down of shops and workplaces, together with the cold of the fall and winter months resulted in the centers of political discussion often being within the home. Electricity was frequently cut off, so family members-- both men and women--would gather around what ever source of heat and light--such as a kerosene stove or lantern-- was available. All would listen to BBC broadcasts at night together and, in the evenings of early December, go up on the roof to join in revolutionary chants and the shouting of "Allah-u akbar." Many women participated in political discussions and heard the same news and interpretations of it as did men. Divisions of space that might otherwise have prevailed between male and female activities did not exist, and the revolution was the only topic of interest to anyone, regardless of age or sex. Despite the privations of that time, there was a great sense of purpose, excitement and elation as it became clear that the revolution would succeed.

Conclusion: The Veil and the Islamic Republic

Most women who participated in demonstrations during the Iranian revolution wore black veils or other forms of Islamic dress. In ordinary circumstances the veil was regarded as an appropriate and proper form of dress according to religious precepts. Though most chose to wear it, others did not. I even heard the veil condemned by a woman who suggested, "It's possible to do a thousand things under one!" However, in the revolutionary context the veil took on another meaning; wearing it became a symbol of rejection of the regime. The regime was seen as fostering Westernization, including Western forms of dress, and also as opposing religion. Even those women who would not wear a veil ordinarily or who would object to wearing one, donned it voluntarily to express their anti-government position and to participate in the marches. Major demonstrations took place on religious holidays or on days of mourning for those who had died supporting the revolution, so it was fitting that black veils be worn. However, the specifically religious content of the Tasu[c]a and Ashura marches, for example, was minimal.[19] Those who were not concerned with the religious implications of marching on the holidays could easily ignore them.

By wearing veils women were able to accomplish the multiple goals of mourning for the martyrs of the revolution, expressing their opposition to the Pahlavi government, and displaying the unity of the opposition. Not all veiled women joining in the demonstrations were veiled during their daily lives; wearing a black veil or scarf on those occasions in no way implied that one intended to continue wearing them in other situations.

That there was a gap between the understanding some women had of their participation in the revolution and the understanding of the women's contribution on the part of the leaders is made very apparent by Ayatullah Khomeini's comments. Even before the founding of the Islamic Republic, Khomeini's appreciation of the identity of women who had supported the struggle became clear.

> We ourselves saw what women developed in Islam
> and what women in the recent century arose.
> Those women who arose were those very modestly
> dressed women [mahjubah] of the south of town
> from Qum and other Islamic cities.[20]

Later, in response to a question by Oriana Fallaci, he elaborated on the subject.

> The women who contributed to the revolution
> were, and are, women in Islamic dress, not
> elegant women all made up like you, who go
> around all uncovered, dragging behind them
> a tail of men. The coquettes who put on
> makeup and go into the street showing off
> their necks, their hair, their shapes, did
> not fight against the Shah. They never did
> anything good, not those. They do not know
> how to be useful, neither socially, nor
> politically, nor professionally.[21]

During the revolution the subject of dress was never publicly discussed; in the midst of the excitement of involvement in the revolutionary process it, like many other topics, was eclipsed by the importance of the major issues of the day. People had varying assumptions about women's dress and the position of women reflected by it. For many, including the religious leaders of the revolutionary movement, modest dress was taken as a fundamental characteristic in the definition of a Muslim woman. They took for granted that a woman should dress "decently;" that is, she should wear loose, unrevealing clothing and cover her hair. The English-language publication Mahjubah: The Magazine for Muslim Women, published since the revolution, shows photographs and drawings of veiled or scarved girls and women involved in various activities --participating in demonstrations, studying, tending the wounded, carrying guns, and placing flowers on the graves of martyrs. The title Mahjubah refers to a modest woman. While the wearing of proper Islamic dress was a

matter of choice during the revolution, and was adopted
by many Iranian women, the situation altered once the
Islamic regime was installed. Veiling became the order
of the day and was equated with decency on the part of
women. Women without veils were officially seen as representing Western values which the revolution had opposed
and which it wished to eradicate in Iranian society.

The unstated assumptions about the significance of
veiling during the revolution and the multiplicity of
reasons for adopting the veil gave rise to a feeling of
having been betrayed on the part of some women after the
revolution. There were women who had adopted the veil as
a revolutionary symbol and others who had adopted it for
the time being, but had not realized that veiling would
become official policy. One woman physician I knew had
dressed in black and worn a scarf on the days of major
demonstrations. Later in 1979, after the success of the
revolution, she objected when she was told to wear
Islamic dress to work. Rather than wear a scarf, she
took advantage of vacation time coming to her and stayed
home. She and her family subsequently left the country
and have taken up residence abroad. Other women protest-
ed in less extreme ways, wearing thin scarves or dressing
in black to mourn what they saw as the loss of their
freedom. Some made a mockery of hijab by wearing colorful headgear and even wearing flowers behind their ears.
I have been told that in these instances the young women
were even more attractive than they had been before
covering their hair. Still others were less vehement in
their response, assuming that their continued work was
most important. They assumed Islamic dress, believing
that although the style of their clothing might be
dictated to them, their opinions would continue to be
their own.

Since the spring and summer of 1979 the revolutionary regime has become further entrenched and more secure.
The ruling ideology is now enforced with greater success,
as indicated by one observer's cynical comment:

> With the mullahs unquestionably in the seat
> of power, the only real program that the
> authorities seem to have is for the total
> covering of women's heads. . . . Indeed, the
> covering of women has become almost a national
> obsession.[22]

The reasons for this program and "obsession" are, I
think, clear. The near universal wearing of Islamic
dress constitutes an obvious symbol of the success of
revolutionary Islamic ideology in Iran. It is difficult
to demonstrate outwardly what is in the minds and hearts
of the population, but the adoption of Islamic dress by
women can be seen as wearing their hearts on their

124

sleeves--symbolizing that Islamic ideology has been accepted. The fact that some women may dress "properly" only under duress is not at issue; the fact is that women are conforming to official desires. Forms of dress are more easily enforced than frames of mind.

In sum, women joined the ranks of those protesting against the Pahlavi regime first as Iranians, eager to change the oppressive circumstances of their political lives. As women, most felt that the government which would come into being following the revolution would respect women's rights. Because the details of proposed change in administrative and legal structure were not discussed, each participant in the revolutionary process could see the future according to his or her own lights. It was only after the Islamic Republic was firmly established that the intentions of the new government's leaders became evident and were revealed to be counter to the hopes of many of those who had aided in bringing them to power.

NOTES

1. Mary Hooglund, "The Village Women of Aliabad and the Iranian Revolution," in RIPEH 4,5 (no. 2, Fall 1980 and no. 1, Spring 1981), p. 32.
2. F.R.C. Bagley, "The Iranian Family Protection Law of 1967: A Milestone in the Advance of Women's Rights," in C. E. Bosworth, ed., Iran and Islam (Edinburgh, Scotland: Edinburgh University Press, 1971) pp. 47-64; Michael M. J. Fischer, "On Changing the Concept and Position of Persian Women," in L. Beck and N. Keddie, eds., Women in the Muslim World (Cambridge, Mass.: Harvard University Press, 1978), pp. 189-215; Behnaz Pakizegi, "Legal and Social Positions of Iranian Women," in L. Beck and N. Keddie, eds., Women in the Muslim World (Cambridge, Mass: Harvard University Press, 1978), pp. 216-226.
3. All women involved in furthering religious education were not of one mind, and a degree of competition existed among them. In Shiraz the established girls' religious school, Maktab-i Zahrā, seemed to feel that its monopoly of girls' religious education was threatened by the establishment of the Ismatiyyeh. The Ismatiyyeh school offered an organized course of study in religion with classes conducted on the weekends. The founder of the school had operated a similar school successfully in Masshad before deciding to open a branch in Shiraz.

Animosity grew to such an extent that the administrators of the long-established girls' school sent "spies" to the new classes with tape-recorders hidden under their veils. They hoped, in recording the classes, to prove that the newcomers were heretical and not deserving of clerical support. When they took the tapes to a high ranking local clergyman, their claims were declared invalid and the women failed in their campaign against the new school. They went so far as to accuse one teacher of practicing mortification of the body as an element of religious life and advocating it to her students. The teacher denied the charge, which was never substantiated.

4. Additional information on Ali Shari^cati is provided in a number of recent publications in English, among them Ervand Abrahamian, "Shari^cati and the Iranian Revolution," MERIP Reports (no. 102, January 1982), pp. 25-28; Shahrough Akhavi, Religion and Politics in Contemporary Iran, (Philadelphia: Movement for a New Society, 1980), pp. 144-158; Mangol Bayat-Philipp, "Shi^cism in Contemporary Iranian Politics: The Case of Ali Shari^cati," in E. Kedourie and S. G. Haim, eds., Towards a Modern Iran (London: Frank Cass & Co., 1980), pp. 155-68; Nikki R. Keddi, Roots of Revolution (New Haven: Yale University Press, 1981), pp. 215-225; Ali Shari^cati, Fatima Is Fatima, Laleh Bakhtiar, trans. (Teheran, Iran: The Shari^cati Foundation, n.d.); Ali Shari^cati, On the Sociology of Islam: Lectures by Ali Shari^cati, Hamid Algar, trans. (Berkeley: Mizan Press, 1979); ^cAli Shari^cati, Marxism and Other Western Fallacies, R. Campbell, trans. (Berkeley: Mizan Press, 1980). Also see the chapter by Marcia Hermansen in this volume.

5. Michael Fischer reports a new school for girls associated with Madrisheh-Yi Haqqani in Qum: "In 1975 it had 30 students and 5 female teachers." Iran: From Religious Dispute to Revolution (Cambridge, Mass.: Harvard University Press, 1980), p. 83. A clergyman in Shiraz told me that he had spoken to the fathers of girls who wished to attend theological school in an attempt to dispel their doubts about sending their daughters off for higher religious education.

6. No woman in present-day Iran has equalled Khānum-i Amīn in theological stature. She has devoted her life to religious learning and teaching and is a prolific writer, having authored a lengthy tafsir (interpretation) of the Qur'an, other works on religious subjects, and books addressed specifically to a female audience. As a mujtahid, her learning has been formally recognized by the clergy, and she has the right to make independent decisions in the interpretation of religious law. However, unlike male mujtahids, her decisions cannot be binding for others. Individual Shi^cis must choose one of the living mujtahids to follow in points of religious law; Khanum-i Amin, because she is a woman, cannot be among them; her decisions are final only for herself. I questioned clergymen in Shiraz about this; they knew of her and held her in high regard, but agreed that her position as mujtahid differed somewhat from that

126

of men who had achieved the same rank in the religious
hierarchy.

7. Unfortunately, it was primarily clergymen, women
in Isfahan, and women highly educated in religion who
were aware of Khānum-i Amīn's existence. Being a woman,
information about her tended to be communicated informally, and she herself signed her works "bānu-yi Isfāhānī"
[an Isfahani lady]. Other women had not heard of her;
when I mentioned the woman mujtahid they were politely
indulgent but convinced that I must be mistaken.

8. For further discussion on sufrehs and the con-
troversy surrounding them see Anne H. Betteridge, "The
Controversial Vows of Urban Muslim Women in Iran," in
N. Falk and R. Gross, eds., Unspoken Worlds: Women's
Religious Lives in Non-Western Cultures (San Francisco:
Harper and Row, 1980), pp. 141-155.

9. Oriana Fallaci, "The Shah of Iran," New Republic
(Dec. 1, 1973): 18.

10. Ali-Reza Nobari, ed., Iran Erupts: Independence,
News and Analysis of the Iranian National Movement
(Stanford: Iran-American Documentation Group, 1978), p. 22.

11. Lynne Shivers, "Inside the Iranian Revolution,"
in D. H. Albert, ed., Tell the American People: Perspectives on the Iranian Revolution (Philadelphia: Movement
for a New Society, 1980), p. 75.

12. Pamela Haines, "Women in Today's Iran," in D. H.
Albert, ed., Tell the American People: Perspectives on
the Iranian Revolution (Philadelphia: Movement for a New
Society, 1980), p. 97.

13. Nobari, Iran Erupts, p. 13.

14. Nobari, Iran Erupts, p. 234.

15. Youssef M. Ibrahim, "Iran's 'New' Women Rebel at
Returning to the Veil," The New York Times, March 11,
1979, IV 2:3. Also see Gregory Jaynes, "Iran Women March
Against Restraints on Dress and Rights," The New York
Times, March 11, 1979, I 1:2.

16. In his book Fatima is Fatima, Shari^c ati
recommends that Muslim women model themselves after the
Prophet's daughter. He rejects the traditional view of
her which concentrates on a few incidents in her life
(Shari^c ati, Fatima Is Fatima, pp. 24-25) and sees her
always in relation to the men in her life as a model
daughter, wife, or mother. Instead he counsels that
women see her for herself and focus on her strength
and personality, knowing her also as "The symbol of a
responsible, fighting woman when facing her time and the
fate of her society" (Shari^c ati, Fatima Is Fatima,
p. 225).

17. Ervand Abrahamian, "The Guerrilla Movement in
Iran, 1963-1977," MERIP Reports (no. 86, March/April
1980), pp. 3-15; Guity Nashat, "Women in the Islamic
Republic of Iran," Iranian Studies 13 (Nos. 1-4, 1980):
173-74.

18. For example,

Pufak namakī shūr i
hukūmat-i Shahanshah zūr i

[Pufak namakī [a snack food popular with
children] is salty
The Shahanshah's government is imposed by
force]
19. The non-religious character of the demonstrations was regarded as irreligious by some devout observers. A man in the Shiraz bazaar went so far as to
suggest that people deserved to stand in line waiting for
fuel and kerosene because they had neglected to mention
Imām Husain on Āshūrā.
20. Ayatullah Khomeini, January 24, 1979, cited in
Mahjubah: The Magazine for Muslim Women 1 (nos. 11 and
12, Rabiᶜ ul-ākhar/Jamadi ul-awwal, 1402 [February/March
1982], p. 38.
21. Oriana Fallaci, "An Interview with Khomeini,"
The Compact New York Times Magazine, October 7, 1979,
p. 7.
22. John Kifner, "Amid Terror and Deprivation,
Islamic Fervor Still Grips Iran," The New York Times,
April 22, 1982, A10.

BIBLIOGRAPHY

Abrahamian, E. "The Guerrilla Movement in Iran, 1963-
    1977," MERIP Reports, No. 86 (March/April 1980):
    3-15.
_____. "Shariati and the Iranian Revolution," MERIP
    Reports, No. 102 (January 1982): 25-28.
Albert, D.H., ed. Tell the American People: Perspectives
    on the Iranian Revolution (Philadelphia: Movement
    or a New Society, 1980).
Bagley, F.R.C. "The Iranian Family Protection Law of
    1967: A Milestone in the Advance of Women's Rights,"
    in Bosworth, C.E., ed., Iran and Islam (Edinburgh:
    Edinburgh University Press, 1971), pp. 47-64.
Bayat-Philipp, M. "Shiᶜism in Contemporary Iranian Poli-
    tics: The Case of Ali Shariᶜati," in E. Kedourie and
    S.G. Haim, eds., Towards a Modern Iran (London:
    Frank Cass & Co., 1980), pp. 155-68.
Beck, L. and Keddie, N., eds. Women in the Muslim World
    (Cambridge, MA: Harvard University Press, 1978).
Betteridge, A.H. "The Controversial Vows of Urban Muslim
    Women in Iran," in Falk, N. and Gross, R., eds.,
    Unspoken Worlds: Women's Religious Lives in Non-
    Western Cultures (San Francisco: Harper & Row, 1980),
    pp. 141-55.
Fallaci, O. "The Shah of Iran," New Republic, December 1,
    1973, pp. 16-21.

Fischer, M.M.J. "On Changing the Concept and Position of
    Persian Women," in Beck, L. and Keddie, N., eds.,
    Women in the Muslim World (Cambridge, MA: Harvard
    University Press, 1978), pp. 189-215.
    _____. Iran: From Religious Dispute to Revolution
    (Cambridge, MA: Harvard University Press, 1980).
Haines, P. "Women in Today's Iran," in Albert, D.H., ed.,
    Tell the American People: Perspectives on the Iranian
    Revolution (Philadelphia: Movement for a New Society,
    1980), pp. 94-107.
Hooglund, M. "The Village Women of Aliabad and the Ira-
    nian Revolution," RIPEH IV (no. 2, Fall 1980) and
    V (No. 1, Spring 1981): 27-46.
Ibrahim, Y.M. "Iran's 'New' Women Rebel at Returning to
    the Veil," The New York Times, March 11, 1979,
    IV 2:3.
Jaynes, G. "Iran Women March Against Restraints on Dress
    and Rights," The New York Times, March 11, 1979,
    I 1:2.
Keddie, N.R. Roots of Revolution (New Haven: Yale Univer-
    sity Press, 1981).
Kifner, J. "Amid Terror and Deprivation, Islamic Fervor
    Still Grips Iran," The New York Times, April 22,
    1982, A 10.
Mahjubah: The Magazine for Muslim Women 1 (nos. 11 and 12,
    Rabi^c ul-akhar/Jamadi ul-awwal, 1402 [February/March
    1982]).
Nashat, G. "Women in the Islamic Republic of Iran,"
    Iranian Studies XIII (nos. 1-4, 1980): 165-94.
Nobari, A.R., ed. Iran Erupts: Independence, News and
    Analysis of the Iranian National Movement (Stanford:
    Iran-America Documentation Group, 1979).
Pakizegi, B. "Legal and Social Positions of Iranian
    Women," in Beck, L. and Keddie, N., eds., Women in
    the Muslim World (Cambridge, MA: Harvard University
    Press, 1978), pp. 216-26.
Shari^{c}ati, A. Fatima Is Fatima, L. Bakhtiar, trans.
    (Tehran: The Shariati Foundation, n.d.).
    _____. On the Sociology of Islam: Lectures by Ali
    Shari^{c}ati, H. Algar, trans. (Berkeley: Mizan Press,
    1979).
    _____. Marxism and Other Western Fallacies, R. Camp-
    bell, trans. (Berkeley: Mizan Press, 1980).
Shivers, L. "Inside the Iranian Revolution," in Albert,
    D.H., ed., Tell the American People: Perspectives
    on the Iranian Revolution (Philadelphia: Movement
    for a New Society, 1980), pp. 56-78.

8
Revitalization: Some Reflections on the Work of Saffar-Zadeh

Farzaneh Milani

Hidden by the veil, restricted by masculine decrees, and reduced to an all-but dimensionless character, the Iranian woman has suffered yet another distortion of her identity--the critical negligence that has surrounded her poetry. And yet, for centuries, poetry has been one of the few fields where her voice can be heard loud and clear. It is here, in her poetry, that she speaks for herself and provides a fresh perspective on her life. Here, she refuses to be an artful creation, a functionless presence, or a phantom personality. In short, it is here, in her poetry, that she transcends her limited definition and violates the prevailing notion of her pale image.

It is as poets, and, for that matter, as some of the foremost poets of Persian literature that many of these women continue to deserve acclaim and admiration. Their work is too intricate to be viewed from the single vantage point of their femaleness and such remarkable craftsmanship and complex vision must necessarily attract more than a limited critical interest. The tradition of women's poetry in Iran is not only an expression of highly artistic sensibilities, or a sanctuary where many a sensitive reader may seek inspiration, but also a valuable adjunct to history.

"Good poets are the most honest historians of their times"[1] argues Tahireh Saffar-Zadeh, a contemporary woman poet. And certainly her own work takes its place with others' in demonstrating this point. A great variety of attitudes is discernible in the writing of women in contemporary Iran, and not all have offered the same response to recent events and the establishment of the Islamic Republic. In fact, Saffar-Zadeh proves to be one of the very few among writers and poets to consistently support the Islamic Revolution. However, and in spite of that, her poetry can be seen as one of the most vivid chartings, not only of an individual woman's experience, but also of a collective history.

Not much is known about Saffar-Zadeh's life, and it

is practically impossible to fully reconstruct it from the meager published information. A comprehensive biography, which would be helpful in better understanding her poetry, is nonexistent, and the scattered information about her life leaves many questions unresolved. She was born in Sirjan, near Kirman, in 1939. Upon graduation from high school, she enrolled at Pahlavi University, in Shiraz, and earned a bachelor's degree in English Literature. She published her only collection of short stories, Piyvand-hay-i Talkh [Bitter Unions] along with her first poetry collection, Rahguzar-i Mahtab [Moonlight Passerby] in 1963. Then, divorcing her husband, she left Iran to study creative writing at the University of Iowa, where in 1969 Red Umbrella, a collection of some fifteen poems in English, was published by the Windhover Press. Upon her return to Iran, Saffar-Zadeh published Tanin dar Dilta [Resonance in the Bay] (1971) and Sad va Bazuvan [Dam and Arms] (1972). She started teaching at the National University of Iran, and after six years of silence published Safar-i Panjum [Fifth Journey]. Preoccupations have shifted for the poet, and as a result another kind of poetry has developed, finding its culmination in Biy^{c}at ba Bidari [Allegiance with Wakefulness] (1980).

Earlier social, political, and spiritual journeys undertaken to provide a more unified context for her life had failed, and the poet is drawn into an almost utopian enthusiasm for Islam. Aesthetic demands continually have given way to those of politico-religious ideology, and what was earlier an expression of a complex reality has become virtually one-dimensional proselytizing.

Saffar-Zadeh's work can be divided into three distinct parts, the first of which consists of the poems and short stories published before her departure for the United States of America. Characterized by a subjective lyricism, the work of this period is the rebellious cry of a woman who feels severely limited in both her feelings and experience and needs to make substantial changes in her life; a woman who is the personification of alienation rather than wholeness and integrity; a woman who frantically seeks to emancipate herself from restrictive social codes and lifestyle, and yet defines herself through those very traditional values. Although she has adopted the dominant sex role model, she cannot operate properly within it. She feels isolated and lonely. The poem titled "Lone Tree" epitomizes the forlorn and solitary tone prevalent throughout the work of this period:

A lone tree I am
in this far reaching desert
on this sorrowful plain
I have no soul mate
no one whose steps tread in unison with mine
the friendly murmur of streams

```
the happy rush of springs
die in a space far away
and my ear
fills with parched strains of solitude
in this desert I have terrifying companions;
hail of pain, cloud of fear,
                    and wild downpour of sorrows
within me, the clamour of
howling wolves of loneliness
in this darkness of night my heart does not
      quicken with the thought of tomorrow.2
```

The female characters depicted in the stories of
Bitter Unions, like the poetic personae in Moonlight
Passerby, have a mixed-up, internally discordant personality. Their impulses and aspirations are discrepant, and
their innermost desires collide with existing social codes
and their own internalized moral values. All of the ten
short stories of this book revolve around relationships
between men and women and little else, voicing bitterness
and agony over yet another broken or failed affair. None
of the women protagonists are sucked into the solaces of
conformity and domestic security or are at ease in their
traditional roles and relationships with men. Time and
again they find themselves imprisoned in depressing, mis-
matched alliances. Some, unable to acquiesce to the
limitations placed on them, spend their lives mourning
their irrevocably lost freedom. Others seek refuge outside marriage. However, paralyzed by self-doubt and
guilt, they ultimately become disillusioned by the dis-
crepancies between their romanticized expectations and
their real experiences. The heroine in the short story
titled "Prince Charming" reflects on the tribulations she
shares with many other women protagonists in the book:

```
I carried my unmaterialized desires from my
father to my husband's house. I was innocent.
For one of us women to express passion is con-
sidered so repulsive and hideous that our
desires suffocate under the bell jar of point-
less prohibitions . . . and then we get so
vulnerable to temptations that if one of our
imaginary paramours comes to life and touches
our bodies with knowing finger-tips we get
shocked like those electrocuted. Helplessly,
we surrender . . . should we tolerate the
thirst, wistfulness will never depart from us.3
```

It is interesting to note that those heroines who
transgress prescribed codes of moral and social proprie-
ties, those who show a certain openness before life as
before lust and passion, do so not in accordance with
their inner promptings but rather out of compliance with

outer forces. The dilemmas of those women moving beyond
traditional roles, expectations, and experiences often
start with their chance encounter with new, menacing
factors. Azar, the heroine in "Flight Temptation" writes:

> Like a magic key, every one of her [Bilitis'[4]]
> songs unlatched the sturdy lock of my parent's
> advice. Gradually, I was being delivered from
> all the ludicrous fear and terror they had
> instilled in me.[5]

There is in the work of this early period a sense
of incompleteness--a void--which the author is eager to
escape from. Freedom, though sought energetically, slips
through her fingers. The alienation, frustration, and
the search itself are by far more forcefully realized in
this work than is the ideal which she longs to compass.
Although an actual plunge into the unconventional and the
unknown is resisted and postponed, an implicit sense of
an imminent change can be felt throughout the book. Indeed, the mere act of communicating her pain and fragmen-
tation, her refusal to submit to conformity, and her
struggle not to surrender to silence or stagnation demonstrate her resolve to seize control of her life. This
identification with the strivings of her own sex, however
confused and unlegitimized, is the extent of the poet's
socio-political commitment in her first two books.
Tahireh's vivid perceptions of a woman torn between
the freedom-loving self and the private, traditional one,
her ruthless probing of a soul tormented by restrictions,
led her to a fundamental reassessment of her life. In
her restless pursuit of self-discovery and self-asser-
tion, she had finally come to terms with the breakups of
traditional bonds. She divorced her husband, left her
country, and more vigorously tended her poetic inclinations. Her inner journey coupled with outer mobility
propelled her to the discovery of new ways of experienc-
ing both life and art. In an interview with Muhammad
Huquqi, she referred to the formative influence of her
trip to America:

> I must say my knowing and living with foreign
> poets in American educational surroundings--
> along with my contact with a lively and fervent
> artistic milieu--had an incredible impact on me.
> Witnesses to the evolution of my poetry were
> those contemporaries of mine who did not suffer
> from sexist, nationalistic, or egoistic com-
> plexes.[6]

And evolve it did, the poetry of this second phase
--a poetry not only combining Eastern and Western symbolism, mythology, and techniques, but also characterized by

the desire to bring language and experience closer together than ever before. Wanting to embrace life on different
levels, the poet inevitably comes to feel the need for
new avenues of expression and finds herself forced to re-
linquish classical rules of versification. A strong
poetic voice emerges from beneath all the pressures of
previously untried experiences; no matter what occurrence
is depicted, a powerful sense of the poetic self dominates. The inner landscape of each poem is thus allowed
to reveal itself and to determine the poetic form that
unfolds. On the whole, many of the poems of this period
are a testimony to the poet's new adventure in both life
and art, the chronicle of personal and artistic growth.

If in earlier poems the spontaneity of emotions was
refined by reason or by social prescriptions, the poems
of this second period can be characterized by a certain
intensity and candor of self-revelation. The previous
detached evasiveness is replaced by a more intimate connection between the poet and the emotions depicted,
making the poetic personae not only the observer but
also the participator. In these poems, there is not only
a change occurring in the technical form and poetic content, but a corresponding change occurs in the poet's
relationship to herself. She not only talks freely about
her unconventional experiences and desires, but she
deliberately disregards the dominant standards of her
society. In the following poem, from Red Umbrella,
Saffar-Zadeh avoids abstractions, making open references
to lust and celebrating physical love:

> we travel towards the enjoyment of salty waters
> in a boat with no compass, we travel from nowhere
>   to somewhere from somewhere to nowhere
> cruising in the song of our bodies
> my breasts trust every word that your hands
> --hands with suppleness of the gentle heart--
>   whisper
>
> we drive we drive towards a hot summer noon,
> and yet men are shivering in their heavy coats
> waves transcribe our gestures in the water's
>   cloudy avenue
> thirst is blowing our breath in all directions
> we will die in a moment
> we die in a moment of perfume humidity and sun[7]

The character that emerges from these poems is far
from what one can call a "traditional" Iranian woman.
Guided by internal influences, relentlessly resisting
uncritical adherence to her society's dominant moral
codes, she is rather a woman who wants do develop a self
in the image of her own ideals. Rather than subcon-
sciously repressing, she can now reject the restrictions

of her society. This recognition of and contact with her
anger is part of her self-affirmation. In the poem
titled "Pilgrimage to My Birthplace", the path pursued
by the traditional mother--her passive acceptance of her
lot, her cultural powerlessness and inaction--is rejected
by the speaker, who, in the character of the daughter,
seeks to appropriate a new version of her life and her
identity. If the mother is molded and defined by society,
the daughter needs to revive and subsequently redefine
the autonomous aspects of a woman's existence:

> I have not seen my birthplace,
> where my mother deposited the heavy
> > load of her insides
> under a low ceiling.
> It is still alive,
> the first tick-tick of my small heart,
> in the stovepipe
> and in the crevices between crumbling bricks.
>
> It is still alive in the door and walls
> > of the room
> my mother's look of shame
> at my father,
> at my grandfather,
> after a muffled voice announced,
> "It's a girl."
> The midwife cringed, fearing no tip
> for cutting the umbilical cord,
> knowing there'd be none
> for circumcision.
>
> On my first pilgrimage to my birthplace
> I will wash from the walls
> my mother's look of shame,
> and where my heart began to pound,
> I will begin to tell the world
> that my luminous hands have no lust
> to clench in fists,
> nor to beat and pound.
> I do not yell,
> I do not feel proud to kill,
> I've not been fattened
> at the table of male supremacy.[8]

Anger and revolt seem to be the galvanizing principles behind many poems of this period; poems which
express the resentment of a woman who senses bitterly
society's ills and injustices; poems which have moved
beyond the earlier sense of confinement and now pulsate
with broader concerns. Throughout this period we witness
the poet building up, piece by piece, a new set of moral
and spiritual codes for herself. If Islam enters in

these poems--to however slight an extent--it is not as a
passive imitation of traditional observances, but rather
as an effective guide to action. In fact, there is
reinterpretation and adaptation of Islamic tradition to
new realities. The poet detaches herself from anachron-
istic Islam and brings a modern meaning to it. She
presents Islam as a religion relevant to the changing
conditions of time and not disconnected from it:

> The crisp sound of Azan can be heard
> the crisp sound of Azan
> is like the hands of a pious man
> freeing from my healthy roots
> the feelings of isolation and seclusion,
> no longer an Island,
> I go toward a mass prayer
> my ablution with city air and dark paths of smoke
> my Mecca, events to come
> and my nail polish
> > no barrier
> > for prayer chanting
> > prayer for miracle
> > prayer for change[9]

An element of corruption and frailty govern the
world around the poet which she can neither ignore nor
evade. Surrounded by people bent under the worship of
material luxury and wealth, she laments the political
apathy inherent in their attitude and actions.[10] The
physical, mental, and emotional hardening, and the sense
of moral stagnation which dominate the society around the
poet perturb her. And as she becomes more disillusioned,
she rises further in defense of religion, viewing it as a
social force, a revolutionary banner to mobilize people.
Interest in Islam, not so all-pervasive in earlier
poetry, becomes thus the most distinctive characteristic
of her last two books and a major turning point in her
poetic career. It is indeed a metamorphosis, a "revitalization", discernable in the changing pattern of her consciousness. By "revitalization", a term borrowed from
anthropology, I mean simply a conscious and deliberate
effort to move into a new gestalt. The Westernized,
liberated poet has turned into a devout Muslim and her
poetry into a religious policy.

This upsurve in religious interest is claimed by
Saffar-Zadeh herself to be one of opposition--a political
rather than spiritual reaction against oppression. In an
interview with Muhammad-Ali Isfahani, she identifies
Islam with political positions and associates her increasing interest in it with "the justice-seeking, uncompromising nature of Shicism and the oppressiveness of
our time which inevitably provokes a righteous person to
rebel and strengthens religious inclinations."[11] And

indeed her growing religious zeal seems to be a reclaim-
ing of "indigenous" culture and a desire to create a new
social order.

The religious and the political mingle in the poems
of Fifth Journey, undoubtedly the most political in the
whole canon of Saffar-Zadeh's work. Although her revolt
expresses itself in religious terms, the main focus of
this work is the injustice, corruption, and materialistic
tendencies which are endemic to socio-political structures that must be changed. A vigorous espousal of
political activism characterizes the poems of this
book--a work vibrating with rebellion and militancy.
Extending her hands beyond the boundaries of gender
Saffar-Zadeh writes:

> The verandah of my house
> the size of a tomb
> made of sun and earth
> I sit as if laid out over a tomb
> and I wait
> for the hand of a passerby
> to be the extension of my own hand
> and to break the lock on the house
> the sound of tired shoes can be heard
> sharp voice of a bell
> from the bottom of a staircase
> a visitor has come to say
> today too the weather is gloomy
> today too the weather is bad
>
> In the stifling calm
> comrads repeat
> with more suffering, news from many years
> today too the weather is gloomy
> today too the weather is bad[12]

Involvement with socio-political issues is obviously
nothing new in the tradition of women's poetry in Iran.
Especially with the advent of the modern era, an increasingly undisguised political awareness can be detected.[13]
However, what differentiates Saffar-Zadeh from most other
women poets is her progressive self-effacement and adoption of a neuter poetic personae. In fact, her previous
waves of resentment as a woman are completely extinguish-
ed at the threshold of her religio-political activism.
Such a trend can hardly be traced in the lives and works
of other modern Iranian women poets whose solidarity with
their female audiences grows ever stronger with time.
Qurrat ul-Ain, almost a century before the decree of
forced mass unveiling of women by Riza Shah in 1936
appeared dramatically without a veil in front of a large
crowd as a token of her belief in the equality of men
and women. Her convictions remained unshaken to her

death. To the minister in whose house she was jailed
she said, "Kill me as soon as you like--you cannot stop
the liberation of women."[14] Many women poets, at the
turn of the century, saw the necessity to bring about
fundamental changes in the position of women in society.
They established a sense of kinship and alliance with
their female audiences and used their works as a public
forum, a weapon to effect change. And, last but not
least, Furugh Farrukhzad remained a defender of women to
her last days. "If my poetry, as you mentioned, has a
certain air of femininity," she told Iraj Gurgin, "it is
obviously due to my being a woman. Fortunately, I am a
woman."[15]

In contrast, Saffar-Zadeh's own earlier concerns for
her position as a woman disappears completely in her last
two books, as do her attempts to reconcile her views on
women with the rigors of Islamic laws. In fact, her
individual consciousness becomes indistinguishable from
Islamic, Shi^cite consciousness. If the voice of her
earlier poetry is privileged with refreshing emotional,
psychological, and intellectual complexities, she is now
actuated solely by Islamic enthusiasm. The alienation,
conflict, and displaced spiritual longings of her early
work lead to a series of eclectic inner and outer journeys, whereas the passionate Islamic devotion and efface-
ment of individual identity in the later poems (Fifth
Journey and Allegiance with Wakefulness) perhaps attests
to the failure of the earlier journeys. Religious zeal
becomes so sovereign in these books that it forms not
only the radiant core of her character but the whole of
it.

It should be noted that although religious passion
animates both Fifth Journey and Allegiance with Wakefulness, there is a big difference between the two books.
Previous despair and disillusionment are left behind in
the poems of the latter, and loneliness no longer holds
sway. The experience of conflict (although not the
potential for it) disappears, and considering Tahireh's
history of inner conflict, the poems are alarmingly free
of friction and discords. In short, Islam seems not only
to guarantee an ideal socio-political order but also to
redeem and vivify the poet's inner world, a world which
in the earlier poetry remained an empty wasteland.

In Allegiance with Wakefulness, Saffar-Zadeh's style
proves also to have changed radically. Technically
speaking, there is a great difference between the earlier
poetry and the poems in this book. Only a few sections
of these peoms depart from redundancy and monotony to
embody the earlier careful manipulation of formal elements combined with economy, precision, and thematic expansion. In reading the poems one not only needs a guide
for the plethora of borrowings from Qur'an and the
Islamic tradition, but previously established artistic

138

commitments continually clash against the demands of a
partisan ideology. A repetitive thematic concern re-
places the whole gamut of themes of earlier work.
Attacks on the West--its decadence, corruption, and muddled values--association of Western dominance with
Pahlavi rule and secularism, and presentation of Islam as
the natural ideological base from which to fight these
two inner and outer enemies along with praise bordering
on panegyric for Ayatullah Khomeini form the very core of
this book. Centralized power and the state are no longer
viewed as an instrument of domination, monopolization of
power, or stepping stone to totalitarianism. The crippled economy, massive unemployment, growing factionalism,
and fear of imminent civil war are totally evaded.
Clenched fists, scores of martyrs, and numberless zealots
ready to die for Islam produce a new set of clichés no
more artistically viable than any other cliche. "Height
of Wakefulness" typifies the dominant theme and mood of
this book:

> Oh Guard,
> in the heart of night's cold
> you watch as if from outside
> the house of your own body
> with tired eyelids
> --a night nurse--
> so that the wounded city can rest
> from the plunder of death.
> Your wakefulness comes from earnest faith,
> your sincerety and Al-Asr[16]
> stories of your martyrdom
> like martyrdom of the people
> remain unheard,
> they have no voice, no image, no date,
> they are unannounced
>
> Oh beloved child, light of the eyes,
> oh good
> oh my brother
> oh watchful one
> as your bullets in the air
> break my sleep,
> as if by reflect, I pray for you,
> guardian of the liberating Revolution
> Oh lonely hero,
> watching against the nightly enemy,
> let God safeguard you from calamity[17]

The poet who maintained emphatically "attention to
reality should not eliminate poetic imagination, otherwise journalism, reporting, and poetry will be synonymous,"[18] now sacrifices the very vitality of her art to
make a point, and she never manages to get beyond her
specific topical obsession. Indeed, a poetry which was

earlier a vehicle for expression of the self with all its
ambiguities, its aspirations, and its responses to complex outer realities becomes predictable and hasty chronicle of limited preoccupations. The observing eyes and
the narrating voice no longer intertwine and blend deli-
cately in the aesthetic of these poems, which instead
present an imagination flattened to the level of mere
slogans:

> Walls have started moving
> walls have started talking
> walls of silence and surrender
> walls of servitude that hold up castles
> bent walls of government
> from the blessing of the attack of the masses
> old walls
>   and middle-aged
> these blind witnesses of yesterday's disaster
> these mute witnesses of oppression and torture
> have just started talking
> have just started walking
> but how fast they can walk,
> these children
> who have just started talking
> these old people
> who have just started walking[19]

Even if Allegiance with Wakefulness reflects the
socio-political climate in which it originated or is a
reaction to years of censorship, still poetic imagination
proves to be severely impoverished in it. The poet's
original indefatigable striving toward Azadigi--that is,
liberation from attachment to the vicissitudes of worldly aims such as money, power, or social station--is replaced by the more narrow concept of Azadi--a socio-
political state compressing an institutionalized ortho-
doxy. Even so, there is a dynamic energy and a perpetual movement in the poems of this book which echo those
of the earlier poems. Indeed, if the whole canon of
Saffar-Zadeh's work can be seen as the account of the
apprenticeship to life of a woman who attempts to
restructure her life and her society according to her own
vision and ideal, Allegiance with Wakefulness cannot be
viewed as its conclusion. The process never stops, the
dialectic never rests.

NOTES

1. Tāhireh Saffār-Zādeh, Harikat va Dīrūz [Motion
and Yesterday] (Teheran: Ravagh Publishing, 1357/1979),
p. 162.

140

2. Ibid., p. 23.

3. Tāhireh Saffār-Zādeh, Paivandhāy-i Talkh [Bitter Unions] (Teheran: Ittilāᶜāt Printing, 1341/1963), p. 217.

4. For the life and poetry of Bilitis, see The Songs of Bilitis, translated from the Greek by Pierre Louiys, privately printed for the Parnassian Society, 1920.

5. Saffār-Zādeh, Bitter Unions, p. 217.

6. Saffār-Zādeh, Motion and Yesterday, p. 131.

7. Tāhireh Saffār-Zādeh, Red Umbrella (Iowa: Windhover Press, 1969), p. 12.

8. Tāhireh Saffār-Zādeh, Tanīn dar Diltā [Resonance in the Bay] (Teheran: Amīr Kabīr Publishing, 1349/1971), p. 110.

9. Ibid., p. 94.

10. Oh bent slave
bent under masses of payments
                                monthly
                                    yearly
                                        eternal payments

11. Saffār-Zādeh, Motion and Yesterday, p. 162.

12. Tāhireh Saffār_Zādeh, Safar-i Panjum [Fifth Journey] (Teheran: Ravagh Publishing, 1357/1979), p. 100.

13. The two major reasons for this widening of the poetic horizon can be seen not only in the changing backgrounds and classes of the modern poets, but also in the newly developing opportunities for women in society. Until the Constitutional Revolution (1905-1911), with few exceptions, only educated women of the court and high aristocracy were allowed to develop their potential into a vocation. Of the 107 poets of Kishāvarz-i Sadr's anthology, Az Rabiᶜeh tā Parvīn, 43 are members of the courts, and the rest belong almost exclusively to the upper class.

14. Martha L. Root, Tahireh the Pure (Los Angeles: Kalimat Press, 1981), p. 98.

15. Iraj Gurgin, an interview with Furūgh Farrukhzād, Arash, ed. Sirūs Tāhbāz (Teheran: Darakhshān Publishing Co., 1345/1968), p. 33.

16. She is referring to Al-Asr Sura, revealed in Mecca.

17. Tāhireh Saffār-Zādeh, Biyᶜat ba Bīdari [Allegiance with Wakefulness] (Teheran: Hamdamī Publishing, 1358/1980), p. 59.

18. Saffār-Zādeh, Motion and Yesterday, p. 158.

19. Saffār-Zādeh, Allegiance with Wakefulness, p. 61.

9
Poor Women and Social Consciousness in Revolutionary Iran

Janet Bauer

Introduction

The images of women protesting in the streets of Teheran were puzzling to many in the Western world. Such behavior contradicted notions of what life was like for the stereotyped "secluded" women of the Middle East, protected by male relatives and extended kin relations. Why were these women protesting, how were they allowed on the streets to do so, and what were the differences between the veiled and unveiled women who joined in?

An investigation of the case of women, especially of poor women, is very useful for understanding the way in which the revolutionary movement took shape in Iran. Neither the "reaction-to-modernization" nor the class struggle approaches are adequate for explaining the involvement of women from different social classes in the revolution. In order to understand the participation and behavior of women in these social/political events and the relationship between their participation and macro level political occurrences, it is necessary to closely examine the lives of women (and men), the conditions under which they lived, and their relationships to other groups in society. To what extent had their social/political awareness developed and to what extent did this motivate them to take part in public protests? To answer these questions we must describe both the cultural/ideological factors and the social/material conditions which contributed to the reproduction of existing social life and class differences, in the period leading up to the revolution.

The linkages between micro level social practices and the larger context of the revolutionary movement are explained not by a refined political or religious ideology but by the role of social relations in the manipulation of information, symbol, and context. These findings challenge accounts of revolution that depend upon a concept of consciousness or ideology to mediate context and action or that give emphatic roles to the poor. Differences in information, which accompanied differences in material

circumstances or class differences, affected the development of social and political consciousness and participation in revolutionary activities on the basis of both
gender and class. Consequently poor women took part for
very different reasons, in different ways, and at different times than did more middle class women.[1]

The Context of the Revolution: Focusing on the Poor

Attempts to explain revolutionary movements such
as the one experienced in Iran often focus on the involvement of the poor. Theda Skocpol, in her recent
book States and Social Revolutions, suggests that the
peasants (and by extension I include the urban poor)
always have reason to revolt. The question is under what
conditions do they act and how is this achieved within
specific revolutionary situations. Skocpol goes beyond
a class analysis and focuses on the relationships between
various groups in society to each other and to the state,
with emphasis on the role of the poor along with the
intellectual elite in creating revolutionary transformations in social and economic structures.[2]
Giving attention to these networks of social relations underscores the enigma of economic development.
Although there were escalating class and social differences, the Iranian revolution was neither a class
conflict nor a struggle between the Westernized and the
more traditional sectors of the population. It was not
the poorest or the most "traditional" Iranians who
initially rose up to march and demonstrate.[3]
Several important infrastructural changes contributed to the role of social relations in both the social
reproduction of existing differences and eventually to
the organization of the revolution. These include 1) the
development of communication and transportation facilities
and of interpersonal networks maintained through migration and travel; 2) structural changes in population
demography with respect to both geographical and age
distributions; and 3) the comparative rising security
of the urban masses, accompanied by growing gaps in
resources among different social groups and increased
pressures created by a Western, industrial approach to
economic development. Although the Pahlavi shahs had
intended to broaden the base of their support by extending social services to the urban poor and to rural inhabitants, they were not very successful in doing so.
There was increasing differentiation between groups in
society. There was also an increased dependency upon
personal networks for survival and adaptation among the
poor. These networks created channels for exchange and
emulation between people with different lifestyles in
different classes and geographical locations, and
provided the impetus for both perpetuation and change in
social conditions. The urban poor were pivotal in main-

taining ties with both the middle class urban households
and with rural relatives in the provinces. It is therefore important to describe the conditions under which
the poor urbanites lived and their relations with other
groups in society during the period called the "white
revolution."[4]

With land reform, industrialization, and the booming
oil economy, large numbers of rural Iranian families had
migrated to urban places, leaving behind friends and
relatives with whom they continued to maintain contact.
In many cases, interaction was stronger between households in different geographical locations than within
the local community, since villagers did not have time to
socialize and urbanites did not always "trust" their
neighbors. Tehran became the hub of industrial enter-
prise and employment opportunities. It was also the
educational and cultural center of Iran. Recent migrants
to Tehran lived in crowded neighborhoods, mostly in the
southern part of the city, sometimes without running water
or electricity. It has been estimated that about four-
fifths of Tehran's 4.5 million population lived in these
southern migrant neighborhoods[5] which were largely poor.
The families there enjoyed few of the amenities available
to the upper and upper middle class residents further
north--cooler temperatures, green trees, clean water,
decent movie houses, and access to recreational facilities
for family leisure. Not everyone could find permanent
employment or housing. Consequently there were inter-
mittent confrontations between the residents of south
Tehran and government functionaries over the building of
houses without permission or the erection of temporary
tents and shacks. There were places throughout south
Tehran where young male laborers wandered about shift-
lessly, waiting for an employer to offer temporary day
labor. Even among the settled residents (as opposed to
seasonal migrants), men usually worked in unskilled, often
temporary jobs as construction workers or menials in
government and business offices; others were independent
drivers and small shopkeepers (cf. Hemmasi 1976; Kazemi
1979; Women's Organization of Iran 1977).

Most of these poor urban households did have
periodic cash incomes and, therefore, the means to
purchase such consumer goods as televisions, refrigera-
tors, clothing, and sometimes even automobiles. Available health care, social health insurance, educational
facilities, electricity, and water supplies, no matter
how unsatisfactory, were improvements over the living
conditions in the rural areas where these families had
originated. New arrivals constructed houses or rented
rooms with glass windows, carpets, and the latest cooking
utensils. Seasonal variations in food supplies and the
availability of prestige foods like rice also enhanced
the prospects of urban living.

By comparison, in the villages few of these goods
and services were available. Despite the large number of
agencies on paper designed to cater to the rural popula-
tion--literacy organizations, co-ops, clinics, and schools
--few were actually operating at the local level. In the
nine villages which I surveyed, only the schools and the
sipahi [the government corpsmen and women], who provided
educational, health, and community services to local
villagers, were active. None of these villages had piped
water or electricity. Village households had less and
more sporadic access to cash income than urban relatives.
Often the income from farm activities was supplemented
by remittances from children who had moved to the city
or had entered military service. In return, village
relatives provided places to stay on holidays and fresh
produce for urban kin. Because of outmigration of the
former landlords and wealthier households, economic
differentiation within the rural areas was not as
exaggerated as in the cities.

Even though villagers had remained in the rural
setting, they experienced increasing exposure to changes
occurring in other sectors of the economy. With travel
to nearby towns and visits from urban relatives who had
migrated to larger cities, rural men and women were in
contact with new attitudes, lifestyles, consumer goods,
and different styles of social interaction. Migrants
maintained contact with village relatives, depending upon
the distance of their village of origin from Tehran.
Actual frequency of these visits depended upon the particular occasion and the occurrence of lifecycle events like
weddings and funerals. Their return to the villages was
always marked with jubilant celebration and a great deal
of status deference on the part of rural kin.

Through these channels information about urban
living was transmitted to outlying populations. Thus,
most rural men and women voiced preferences for city
living, which was easier, with kinder winters and a more
varied social life. The outflow of the young for various
reasons--employment, education, military duty, and mar-
riage--skewed the age composition of the villages toward
the extremely young and the rather old. Older inhabitants
recalled the days when the countryside was plagued with
tribal raids, famine, and high mortality rates. The
suppression of pastoral nomads by the government and the
subsidies provided on foodstuffs had increased the relative security of these villagers. Of course, there were
hardships of other kinds--shortages of water, labor power,
and markets for locally-raised produce.[6] Still, the older
inhabitants tended to compare the present with the past,
finding the present a little better. The young, on the
other hand, were seduced by what they considered to be
much better than the hardships of the countryside--the
rewards of city living.

And what about poor urbanites? Although they had
contact with the middle and upper classes of Tehran
through the media, kin relations, and service agencies,
they often compared their situation with less fortunate
kin in the village, with whom they probably had had more
consistent and personal interaction. They perceived
rural work to be a drudgery and unhygienic and town life
to be more exciting than the farm. Despite disappoint-
ments, few seriously intended to return home. Thus,
while the crowded competitive conditions of the urban
places provided a potential context for unrest and protest, these contacts among social groups initially
served to "whet" the appetites of the poor for the good
life rather than to politicize them to injustices or
differences that were being exacerbated with "modernization." By contrast, the middle classes, religious and
intellectual, suffered more directly from state repression. Moreover, they had the financial means and the
informational arsenals to seek to do something about it.

Women's Lives in the Poor Neighborhoods

All of these conditions provided a framework within
which the participation of poor women in national political and social life must be understood. While attention
here is drawn first to the situation of low income urban
women and their households, the relationship of these
women to their rural relatives, as well as to middle
class urban women, is essential to portraying the unfold-
ing of the revolution.

Women's daily activities, the details of their
lives, and their social relations in the period prior
to the revolution varied by class and geographical location.[7] Like poor men, most poor women were not engaged
in the kind of extradomestic labor activities that were
conducive to achieving some conception of their position
in relationship to other classes. Most were engaged in
work and social activities in their own households or
within the local neighborhood. Given this situation,
social relations with kin and neighbors were the major
"relations of production" mediating individual experiences
and awareness. Describing the development of these networks within the larger structural conditions in pre-
revolutionary Iran gives some insight into women's
attitudes toward their own lives, as well as to the reasons they did or did not take part in the revolution.

In south Tehran, women spent most of their day
behind their compound walls or those of their neighbors.
The majority of women resided in nuclear family households, sometimes sharing a compound with other related or
unrelated families. About 25 percent lived in extended
family households, with other than nuclear family members
present. Women had a hand in the management of the household, particularly on a day-to-day basis. They often had

control over the distribution of some portion of their
husband's income (which averaged 15,000 rls/month in the
households I surveyed and 18,000 rls/month in the Women's
Organization of Iran's survey in 1977). Women differed
in the extent to which they controlled their husband's
earnings, and most had no source of personal income.
Within the home, women were responsible for the maintenance activities--cooking, cleaning, washing, carrying
water from fire hydrants or pools--and rearing the
children. They also established contacts for the household with agencies like health clinics and schools in
the neighborhoods.

As women became more confined to the domestic
sphere, their workload within the physical confines of
the home became more burdensome due to increased household size and better means of entertaining guests. The
size of these households in the low income areas of
Tehran (averaging five to six persons per household in
my sample) was slightly larger than in the rural areas,
partly due to immigration from the countryside.[8] Adult
men made few contributions to household labor. They were
usually absent from the household during the day,
engaged in their places of employment. Most worked about
one hour's travel time from their place of residence,
although a substantial number had small shops and garages
near their homes. In fact, these shops were partly
responsible for bringing in unfamiliar young men from
other neighborhoods to loiter about the streets.

Male members of the household continued to make
most of the decisions concerning larger purchases,
travel, and the children's education. At least, women
verbally attributed "the last word" on most matters to
their husbands or fathers. Women's actual degree of
autonomy over decisions varied, however, depending on
the topic. Women had to receive at least implicit permission from menfolk to engage in most activities outside
the home. Of course, women also reported ways of "getting around" their male relatives' opposition on various
matters.

The household's joint activities included evening
meals and chats in addition to about five or six hours
of television viewing each afternoon/evening. On holidays and weekends, they entertained or visited with other
kin living on adjacent streets or living in other neighborhoods of the city. Whether the family guests came
from outside the city or from a distant (usually more
middle class) neighborhood of Tehran, the conversation
revolved around news of other kinspeople, new consumer
items, and occasionally recent events.

A woman's activities outside the household included
daily sojourns along the streets to visit with nearby
neighbors either inside their homes or in the doorways
and attendance at rowzehs [religious services which were
held in women's homes, in contrast to many male religious

activities which were held in local mosques]. Neighborhood chats were very informal. No tea or fruits were
served, and women dressed in baggy pants and tops, covered by their veils. They exchanged gossip about their
neighbors, described recent dreams, and discussed omens.
They were concerned about observing ritualistic practices
they attributed to Islam teachings (not dyeing one's hair
on certain days, for example). Rowzehs varied in degree
of formality, but tea was almost always served. Women
were more likely to wear better clothing and heavy black
veils. Between religious readings, when mullahs or
female readers recited the stories of Husain's martyrdom,
the women ate, drank, and chatted about everyday affairs.
Rowzehs were held almost daily somewhere in these poor
neighborhoods, and to host one was an indication of social
status.

Younger women often attended educational classes
either in a formal educational institution or at the
women's center, but outside the classroom situation they
had little opportunity to exchange visits with their
friends. A few women in the neighborhood were engaged
in wage labor outside the home. The more unskilled women
came from the poorest households and were employed either
as domestic workers, a shameful occupation, or at the
women's center doing the cooking and cleaning. Some
younger, more educated women from slightly more affluent
households worked as teachers or office workers, another
job held in low moral esteem by neighbors (cf. Davis 1978)

Women also went about the neighborhood on errands.
However, as much as possible, young children and teenage
boys were sent on errands to the local shops. Women who
ventured along the streets were careful to veil themselves and to walk along the least-traveled kuchehs.
Still they were frequently subjected to verbal harrass-
ment from men. Relative strangers were everywhere outside the compound, and neighbors were often distrusted.
Occasionally, women also made visits to the local women's
center. The Women's Organization of Iran maintained
several centers in Tehran and a few regional towns. In
the neighborhood of South Tehran where my study was conducted, the center provided classes in a variety of
subjects, as well as day care for the small children of
working women and employees. These were popular places
for young girls who were no longer in school to spend
part of their day in the company of other young women.
While the instruction was aimed at preparing young women
for some kind of economically productive employment, the
instruction offered was usually limited to basic dress-
making, dollmaking, and sports activities. Older adult
women most often made use of the legal services and the
health clinics attached to the centers. There they had
to interact with the upper middle or middle class women
who staffed different levels of the center's operations.

When women ventured outside their own neighborhoods
to visit urban or rural relatives, to go to parks with
their families, or to visit religious shrines, they were
accompanied by other family members or female friends.
When they visited rural kin they stayed with women whose
daily lives were consumed from morning until evening with
agricultural chores. Their village kinswomen were responsible for milking animals, preparing breads and cheeses,
and helping with the harvest, in addition to regular
household chores.⁹ These women had less free time than
urban women and fewer places to go. They sometimes wore
the veil but in a less restrictive manner, leaving their
faces and hands free to perform outdoor tasks (cf. Beck
1978; Jeffry 1979; Davis 1978). There were fewer formal
events like rowzehs to attend and fewer strangers from
whom to cover oneself. The villagers complained that
weddings were less festive than in the past and that the
custom of visiting neighbors in the evening had declined
Religious services for women were held only once or twice
a year in the religious months of Ramazan and Muharram
when the mullahs [religious clerics] came out from the
towns and cities to lead them. It was during these few
times a year that village women had access to current
religious information.

Urban relatives preferred to stay with their more
affluent village relatives. Most village households had
fewer comforts than those in the towns. Homes were
usually constructed of adobe brick, and water was carried
from the local stream or spring. Foods were mostly local
and seasonal in availability. As in the poor urban areas,
households were nuclear in composition. In the village,
women had daily contact with neighbors, much as poor urban
women did, but very often those in adjacent households
were also kinspeople. Women gossiped in doorways and
baked bread together. Such gatherings and talk among
women were more frequent in villages closer to Tehran
where agricultural chores were minimal, and the household
could survive on the husband's wage labor in the city.
While village women had to seek permission to travel outside the village (and rarely did so), there were fewer
activities in the village itself which would require such
permission. There were no health clinics, high schools,
or big markets in the village. Girls had just recently
begun to attend elementary school.

Only women from the wealthier households sometimes
made trips to the city to visit relatives. Village men,
on the other hand, had traveled extensively outside the
village to conduct business, to make purchases, or to
serve in the army. What rural women looked forward to
most was a visit from city relatives. When town relatives
arrived, there was much excitement, a great many questions, and much awe over the news and presents brought
from the city.

Less frequently, poor urban women might have a
chance to visit in the homes of middle class relatives or
acquaintances who were holding religious services. Middle class homes were better equipped than the migrant's
household and were more likely to be furnished with
indoor toilets, baths, and furniture. Middle class women
spent more money on meals, entertainment for friends and
family, consumer products, clothing, and education for
both male and female children. Some of these women
worked as teachers or government employees, but most were
full-time housewives. They had more opportunity to
travel around the city, to take vacations, and to meet
people from different and even higher social classes than
low income women did. They were more likely to have
studied formally and also to regularly attend religious
meetings based on discussion rather than ritualistic
observance. These women were likely to know some of
their neighbors but to spend little time on the streets
or in the doorways with them. More socializing occurred
within the household and with friends of different sexes
in different parts of town. This was true among both
the more religious and the more secular middle classes.
Some of the women wore veils; some wore stylish Western
garments. Lower income women were often formal and
cautious in their presence.

The specific activities of individual poor women
varied by age and marital status. Some had more contact
with village women and recent in-migrants; others had
more occasion to interact with middle class women.
Younger women were more likely to spend part of their day
in school, where they had daily contact with educated
individuals from other neighborhoods. Their mothers were
less likely to have these contacts. In fact, in the
urban areas about 36 percent of the younger women (aged
10-24)[10] spent some of the day with individuals from
higher social classes. Only 29 percent of the women in
the middle age group (25-49) and even fewer of the oldest
women did so. A few of the younger women worked or
attended classes further north in Tehran. Most older
women who worked outside the home were employed by the
local women's center. On the whole, younger women had
both the educational exposure and the social experiences
which gave them an edge on knowledge and information, as
demonstrated in recent changes in women's authority roles
over the course of their life cycles[11] and the age
differences in the participation of women in the revolution.

However, the contacts of most adult women in south
Tehran consisted of family and neighbors very much like
themselves. Though they may have come from different
parts of the country and speak different languages, they
were interested in reinforcing similar beliefs and
practices. These networks of neighbors and geographical-
ly proximate kin were important in regulating women's

behavior, particularly since many extended family members
lived outside the neighborhood, and male relatives had
little daytime contact with their women. Women themselves
reported that while the approval of husband, father, or
brother was important, the most effective constraints on
their behavior were imposed by the expectations of others
in the neighborhood, even people with whom they had no
verbal contact but who were likely to be acquaintances of
acquaintances. When women gathered to talk, they exchanged information about other women and their behavior
(cf. Wikan 1980; Jeffry 1979). One young woman, Azar, was
the butt of many disapproving comments when she began to
appear more and more often in the streets, wearing her
chadur[12] loosely about her shoulders and talking loudly
with men. This kind of behavior was reported by others
to potential suitors and was partly responsible for Azar's
parents quickly arranging her betrothal to a second
cousin.

Feminism and Women's Consciousness

The extent to which women were conscious of the
social circumstances under which they lived--particularly
of the way in which men had dominant roles in public life
--depended upon women's access to information and their
range of personal experience. Consciousness as I use it
here recognizes that there are different levels at which
one can interpret one's own life. At the most practical
or basic level, consciousness involves knowledge of the
cultural and social rules that facilitate everyday life
and social interaction, whether or not one has the ability
to discuss these issues or verbalize them. At more removed levels of interpretation or reflection upon one's
life, particularly in relation to larger social and political spheres, different kinds of information are needed.
Refined ideologies exist at this more "discursive" and re-
flective level (cf. Giddens 1979; Therborn 1980; as well
as later sections of this chapter). Sensitivity to
women's issues or to political affairs was dependent upon
a woman's learning to think about her own circumstances
and put these into a perspective beyond everyday concerns.
While poor women were aware of or understood the immediate
realities of their lives, they did not have a formal ideological framework for interpreting their own social existence in terms of gender differences or class relations.
There was no feminist movement that touched the lives of
poor women.

Because women's experience and education varied, so
did their information for drawing conclusions about their
own lives and those of others. The poor younger women
(both urban and rural) with more education or in better
economic circumstances had more access to print media and
to contact with higher status individuals. Most adult
urban and rural women were illiterate and few traveled

more than 15 or 30 minutes from their homes. Poor
women's available role models and information about women
in other social classes came from a variety of sources.
In the urban areas, women watched television programs,
looked at newspapers and women's magazines, and had some
contact with women in other neighborhoods, particularly
in the women's centers. These poor urban women, in turn,
provided role models and information to migrant relatives
during their visits in both town and village.

Exactly what kinds of women/social lives were portrayed in these sources, or what did poor women perceive
the lives of these "models" to be like? The women on
television, in the printed media, and working in urban
institutions lived lives more typical of women in the
more "Westernized" upper or upper middle classes of the
city--in contrast to the lives of poor women of South
Tehran and their village relatives. These women were
likely to be unveiled and to lead somewhat independent
lives, working in professional or entertainment jobs,
driving automobiles, and dating and talking with unrelated men. Television programing and the stories in women's
magazines were often imported from the West, translated
directly from foreign sources. The women's organization
was especially active in disseminating the Western image
of unveiled and active women among the poor. It did so
partly by preferrential hiring of these people for positions of responsibility within the organization and its
centers. Yet women in the poor urban neighborhoods had
only limited contact with these women's center employees.[13]

In addition to these "new" sources of role models,
there were the women described in the religious stories
and tales, who were more similar to the women in the
religious middle classes in the cities. During rowzehs
the mullahs and speakers extolled the virtues of the
chaste mothers and daughters of Islamic religious
figures. The descriptions of Fatimeh, for example, the
Prophet's daughter, emphasized her pure, generous
qualities and her devotion to her husband, children,
and Islam.

Women's preferences for various types of behaviors
and social relationships reflected the degree to which
they had contact with new role models and women in higher
status classes, as well as their respective ages.[14] The
media input and formal education clearly had a stronger
impact upon younger women, while older women were influenced by the religious characters. Young women in south
Tehran were attracted to the images of women in Western
clothing, having some autonomy over their lives, working
in status professions, and enjoying the material comforts
of life. Older women were also attracted to these images
but the religious models had a stronger influence on
their lives. This was especially true of women from the

poor households in the low income neighborhoods. Women
in the villages sought to emulate the veil-wearing
relatives who came to visit them in the countryside. In
general, women selected as models women who had higher
status, either social or economic, while at the same time
comparing themselves to those around them who were less
fortunate or more simlilar to themselves.

When migrant relatives went to the village or when
their country relatives spent time with them in the city,
they were struck by the meagerness of the homes, the
drudgery of farm labor, and the uneducated bearing of the
rural women. They found their own lives "cleaner" and
easier than that of their village cousins. For the most
part, the village women agreed. City women often exaggerated urban behaviors in the presence of these village
kin and gave them advice on many matters in their lives.
Said one village woman, "We just observe and listen when
they are here." As a result, when possible these village
women sought to avoid working outside the home in the
fields and to style their wedding practices after these
low income urban customs. Most village women wanted to
marry and to live in the city.

While women might like to emulate the ways of life
they saw or thought they saw among higher classes, most
poor women were working hard to maintain their own status
within existing social circumstances. Particularly in
the low income urban areas the expectations not only of
male relatives but also of networks of neighbors and kin
encouraged women to observe culturally approved behaviors
--that is, the more restrictive female behaviors.[15] This
often meant accomodating one's behavioral choices in
marriage, career, and friendship in the meantime. One
result of women's seeking to uphold status-producing
behaviors was the reinforcement of differences between
men's and women's opportunities and behavior. Another
effect was the erosion of women's confidence in their own
abilities. Some women did attribute superior male
judgement to male advantages in travel and education, but
many women assumed that women were innately inferior to
men. Men were considered to be more intelligent and
capable than women. Both men and women used these
stereotypes to keep other women from engaging in those
activities and experiences which could have had an effect
on increasing women's personal efficacy.

Of course women were at the same time seeking to
attain middle class or higher standing if possible. As
a result of their desire to imitate behaviors demonstrated in higher classes, changes in approved behavior occurred. However, there were also pragmatic limitations of
material and structural nature in addition to social/
cultural ones which affected women's emulation of
behavior. Thus, there were lags in the emulation of
status behaviors over time and geographical space so that

class differences were continually perpetuated by this
interaction between changing cultural expectations for
behavior and the social/material circumstances in which
one lived. By the time lower class individuals were in a
position to recreate certain practices, these were
already outdated among the higher classes. This gave the
lower class women a false sense of rising mobility.

To what extent were women aware of the discrepancy
between their own preferences and their actual behavior
or of the processes that sustained gender and class
differences in Iranian society? Some women verbally
acknowledged that their activities were limited by the
social milieu in which they lived, not by male dominance
alone. They remarked that if the household were to
re-locate in another part of Tehran where people lived
and behaved differently, the expectations of their own
male kin would be altered accordingly. However, similar
to the split among middle class women, other poor women
attributed their behavior to religious prescriptions
rather than to social constraint. Some women were also
aware of differences between rich families and poor ones;
a few even lamented vaguely about the changes that had
occurred in social life with the advent of "modernization." However, most of the poor women did not have the
information for putting their perceptions or dissatisfactions into a religious or a political framework for
explaining gender or class inequality. Certainly they
did not understand the extent to which their own behaviors and cultural beliefs exacerbated these inequalities
at other levels.

The following examples reveal the thoughts of some
poor urban women about their own lives. Those with more
education and exposure typically had given more consideration to the relationship between men and women in their
neighborhoods and of the relationship of their neighborhood to others in the city.

Rubab. Rubab was in her late thirties and had six
children. She had received a high school education
before her father arranged her marriage to a man many
years her senior. Rubab's relationship to her husband
was a unique one, and he allowed her to have a hand in
making many decisions. She and her husband considered
moving out of their present neighborhood because of the
restrictions placed upon them by their migrant neighbors.
Her husband, she said, did not insist on her being veiled.
Look at her own daughters who went about unveiled. Still
Rubab wore the veil and was very careful that her daughters should veil when they returned to her husband's
village on visits. Rubab wanted her daughters to receive
as much education as possible and had rejected suitors
for her oldest daughter, in the hope that she could be
accepted into a college in a few years. Rubab believed
that parents should not strike their children but should

talk and reason with them. Rubab read women's magazines
and her children's school books. She was attentive to
television programs and women that she met in other parts
of Tehran.   She believed that women in the poor neighborhoods exacerbated their own situation by reporting on
other women and telling tales about them. "We cannot
help it," she said. "Rich women can drive around in cars,
go to work, and enjoy other activities. We have nothing
to do all day but to sit in our homes and spread rumors
about one another." Rubab, for example, wanted to open
a tailoring shop in her compound. She also wanted to
allow her daughters to go on outings with a male cousin
who used to take them all to the park in his automobile.
Because of neighborhood opinion, however, Rubab's husband
would not allow her to open the shop, and eventually he
asked his male cousin not to take his family on outings.
Rubab had some thoughts about the negative impact of
urbanization on family relations but generally believed
that women were capable and should be allowed to engage
in more activities outside the home.

Fatimeh. Fatimeh lived in the same neighborhood as
Rubab. She was about the same age and was married at
about the same age, sixteen. She had only two children,
and her mother-in-law resided in the house. She worked
at the local women's center, preparing tea and running
errands. Like Rubab, she was bright and articulate.
However, she had no formal education. Fatimeh realized
that her neighbors and co-workers were important to her
social standing. Still she deplored the way in which
gossip was used to condemn women on the basis of superficial evidence. If women were at fault, she said, it
was because men and women's families had made them this
way. Men liked to think that women could not do anything
and that women did not or should not enjoy sex. They did
not realize that women had sexual feelings too and that
women liked to be complimented and appreciated for their
achievements. Fatimeh wanted her daughter to receive an
education and felt very strongly that young men and young
women should have the chance to know one another before
deciding to marry. Fatimeh was influenced greatly by her
sister who lived in north Tehran in a house with running
water. She knew that women in north Tehran lived more
comfortable lives, yet some were not so very different
from herself--take her sister, for example. The biggest
difference was in the quantity of material goods and in
the different expectations of the people who lived in
those neighborhoods. However, Fatimeh did not criticize
the urbanization or "modernization" of the country.

Azar and Jamileh. Azar and Jamileh were school-aged
girls who had dropped out of school. They were enticed
by the Westernizing influences around them. Azar was
about to be married because of the gossip about her in

the neighborhood. She thought little about the social
realities of the world around her. She was interested in
finding a good husband and having a nice house. She would
have liked to have traveled more. When the activities of
1978 became more persistent and violent, she commented
that Khomeini was doing this to put the veil back on women
and to make them proper again.

Jamileh was about the same age as Azar. She failed
her last year of high school and out of shame elected to
quit school and stay at home. She had only minimal household chores and liked to go to the market so she could
get out of the house. Neighbors had begun to gossip
about her. We spent hours together talking about her
aspirations in life. Marriage was not that important to
her, at least not right away. If she did marry, Jamileh
intended to find someone who shared many of her own goals
in life. She preferred first, however, to find a job
that interested her. Perhaps she would even go back to
school. She wanted to be independent of her family. But
in early 1978 a suitor came to her home and asked to marry
her. She had no opportunity to talk with him about his
plans in life before the arrangements were made. She
agreed to the marriage, and the ceremonies were completed
in late 1978.

Zahra. Zahra was a woman of about fifty who was
born in the provinces and married late in life. Only two
of her children had survived. She was completely illiterate but had some status, having lived in the neighborhood
for ten years. Zahra, with no educational exposure at
all, was very dependent upon her children and other neighbors for interpretations of various religious and social/
political events. She was very careful to maintain the
image of her husband as head of the household and once
mentioned to me that one should be so lucky as to remain
single so as not to have someone "over one's head." However, Zahra herself apparently ran the household's affairs
and shared household responsibility equally with her husband. During the events of 1978, she was influenced in
her thoughts to a large extent by neighborhood opinion on
the matter. At the same time she felt that the neighbors
themselves were bad and had a corrupting influence on her
children.

Rural women had fewer sources of comparison and fewer
role models than did poor urban women. They also realized
to some extent that their activities were even more
limited by the conditions of village living--the lack of
schools and facilities, for example. They quickly insisted that they could not respond to certain questions that
I asked them because they did not have enough information
to do so. While they had effective control over domestic
affairs and while rural men were obviously dependent upon
their domestic services, rural women too deferred to the

156

"superior" position of men. Theoretically men could even
beat their wives if the women were at fault. What could
women do about men? Well, men were hardly ever to blame.
As for class issues, it was only the very poorest of
village women who railed against the religious and cultural preferences they were supposed to uphold but which
could not mitigate the realities of their unending poverty. At the same time, many of the wealthier found city
influences corrupting (city children were ill-mannered)
while the poorer felt that their lot might be improved in
the city.

The urban middle class women with greater financial
means were able to achieve the ideal of housewife/mother.
However, they also had more education and contacts among
the upper classes so that their perception of gender and/
or class differences were seen in different context from
the poor women. There were two groups of young middle
class women who were to become especially active in the
revolution. One included those in the religious middle
class, many of whom had not finished high school but who
had more education than women in the lower and lower middle class; these women were more "scientific" about their
religious studies, investing a great deal of time in
selective readings and in meetings which involved discussion groups and speeches on religious topics. The
other group consisted of students attending universities
and junior colleges.

The role of women advocated by the religious middle
class women was a separate-but-equal one in household
matters and public affairs. However, men were still to
be the heads of the household and have the responsible
social positions. In their religious meetings these
women advanced a "tri-partite" image of women. Upper
class women who wore Western clothes and enjoyed a great
deal of autonomy were considered to be "painted dolls"
who had betrayed their religion. They described the poor
women in the migrant areas and the women in the villages
as uneducated and superstitious. But they saw themselves
as the "new Muslim women," representing the true image of
womanhood. For the most part these women did wear the
veil, but they were more experienced and independent than
the lower class women. It was among these women that a
clearer conception of class differences was presented not
in terms of a simple dichotomy between rich and poor, but
by the ranking of occupational classifications. Those
women also asked many questions about class differences
in America.

The students that I interviewed were mostly from the
Women's Organization's School for Social Work. They
lived in more middle class neighborhoods than most of the
families I interviewed and had a great deal of contact
with students from other universities, many of whom were
neighbors or relatives. They were largely secular

in their approach to the political events of 1978,
although many adopted a veil or headscarf to identify with
the Islamic spirit of the revolution. Many were not
religious themselves, and some even had siblings who were
active in underground political organizations. They
anticipated outright equality between men and women, and
their perceptions of class differences and the plight of
their country were rooted not in a religious framework so
much as in political ideologies influenced by Marxist and
socialist thinking.

These middle class women--both religious and "intellectual" were more aware of gender and class differences
and had the information for interpreting both. Most poor
women did not have a framework for understanding the
underlying dynamics of either "patriarchy" (in the sense
of male advantages) or "class hegemony." Those with more
education and mobility did have some awareness of these
issues and along with the more middle class women began
to participate in the early stages of the revolution.
However, most women, poor or not, became involved in the
marching and protests, discussions and organizing only to
the extent that personal situations provided the role
models, information and support which made it efficacious
for them to take part.

Women's Roles in the Revolution

The revolutionary events of 1978 established the
context for a fairly predictable cycle of demonstrations
in many urban areas of the country. A series of individual incidents in late 1977 and early 1978 set off protests and subsequent killings, which then led to other
demonstrations and the 40th day commemorative marches for
those who had died, at which time still others would be
killed. These events were accompanied by strikes in
which shopkeepers, teachers, and students marched for a
variety of reasons. The initial protests were covered in
the media, but official versions of these incidents were
given little credence by the public. It was the religious and interpersonal networks described in the previous
sections that disseminated information about recent killings, upcoming marches, and Ayatullah Khomeini's latest
directive. In most cases, the inverse of what the
government reported was believed to be true. This made
the deciphering of actual events very difficult. The
stories which circulated in this manner were reinforced
by anti-foreign sentiments, appealing to nationalism,
and by religious fervor, appealing to the example of
Husain, the Prophet's grandson, martyred at Kerbala.[17]

Women did play an instrumental role in the success
of the initial protests which took place throughout 1978
and into 1979. However, most of the early participants
were wives, mothers, and sisters from the more middle
class homes. During 1978, in gatherings of the women's

center staff, in religious meetings, and among their
families, women reported incidents they had heard of,
the tales of neighbors or friends whose sons had been
killed or imprisoned, and the sights they had witnessed
during their travels to regional towns on regional holidays such as Now-ruz [the Iranian New Year]. "In Yazd
all the shops in the bazaar were closed in protest," or
"My cousin saw many Israeli soldiers on the front lines
shooting protestors." Women in chadurs carried messages
and instilled uneasiness in military personnel with the
possibility of concealing weapons beneath their veils.17
Women's religious classes provided an effective forum for
exchange of information since these activities were less
likely to be held in the more "public" mosques, where
government informants could attend. Students like Laila
(see below) exchanged information among themselves and
circulated reports of what other students were doing.
People in different places were striking for and demanding different things--changes in the oil prices, school
lunch programs, and freedom of speech.

Mina. Mina was college-educated but very religious
in her life style and demeanor. She attended relgious
classes in different places about four times a week. She
advocated the separate but equal approach to men and
women's roles and the tripartite image of women. When
the events of 1978 were underway she was traveling back
and forth between different religious meetings in
Tehran and to the provinces to visit relatives during
holidays. She engaged in a great deal of discussion and
passed on information to her friends and relatives in a
careful and guarded manner. The first active steps Mina
took occurred after her younger brother was picked up by
the police when he stood outside a mosque where leaflets
were being distributed and he chanced to pick up some to
read them. Mina became involved in working for his
release from jail. For Mina, the important issues were
focused around religious interests, but her own participation was motivated by the events affecting her family
and friends.

Laila. Laila was a student in a junior college
course, preparing to become a social worker. Her parents
were in-migrants to Tehran, but they lived in a middle
class neighborhood to the north of the city. She talked
every evening with a male cousin who attended another
university in Tehran. They compared notes about the
issues students at their respective institutions were
striking for. Laila was respectful of religion but also
advocated a fully equal role for women. While a number
of her male relatives had been killed in street demonstrations by mid-1978, Laila herself had only participated in the strikes at her college.

These middle class women were important in passing

on information to lower income women. Many poor women
had middle class relatives. Others overheard conversa-
tions by the staff in the women's center or attended
rowzehs where these other women chatted guardedly about
the revolution. How did poor women in south Tehran view
these events? Their orientation revolved around religious justifications or explanations for various political
events (partly because they had more contact with the
religious middle class) although they espoused no system-
atic religious position. They focused on their own
errant religious practices and the necessity for correcting their own behavior. Some felt, like Azar earlier,
that this was all a fight to put women back in the chadur.
Rubab, usually the forward-looking one, felt that the
killings were terrible but that the implication of this
for families like her own was that one should not be too
lax in demonstrating religious behaviors like the wearing of the veil. Subsequently, her daughters began
wearing the veil to school. Women who did not wear the
veil, it was said, would have acid thrown in their faces.
The arguments of many of the younger, more educated
religious women concerning the corrupting influence of
the West on women and the family were picked up and
repeated. The West, they said, and particularly the
United States, had copied what was good from Islam and
used it to advance themselves. Iran could prevail if she
returned to Islamic practices!
Out of habit or perhaps tradition, many women were
influenced by the appeal to religious martyrs and the
talk of following Ayatullah Khomeini into jihad [holy
war] if necessary. However, they had ambiguous feelings
about the clerical establishment. While poor women had
shown deference toward the mullahs, they talked openly
about the corruption of these men while reserving admiration for the more learned and distant religious figures.
"The mullah tells us not to watch television, but he has
five of them in his house," explained one woman. Another
woman told me the following story, which reflects the
extent to which a religious leader like Ayatullah
Khomeini was held in respect even though the ordinary
mullahs were not:

> There was a man whom Ali [the Prophet's son-
> in-law] told to walk forward into a clearing.
> There the man saw streams that were full of
> water. Then suddenly the streams dried up.
> The man saw all varieties of fertile trees with
> fruit but when he went to eat the fruit, black
> worms came out of it, and birds were eating the
> flesh of dead animals. The man came out of the
> garden unable to understand what he had seen.
> Ali said to him that there would be a time
> thirteen centuries later when the world would
> be nice on the outside but inside everything

would be corrupt. This would happen not just
to one country but to all of them.

The bird, explained my friend, was a mullah. Mullahs are
corrupt. Even the one who came to her house slept with
different women. But the mujtahids [the learned mullahs]
were different. They could be respected.

As more and more people were affected by the killings
of friends, acquaintances, or neighbors and as more of
their relatives and friends joined in, the stories
reached closer to home: "Did you know that Rashidi's
neighbor's son was shot for not firing on demonstrators?"
"Did you know that enlisted men are now firing on their
own officers for making them shoot fellow Iranians?"
"Did you hear that . . .?"

More people returned from Qum with tapes of Ayatul-
leh Khomeini's speeches. There was a gradual snowballing
of participation, instigated in the minds of many by the
events of Black Friday.[18] As more and more people died
and rumors continued to spread, more and more women and
men were provided with personal role models and the
religious and social contexts for feeling efficacious
about acting. Most people were not motivated by a
coherent religious or political ideology. The same networks which had fostered emulation between classes and
had perpetuated the differences between those classes and
geographical areas became important in providing the
information and examples for interpreting conditions in
terms conducive for taking action.[19] Some even felt
constrained by social pressure to participate. However,
up through the end of 1978, relatively few women (or men)
from the lowest income neighborhoods of Tehran were
actively participating in street events. In the rural
areas, there were few events at that time for women to
participate in. The breaking of school windows, often the
only government building, did occur in some villages.
Those rural residents who took an active part in the
demonstrations were usually the more mobile young men
who traveled frequently to regional towns or who lived in
villages near them.

The Continuing Revolution: Gender and Class in Iran

The revolution was organized and succeeded due to
the unraveling of a series of events beginning in late
1977, the effectiveness of social networks and religious
symbols in providing a context in which increasing numbers of poor could act, and the state's vascillation in
its reaction to the demonstrators. One day freedom to
march would be allowed, and the next day protestors would
be greeted with bullets. Such inconsistency in reinforcement gave individuals the encouragement to continue. As
a result of the sporadic success of the largely unarmed
demonstrators and the inclusion of more and more people,
the Shah capitulated. People had joined in the movement

for very diverse reasons.[20] While class differences alone
cannot explain the emergence of the revolution, differences on an economic basis were important in explaining
the variations in participation. Among the poor, the
manipulation of religious symbols and interpersonal context were most important in determining who participated
and when. In general, those "marginal" people in both
urban and rural areas were the last to join in.

The first to participate were those in more secure
financial positions and with greater access to information about the political implications of these events,
linking them to larger national and international issues.
A great deal of social-psychological research on revolution and protest, as well as empirical evidence, confirms
the observation that it is usually not the poorest who
rise up and carry through with the revolution.[21] Often
the earlier participants from the poor neighborhoods
were young men, and sometimes young women, who had more
opportunity to roam about the city.[22] They went daily
from their own neighborhoods to the University of Tehran
to see what the protest agenda for that day would be.
Their comments about their own roles in the revolution
indicated that they had initially taken part out of a
sense of excitement and curiousity rather than out of
strong ideological conviction. I asked one young ambu-
lance driver who had "gone to see what was happening" how
many people he saw killed at Maidan-i Jaleh on September 8; he replied that when the shooting began he had
turned to run away and did not see.

However, by talking to participants, particularly
college students, many young people were made aware of
the social/political issues at stake. Younger family
members argued with their older relatives about these
matters, even though the parents did not at first compre-
hend or agree. The poor, as exemplified by poor women,
had some "practical" understanding of their own life
circumstances, but they could not always talk about this.
More importantly, however, they did not always have the
information necessary to perceive their immediate situation in ways that linked these experiences to different
classes, to the state, or to international events beyond
their own lives. Contacts with other classes had generally tended to encourage status enhancement rather than
evaluation of contrasting positions. The events of the
revolution provided poor men and women with the opportunity to gather the information for making more critical
comparisons, emphasizing the importance of activity and
of exposure to social contacts in the formation of
thought and perceptions.[23]

Before the return of Ayatullah Khomeini in 1979,
many poor and middle class Iranians admitted that they
had not given much thought to what would happen after the
Shah. "Anything would be better than what we have now,"

162

they said. While no coherent ideology or ability to discuss these issues was necessary to motivate people to act
en masse against the government, the definition of con-
sciousness--what it meant to be Iranian or what Iran was
to be--became important in determining how, if at all,
the revolution would transform social and economic life.[24]
Consequently a struggle developed between the religious
factions and intellectuals on the left to define what
this new "consciousness" or the national goals would be.

As a result, discussion of these issues was taken to
those people in the poor urban areas and the remoter rural
areas, who were not so actively involved in the earlier
activities. Although it is not clear who is responsible
for speaking to these people, it is clear that women in
the southern neighborhoods of Tehran (and perhaps the
villages) are being educated and awakened to larger
political concerns through public lectures, meetings, and
films.[25] During early 1978, the women I interviewed
showed very little understanding of "international imperi-
alsim" or "Zionism." Even in their religious orientation
these women were directed toward an almost ritualistic
re-creation of various acts rather than toward the application of religious principles or doctrines to their own
lives. The letters I have received since that time
(1979-1981) indicate that women are being exposed to new
political terminology and religious information that will
be useful in continuing the course of the revolution--
whether it takes a political/social or continues in a
religious direction.[26]

The emphasis to date appears to have been on the
consolidation of national or religious sentiments rather
than feminist or class-based ones, even though class and
gender equality are strongly supported in Islamic tradition. In the case of gender, the mullahs were constantly
reiterating to me that Islam provides equality for women.
Despite official pronouncements and explicit sections of
the new constitution guaranteeing women's equality, the
rights of women have been placed within the very specific
context of household and kin groups, where women's roles
and duties are narrow defined. Likewise, religious
teaching provides a basis for class equality. Poor women
used to repeat stories about Ali's and Fatimeh's kindness toward their servants, pointing out that brotherhood
between servant and master is essential to the spirit of
Islam. Yet little appears to have been accomplished
toward altering the distribution of property or changing
the material conditions in which the poor live.

What has happened to the lives of "veiled" and
"unveiled" women in the new Islamic Republic? Has the
revolution made any difference in their daily lives?
Middle and upper class women provided role models for
many of the lower class women during the earlier stages
of the movement. As already noted, the more active women

often donned veils during the early protests, while some
had always worn them. These were publicly active women
garbed in costume acceptable for lower class women.
Among lower class households/families, the participation
of women in public activities was deemed respectable if
the women were properly dressed, especially when the
activity was in support of religious goals, as the
revolution was often purported to be. Following the
establishment of the Islamic Republic, many new Muslim
feminists appeared in public roles, dressed in veils.
Reports in magazines and newspapers made these women
leaders in Islamic dress publicly visible. Some poor
women turned out for religio-political meetings at the
University of Tehran and for demonstrations at the
American Embassy. If the revolution could have provided
additional contexts for these veiled women to become
publicly active, to be educated, to seek professional
employment, then the veiled image might have been an
effective transitional role model, providing women with
the opportunity to demonstrate their abilities and to
gain confidence in themselves.

However, the middle-class women who temporarily
donned the veil and later took to the streets unveiled to
push for Western-style equality for women have been
silenced. What are the poor women whom I interviewed
doing? Rubab who berated herself for having so many
children and who used contraception has had another child.
Azar, Jamilleh, and other young women have capitulated to
their families' choices of marriage partners. One young
woman who wanted to attend the university to study
medicine is now a teacher of religious classes.

While women like Rubab were beginning to make sense
of their social situations, the recent attempts to formally define in "religious" terms what is acceptable
behavior for women means a continuation of the middle-
class-housewife status quo that the majority of Iranian
women were either already engaging in or aspiring to.
As long as both the material and the social conditions of
their lives remain the same, differences of gender and
class will be perpetuated. The influence of family networks has only been increased through appeals to good
Muslims to report family and friends for acts of "treason"
to the state and to Islam.

At the same time, the conditions which organized the
successful creation of a revolutionary movement--the
interpersonal networks and the political groups (like the
student left)--remain a potential channel for continuing
the revolution into other areas of Iranian life. The
experience of Iran emphasizes again that unless deliberate
efforts are made to change existing social and economic
structures, people can take part in revolution without
significantly changing their own status.

164

NOTES

1. The material on which these observations are
based was collected during 18 months of anthropological
fieldwork in south Teheran and in four rural areas from
which migrant families originated. Two of the rural
areas surveyed were in Azerbaijan, one was in the Central
Province, and one was on the border between the Central
Province and Hamadan. The data was collected by means of
participant observation, case studies, and directed
interviews during a period from July, 1977 through late
1978. Data from later periods is based on correspondence
which I received from individuals in the original sample
through September, 1981. The total sample used in the
final analysis included 287 women and 236 households.

2. Skocpol (1979) points to the following conditions and relations as important for understanding how
revolutions take shape: the crises of the state in relation to international situations and to groups within its
own society, the situation of the poor, and the ability
of the intellectuals to direct uprisings of the poor.
The type of revolution which Skocpol analyzes is defined
by Skocpol herself as social in nature or involving the
basic transformation of the class structure of the society (pp. 4-5). While the conditions she describes as
central did exist in pre-revolutionary Iran, to date the
Iranian revolution has not achieved a class transformation. Noticeably the role of the poor and the way in
which the intellectuals have directed the sentiments of
the revolution differ from that which Skocpol describes
for France, Russia, and China and will be important in
determining whether or not critical changes do occur in
the Iranian case. (Cf. Cottam 1979 and Abrahamian
1979 on conditions leading up to the Iranian Revolution.

3. The popular press has seemed especially inclined
to emphasize the importance of "traditional" religious
sentiments and disdain for modernization, while others
have tended to underscore class divisions and the growing
economic gaps between the mainly urban Iranians and the
poorer, more rural dwellers. The relevance of these
speculations will be discussed in the text. However, to
assume that sentiments or awareness arising from these
conditions are sufficient to explain participation in the
revolutionary demonstrations is misleading (cf. Keddie
1980 for descriptions of the "two cultures" in Iran).

4. The white or "bloodless" revolution was the name
given by the last Pahlavi Shah to his "modernization"
programs, designed to industrialize and nationalize the
country.

5. This particular statement was made in the Persian edition of the Kayhan newspaper in September 1978.
These neighborhoods were considered as "migrant" (by cen-

sus definition) because a majority of the persons there were born in provincial towns and villages. Many of the households were recent arrivals to the area; others had been resident in Tehran for some years, moving from one neighborhood to another seeking better accomodations or more agreeable landlords. "Of course everyone wants a place of their own" was a common response to queries about multiple moves. Ideally, a household moves until it finds affordable lodging which it can purchase as its own.

Migrant enclaves were found scattered throughout other parts of the city, but most were found in south Teheran. It is difficult to confirm the exact proportion of the population residing in the southern neighborhoods because the most recent census figures (1976) do not report residence by district in Tehran. However, Hemmasi (1977) reports that 88 percent of the families in Tehran (based on 1966 data) lived in the lower and lower middle class neighborhoods throughout the city.

6. Shortages of water were created through the mis-use of mechanized pumps and wells such as those supplied on government projects. Labor was drawn away to the cities. The government's failure to develop adequate marketing infrastructures for agricultural products and its subsidies of imported staples like rice and wheat meant a reduction in the farmers' incentives to plant certain kinds of crops in amounts beyond that needed for their immediate household or family.

7. The sample of households in my study was divided into groups by economic class and geographical location, differing in distance from Tehran. Signifi-cant differences in behavior and thought were found to exist on the basis of these "geo-social" groupings.

8. There was a great deal of variation in the household size of the rural sample according to the status of the household. In the remoter rural areas, both the richest and the poorest households often had fairly large households (averaging around eight persons), but for different reasons.

9. This information about village women, of course, refers specifically to women interviewed and observed in the areas described in note 3. Contrasting information about village women's lives in the north of Iran (the Caspian area, for example) and among nomadic groups may reveal some differences. However, much of the available information from other parts of Iran supports the con-clusions reached about rural women in this sample (see Beck 1980).

10. While no women under the age of 15 were formally interviewed in this study, it was foreseeable that some might be included since 13- and 14-year-old married women were interviewed informally during the study.

11. With in-migration to the cities and the increas-ed educational exposure of younger women, older women

were coming to live in the homes of daughters-in-law who were much better prepared to deal with contemporary living. As a result, older women had less authority in family and interfamilial affairs than they held in the past.

12. The <u>chadur</u> (veil) worn in Iran today is less restrictive than the style worn in the past or that worn by women in other parts of the Muslim world today. The <u>chadur</u> is a semi-circular piece of cloth which is worn from head to foot, wrapped around the body and held in place by the hands.

13. The Women's Organization of Iran placed more emphasis on the images it was propagating than upon changing the actual conditions which made certain roles and behaviors the only reasonable choices for poor women.

14. Simple statistical indices were developed to describe this relationship between women's contact with other social classes and experiences and their behavioral preferences.

15. The behaviors imposed upon women in the lower classes of the city were more restrictive than in many rural areas both for economic and social reasons. There were more strangers in the city, creating a situation which necessitated the recourse to more formal behaviors like veiling. In addition it became economically feasible in the cities to restrict women to their households, since their productive labor outside the household was not so crucial to the survival of the family.

16. References have been made in other recent works to the influence of "gossip" networks during the revolution (see Pliskin 1980).

17. The similar participation of women in earlier Iranian political movements such as the Constitutional Revolution, 1911 (see Bamdad 1977) and in movements in other parts of the Middle East/North Africa suggest that women's role in this kind of public activity is not a new phenomenon in the Muslim world.

18. Black Friday is the name given to September 8, 1978, the day on which a large number of Iranian protestors were killed when government troops fired upon them. (see M. Fischer 1980 for a more complete chronological listing of revolutionary events.)

19. J. A. Barnes' work (1969, p. 52) represents an early anthropological attempt to apply network analysis at a micro-level to understanding political process. While references have been made in this paper to the importance of social networks in explaining participation in the Iranian Revolution, the material on which these suggestions are based is drawn from network material collected among poor urban and rural Iranians in the period leading up to the revolution (through early 1979). There is little empirical data on the use of these networks to organize specific revolutionary events, particularly by the religious and intellectual middle classes,

during late 1978 and into 1979.

20. Among the upper and upper middle classes there were many persons who opposed the government but for a variety of different reasons. Many of these individuals provided only tacit support for the street activities, never actually marching themselves.

21. Bandura's research (1979) shows that it is usually the middle class individuals or those from slightly wealthier backgrounds who rebel first or lead movements and strikes. Reports from the Watts riots also show that these young people who were the first to demonstrate were not from the poorest quarters but from the better-off households (Stoll 1973). And a note is made of a similar occurrence in political struggles in India. "According to Dr. Arparna Basu, the movement initially attracted women from the urban middle classes, but as the nationalist movement gained in strength industrial workers and certain sectors of the peasantry also participated in it." (Srinivas 1977).

22. Participation in the revolutionary events reflected differences in information and experiences between men and women of different ages and women from different social classes. Men had more education generally than did women; the poor remained less exposed than the wealthy. For example, among the poor urban and rural women I interviewed, 52.3 percent over the age of 15 were illiterate, whereas only 27.2 percent of the men from the same households could not read or write. Among the sample of women, only 4.5 percent of the poor women traveled more than 60 minutes from their homes daily; almost 42 percent of the men did. It was differences such as these that helped to create differences in social contacts and available information. In contrast only 22.2 percent of the middle class women over age 15 were illiterate. The great majority of these were in fact older women, age 50-85. In addition, about 37 percent of these middle class women traveled more than an hour from their homes daily.

23. There is a whole literature on Marxist conceptions of praxis and the relationship between activity/ experience and the formation of thought and consciousness. Giddens (1979), Bologh (1980), and Marx himself discuss the degree to which thought and awareness are grounded in experience and living. See Therborn (1980) for further discussion of this as well as a precedent for considering consciousness and ideology as variations in kinds of information.

24. See Giddens (1979) and Therborn (1980) for conceptions of "discursive" consciousness--that level of awareness about which individuals can discuss vs. that which is practical and motivates daily life without being verbalized or thought about objectively. These writers as well as others have discussed at length the "politi-

cal" nature of consciousness and the extent to which the
definition of consciousness is a political act.

25. As already noted, Skocpol has made the role of
an intellectual elite or organized revolutionary group
central to the transformation of a political movement
into a social revolution. This conceptualization of
social revolution acknowledges the extent to which certain groups in society have different kinds of information and frameworks for viewing these struggles. In
the case of Iran, however, cadres of organized revolutionaries have not yet led on the lower-class workers
and peasants to transform society. I suggest that Skocpol probably put too much emphasis on the spontaneity of
the uprisings from below that were to be led by revolutionary elite and that more emphasis should be placed on
the way in which such organized groups are able to work
at manipulating situations of revolutionary potential.
For example, in the case of China, recent work highlights
the effort made by revolutionary cadres in encouraging
peasants to act against landlords and to participate in
other revolutionary activities (Yung-Fa Chen [personal
communication]).

26. It is difficult to ascertain the effect of these
meetings and discussions on women's perceptions of the
relationship of the revolution to their own lives. In
their letters women have focused on descriptions of the
details of their personal lives, making political comments only under the guise of jargon.

BIBLIOGRAPHY

Abrahamian, E. "The Causes of the Constitutional Revolu-
tion in Iran," International Journal of Middle East
Studies 10 (1979): 381-414.
Bamdad, Badr ol-Moluk. From Darkness into Light: Women's
Emancipation in Iran, F.R.C. Bagley, ed. and trans.
(Hicksville, N.Y.: Exposition Press, 1977).
Bandura, A. "Self-Efficacy: An Integrative Construct,"
Invited Address, Western Psychological Association,
San Diego, California, April 1979.
Barnes, J.A. "Networks and Political Processes," in J.C.
Mitchell (ed.), Social Networks in Urban Situations
(Manchester: Manchester University Press, 1969).
Beck, Lois, "Women Among the Qashqa'i Nomadic Pastoralists
in Iran," in L. Beck and N. Keddie (eds.), Women in
the Muslim World (Cambridge, Mass.: Harvard Univer-
sity Press, 1978), pp. 351-73.
Bologh, Roslyn. Dialectical Phenomonology. Marx's Method.
(London: Routledge and Kegan Paul, 1979).
Cottam, R., Nationalism in Iran, updated through 1979
(Pittsburgh, Pa.: University of Pittsburgh Press,
1979).

Davis, Susan. "Working Women in Moroccan Villages," in L. Beck and N. Keddie (eds.), Women in the Muslim World (Cambridge, Mass.: Harvard University Press, 1978), pp. 416-33.

Fischer, M. Iran. From Religious Dispute to Revolution (Cambridge, Mass.: Harvard University Press, 1980).

Giddens, A. Central Problems in Social Theory (Berkeley, Calif.: University of California Press, 1979).

Hemmasi, M. "Tehran in Transition: A Study in Comparative Factoral Ecology," in J. Momeni, (ed.), The Population of Iran. A Selection of Readings (Tehran: East/West Center and Pahlavi University, 1977).

_____. "Migration and Problems of Development: The Case of Iran," in Kh. Farmanfarmian (ed.), The Social Sciences and Problems of Development (Princeton, N.J.: Princeton University Press, 1976).

Jeffrey, Patricia. Frogs in a Well. Indian Women in Purdah (London: ZED Press, 1979).

Kazemi, Farhad. Poverty and Revolution in Iran. The Migrant Poor, Urban Marginality, and Politics (New York, N.Y.: New York University Press, 1980).

Keddie, Nikki. Iran: Religion, Politics and Society (London: Frank Cass, 1980).

Pliskin, Karen. "Camouflage, Conspiracy and Collaborators: Rumors of the Revolution," Iranian Studies 13 (1980): 55-82.

Srinivas, M.N. "The Changing Position of Indian Women," Man 12 (1977): 221-38.

Skocpol, Theda. States and Social Revolutions. A Comparative Analysis of France, Russia and China Cambridge, Mass.: Harvard University Press, 1979).

Stoll, Estie. "Crowding," in T. Weaver (ed.), To See Ourselves. Anthropology and Modern Social Issues (Glenview, Ill.: Scott, Foresman and Co., 1973).

Therborn, G. The Ideology of Power and the Power of Ideology (London: Verso Editions and NLB, 1980).

Wikan, Unni. Life Among the Poor in Cairo. Ann Henning, trans. (London: Tavistock Publications, 1980).

Women's Organization of Iran. Araneh Sima-yi Yakchiabad. (Tehran: 1977).

10
Aliabad Women: Revolution as Religious Activity

Mary E. Hegland

An apparent paradox of the Iranian Revolution has
been the tremendous participation of Iranian women in the
revolution, in terms of the numbers of women who were
active in demonstrations, contrasted to the subsequent
setbacks in the position of women in Iran and their de-
creasing participation in public life. In this chapter, I
argue that the great majority of women participating in
the revolution did not consider their actions to be outside of traditional social, cultural and religious parameters.[1] Neither did they expect their participation in
the revolution to be the first step in gaining improved
status and more important roles in public life. Before
the revolution, the great majority of Iranian women
remained outside the modern work force and were not educated. They were still constrained by traditional expectations; their primary responsibility was to children,
home and husband. Ideally, any outside activity was
restricted to socializing among neighbors and kin or was
contained within religious activity. Such women, although
participating in the revolution for much the same reasons
as men, were able to take part because revolutionary
activity was defined as religious activity. As such
women were accustomed to participating in religious activities and containing their activity outside of the home
and their socializing within a religious framework, they
felt little social pressure or self-censorship against
participating in this new type of "religious" activity.
Because the women themselves as well as the religious
leaders who subsequently took over control of the country
did not perceive the revolutionary activity of women to
be outside of the traditional cultural and religious
framework, it is not surprising that such activity did
not result in increased activity of women in the public
sector.
Material for this paper was gathered mainly in the
village of Aliabad,[2] located half-an-hour away from the
outskirts of Shiraz, capital of the southwestern province
of Fars; also included is information from interviews

with women in Shiraz and elsewhere in Iran between June
1978 and December 1979. It should be noted that the village of Aliabad is something of an exception to the
majority of Iranian villages. It enjoys a high level of
economic prosperity due in large part to its close proximity with Shiraz, which allows the men to commute to
jobs in nearby factories and in the city. A long time
association with the bazaar and with religious and educational circles in the city was part of the reason for the
relatively high level of participation in the revolution
by men and women in the village. Although this paper
deals mainly with those women who took part in demonstrations, it is important to remember that such women were
in the minority; most women of Aliabad did not join in
revolutionary activities. Most of the women who did
participate found it possible to take part in the revolution because it was defined as religious activity and
therefore as legitimate for them.

In the first section I discuss pre-revolutionary
conditions for the women of Aliabad. Next I describe
the involvement of the women in the revolution and their
attitudes concerning this involvement. Finally, I look
at the position of the women during the months following
the revolution while I was still present in the village.

Pre-revolutionary Conditions for Women in Aliabad

Previous to the revolution, few women in Aliabad
worked or were educated beyond a few years of elementary
school. As the following table shows, there were eleven
women out of almost 500 in the village who either earned
enough income to make them self-sufficient or to contribute a substantial part of their own support.

WOMEN OF ALIABAD WORKING OUTSIDE OF THE
HOME DURING 1978-1979

Kindergarten teachers	2
Cloth salesperson	1
Seamstress	1
Hammam [public bath house] attendant	1
Kindergarten cook	1
Midwives	2
Baker of bread	1
Keeper of dairy cows and other animals	1
Opium smuggler	1
Total	11

The opium smuggler was the only woman working outside of
her home who was not forced to do so through economic
necessity. Most working women were widows, although the
kindergarten cook was married to an incompetent man, unable to support himself and his family. The two kinder-

garten teachers were young siyyid women in their early
twenties, somewhat older than the average age of village
women at marriage. Since they were siyyids (purportedly
descendants of the Prophet through his daughter Fatimeh)
and therefore reluctant to marry non-siyyids, there were
few potential husbands for them in the village. Furthermore, neither of them had either beauty or a winning personality. Therefore, since they were poor, there was no
recourse for them except to support themselves, which they
did by teaching kindergarten.

On the whole, employment outside the home was considered an indication of low socio-economic position and
a source of shame both for the women involved and for
their relatives.[3] The female opium smuggler was envied
for the quantity of gold jewelry she wore, reportedly purchased with the proceeds from her illicit trade, but many
villagers disapproved of her trading activities, although
they did not display their disapproval openly because of
the close relationship between the woman's husband and the
powerful Askari brothers, who ran the village.

The one financially rewarding activity for women
commonly accepted among the villagers was the crocheting
of cotton uppers for the hand made shoes sewn by some men
in the locality and usually sold to migrating Qashqa'i.
Such crocheting could be done in a woman's own home, in
time she could spare from housework and child care. However, the demand for the hand made shoes was rapidly declining, and women in general were no longer very active
in crocheting. In the past, young unmarried girls would
have brought in some income by crocheting. Since the market had lessened in recent times, that option was no
longer open to them. They could go to school if their
families would permit them to; they could stay at home,
perhaps doing a bit of knitting or other handicraft, but
relatively idle; or they could go to work at the carpet
workshop owned by the Askari brothers.

Some twenty girls from less-well-off families worked
at the workshop. If they were masters, those who could
call out the pattern and the colors to be used, they
earned 500 tomans; the girls with less experience earned
300 tomans a month.[4] They worked from 5 to 1 and from
1:30 to 6 six days a week. Although there was no rule
against employment of married women, none worked at the
workshop. The girls from the workshop who married while
I was in the village stopped working.

Although education for boys was greatly valued, villagers were not enthusiastic about educating their girls.
Most fathers were not adverse to allowing their daughters
to attend school for a few years, but most girls left
school before puberty. Only persons from the upper socio-
economic class of the village allowed their daughters to
attend high school. Among the siyyids from the Lower
Neighborhood (the most prosperous section) of the village,

only the daughters of the three Askari brothers, the
political bosses of the village, attended high school in
Shiraz. The daughter of one of the brothers, Siyyid
Ya^{c}qub Askari, had received a high school diploma and
was a teacher. She had married and moved away from the
village. Siyyid Assadullah Askari's daughter attended
high school in Shiraz, living at the home of her uncle,
Siyyid Ibn Ali Askari, whose daughters were also in
high school there. Six to ten girls from the Upper Neighborhood also attended high school in Shiraz, living in
homes owned by their fathers or with relatives. These
girls were the daughters of Aliabad teachers or families
with more progressive attitudes toward the education of
women. However, there was strong pressure against the
continuing education of these girls. Shirin, the leader
of this group of girls and the best student among them,
was determined to attend a university and to have a
.career. Her fiance had earned a diploma and worked in the
administration of a nearby factory; he was only mildly
opposed to her plans, but her future father-in-law was
immovable. Any daughter-in-law of his would certainly not
work outside of the home; his son was quite capable of
supporting her. Opposing opinions on the matter almost
caused the engagement to be broken, and the conflict had
not been settled by the time I left the village.
     Since most people did not anticipate that girls would
have jobs in the future, but would be wives and homemakers, little value was placed on education for women by
the majority of villagers. The 14-year-old daughter of my
courtyard neighbor had been taken out of school. When a
visitor suggested that she start work at the carpet workshop, she replied that she wanted to go to school. "Why?"
the visitor asked, "No matter how long you go to school,
you'll still end up doing just what the rest of us do."
And indeed, the girl was engaged shortly afterwards.
     Changes supposedly brought about by the Shah's gov-
ernment had not affected village women to any great degree.[5] Although the Family Protection Law of 1967 stated
that women could not marry before the age of 15, with ex-
emptions allowed, it was not unknown for girls to marry
at the age of 12 in the village of Aliabad. Various
means, such as obliterating the age on the identity card
or using the identity card of an older sister, were used
to circumvent the law.
     As far as I am aware, there had been only four cases
of men with two wives in the village in recent times.
Two cases were of long standing. In a third case, which
occurred a few years before I came to the village, a
woman had committed suicide when her husband took a
second wife. In the fourth case, the law which stipulates
that a wife must give her written agreement before her
husband takes a second wife failed of its intended effect
when an outsider working in the village as a welder
changed his identity card and married a local woman with-

out either woman being aware that he had two wives. The authorities were subsequently informed, and he was threatened with either a large fine or six months imprisionment. However, he had managed to retain both wives without suffering any consequences at the time I left the village.

For most village women, being supported by a husband was the only option in life. When the brother of a 13-year-old girl objected to her marriage to a young man whom he suspected would make a poor husband, his step-father asked him, "Are you going to support her for the rest of her life then?"

In the case of marital unhappiness, likewise, little choice was available. A woman could either put up with abuse, make a suicide attempt, or return to her father's house, if her father was willing, with an eventual return to her husband's home or a divorce. In her father's home the separated woman had to comply with her father's wishes. If she chose suicide or if she divorced, a woman could be quite certain that her children would suffer; it was unusual for a person other than the mother to show loving attention to a child. A divorced woman generally had no option but to hope for a second husband. However, one divorcee from the village was teaching kindergarten in Shiraz, leaving her children in the care of her mother in the village and returning to see them on her day off.

In the case of the death of a husband, village women informed me, the widow must go to court shortly after her husband's death and declare that she would give over guardianship of her children to her husband's father. Or if she wished to keep guardianship herself, she must promise not to marry again. In the latter case, she must then solve the difficult problem of how to support herself and her children.

On the whole, the reforms of the Shah's government did not have much effect on the lives of village women, although there were several women whose male relatives worked in town and who were thus more aware of the legal possibilities for protecting their rights. They were beginning to use the court system; it is likely this tendency might have increased in the future.

The social activities of women were restricted. The rightful business of women was to attend to their children, homes, and husbands. Women were concerned about fulfilling their expected roles in order to earn good reputations.[6] Several siyyid women prided themselves on rarely leaving their own courtyard. One of the kindergarten teachers was so modest in behavior that she did not even attend the weddings of kin unless they were very closely related. Required to be circumspect about any activity outside of their homes, women were anxious to avoid the reputation of poor worker or of "stray" or runabout.[7] Women could sit in the sun and chat with their neighbors as they crocheted cotton uppers when their housework was completed, or they could make visits to the

homes of close female relatives, but they felt constrained from visiting elsewhere. One woman, in explaining why
she did not come to visit me in my new village home
located outside of her own neighborhood, said,

> I couldn't come to your neighborhood. I've never
> been there, except a couple of times for mourning
> ceremonies, like Ali Naqi's last year. I would
> feel as if I were stealing something. It would
> be zisht [socially inappropriate].

Women generally were allowed to attend weddings and
other life-cycle celebrations of relatives, although
sometimes their husbands would prevent them from these
activities. The best excuse for leaving the house,
socializing, and escaping from the responsibilities of
children, housework, and husbands was religious activity.[8]
The siyyid women, whose husbands were primarily traders
and thus influenced by the religious culture of the
Shiraz bazaar, were far more active in religious observances and ritual than other village women. What follows
is a description of their religious activities which
provided a background for their participation in the
"religious" activity of revolution.

Many village women, especially older women, widows,
and other women free from the care of young children or
from the constraints of husbands, attended evening prayers
at the mosque. They enjoyed this session as a major
social activity of the day and a chance to catch up on
news and gossip. The siyyid women, however, and those
women more careful about modest behavior did not go to
the mosque. To attend the mosque would entail going outside of their own neighborhood and mixing with village
men who were not relatives or even neighbors. The
women's section was curtained off, but men and women came
and went together through the mosque courtyard.[9]

The siyyid women and their social circle took part
only in religious activities which could be held in their
own or neighboring homes and which were completely segregated from men. Regular prayers provided the women with
some time to themselves, since they were not supposed to
be interrupted. Rowzehs, the chanting of the passions of
the Imams, were conducted in homes and attended by close
female relatives and neighbors. Generally the only man
present was the rowzeh chanter. Women would gather to
drink tea and smoke a water pipe, exchange news, and chat
about household matters or village affairs. During the
revolution this list of topics was expanded by the addition of news about political and religious matters.
Sessions conducted by teachers and students from the
Zahra Religious School in Shiraz were also held in a home
in the siyyid neighborhood for members of the social
circle of the siyyid women. When it was suggested that
the meetings be held in a public place such as the kindergarten so that other village women would feel free to

attend, the siyyid women replied that they would be unable to attend if the meetings were not held in a home in their own neighborhood.

Joining in mourning was perceived to be a religious duty, bringing religious credit to the participant. Women thus felt quite free to attend the mourning gatherings of other villagers, generally walking to such gatherings in the company of their neighbors and kinswomen. Women's mourning gatherings were held in homes, separate from the male gatherings which were held in the mosque or in a separate courtyard. Thursday afternoons were set aside for visits to the cemetery in remembrance of the recent dead. Cemetery visits and paying respect to the family of the dead at their home were important social activities for women. As one woman on her way to the cemetery aptly commented, "And this is what we women have for recreation." No men participated in the Thursday afternoon cemetery visits, so women who were not allowed to go to the mosque for evening prayers or who did not wish to go for fear of being seen in public with men not related to them felt no constraint in going to the cemetery on Thursday afternoons.

Pilgrimages to nearby shrines or to shrines in Shiraz[10] also served a social as well as religious purpose. On these trips women would join together with several relatives or neighbors, usually taking tea and snacks. Visits to more distant shrines, requiring private transportation and possibly even an overnight stay, were family affairs rather than exclusively female preoccupations. A pilgrimage, whether with other women or with husband and family, allowed a woman to escape from her daily routine for some diversion and exposure to new sights and experiences. The trip to Mecca, actually completed by several village women, was also greatly valued. Women told me that the permission of one's husband was not required for making the hajj, although for every other destination or activity women had to obtain their husbands' permission.

Tasu^ca, the ninth, and Ashura, the tenth of the holy month of Muharram, anniversary of the martyrdom of Imam Husain (d. 681), were also perceived by women as offering a legitimate opportunity to get out of the house and find release from household labor. Village women believed it was their religious duty to listen to the lamentations for Imam Husain and to cry. Ashura was the one day of the year when women were forbidden to work.[11]

Such religious activities allowed only a brief reprieve from responsibilities and drudgery. In actuality, even religious activity did not generally allow escape from child care. If there were children, women had to take them along to mourning ceremonies, to rowzehs, and on pilgrimages. Even on Ashura women had to attend to their children and cook for them. The pri-

mary task of the Muslim woman was the raising of her children, a duty even more important than participation in
religious activity.[12]
  Women could participate in religious activities more
easily when they were held in their own neighborhood.
Wearing their veils, they could take their children, come
and go rather informally, and do household tasks inter-
mittently. Unlike the daily prayer and attendance at the
mosque, the neighborhood activities did not require a
state of ritual cleanliness. Thus, menstruating women and
mothers in constant contact with the soiled clothing of
their babies were free to attend. Since these activities
were defined as religious, participation by women was
sanctioned by social, cultural, and religious norms of
of behavior. Partly because of this previous experience
in religious activity, women overcame reluctance to join
the revolutionary demonstrations when religious leaders
defined their activity as religious.

Aliabad Women and the Revolution

  Attitudes of Aliabad women towards the revolution
fell into several categories. The wives of the political
elite (a total of five or six families) were firmly
against the revolution. One of these women berated young
men who took part in the revolution and scolded their
mothers for allowing them to do so. Another fought con-
tinuously with one of her sons over his involvement in
revolutionary activity. These women and their husbands
had reason to be pro-Shah. They owed their power and
prominence to their support for the monarchy, and their
efforts to encourage sympathy for the regime and to
prevent dissension.
  The poor peasants in the village, both men and women,
remained cynical towards participation in the political
struggle. They considered revolutionary activity periph-
eral to their own lives.[13] Their cynicism did not lessen
when the struggle was couched in religious terms. They
were convinced that the best action was no action and that
risking their lives in support of the revolution was
fruitless. Shortly before Ayatullah Khomeini's arrival
in Tehran from Paris, I heard a peasant remark to his
mother, "Khomeini's supposed to come soon."
  "So," his mother replied, "What's he bringing with
him?"[14]
  The peasant women and other poorer village women did
not engage in the round of religious and social activities
enjoyed by the siyyid women; they participated in far
fewer gatherings of any sort. Their social networks were
smaller and less cohesive, and their social interaction
was more confined. They seemed far less well informed
and articulate about national level politics than the
siyyid women. It seems likely that because these poorer
women rarely participated in organized religious activity

they would not be easily influenced by religious figures.
Similarly, because they were cut off from any network,
they were not widely exposed to the interpretation of
revolutionary activity as a required [vajib] religious
duty. However, it is unlikely that they would have found
that argument persuasive because they were far less accustomed to involvement in religious activity.

The peasants were not turning their backs on their
religion by declining revolutionary involvement. They
considered themselves to be good Muslims, but their
emphasis was more on general belief and moral behavior
than on the ritual and organized religious activity
stressed by the siyyids and traders.[15] If anything,
peasants had a rather suspicious and derogatory attitude
toward persons who emphasized ritual. For example, they
felt that shopkeepers accumulating enough money to go on
hajj were obviously cheating customers.

A difference could be discerned between the older
peasant women and their daughters who had moved to the
city or associated with relatives in Shiraz. The latter
seemed far more articulate and informed about the national
events. Several of these were quite enthusiastic in their
attitudes towards the "Aqa" (Ayatullah Khomeini) as early
as October 1978, even if they did not actually participate
in demonstrations.

Some of the wives of commuters into Shiraz or to
nearby factories became politicized during the fall and
winter months of 1978 as their menfolk began to bring
back information about the on-going revolutionary process
and condemnations of the Shah's regime. Although some
of these women eventually joined the nightly demonstrations in the village initiated by the siyyid women early
in January of 1979, very few of them traveled to Shiraz
to participate in demonstrations in the city.

Eight or ten young unmarried women from the Upper
Neighborhood of the village were the first women of the
village to become involved in the revolution. Students
in high schools in Shiraz, they were influenced by their
fathers, most of whom were teachers, and brothers as well
as by the other students in their high schools. In
addition, they attended Qur'an classes led by a visiting
mullah from Qum during the summer of 1978 and that fall
and winter during the school strikes. During one class
in February of 1979, before the fall of the government,
Shirin, the leader of the high school group, asked the
mullah if political parties were to be free under the
future Islamic Republic. The mullah responded that political parties which are in accordance with Islam would be
free. Shirin looked dubious and commented that she had
understood all political parties should be free.

Shirin held her own Qur'an class for younger girls.
In a meeting on February 2 she exhorted the younger girls
that just praying and knowing the Qur'an was not enough,

that the Shah's government had taught exclusive attention
to these matters in order to keep people from becoming
involved with political matters. Rather, she told them,
one should both know the Qur'an and put it into practice.
Imam Ali was both religious and political. One should be
both. She cautioned that such television programs as
"Little House on the Prairie" were used for the same
purpose as attention to religious details--to entertain
people and keep them from becoming involved in politics.
She also spoke in favor of education for girls:

> Don't accept it if your mothers say that
> the Qur'an is against girls studying. Some
> people say that since Fatimeh the pure
> didn't study, girls today shouldn't study
> either. But Ali said, "I have responsi-
> bilities and my wife must have responsi-
> bilities too." Girls should study.

The high school girls from the Upper Neighborhood
began participating in demonstrations in Shiraz even
before the Ashura demonstration in December 1978.
Probably they would have participated in revolutionary
demonstrations whether or not they had been given a
religious connotation. As high school students in the
city, they were accustomed to public life, and they
planned careers for themselves (whether or not such plans
would have become reality is not at all certain). They
did not require the legitimization of a religious framework for their participation in activity outside of the
home.

The largest group of female activists was made up of
some twenty to thirty siyyid women from the Lower Neighborhood of the village. These women were influenced by
their husbands, brothers, sons, and fathers, who were
traders or businessmen in Shiraz. The religious emphasis
placed on the revolution was a drawing factor for them,
with their identification with religious ritual, activity
and symbolism and their feelings of religious identity and
desire to fulfill the religious expectations of their
social group.

The major topic of conversation for the siyyid women
during the winter of 1978 was the events of the revolution. Women would sit with men during the constant discussion of political conditions, even when male visitors
were present. Male relatives and associates or customers
of husbands, brothers or sons would visit, and women
would quiz them on recent occurrences, even in the
absence of the men of the house. Mothers and sisters
likewise carefully questioned boys coming home from
school for the latest news. For example, the brother
of one young widow, Ismat, was a tailor in Shiraz and
belonged to a group studying the Qur'an and engaging in
religious-political discussions. Ismat declared that

everything she knew she had learned from her brother.

An important part of the revolutionary effort was the dissemination of information about on-going events, which served to arouse the outrage and determination of the populace, and interpretations of the events, which would likewise be persuasive in urging revolutionary action. Women were active in this dissemination of information and interpretations, which brought about a change in women's perceptions and attitudes before they actually became active in demonstrations. Upon hearing some news, women would rush to tell neighbors and relatives. Literacy was not necessary for the accumulation and spread of information. Much news passed by word of mouth. Women listened to BBC and to tapes collected by their sons and other male relatives, lending them to friends, neighbors, and relatives as well. Women learned the revolutionary couplets, chants, and songs; they collected the I^clamiyyehs [the mimeographed revolutionary announcements]. Those who could not read themselves would ask sons or male neighbors to read the announcements to them. Women's gatherings, religious or otherwise, also served as opportunities to pass on news about current events. For example, after the chanting of a rowzeh on December 28, 1978, the rowzeh chanter gave a full report of the BBC news from the night before, concentrating on an interview with Ayatullah Shari^cat-Madari, and a discussion followed.

Towards the end of December 1978 and beginning of January 1979, a photo exhibit dealing with the revolution was held at the Aliabad mosque, with times set aside for viewing by women. A slide show about the revolution was given at the mosque one evening with women sitting on the floor behind the men. Aliabad women also went to the exhibit held at the university in Shiraz, where ropes served to separate the women moving along close to the photos from the men viewing at a distance of two feet. When the SAVAK building in Shiraz was attacked and taken over by the people in early January 1979, a group of women from the Lower Neighborhood went in to view the photos of torture victims, implements of torture, fingernails and pieces of human skin put on display. These women shared in the horror and great sorrow of realizing through first hand evidence what had happened to their countrymen. Some women reported that after seeing these gruesome sights they wept until late into the night, unable to sleep.

Most of the Aliabad women who participated in revolutionary activity accepted the prevalent religious interpretation of the struggle, that the duty of each Shi^cite is to struggle against tyranny, that the Shah was the Yazid of the age and that Ayatullah Khomeini was the Imam Husain of the age*, and that they should support Ayatullah

---

*Editor's note: It was during the reign of Yazid

Khomeini in his struggle against tyranny, repression and the corruption of religion.

In joining revolutionary demonstrations, women were not violating social, cultural, or religious constraints on women. Rather, those "traditional" women who took part could do so because their participation was defined as being within the bounds of traditional constraints and was sanctioned by their menfolk, by religious leaders, and by other women in their social control units. In a number of different ways women repeated to me the language used by religious leaders, stressing the importance of action rather than status: "The best one of you is the one who does the best deed." "In Islam, action is more important than whether you are a man or a woman." "Whoever follows the orders of God and does the same work that Ali and Muhhamad did can be an imam for him or herself." "The highest point of human and religious attainment is to become a martyr. A martyr becomes his own mediator with God."

The siyyid women of Aliabad began demonstrating early in January 1979.[16] While he was still in France Ayatullah Khomeini had declared Friday, January 5 a day of mourning for the many persons martyred during the month of Muharram clashes between the demonstrators and the military and police forces. In the afternoon of that day a group of siyyed women were sitting outside chatting as they crocheted cotton uppers. They began to discuss the demonstrations in the cities and the day of mourning.

Laila, a young wife and mother, said, "We should shout chants too!"

Ra^{c}na, the leader of this social group, replied, "In the city this is okay, but in the village it is zisht [improper].

"No, it's not zisht. Are the women in Shiraz better than we are?" Laila insisted.

Akhtar added, "If we had any courage, we'd go too."

So the women agreed to go on their own demonstration after dark, about 7:00. When the time came, some of the women were having second thoughts, but a few resolute ones gathered the whole group together, and they started out.

They walked up the alley shouting their chants.

(680-684) and at his instigation that Imam Husain, the grandson of the Prophet Muhammad and the third Shi^{c}ite Imam, was murdered. In Shi^{c}ite view, Yazid's reign exemplifies injustice, calumny, oppression, and the greatest deviation from the teachings of Islam while Imam Husain is the personification of a great hero who died unjustly in defense of his principles. Shi^{c}ites annually commemorate his martyrdom during the first ten days of the month of Muharram, culminating in Ashura, the day he was killed.

When the men heard their voices, they came out and joined
in shouting slogans. The women were somewhat nervous, but
they were also pleased, excited, and very proud of themselves.

The following evening the women again assembled to
march. This time they were joined by a few men and a
group of teen-age boys. Their slogan shouting began to
follow a pattern: the men and boys, marching together in
the front, shouted the first phrase in a revolutionary
couplet; the women and girls, marching behind, responded
with the second phrase. Others joined the marchers as
they proceeded through the village; even some of the most
pious and modest women ventured out. The demonstrators
gave special attention to shouting slogans when they
passed the courtyards of known Shah-supporters. This time
the marchers covered more distance than they had the night
before. The women began to feel that much was possible.

Each succeeding night the women found courage to
venture further through the village, until finally they
were making an entire circuit around the village two or
three times an evening. The demonstrations became large,
with both men and women joining in; they become more
organized and less spontaneous. Routes were planned, and
boys with flashlights were stationed at rough places in
the path to make sure no one fell where the footing was
poor.

The day after the second evening of marching and the
following day had been declared days of mourning; the
women decided that they would go to Shiraz and join the
huge demonstrations to be held there. Ra^{c}na described
what happened:

> They said that women in Shiraz were march-
> ing and shouting slogans. I wanted to go and
> see what it was like. So we went to Shah-
> Chiraq Shrine. A lot of people were sitting
> there. The women were separated from the men
> by an iron fence that had been put up. The
> son of an important religious figure in Shiraz
> gave a speech, saying, "Shout slogans as much
> as possible for your own benefit. Don't give
> money to the government for kerosene, electric-
> ity, natural gas, or telephone. I don't ap-
> prove of burning houses. Don't ruin houses,
> banks, or shops. Don't bother people. Don't
> be destructive. Whenever you see our brothers
> the soldiers, be respectful; they are our
> brothers."
> When he was finished, he gave orders to go
> on a march. He himself didn't come because
> the Prime Minister had announced it was to be
> a day of public mourning, so we didn't want
> to commemorate the dead on that day, but on

the following day. So he said to march a
little bit that day, but that the day of
mourning would be the following day, and we
should prepare ourselves for the following
day. Everyone should come, brothers and
sisters.

So we marched. Then we ate kabob, which
was delicious, and then we came home. In
the village we saw that women were shouting
slogans, with the men in front, so we went
too. Because it was a day of mourning, the
women could march during the daytime.

On the second day, I said to my brother,
"You must take us again today. Yesterday
wasn't so interesting because there weren't
many people."

As Ra^cna's account indicates, women took part in
demonstrations and marches as a religious duty. They
took participation seriously, knowing that there might
be danger. They were either nervous and frightened, or
they were so angry that the possibility of danger didn't
matter. The relationship with mourning served to further
legitimize participation because joining in mourning was
a religious duty in which women could take part without
adverse comment. The first day the siyyid women demonstrated in the village was a day of mourning. Likewise,
the first two days women went to Shiraz to demonstrate
were days of declared public mourning for people killed
in the revolution. In addition, participating in demonstrations did not require any deviation from other forms
of religious activity in which the siyyid women would
customarily engage. They could wear their veils,[17]
participate segregated from men, and could take their
children. The atmosphere was relatively informal so that
they could interrupt their chanting to tend to their
children, or they could drop out of the march for a
while, rejoining it whenever they wished. Likewise,
they could participate protected from suspicion of impro-
priety through the presence of the customary companions
who formed their unit of social control.

Over and above the religious aspects of marching,
taking part in the marches became a major form of diversion and recreation, adding excitement and interest to
the daily routine. Marching provided an excellent excuse
to get away from the house and housework, to join companions for a day of socializing, and to see other acquaintances on the route. Food, drinks, and sweets were distributed to the marchers by Shirazis who supported the
effort, adding to the enjoyment and festivity of the
day.[18]

In explaining the new involvement for women, Ra^cna
told me,

> The religious scholars and the ayatullahs
> have said that men and women must revolt to-
> gether, and must demonstrate together for
> religion and for freedom for all. Islamic
> government is for everybody, and the Islamic
> struggle is for everybody. Before, women
> didn't do this. People didn't believe the
> students when they criticized the Shah's
> regime until Khomeini also said the same
> things. If we don't speak, this government
> will go on for hundreds of years more. It
> is the will of God that the Shah has run
> into problems.

Although women declared that their role in the revolution
was just like that of men, and that everyone, man or
woman, could become like Imam Husain, actively and directly struggling against tyranny, the actual role of women
during marches could be seen to differ somewhat from that
of men. The attitude toward the involvement of women was
one of protectiveness, particularly in the larger demonstrations in the city.[19]

On February 11, 1979, the day of the final overthrow
of the monarchy, the Aliabad women did not go into
Shiraz to take part in the uprising. Many of the village
men and boys went to Shiraz and joined the attacks
against the central police station, the government troops
in the old Zand Prison, and smaller police stations
throughout the city. Aliabad women attempting to go to
the city were prevented by people at the village gate,
on the grounds that it was too dangerous for women.

A discussion with Sima, daughter of a religious
Shirazi family, helped to explain this attitude of protectiveness. She intended going to the religious observance at Habib Mosque. Because of a rumor that soldiers
were going to attack the Mosque (a rumor which proved to
be true), her father was against her going. The ensuing
argument with her father ended when he ordered her to
stay at home because of her children. It was of greater
importance for her to live and continue to raise and educate her children than to risk her life participating in
a religious and political event. There is no duty more
important for the Muslim woman than raising her children;
no religious or other activity can take precedence over
them. Her primary role in the revolution was to raise
her children and indirectly influence society through the
teaching of values that would inculcate revolutionary
sentiments. A woman told me, "If a woman wants to go on
a jihad [religious war] but can't because of her children, she will be more rewarded than if she had actually
gone."[20]

Women were believed to have a special and very important role in the revolution because they had raised
the brave young men who were willing to sacrifice their

186

lives for the good of the country and their religion. A
common phrase of sympathy and consolation offered to
mothers of young martyrs was "rahmat beh shirat" [blessed
be your milk], a way of congratulating the mothers for
having raised their children well.

After the Revolution

The more progressive high school students from the
Upper Neighborhood were the first to become disillusioned
with the direction of the revolution, not long after the
actual overthrow of the monarchy on February 11, 1979.
Early in October, Shirin, the leader of this group, indicated deep unhappiness with conditions, asking, "Has
anything really been accomplished?" She was distressed
that government was in the hands of the akhunds, adding
that Taliqani was the only good one among them. She was
sorry for the guiltless Kurds who were being killed and
was increasingly sympathetic to leftist forces. Mention-
ing that Shaikh Izziddin Husaini, a Kurdish religious
and political leader, is a socialist, she declared that
it is possible to be both socialist and religious.

The women of the politically elite families were not
at all happy with post-revolution conditions. The wife
of Siyyid Ya^cqub especially complained about the unavail-
ability of gendarmes to settle "difficulties" in the village. When her son was wounded in May 1979 by a member
of the opposition faction in the village, she bitterly
questioned, "And who can we go to to complain? The
courts? Mr. Ruhani (the visiting mullah from Qum)?
If this had happened before, we would have taken this
person to the gendarmes, and he would have been put in
prison right away. Now we can't do anything."

Peasant women and their husbands were concerned
about the increasing insecurity. One peasant couple was
greatly distressed over the theft of several animals
from their courtyard. Mr. Ruhani told them to forget
about it; nothing could be done.

Some months after the revolution, the wives of
commuters began to complain about economic conditions.
"Before," they would say, "At least there were factories
and jobs." The mothers of younger men were concerned
that their sons could not find work. Unemployment,
especially among the younger, unestablished men became
a growing problem.

The members of the siyyid social circle of women
were also concerned about the lack of security. Stories
of abductions of children and girls in Shiraz circulated;
the number of local robberies increased. Most of these
women retained their loyalty to Ayatullah Khomeini and
to the Islamic Republic, however, and their faith in the
eventual success of the revolution was unshaken when I
left in December 1979.

At the height of revolutionary activity the siyyid

women began to wear the solid-colored "Islamic" scarves, which frame the face and conceal the hair. Some women began wearing the chadurs even at home, tied around themselves as they went about their work. However, after several months, interest in this new modesty began to wane, as did interest in participating in marches in Shiraz.

In a spasm of piety, hosts of several post-revolution weddings did without "unIslamic" music and dancing. Soon, however, this proscription was being ignored. The wife of Siyyid Muslim, an important revolutionary activist who had herself become entirely imbued with the spirit of Islam and the revolution, commented, "I'd like to know why, if dancing is such a sin, men can do it." The visiting mullah from Qum finally left the village in exasperation, partly over the refusal of villagers to give up music and dancing at weddings.

Cynical comments could be heard from some of the siyyid women and other pro-Khomeini women in the Lower Neighborhood. In March of 1979, one of the kindergarten teachers, a pious, modest, and fervently revolutionary young siyyid woman, dropped her Naw Ruz [New Year's-- March 21] bonus, a roll of bills, while standing in line to buy goods at an Islamic cooperative store in Shiraz. Her contacts with the religious organization and the kumitehs in Shiraz in her subsequent unsuccessful attempts to get her money back left her cynical and bitter about those holding positions of authority in the new regime.

During the rest of my stay in Aliabad, this loss of faith in the honesty and integrity of lesser figures in the new regime felt by the women who had supported the revolution did not generally extend to Ayatullah Khomeini himself. The former village boss, Siyyid Ibn Ali Askari, was put in prison; his brother Siyyid Ya^{c}qub went into hiding along with other close supporters, and the peasant faction took over and planted the land of Siyyid Ibn-Ali.[23] The siyyid women blamed the opposition faction in the village for the predicament of their relatives and not Ayatullah Khomeini. One of the kindergarten teachers, the grandniece of Siyyid Ibn-Ali, commented,

> If Ayatullah Khomeini knew what was going
> on here, he wouldn't like it. Islam says to
> respect private property. Siyyid Muslim
> (Siyyid Ya^{c}qub's son) was so active in the
> revolution, and we went in to demonstrations
> everyday too. Now look how we are being
> treated.

On the whole, the attitude of the pro-revolution women from the Lower Neighborhood, up until I left in December, was summed up in the words of one of them:

> We did it for religion. Most of the

village women who went to demonstrate had no
purpose in mind other than religion. We
didn't think that things would improve for
us necessarily. Like myself. I had no expectation of better schooling for my children
or property for myself or that the government
would help me. And now I have no expectation
either. My efforts were for Islam.

I was not in the village long enough after the
revolution to see the extension of the power of the
regime into the village. However, one incident which
took place in the village might have been an indication
of things to come.

In March of 1979, the welder from Zargun who lived
in the village and had taken a village woman as a second
wife was visited by his cousin, her fiance, and another
young man. The young woman was very properly seated in
the back of the car and wore a chadur, while the two
young men sat in the front. When the young people got
out of the car at the village gate, people stopped them
and accused the young woman of being a "madam". The
three were able to reach the welder's home, although they
were taunted along the way. A group of some thirty men
and boys gathered outside of the courtyard, shouting and
swearing at the welder's village wife and claiming that
she was lying, that the young woman was a prostitute and
not the welder's cousin. The three young people claimed
membership in the kumiteh and tried to get the village
men to call the kumiteh from the gendarme station in the
neighboring village. When the men finally did make the
phone call, they were told that the three were respectable people and associated with the kumiteh.

Later, Ra^{c}na, a leader among the siyyid women,
commented that while the men and boys were wrong to
harass the visitors, according to Islam a young woman
should not go anywhere with a young man unless he was
her husband or brother. Although control by outsiders
such as the visiting mullah from Qum proved ineffective
up until the time I left the village, it seemed clear
that the trend was in the direction of self-policing by
the more conservative and ardently "Islamic" members of
the village community.

Other effects of the revolution also seem probable.
Education for women in the village will apparently suffer. There will not be enough teachers to hold the
sexually segregated classes now required for boys and
girls at the junior high school level, so classes for
girls will be discontinued. It will be necessary for
girls to go to Shiraz if they are to continue their
education. The declining opportunities in education and
employment for women could mean that those village girls
attending high school before the revolution will not be

able to attain their hopes for higher education and careers. However, it seems unlikely that such plans would have materialized in most cases even without the changes brought about by the revolution.

Before the revolution, villagers were gradually becoming aware of the usefulness of the Family Protection Law in providing some protection for women; at least two young women with knowledgeable brothers had used the courts in disputes with their husbands. This incipient utilization of the courts will also likely be stopped.

Conclusion

"Traditional" women from the village of Aliabad who felt required to place their extra-home and social-izing activities in a framework of neighborhood, family, kin, or religious activity were able to participate in demonstrations during the Iranian Revolution because those demonstrations were defined as religious activity. This did not mean, however, that the women could abandon their primary Shi^cite duty; it was still necessary to take care of their children, even during demonstrations. Women were protected in order to survive and raise their children, and their involvement was defined in relation to their children.

However, the demonstrations were very different from the other religious activities in which women had participated in the past: the rowzehs, the Zahra School meetings, pilgrimages to shrines, and the Thursday after-noon visits to the cemetery. Such activities were generally exclusive to women. During the Ashura com-memorations women played a passive role, standing in informal neighborhood and/or kin groups, watching and weeping on the sidelines while men marched in organized groups in a procession, beating themselves and stepping in time, chanting Ashura couplets. During the revolu-tionary demonstrations, however, including the Ashura march of December 1978, men and women both engaged in the very same form of "religious" activity. Both sexes marched in the procession, chanting couplets and often raising their fists in cadence. Men and women partici-pated at the same time and place, although they were separated into different groups.

Interpreting the participation of women in demon-strations as religious activity and thus legitimate for Muslim women served to obscure the fact that such demon-strations were a new kind of activity for these women. It was entirely unprecedented that such great masses of "traditional" Iranian women, normally constrained by cultural and religious limits on their public behavior, should openly and directly participate in national level politics. In sanctioning the participation of women, religious leaders were obscuring changes in permitted female activity by a pretense of continuity.[22] After the revolution, then, it was quite simple to take the

190

attitude that the participation of some women in the
revolution had been within the limits of expected behavior for Shi[c]ite women. Their participation in the
revolution should, therefore, by no means be taken as an
indication that new ground had been broken, or that
Iranian women would continue in their public role of
directly and openly influencing political events. Given
an understanding of those religious figures now in
authority in Iran as well as of the large majority of
Iranian women who participated in the revolution about
their participation, it is not surprising that the
increasing restrictions on the public activity of women
have been enforced with relative ease.

NOTES

    1. Azar Tabari likewise notes,

        Contrary to the presumptions of some
    Western feminists, the militant participation
    of women in the struggles against the Shah
    and their current involvement in the so-called
    "battle of reconstruction" do not conflict with
    their traditional seclusion and treatment as
    second class citizens, and their roles as
    obedient wives and daughters. So long as the
    participation of women remains within an Islamic
    framework, the limits of their responsibilities
    can be wide and the variety of roles they assume
    numerous." (Tabari, 1982, pp. 25-26)

Lois Beck states, "[Women] had and have in the
revolution a ready-made set of religious institutions
and customs which allow their public participation."
(Beck, 1979, p. 8)
    See also Hooglund [Heglund], 1981.
    2. Research was made possible by a grant from the
Social Science Research Council and the American Society
of Learned Societies. The names of the village and of
persons have been changed in the interests of privacy.
I owe a great debt to the many kind and open-minded
Iranians who offered their friendship and assistance.
    3. Erika Friedl, in her study of the roles and
status of women in the Boir Ahmad area, also points out
that a woman's

        overall status in the community is largely
        determined by how well she is taken care of
        and provided for by . . . the closest man whose
        economic (and moral) responsibility she is. . . .
        An older woman or widow who relies in part on
        income derived from, say, midwifery, shows that
        her own sons neglect her or else cannot provide
        for her adequately. (Friedl, 1981a, pp. 14-15)

4. In 1978 the rate of exchange was about 7.5 tomans to the dollar.

5. Benard states,

However, except for a small stratum of "middle class" urban women, the implementation was difficult and not very effective. Laws were circumvented or ignored, and studies of Iranian rural areas showed that the median age of marriage for girls was between thirteen and fifteen. (Benard, 1980, p. 17).

See also Gulick and Gulick (1979, p. 509).
Momeni (1972) documents the fact that actual age at marriage of women in Iran has not been very much affected by legislation.

6. As Janet Bauer (1978, p. 30) points out, "Women see that their only form of security lies in measuring up to the cultural and social standards of proper female behavior . . . ."

7. I was also subject to such social pressure. I felt pleased when, upon spending time cleaning after moving into my village home, I heard comments that I was a good worker. On the other hand, I felt the rebuke in the rowzeh chanter's comment made while I was attending his rowzeh. Looking at my watch, I noted, "My watch doesn't work."
He shot back, "You don't work either," suggesting thereby that my interviewing activities resulted in neglect of my household and child. Erika Friedl (1981a, p. 15) noted the same social pressure on herself.

8. Anne Betteridge has likewise pointed out that especially for lower-class women and for those who come from more traditional families, religion offers a much-needed opportunity to assemble. . . . [Women] are obliged to justify their socializing by placing it in a religious framework. (Betteridge, 1980, p. 154-55).

See also Betteridge (1981); Benard (1980, p. 15); Bamdad (1977, p. 10); and Fernea and Fernea (1978, p. 401).

9. See Betteridge (1980, p. 3-4) for an explanation of other factors hindering the attendance and attention of women at mosques.

10. See Betteridge (1976, 1981) and Friedl (1980) for further information on women and pilgrimage.

11. Thomas Thompson (1979, p. 200), in his dissertation on a village in Mazandaran, also notes, "[The commemoration of Ashura] is one of the few occasions during the year that women and girls can legitimately stay away from their homes for hours . . . ."

12. This point was clarified to me through a comment made by Isa Helfgott (personal communication, November 1981).

192

13. The report of A Special Correspondent (1982, pp. 27-28) about another area in southwest Iran indicates that peasants in that area as well were not enthusiastic about the revolution. The relatively low level of involvement of poorer peasants in the Iranian Revolution tends to support the conclusions of Wolf (1973, pp. 290-91) and Alavi (1971, p. 123; 1973, pp. 332-34) that poorer rural groups generally do not have the resources and are unable to risk revolutionary involvement.

14. This material, as well as some of the material following is taken from Hooglund [Hegland] (1981). I am grateful to the editors of RIPEH for permission to reprint these sections.

15. Erika Friedl (1981b, p. 3) also notes that peasants emphasize moral behavior rather than ritual in their religion.

16. The section on women's demonstrations in Aliabad is taken from Hooglund [Hegland] (1981, pp. 38-40).

17. See Bauer (1980b) for discussion of how the veil allowed "traditional" women to enter into public activity during the revolution.

18. As Betteridge (1980, p. 155) points out, referring to meals connected with religious vows, "To separate religion from social life would be to make a distinction not recognized in practice by many Islamic women." In the context of revolutionary marches, too, I feel that recognizing the social and recreational aspects does not necessarily question the seriousness of the religious and political motivation.

19. For more on the protective attitude toward women during revolutionary activity, see Hooglund [Hegland] (1981, pp. 41-44).

20. It is not surprising that women would accept the pronouncement that their primary function was as mothers and attempt to find self-worth and fulfillment through this role. In all other roles women were considered to be substitutable--identical to or at least similar to other women, and therefore interchangeable. As mothers, however, they were considered unique. If a home was left motherless through death or divorce, there was generally no one willing to assume care of the children, and it was not uncommon for the children to be sent to an orphanage. A step-mother would be inclined to be inattentive to the children of a previous wife.

21. For a description of this situation, see Hooglund [Hegland] (1980).

22. See the discussion in Kertzer (1982) of how "ritual continuity" is used to obscure "political changes".

BIBLIOGRAPHY

Alavi, Hamza. "The Politics of Dependence: A Village in
    West Punjab," South Asian Review 4 (1971): 111-128.
    _____. "Peasants and Revolution," in Gough, K. and
    Sharma, H.P. (eds.). Imperialism and Revolution in
    South Asia (New York: Monthly Review Press, 1973),
    pp. 267-90.
Bamdad, Badr ol-Moluk. From Darkness into Light: Women's
    Emancipation in Iran (Hicksville, NY: Exposition
    Press, 1977).
Bauer, Janet. "New Models and Traditional Networks:
    Migrant Women in South Tehran, Iran," Paper pre-
    pared for the IXth World Congress of Sociology,
    Uppsala, Sweden, 1978.
    _____. "Some Brief Comments on the Post-Revolutionary
    Consciousness of Lower Income Women in Tehran,
    Iran," MERA Forum 4 (1980): 6-8 [1980a].
    _____. "Women, the Veil and the Islamic Revolution in
    Iran." Paper prepared for the 4th Annual Women in
    Anthropology Symposium, Sacramento Anthropological
    Society, California State University at Sacremento,
    March 7-8, 1980 [1980b].
Beck, Lois. "Women in Revolutionary Iran." Paper pre-
    sented at the Women in Islam conference, Scandinavian
    Institute of Asian Studies, Copenhagen, Denmark,
    November, 1979.
Benard, Cheryl. "Islam and Women: Some Reflections on
    the Experience of Iran," Journal of South Asian and
    Middle Eastern Studies 4 (1980): 10-26.
Betteridge, Anne. "Ziarat: Pilgrimage in Iran." Paper
    presented at the Tenth Annual Meeting of the Middle
    East Studies Association, Los Angeles, California,
    1976.
    _____. "The Controversial Vows of Urban Muslim Women
    in Iran," in Falk, N. and Gross, R. (eds.). Un-
    spoken Worlds: Women's Religious Lives in Non-West-
    ern Cultures (San Francisco: Harper and Row, 1980),
    pp. 141-155.
    _____. "Muslim Women and Shrines in Shiraz." Paper
    prepared for Islam: Spiritual Foundations and Modern
    Manifestations, Brigham Young University, October
    22-23, 1981.
Fernea, Robert and Fernea, Elizabeth. "Variation in
    Religious Observance among Islamic Women." in
    Keddie, N.R. (ed.). Scholars, Saints, and Sufis:
    Muslim Religious Institutions since 1500 (Berkeley:
    University of California Press, 1978), pp. 385-401.
Friedl, Erika. "Islam and Tribal Women in a Village in
    Iran." in Falk, N. and Gross, R. (eds.). Unspoken
    Worlds: Women's Religious Lives in Non-Western Cul-
    tures (San Francisco: Harper and Row, 1980), pp.
    159-73.

Friedl, Erika. "The Division of Labor in an Iranian Vil-
    lage," MERIP Reports (March/April, 1981) [1981a].
    _____. "State Ideology and Village Women in Iran."
    Paper prepared for the Middle East Studies Associa-
    tion Conference, Seattle Washington,
    1981 [1981b].
Gulick, John and Gulick, Margaret. "The Domestic Social
    Environment of Women and Girls in Isfahan, Iran." in
    Beck, L. and Keddie, N. (eds.). Women in the Muslim
    World (Cambridge, Mass: Harvard University Press,
    1979), pp. 501-21.
Hooglund [Hegland], Mary. "One Village in the Revolu-
    tion," MERIP Reports (May, 1980), pp. 7-12.
    _____. "The Village Women of Aliabad and the Iranian
    Revolution," RIPEH (nos. 4 and 5, 1981): pp. 27-46.
Kazemi, Farhad. Poverty and Revolution in Iran: The
    Migrant Poor, Urban Marginality and Politics (New
    York: New York University Press, 1980) [1980a].
    _____. "Urban Migrants and the Revolution," Iranian
    Studies 8 (1980): 257-78 [1980b].
Kertzer, David. "The Role of Ritual in Political Change."
    in Culture and Political Change. Political Anthro-
    pology Yearbook, Vol. 2 (New Brunswick, N.J.:
    Transaction Books, 1982).
Nashat, Guity. "Women in the Islamic Republic of Iran,"
    Iranian Studies 8 (1980): 165-94.
Momeni, Djamchid. "The Difficulties of Changing the Age
    at Marriage in Iran," Journal of Marriage and the
    Family 34 (1972): 545-51.
Ramazani, Nesta. "Behind the Veil: Status of Women in
    Revolutionary Iran," Journal of South Asian and
    Middle Eastern Studies 4 (1980): 27-36.
El Sadaawi, Nawal. "Arab Women and Western Feminism: An
    Interview with Nawal El Sadaawi," Race and Class 12
    (1980): 175-82.
A Special Correspondent. "Report from an Iranian Vil-
    lage," MERIP Reports (March/April, 1980): 26-29.
Tabari, Azar. "The Enigma of the Veiled Iranian Woman,"
    MERIP Reports (February, 1982): 22-27.
Thompson, Thomas. "A Persian Miniature: The Value of
    Tradition in a Mazandaran Village," Ph.D. disserta-
    tion, The University of Texas at Austin, 1979.
Wolf, Eric. Peasant Wars of the Twentieth Century (New
    York: Harper and Row, 1973).

11
Women in the Ideology of the Islamic Republic

Guity Nashat

One of the principle objectives of the leaders of the present Iranian regime has been to restore women to what they consider women's primary role in society: domestic responsibility. In their view such a role is in keeping with the teachings of Islam. At first the efforts to keep women in their "place" on the part of a regime that was enormously helped in coming to power by women's support might seem surprising, if not baffling. However, as the new leaders see it, while it was the religious duty of both men and women to rise up against oppression under the Shah, now that the "right type" of government is in power, women's religious duty requires that they concentrate on fulfilling their real task of taking care of their husbands and children, and that they allow the men to run the affaris of government. Therefore, while extolling the role women played in overthrowing the Shah, the government is urging women to resume their traditional duties as wives and mothers.

The leaders of the regime have resorted to a variety of methods, both positive and negative, to convince women of the soundness of this argument, which they claim will serve the interest of the women themselves as well as of society. Judging by the results over the past three years, their efforts to push women out of public life and back into the home have been successful.

This chapter will focus on the ideology of the regime toward women and will present some of the arguments used in support of this ideology. Some of the specific policies carried out by the government to implement this ideology will also be reviewed. Finally, the reasons for the compliance of women with policies which some have termed "turning the clock backward" will be briefly mentioned.

In an address directed to Iranian women on the occasion of Women's Day, May, 1980, the Ayatullah Khomeini said that the previous regime had encouraged the spread of immorality and prostitution among young women in the name of progress and liberty. He urged the young women of

Iran to abandon the ways and behavior of the time of
taqut [the Tyrannical Shah] and to return to the purity
of the pre-Pahlavi period.[1]

The strong language used by the Ayatullah in describing the changes women had undergone during the
Pahlavi regime should not be taken to indicate that
immorality had become rampant among Iranian women, but
it demonstrates the deep repugnance the Ayatulla feels for
the types of changes that had occurred in the lifestyles
and roles of Iranian women, especially during the sixties
and seventies. These changes were both extensive and
striking. They went beyond the women who adopted a
Western lifestyle and also affected those whose outward
lifestyle was charaterized by the more traditional chadur
[veil], in urban as well as in rural areas. The transformation of women's lifestyle occurred in three generations.
Like countless generations of women before them, few women
in the early twentieth century could read or write. Even
fewer attended the schools that had been opened for the
daughters of the rich or for the daughters of Christian
minorities. Woman's destiny was thought to be marriage,
usually between the ages of 9 and 13, usually to a man in
his thirties or forties, followed by childbirth and a
lifetime of caring for her husband and children. Few
women could leave the confines of their homes except on
great occasions, and then they had to be wrapped completely in the long black shroud that covered them from their
heads to their feet. Their primary raison d'etre was to
fulfil the wishes and needs of their masters and lords--
their husbands.[2] But the horizons and options for the
young women of the seventies looked radically different.
Although in some rural areas girls as young as 13 might
still be married, in most urban areas a girl of 13 was
considered a mere child, even if she was not lucky enough
to be at school. And many thousands of young girls, two-
and-a-half million of them, were enrolled in elementary
schools, some of these in remote rural areas. To be sure,
by most families, and even by the girls themselves, marriage was considered the best and most secure future for
a girl, but a girl with ability could postpone marriage
until she had received high school or even university-
level education. Many young women, including a great
number from traditional families where the mother still
donned some form of veiling, looked forward to having
careers as teachers, white collar workers, sales girls,
technicians, or many other types of service employment.
Some hoped to keep these jobs after marriage, at least
until the first child arrived. Most also were certain
that they would have some say in the choice of the man
they would marry.

These lower level jobs were not the only ones filled
by women. There were also many women physicians, lawyers,
judges, university professors, top level administrators,
and members of parliament. Women had become an important

part of the work force.[3] Women's improved employment
opportunities were the result of rapid economic growth
of Iran during the 1960s and 1970s.[4] The labor shortage
thus created could not be filled with the available pool
of qualified men. One of the remedies sought both by the
government and by private industry was increased employment of women. To facilitate women's working, many day-
care centers were founded, and employment laws for women,
such as maternity leave, were improved.[5]

The participation of women in professions hitherto
reserved for men, such as medicine, engineering, law, and
various types of government employment had important
results. It began to break down the built-in social and
psychological barriers against women's participation in
activities outside the home. The growth of employment
opportunites during these decades also spurred the spread
of education not only among the daughters of the more
modernized middle class families who tended to be secular
in outlook, but also among the more traditional religious
families where women still wore the veil and led more
secluded lives. The greater educational and employment
opportunities for women, both the modernized and the more
traditional middle class, in turn set off a fundamental
change in the outlook of the younger women, and their
perception of themselves as individuals and members of
society. They began to perceive themselves not merely as
passive objects to be subordinate to and manipulated by
the male members of society--father, husband, or the male-
dominated state--but rather as active members who should
participate in changing the rules by which society functioned.

These changes in educational and occupational opportunities were accompanied by changes in the legal status
of women. In 1963 women were finally granted the franchise by an act of Parliament. Although elections were
not free, this was a recognition that women's domain of
interest should not be confined to the affairs of their
homes. Then in 1967, the Parliament passed the Family
Protection Law (amended in 1975) to ameliorate women's
civil rights in marriage, polygamy, divorce, child custody, and employment.[6] The law stipulated 15 as the minimum age of marriage for girls; this was raised to 18 in
1975. Permission for men to have up to four wives was
restricted, and consent of the first wife became mandatory before a man could take an additional wife. The law
also improved a woman's right to seek divorce and placed
restrictions on the husband's unlimited ability to divorce his wife at any time or place without her knowledge
or consent. Henceforth, the man or the woman seeking a
divorce was required to proceed by petitioning the family
court system, which had the right to approve or reject
the petition and to determine the amount of alimony and
child support. The court would also decide which of the
two parents was better suited to have custody of the

children. This last provision was a radical departure from the provisions of previous codes, derived from Shi^{c}i Shari^{c}a law, under which a woman automatically lost her children to her former husband, boys at age two and girls at age seven, when she was divorced. Although the rate of divorce was low in Iran before the passage of the law, and not many men exercised their unlimited and one-sided right to divorce easily, women's knowledge that their husbands had such power kept many women "in line." It was in effect a veto power men had to completely subordinate their wives. Finally, the Family Planning Law improved the right of women to seek gainful employment.

It should be stressed that the application of these laws was slow at first, and many men found ways to circumvent them. Furthermore, the weight of social pressure was so strong that even women familiar with the laws were reluctant to exercise their legal rights. Nevertheless, knowledge about these laws, especially the Family Protection Law, began to spread slowly but surely, so that by the end of the 1970s even women in rural areas had some familiarity with them, although usually those women lacked the knowledge and the financial means to make use of them. The 1970s was also a decade in which the authoritarian regime of the Shah arrogantly stepped up its effort to reorganize society after an illusive Western model. These efforts, which resulted in more rapid change, were accompanied by rampant corruption, increased inequity, and widened class and individual gaps in society. Not surprisingly, larger and larger groups began to resent and to resist these changes-by-fiat, and, consequently, the ranks of the opposition to the regime began to grow by leaps and bounds. As tension heightened and conflict between the regime and the diverse groups of oppostion deepened, various policies of the Shah's government came under attack. The dramatic changes in the status and role of women were closely identified with that regime; they began to be criticized by old anti-Shah and anti-Western voices, led by the ulama, who were now joined by some new critics, a growing number of women themselves. The female critics were mostly younger educated women from the universities and institutes of higher learning, and professional and working women.

These women came from diverse social backgrounds.[7] There were ideologically secular women from urban professional families of the middle and upper-middle classes whose women had entered the mainstream of society for two and three generations. Many of them had been educated in European or American universities; for the most part they tended to be ideologically oriented to the left. Too young to remember how their grandmothers and great-grandmothers had lived, they mistakenly attributed all the changes in the condition of women to the Shah's regime and dismissed these changes as mere window dressing. They argued that only a regime they could trust would

improve women's condition. Hence, they joined the ranks
of the growing opposition, including the Fida'iyan-i
Khalq, to bring about the downfall of the Shah. Other
women came from more traditional middle or lower-middle
class backgrounds; they tended to join a movement that
has been loosely termed "Islamic Modernism." Briefly,
the diverse groups that made up this movement blamed much
of society's ills on its deviation from the true teachings of Islam and the blind imitation of alien, especially Western, ways and ideology. They held that society's
health could be restored only when Islamic values were
revived. Thus, the women who adopted this philosophy
rejected the changes in the status of women as mere aping
of superficial and corrupting Western influences. To
symbolize their rejection of the regime and to express
faith in their own cultural heritage, many of these women
began to wear a scarf or even a <u>chadur</u> to the university
or the workplace. They also began to join various clan-
destine political groups, especially the Mujahidin-i
Khalq.[8]

Many of these younger, politically active women were
in the forefront of revolutionary activity and were instrumental in drawing the less politicized women (both
the professional and the traditional ones) into the
street demonstrations. The participation of large numbers of women and their massive demonstrations were important to the success of the revolution and its largely
nonviolent character. The women's presence served as the
most important factor in disarming the soldiers placed
there by the regime to contain the mobs and to shoot at
them if necessary. However, few of the thousands of
women who took to the streets carrying a child or a
machine gun did so because they had any objectives for
themselves as women. They were motivated by the same
deep-seated malaise that had driven the men into the
streets. The lack of any specific feminist platform was
true even of the most politicized women activists. Despite their effective contributions to the various political and guerrila movements, exemplified by the sizable
number of women who were killed during the anti-regime
activities, few of the activists made a distinction between the more general social and political issues and
those that affected them as women per se. Although they
vehemently criticized the wide-spread iniquities practiced against women, they blamed the regime for these.
They failed to recognize the centuries-old underlying
social, cultural, and economic biases against women.
This failure to perceive that women's condition would not
automatically improve merely by a change in regime partially explains their subsequent failure to react promptly to the policies of the next regime, which many have
come to view as a great setback for all women. Therefore,
despite the radically fundamentalist Islamic coloring
that the revolutionary leadership had assumed during the

final months of 1978 and early months of 1979, few women,
including the ideologically secular, stopped to think
what the change would bring them. Even fewer tried to
develop any specific platform that would at least protect
if not enhance their existing rights and status.

However, it was not only the women who failed to ask
what would take the place of the regime that both sexes
strove so long and hard to overthrow. Perhaps no one
thought that it would be possible to accomplish such a
feat. Once the old regime was swept aside, there seemed
to be little reason for worry; everyone assumed the
future could only be better. This optimism was apparent
in the spontaneous jubilation and frenzy with which
Ayatullah Khomeini, the newly emerged leader of the
revolution, and for many, its symbol and conscience, was
greeted on his return from exile in February, 1979.
Their expectations had been encouraged by his numerous
messages from abroad and by his assurances that a better
and more equitable future would prevail in a society run
under his guidance. This confidence was also shared by
women, who felt certain that because of the role they had
played in the revolution they would have an active voice
in determining this brighter future for everyone.

In several of his messages and interviews from Paris,
Ayatullah Khomeini had taken pains to reassure women that
they would have nothing to fear from his leadership. As
if addressing those who might remember his opposition in
1963 to extending the franchise to women, he repeatedly
stated that women would have everything to gain in the
society he envisioned. "Because," he declared, "not only
does Shi^{c}ism not exclude women from social life, but it
elevates them to a platform where they belong, a higher
platform."[9] However, if women had paid sufficient attention, they would have perceived the underlying import of
the Ayatullah's statement: negation of the principle of
the equality of men and women. But no one drew the
logical conclusion from his statement: if women can be
raised to a higher platform, they can also be pushed down
to a lower platform. Therefore, what women should demand
is equality. Even fewer of the women who enthusiastical-
ly put their stamp of approval on the Constitution prepared under the close guidance of Ayatullah Khomeini and
the main stream of Shi^{c}ite ulama seemed to have much
familiarity with what these leaders had been advocating
for women.

The views of Ayatullah Khomeini and other influential idealogues of the regime reflect the long-standing
beliefs of the Iranian-Islamic culture about women and
their role in society.[10] They generally believe that the
division of labor in society should be based on gender:
women should confine themselves to activities in the
private domain, and men should concern themselves with
activities in the public domain. They also hold that

this division of labor is determined by inborn differences which are in harmony with the dictates of natural
law and the command of God as revealed in the Shari^ca.
According to one theologian, Hujjat ul-Islam Nuri, "These
differences do not result from social and cultural con-
ditioning, but they appear in accordance with higher wisdom and command in harmony with the particularities of
the law of creation. Hence they are innate and natural."[11]
These differences are also demonstrated by the physical,
intellectual, and emotional make-up of each of the two
sexes. A woman differs from a man by her "beauty and
fine bone structure, her pleasant voice, and the weakness
of her physique." Whereas women excel men in physical
beauty, men excel in physical and mental ability. Another major difference is in their psychological natures.
Wemen are more sensitive and emotional, and they judge
hastily and unwisely. Due to their superior intellect,
men have the ability to reflect and assess difficulties
more rationally. Therfore, men are better suited to have
control of major decisions both within the household and
without. This is why women are ill-suited to be law-
makers and judges, or to occupy high positions in society.
According to Hujat ul-Islam Nuri, the differences in
physical and emotional makeup of men and women account
for their different treatment in the laws of Islam. He
states, "The responsibilities of men and women sometimes
correspond and sometimes differ, and the difference was
designed to safeguard the good of the community as well
as of the individual."[12]

In a few commentaries the authors show an awareness
of women's modern sensibilities and their desire for
equal treatment; they have tried to sooth and appease
women by raising the old arguments in a new guise. They
claim that women's inferior status is merely a reflection
of the differences between women and men. For example,
it is argued that women have been barred from acting as
judges because of their emotional nature. Furthermore,
the reason the testimony of one man is equivalent to the
testimony of two women [in the Shari^ca] "is not to
denigrate women and to render them inferior, but because a higher purpose is involved and that is the respect and great importance attached to the rights of the
people to ensure that all loopholes and ways in which
people can be hurt are closed and all caution is taken
into account."[13] It is to protect women against their
own lack of judgement that they have been placed under
the guardianship of men. Before marriage, the welfare
of a female must be protected by her father, or in his
absence, by other male relatives; after marriage, by her
husband.[14]

Some authors have resorted to the use of psychology
to convince women of the merits and the necessity of
men's superiority over women within the family, and by extension, in society. Hujjat ul-Islam Nuri, for example,

has suggested that in households where equality between
husband and wife prevails, children could suffer irrep-
arable confusion and emotional damage as a result of disagreement between their parents. He also asserts that
women themselves like to be dominated by men. Hence, he
states, "placing women under the authority of men would
make women happier."[15] Although women are deficient in
intellect and do not qualify for careers that require
cool judgement and strength of character (such as being
judges, high administrators, etc.) their natural makeup
renders them the more suitable of the two partners within
the family unit for a very important task: motherhood
and the raising of children.[16]

It is important to place women's exclusion from
activities outside the home in the context of the emphasis attached to their role as mothers. In the thinking
of the Shi[c]ite ulama, as with other Muslims, irrespective
of their schools of law, the family is central to the
Muslim devotional scheme. Islam is based on the belief
that the duty of the individual is total submission to
the will of God. Both men and women manifest submission
by following the Godly life, which is prescribed for the
individual Muslim in the Shari[c]a [the religious law].
Although each individual is responsible for his or her
own acts and ultimately faces the Creator alone, the
society and family within which the individual functions
are of the utmost importance in preparing him or her and
providing the guidance and support needed to lead a life
that is pleasing to God. The early years of childhood
can provide the child with the opportunity to be correct-
ly initiated into this path.[17]

However, not every woman is capable of fulfilling
this primary task. In fact, one particular type of woman,
the traditional type who has not been corrupted by modern
values and is endowed with modesty, piety, and moral purity, should be entrusted with the grave task of "feeding
the child with the milk of religion." In contrast,
modern, Westernized mothers, despite their diplomas, bac-
calaureates, and even doctorates, are not fit to be
mothers and wives. "These women do not listen to their
husbands and do not value them. They go anywhere they
want and with whom they please. They go to the cinema,
the theater, gatherings of prostitution and what religion
forbids, and might even breast-feed their child in a
state of drunkenness." Children raised by these modern
women, this same author warns, "turn against religion,
. . . become traitors to their country and people, and
. . . make suitable agents of colonialism." It is not
surprising then, he continues, that there are no longer
men of the caliber of Khwajeh Nasir ud-Din Tusi, Ibn
Sina, and Shaikh Murtiza Ansari to be found in present-day
society. "Every single one of these men was raised by a
woman who was illiterate but pious and virtuous."[18]

Unlike those corrupted modern women, a truly proper

Muslim woman would take pride in herself and abide by the
rules of her religion, which require that she adopt the
veil, or the hijab. In the view of the ulama, the hijab
is the hallmark of the Muslim woman. As one of its
numerous advocates states, "The hijab is the most effective protection of the chastity and character of the individual and society. It is a strong fortress against
the onslaught of marauders of chastity. The hijab is the
highest symbol of the respect of Islam for women's position so that they do not become playful objects of sex-
ridden sensualists, and corrupt individuals."[19] This
point of view has appeared in the writings of ulama in
the past and appears in the writings of many of the ulama
today. These arguments are usually accompanied by the
famous Qur'anic verse enjoining men and women to view
each other with modesty and commanding women not to
reveal their attractiveness.

> Tell the believing men to lower their gaze and
> be modest. That is purer for them. Lo, Allah
> is aware of what they do. And tell the
> believing women to lower their gaze and be
> modest, and to display of their ornament only
> what is apparent, and to draw their veil over
> their bosoms, and not to reveal their ornaments
> save to their own husbands or fathers or hus-
> bands' fathers, or their sons, or their hus-
> bands' sons, or their brothers or brothers'
> sons or sisters' sons, or their women or their
> slaves, or male attendants who lack vigor, or
> children who know naught of women's nakedness.
> And let them not stamp their feet so as to reveal
> what they hide of their adornment. And turn unto
> Allah together, O believers, in order that ye
> may succeed. (XXIV, 31)

Although the Qur'anic verse is addressed both to men
and women, in the arguments of the pro-hijab ulama the
burden of complying with its provisions is placed entirely on women. This shift of responsibility to women is
not surprising since all the commentators on this verse
of the Qur'an have been men. Not one of these commentators has paid any attention to the first part of this
verse, which is addressed to men, nor has made any recommendation for modest behavior by men. They have merely
argued that women should leave their homes as little as
possible to minimize contact with male strangers. Furthermore, when women go out, they should make every effort
to veil themselves so as not to distract and mislead men.
These arguments for the necessity of the veil are derived
from the assumptions mentioned earlier about the nature
of men and women. They also reveal conflicting attitudes
toward women, portraying them as weak and sexually pas-
ive, yet dangerous and conniving. Thus, while women are
regarded as creatures in need of security and protection

204

by men, they are also conceived of as dangerous beings who
use their sexuality as a lure to attract and entrap men.
But the commentators' view of men is not any more
flattering since it presents men as creatures primarily
and hopelessly controlled by insatiable and enormous
sexual instincts. According to the late Ayatullah
Mutahhari, one of the leading idealogues of the present
regime,

> It is a mistake for us to imagine that a man's
> sensuality when satisfied to a certain limit
> will attain rest. In the same way that a per-
> son, whether male or female, cannot be satisfied
> with wealth and power, no man ever has enough
> of possessing beautiful women and no woman enough
> of attracting the attentions of men and posses-
> sing their hearts. Finally, no man's heart is
> satiated by sexual pleasure.[20]

The implication in such statements is that men are
basically weak, hence the need to keep women away from
them lest they lose control at the sight of an attractive
woman. Therefore a mechanism (i.e., the veil) is needed
to protect men against their own dangerous animal nature.
In the words of Ayatullah Mutahhari,

> Where would a man be more productive, where he
> is studying in all male institutions or where
> he is sitting next to a girl whose skirt
> reveals her thighs? Which man can do more
> work, he who is constantly exposed to arousing
> and exciting faces of made-up women in the
> street, bazaar, office, or factory, or he who
> does not have to face such sights?[21]

Holding these assertions about the nature of men and women to be facts, the author concludes that the society's
and men's interests (and, by extension, women's interests)
are served best if women stay out of men's sight, in the
seclusion of their homes.
The male point of view dominates discussions of
conjugal duties and responsibilities. In these discussions once again certain specific Qur'anic passages have
been used for the development of elaborate laws that demand complete subservience of the wife to her husband.
A woman's obligation to obey her husband is total and
extends even to such trifling matters as a visit to her
mother's house.[22] However, it is in the interpretation
of a woman's sexual obligations to her husband that the
one-sidedness of these interpretations becomes glaringly
apparent. A wife must submit herself entirely and at all
times to her husband's sexual demands and needs, in any
way he sees fit. In return for her subserviance and her
services, a wife is entitled to sexual intimacy once
every fourth month and full maintenance according to her
husband's means.[23]

Ayatullah Mutahhari uses men's allegedly unbridled sexual needs as one of his main arguments in defense of polygamy. Like other advocates of this practice, he pays lip service to the Qur'anic injunction for the need of equal treatment of the wives in polygamous marriages. Although he acknowledges that the kind of treatment required by the Qur'an is very difficult, if not impossible, he argues that the social and psychological benefits of polygamy outweigh that drawback. In his view, if men were not allowed access to another wife during menstrual periods or during childbearing, then men would be forced to go to prostitutes. This, in turn, would lead to the spread of prostitution. Another justification he offers for polygamy is men's great desire for children, which can no longer be satisfied when a wife reaches menopause. However, women are not forgotten in this discussion. Ayatullah Mutahhari argues that in the absence of polygamy the extra women in society will be deprived of the care and protection of men since he alleges that there are more women than men in society.[24]

More than any other discussion of male-female relationships, mut^{c}a [temporary marriage] reveals the degree to which the male point of view has dominated the cultural and moral outlook of Iranian society. In the past, commentators simply accepted mut^{c}a as a religious sanction for alleviating men's urges and their need for variety.[25] Contemporary advocates of mut^{c}a have made an effort to provide socially and morally justified arguments for this type of union, which permits sexual intimacy between a mature male and a mature female for an agreed-upon specified period with the payment of a mutually agreed-upon sum to the female. Legal maturity according to Shi^{c}i religious law is defined as the age of fifteen for males and the age of nine for females. The most serious attempt to defend mut^{c}a was made by Ayatullah Mutahhari, who argued that mut^{c}a prevented the spread of prostitution by offering men a legitimate method of satisfying "their unbridled sexual desire." It was also Ayatullah Mutahhari who advocated propogation of mut^{c}a among adolescents. He held that mut^{c}a would harness their strong sexual urges in a legitimate manner. In his view, the legitimacy of this type of union was an indication that Islam was cognizant of the emotional and psychological needs of young people. Therefore, he considered mut^{c}a to be one of the proofs of Islam's progressiveness and its compatibility with modern conditions.[26] The recent campaign by the leaders of the Islamic Republic to propogate this type of relationship among high-school-age children derives from Mutahhari's argument. It should, however, be noted that the concern about men's sexual drive is limited to Shi^{c}i Islam. Sunni Muslims consider mut^{c}a the same as prostitution; hence the practice is banned by all Sunni legal schools.

Despite their efforts to develop an acceptable defense of mut^ca, none of its male commentators and advocates has concerned himself with the deeper moral and social implications of this practice. They have ignored the fate of mut^ca women, who are stigmatized because their society places a premium on virginity of women, and its men seek "unsoiled" brides. They have also disregarded the physical and psychological harm to a young girl, often under thirteen, of intercourse with a much older man who may be anxious to get his money's worth by indulging his sexual fantasies with the blessing of his religion. They have been silent on the role played by mut^ca in driving women who become stigmatized following several such relationships into houses of prostitution. They have failed to perceive the inherent injustice of an arrangement whilch allows a man to have as many temporary wives as he can afford whenever and wherever he desires, but restricts a woman to only one such relationship at a time and requires that she observe idda [a two-menstrual-cycle waiting period] after each mut^ca relationship, even if no more than one act of intimacy takes place. Finally, the advocates of mut^ca fail to appreciate the adverse effect on poorer men. If this practice became widespread, richer men would attract most of the single women, and poorer men would have difficulty competing against them!

However, the religious leaders had more pressing issues than mut^ca on their minds during the late 1960s and 1970s. They became preoccupied with what they considered the deterioration of the moral and political health of society. In their view, the policies of the increasingly unpopular and repressive regime were undermining the traditional Islamic foundations of society and attempting to replace them with the alien and Godless culture of the West. The weakening of family ties and the rising tide of crime, alcoholism, and prostitution, especially among urban youths and migrant workers, pointed in that direction. But the worst sign of the onslaught of Western culture, according to the religious leaders, was the brutalization and exploitation of women, who were encouraged to flaunt their sexuality publicly in in the name of equality and progress.

In the wake of the quadrupling of oil prices in 1973, as the regime stepped up its Western-inspired transformation of the social structure, dissatisfaction among various groups began to mount. For a growing number of intellectuals and educated men and women, disenchanted with both the Western and Socialist ideologies, the Islamic solution seemed to present the only hopeful alternative for individual and social regeneration. Therefore, it was not only the religiously inclined who turned to the clergy for leadership. As political turmoil heightened, even secular groups, including those traditionally hostile to religion, such as the various Marxist factions,

joined ranks with the religious opponents of the Shah's
regime. The influence of the religious leadership was
further consolidated as Ayatullah Khomeini emerged as
the unchallenged leader of the revolution during the last
months of 1978.

Once the revolution had attained its immediate goal,
the ouster of the Shah, the secular groups, not antici-
pating such a quick victory and lacking a precise agenda
for action, splintered into many squabbling factions.
However, the religious leaders had a definite plan of
action: the establishment of an Islamic society according
to the outline envisaged in Ayatullah Khomeini's
Vilayat-i Faqih [The Rule by the Jurist] and under his
supervision. These two factors account for the speed
with which the religious leadership moved to establish
control over society and to fill the political vacuum
left after the collapse of the Shah's regime. The reason
women received high priority in the programs planned by
the religious leadership stemmed from their desire to
restore, at least outwardly, the Islamic character of
society.

Aided by the enormous popularity of Ayatullah
Khomeini, many members of the ulama filled positions of
power, including membership in the Constituent Assembly
entrusted with the task of writing the new constitution.
The decision of some important secular groups (e.g., the
National Front) to boycott the Constituent Assembly provided the ulama and their supporters a free hand in
drafting the constitution and incorporating their particular brand of Islam, especially as far as the role of
women in society was concerned.

The preamble to the constitution declares that the
Islamic foundation of the state will be derived from
Vilayat-i Faqih. Three sections of the constitution are
of special significance to the role of women. Under the
heading "Women and the Constitution," the preamble reveals the new emphasis placed on the family and the role
of women. It states,

> The family is the cornerstone of society and
> the primary institution for the growth and
> improvement of the individual; concensus and
> ideological belief in the principle that the
> formation of family is fundamental for the
> future development of the individual is one
> of the main aims of the Islamic government.

The relationship between the right kind, i.e., the Islamic kind, of family and women is revealed in the next
sentence, which adds,

> According to this line of thinking regarding
> the family, women will no longer be regarded
> as mere objects [instruments] in the service
> of consumerism; but, while being restored to

the worthwhile and responsible task of motherhood, they will be primarily responsible for the
raising of committed individuals.

This emphasis on motherhood in a country where most women,
even women with professions, are mothers first no matter
what else they might be, is significant because it implies that the regime will exert every effort to ensure
that women do not entertain other ambitions.

Article Four expounds the extent to which this
Shi^{c}ite interpretation of Islam shall pervade society.
It states,

All the laws and regulations concerning civil,
criminal, financial, economic, administrative,
cultural, [and] military affairs must be based
on the Islamic standards. This principle will
be applied to all the articles of the constitution and all other laws and regulations.

Article Twenty, on the other hand, pronounces the separate treatment of men and women and enacts this principle
into law. It states,

All members of the nation, be they men or
women, enjoy equal protection of the law
and will be entitled to human, political,
economic, and cultural rights according to
the laws of Islam [emphasis mine].

These two articles make absolutely clear that what women
should not expect is equality under the law, since
Shi^{c}ite law does not recognize the equality of men and
women but holds women inferior to men. The constitution
also builds into the law of the land the belief in the
inferiority of women.

Having succeeded in embodying their particular view
of women as inferior to men into the constitution, the
new leaders of the country have proceeded to enact these
beliefs into actual laws. The regime has launched an
extensive effort to restore women to their Islamic roles
of full-time mother and submissive wife. This is being
done by a variety of means, the most important of which
follow.

Many of the laws passed during the 1960s and 1970s
have been abrogated. These laws only partially closed
the traditional gap between men and women within the
family and society. The most important of these was the
Family Protection Law. Among other things, the repeal of
this law resulted in lowering the minimum marriage age
for girls from 18 to 13.

An important new law barred women from acting as
judges; hence all women judges were dismissed. Following
the barring of women from judgeships, scores of women
were removed from top level government posts; they were
forced either to accept lower level jobs or to retire

completely.

The regime has also passed a number of laws to
encourage women to return to the home and to ensure that
they remain there. Various retirement programs allow
women who have worked as little as fifteen years to retire without loss of benefits. Later, another law was
passed allowing working couples to enjoy the full benefit
of the wife's salary if she decided to stay home. Many
day care centers which had been opened in various government agencies and in factories under the previous regime
were closed. In the area of criminal law, the passage of
the Bill of Retribution further codified the regime's
belief in the inferiority of women by declaring that the
blood money to be paid for a female victim would be only
half that paid for a male. Women's testimony in court is
accepted as having only half the value of men's testimony.

The regime has also undertaken a long range plan to
ensure the success of its ideology for women. The central feature of this program is their imposition of the
hijab [veil]. This intention to make the veil mandatory
for women was first proclaimed by Ayatullah Khomeini two
weeks after his return to Iran in March 1979. He spoke
of the need for wearing the veil to separate the real,
committed Muslim women from the corrupt lackies of the
previous regime. Women reacted to these remarks with
large demonstrations the day after he had made them,
protesting that choice of dress is a basic right of women
and should not be determined by governmental decree.
These were spontaneous demonstrations by large numbers of
women; a cross-section of society was represented, including religiously-oriented women who believed in wearing
the veil. The atmosphere of freedome that still prevailed allowed these women to express their opposition openly.
The authorities retracted and announced that the Ayatullah was merely making a suggestion. After the initial
failure to make wearing the veil mandatory by fiat, the
leaders of the regime abandoned the plan for immediate
and universal imposition of the veil and adopted a gradual policy. Diverse factors accounted for the government's persistence in imposing the veil. In addition to
the theological arguments which view the veil as the
hallmark of the Muslim woman, its imposition would accomplish several other stated goals of the regime. First,
the wearing of the veil would give the country the
appearance of being Islamic. Second wearing the veil
would make it more difficult for women to practice some
professions (e.g., surgery), Finally, it would serve as
a constant reminder to women of their place in society,
secluded and isolated.

The new tactics were more successful. The regime
started by imposing the veil on a piecemeal basis, beginning with various governmental departments and
ministries. Each department issued its own dress code.
At the same time government spokesmen and religious dig-

nitaries launched a campaign in the press and on television in support of some form of veiling. Women who
joined in the chorus were greatly rewarded. One such
example was Mrs. Zahra Rahnavard, an obscure writer, who
was appointed editor-in-chief of Ittila^cat-i Banuvan [In-
formation for Women], one of the two leading magazines
for women, a month after she wrote a lengthy article in
defense of the veil.[27] On the other hand, women who did
not comply with the dress codes were dismissed from their
jobs. The threat of dismissal effectively silenced many
women whose incomes were needed to support their families
in a time of galloping inflation and worsening economic
conditions.

As the government stepped up its effort and its
design became obvious, some women did try to organize
demonstrations. The reaction of the regime to one such
demonstration was typical and explains why such efforts
were not successful. In July 1980, rumors circulated
that the government intended to pass a law making the
veil mandatory for all government employees. A demonstration by several thousand women was organized to protest. The demonstrators were surrounded and followed by
club-wielding members of Hizbullah [The Party of God] who
assailed the women with bottles and stones and hurled
such epithets as "prostitute" at them. Some of the demonstrators were arrested on charges of disrupting the
peace. Newspaper reports of the incident labeled the
demonstrators as a group of CIA agents, aristocratic and
corrupt women, sympathizers of the former regime, and
cabaret dancers and prostitutes. These reports went on
to commend the Hizbullahis for expressing their patriotic
and Islamic sentiments.[28]

Not all supporters of the regime approved of these
coercive efforts by the government to impose the veil on
women. Some even criticized these measures openly. Mrs.
A^czam Taliqani, one of the two female members of Parliament and the daughter of the late Ayatullah Taliqani,
denounced these efforts as discrimination against women
and demanded that such a code not be imposed on women
unless a similar code was enforced on men. But in the
end it was the advocates of the mandatory veil for women
who emerged victorious. A visitor to Tehran in July 1982
found no signs of bareheaded women.[29]

Another important policy of the government to bring
about the segregation of men and women is the revamping
of the entire educational system. This effort began by
banning coeducation and all types of coeducational activities such as sports for young boys and girls. School
books have been rewritten to bring them into line with
the different needs of each sex. In the curriculum for
girls' schools the emphasis is placed on subjects that
will prepare girls to be better mothers and housewives
or for careers suitable for women--sewing, nursing,
handicrafts, and teaching in girls' schools. The image

projected in the new school books being published shows
girls wearing the veil and helping their mothers around
the house, whereas boys appear in outside activities with
their fathers.

A new image is also being projected to women through
an extensive campaign in the press. Women are continually praised for the role they played in the Revolution.
Ayatullah Khomeini expressed his gratitude by declaring,
on Women's Day, 1981, "We owe the Revolution to women."
However, he qualified his statement by adding

> . . . to those women who have had an Islamic
> upbringing, the veiled women of south Tehran.
> They were the ones who shed their blood for
> the Revolution and urged their husbands to go
> out into the streets to fight oppression, not
> those who were educated under the regime of
> the Aryamihr [the Shah], the cursed Muhammad
> Riza.

Women are told that their belief in Islam provided them
with the incentive to rise up against tyranny. The relationship between being truly Muslim and participating in
the Revolution is also expounded for women by comparing
them to Muslim heroines of the past; the true Muslim
women were emulating the role played by one of their
favorite saints, the Saint Zainab, sister of the most
popular Shi^cite imam, Imam Husain. When Imam Husain was
martyred by agents of the venal Yazid at Karbala in 681
A.D., Zainab assumed the leadership of her kin because
there were no suitable males left to do so. At that
critical time she put aside her customary role as the
subordinate and obedient woman because her religious duty
required that she stand up to oppression and defy the
tyrannical and corrupt Yazid. The present-day women of
Iran did likewise, the argument goes, and by their defiance they were able to make invaluable contributions to
the downfall of the modern day Yazid, the late Shah. But
since the rule of justice has been restored, women must
resume the role required of them by their Muslim duty.
The model they are urged to emulate for normal [nonrevo-
lutionary] times is that of Fatimeh, the daughter of the
Prophet Muhammad, the wife of the first Shi^cite imam,
Imam Ali, and the mother of the heroic Imam Husain and of
Zainab. It was the exalted Fatimeh's obedient loyalty as
daughter, her devotion as wife, and her loving care as
mother that enabled those exceptional, larger-than-life
beings to fulfill their special destinies. Accordingly,
the most fundamental duty of a Muslim woman, when times
are normal, is to turn to her real task, the raising of
committed individuals. In the words of Ayatullah
Muntazari, widely considered Ayatullah Khomeini's successor, women's duty is truly a grave one: "It is their
[women's] duty to acquaint the new generation with Islamic ideals. This is the duty that the holy Qur'an has en-

trusted to them because women's role in the raising of
children and acquainting them with Islamic teachings and
values are much greater than men's."[31]

The credit for the use of religious figures as revolutionary archetypes must go to Ali Shari^cati; he transformed the traditional images of Shi^ci saints from symbols of suffering, forebearance, and helplessness in an
unjust world into active revolutionaries who put their
commitment to justice and fighting oppression above all
other priorities. However, the present revolutionary
leadership has made use of the same archetypes to restore
women to their traditional roles and to relate their unprecedented behavior of active participation in a major
social event to an acceptable traditional pattern. By
arguing that it is the duty of every Muslim to rise
against tyranny as did these saints, they have been able
to neutralize the tremendous departure from the norm in
the women's behavior. Furthermore, by arguing that these
saintly women only acted as revolutionaries at extraordinary times and then reverted to their customary household and wifely duties, the government discourages the
average traditional women from drawing larger and more
general lessons from their revolutionary experience.

One of the questions the leaders of the present
regime have not addressed as yet is the crucial issue of
franchise for women. Although women have so far been
allowed to participate in elections, it is by no means
certain that they will continue to do so. The present
constitution does not explicitly guarantee them that
right. Part Six, Article Sixty-two of the constitution,
which deals with legislative power, states, "The Parliament will consist of the people's representatives, who
will be chosen directly and by secret ballot. The conditions for the elections and the elected and the manner in
which elections will be held will be determined by law."
To my knowledge, the issue has not yet been determined.
However, if the present policies of the regime are any
indication, we should not be surprised if the franchise
is withdrawn from women; there is reason to believe that
the present government does not approve of the vote for
women.

Ayatullah Khomeini and other prominent religious
figures had opposed suffrage for women on the grounds
that it was contrary to the Shari^ca. Although none of
the prominent religious authorities has openly stated
this view recently, they still uphold the principle that
led to their opposition in the past: women's inferiority
in intellect renders them unsuitable to act as judges.
The present regime used this principle as the basis of
some recent legislation such as that barring women from
judgeships. The ulama have also held the view that discussion of women's rights is irrelevant to Muslim society
since women received all the rights they need fourteen
hundred years ago. Hujjat ul-Islam Nuri has stated, "Only

those women ignorant of their Islamic rights, who have
been misled by imperialism, clamor for human and other
rights."[32] Ayatullah Khomeini recently advised women to
be happy with the status Islam has given them and not to
allow the present day "satans" to deceive them and divert
them from Islam in the name of freedom and human rights.
This hostility to franchise was also expressed in a
work by the editor of the influential Qum-based magazine,
Maktab-i Islam [The Ideology of Islam], Makarim-Shirazi.
Entitled Zan va Intikhabat [Women and Elections], the
work strives to prove two points: that women's participation in the electoral process is contrary to the teachings of the Shari^ca and Islam, and that franchise for
women in Western society has resulted primarily in
numerous social ills.[33]

The past opinions of the ulama and these recently
issued views on the subject do not bode well for the
future of franchise for women in Iran. Two factors, however, may safeguard this right for them in the near
future. First, traditional women have continued to respond to the regime for a show of solidarity with its
policies and actions. Therefore it would be unlikely
that the government would disenfranchise an important
portion of its supporters at a time when it needs all the
support it can get--increased use of censorship and the
secret police indicate that the government faces serious
opposition. Second, the leaders of the regime may not be
certain that the withdrawal of franchise at this particular time would be wise or even necessary; it might lead
to disaffection of many of the traditional women, who
still cherish and value their participation in the
revolution. Furthermore, the present leaders may be
satisfied with the gains they have already made in attain-
ing their goals towards returning women to their homes.
Even women's parliamentary representation has been weakened, reduced to two members in the present session from
twenty-four in the pre-revolutionary Parliament.

The current state of censorship makes it difficult
to know what portion of the Iranian women who approved
the establishment of an Islamic Republic in Iran in 1979
support the policies and laws enacted by that regime in
the name of Islam. Judging by the large number of women
who show solidarity with the regime when they are called
upon to do so, it would appear that the regime still
meets with the approval of the majority. This support
is not surprising. Although participation in the revolution did sharpen the political awareness of many of the
traditional women, the subsequent policies of the present
regime have not really affected their lifestyle or their
perception of themselves as women. To the contrary, the
reinstatement of many of the values by which these women
have lived, such as veiling and subordination to men, may
even seem an affirmation of these values. Probably few
of them mourn the loss of laws such as the Family Protec-

214

tion Law; those laws had not existed long enough to prove
their usefulness to these women. Even their unprecedented
and truly revolutionary participation in the events of
the revolution has now been couched for them into a language that renders it quite traditional.

However, the lessons of the participation by women in
the revolution cannot indefinitely be lost on women, even
the most traditional. The continuous use of Islamic symbolism and Islamic ideals will sooner or later result in
some of the religious supporters of the regime going to
the sources of these ideas, the Qur'an itself. Ayatullah
Mutahhari prophetically foresaw the coming of such a day
when he said

> If, some day, woman fully understands this and
> is enlightened and notices the traps that twen-
> tieth-century man has set in her path and con-
> cealed from her, she will rise in revolt against
> this fraud. That will be the time when she
> finds out that her only protector in all sin-
> cerity is the Qur'an. Of course, that day is
> not far off.[34]

There they will find that nothing is more remote from the
true teachings of Islam and its spirit than the assumptions presented in theological discussions about the inherent inferiority of women. They will also discover that
central to the Qur'anic teachings is the notion that the
individual's worth is determined by God on the basis of
piety, regardless of rank, race, or sex. Such women may
wonder why a standard that satisfies the Divine requirement does not satisfy the interpreters of His Law. They
will also learn of the Qur'an's unequivocal demand for
social justice in society. Yet they will observe that the
laws applied to them in His name treat them as inferior
because they are women and that these laws affecting their
destiny so deeply are written entirely by men. They may
wonder if such a state of affairs is not a flagrant contradiction of what is meant by social justice in the
Qur'an. They will also learn of the Qur'anic condemnation
of Pharaoh, who demanded submission from his subjects.
Will they not be thunderstruck by the arrogance of the
men, no matter how learned they may be, who demand that
women submit to their husbands, when they are told in no
uncertain terms in the Qur'an that only the Almighty
should be the object of their submission and obedience?

How will many of the supporters of the present regime answer these questions when they finally turn to the
Qur'an, the most important source of the law? The future
must determine that. However, the participation of a
minority of the younger religiously-oriented women in
anti-regime activities indicates that some Iranian women
have already decided the answers. The risks they seem to
be taking with their lives reveals the depth of their
disagreement with the interpretations presented to them

in the name of God. The fact that many of the Mujahidin
women have been executed is sufficient proof of the rejection by some women of these assertions about themselves in the name of Islam.

NOTES

1. "The Imam's Message on Women's Day," Jumhūrī-yi
Islāmī, 15 Urdībihisht 1359/ 6 May 1980, p. 1.
2. Badr ol-Muluk Bāmdād, From Darkness to Light,
F.R.C. Bagley, trans. (Hicksville, New York: Exposition
Press, 1977), pp. 7-22.
3. Ahmad Ashraf and Mamideh Sedghi, "The Role of
Women in Iranian Development," Iran: Past, Present, and
Future (Aspen: Aspen Institute for Humanistic Studies,
1976), pp. 201-312.
4. For greater discussion of the changes in the
impact of economic growth on women in Iran, see the
chapter by S. Kaveh Mirani in this volume.
5. "A Brief Assessment of the Women's Democratic
Struggles," Women and Struggle in Iran, no. 1, March 1982,
pp. 22-27.
6. Charles Issawi, "The Iranian Economy 1925-1975:
Fifty Years of Economic Development," in George Lencszow-
ski, ed., Iran Under the Pahlavis (Stanford: Hoover
Institution Press, 1978), pp. 129-167. For a detailed
discussion of the Family Protection Act see F.R.C. Bagley,
"The Iranian Family Protection Law: A Milestone in the
Advance of Women's Rights," in C.E. Bosworth, ed., Iran
and Islam (Edinburgh: Edinburgh University Press, 1971)
pp. 47-64.
7. Azar Tabari, "The Enigma of the Veiled
Iranian Woman," MERIP Reports (February 1982), pp. 22-
27.
8. For greater discussion of these two groups of
women's guerilla organizations, see the chapter by Eliz
Sanasarian in this volume.
9. Interview with a German reporter, November 13,
1978, reprinted in Women and Struggle in Iran, no. 1,
March 1982, p. 3.
10. For more discussion of the traditional attitudes
toward women, see the chapter by Amir and Adele Ferdows
and the historical overview by Guity Nashat in this
volume.
11. Hujjat ul-Islām Yahyā Nūrī, Huqūq va Hudūd-i Zan
dar Islām [The Rights and Limits of Women in Islam]
(Tehran: Shams Publishing, n.d.), p. 54.
12. Ibid.
13. Ibid., p. 92.
14. Ibid.
15. Ibid., pp. 115-16.
16. Ibid, pp. 56-56.
17. Guity Nashat, "Women in the Islamic Republic of
Iran," Iranian Studies 13: 165-95.

216

18. M.A. Ansāri, Difā^C Az Islām va Rowhānīyyat [In Defense of Islam and the Clergy], (Qum: 1351/1972), pp. 219-20.

19. Nūrī, Huqūq, p. 82.

20. Ayatullāh Murtizā Mutahharī, Mas'aleh-yi Hijāb [The Question of the Veil] (Tehran: Anjuman-i Islāmī-yi Pizishkān, 1347/1968), pp. 70-71.

21. Ibid., p. 69.

22. Ayatullāh R. Khomeinī, Towzīh ul-Masā'il [Explanation of Problems](Tehran: Piruz, 1979), p. 80.

23. Ibid., p. 386.

24. Ayatullāh Murtizā Mutahharī, Ta^{C}addud-i Zowjāt [Polygamy] (Tehran: n.d.), p. 35.

25. For greater discussion of the policies of the present regime regarding mut^{C}a, see the chapter by Shahla Haeri in this volume.

26. Ayatullāh Murtizā Mutahharī, "The Rights of Women in Islam," in Mahjubah, the Magazine for Muslim Women 1 (no. 8, Muharram 1402/October-November 1981): 52-56.

27. Newspaper articles, Ittilā^{C}āt, 16180-82, 12-15 Tīr 1359/5-8 July 1980.

28. Ibid., 15 Tīr 1359/8 July 1980.

29. Newspaper article, New York Times, 13 July 1980.

30. Newspaper article, Jumhūrī-yi Islāmī, 16 Urdī-bihist 1359/6 May 1980.

31. Article, Piyām-i Imām [The Imam's Message], Urdībihisht 1360/April-May 1981, p. 10.

32. Nūrī, Huqūq, p. iv.

33. Nāsir Makārim-Shīrazī, et al., Zan va Intikhābāt [Women and the Elections](Qum: Tabātabā'ī Publishing Co., n.d.), pp. 109-10.

34. Mutahharī, "Women," p. 55.

12
State Ideology and Village Women

Erika Friedl

Listening to discussions about women in Iran today, one learns that the present fundamentalist ideology of the government means either a return to medieval subjugation for women or a progressive liberation from the yoke of evil Western ways, depending on whether the speaker is a liberal modernist or a Muslim fundamentalist.[1] As such sweeping statements go, we can guess that one or the other is probably true for some women, especially those in larger cities, but that for many more neither is accurate.

The question arises of how much influence state-propagated ideology has on the lifeways and philosophies of the ordinary people--those not engaged in the ongoing ideological and power struggles of the politicized elements. Do they keep doing what they have always done, bound by tradition and deaf to the noises around them? Do they become politicized by learning the new language? Do local conditions change essentially in the wake of national consciousness raising? The masses of peasants, wage laborers, small craftsmen, women, and children--the resonant body of a society on which politicians, intellectuals, and ideologues play their tunes--are not the focus of public attention at the quietest of times, and are even less so in times of crises, unless they emerge as refugees somewhere. This paper deals with some of these ordinary people in times of extraordinary ideological pressure: the women in one village in postrevolutionary Iran.

Most of the vocal women on either extreme of the Islamic-liberal-leftist spectrum in Iran are educated urban women, participants in a subculture that has, over the past 15 years, become increasingly riddled with discontent. Indeed, one can argue on the basis of strain-theory that the incongruities brought about by fast culture change and the stress created on the adaptability and validity of cultural values which had held together Persian society in the past--such values as hospitality or an authoritarian family structure with a tight fabric of mutual responsibilities--paved the way for an ideology

promising peace of mind by providing absolute values and
by relegating to the sphere of evil all forces blamed for
the painful breakdown of the old order.[2]

However, the great majority of women in Iran are
tucked away in villages, isolated, illiterate, unheard
and unspoken of outside their own small worlds; therefore
they were probably never quite as confused by the shake-
up of cultural symbols as urban women. What effects do
the recent politico-ideological changes have on the
village women?

The data for this paper were gathered during an
extended stay in a large village of over 2,500 inhabitants in West Iran in 1981. Although I cannot claim this
village to be representative of rural Iran in general, I
do not think that the views expressed by the women of
the village are exceptionally radical or odd. Similar
opinions frequently were expressed to me by women of all
walks of life in other villages, towns, and even cities.
To guard the anonymity of the village, no names are
mentioned, and all references pertaining to the village
in the literature are omitted.

At present in Iran, religious and political ideology
are firmly interlocked: religion is used as a political
basis by the government. Political decisions are justified by theological arguments. The ruling elite's view
of the nature of man, or reality, is Qur'anic. The ultimate goal of governmental actions is phrased in religious
concepts: to install God's order in the world, to uplift
morality, to wipe out evil and evil-doers.[3] In the
attempt to realize these ideals, the goal is said to
justify any acts the rulers deem necessary. Shi^{c}i clergy
formulate the goal, control the implementations of rules
to attain the goal, and judge the performance of all per-
formers in the enactment of the resulting drama.

Shi^{c}i Islam--even fundamentalist Shi^{c}i Islam--is not
at all new to village women. Indignantly they point out
that village women have been "true Muslims" for hundreds
of years and had remained faithful during the morally
loose times of the Shah. Therefore, they resent the
present attempts to "reform" them. The dogmas of their
faith are not new; what is new is the fact that fundamentalist Shi^{c}i principles are propagated as all encom-
passing regulations of every aspect of life. In the
village, religion had always been an intimate affair
between God and person, a free act of acceptance of God's
will and order. Under the new regime religion is no
longer a private affair. Rather, one's proclamation of
faith and one's religious behavior must meet standards
firmly set by outside agents, and both are open to public
scrutiny. This gives the otherwise familiar religion a
whole new outlook. However involuntarily given, adherence to the new standards changes the quality of life in
the village.

For villagers generally, and for women especially,
Islam was and still is foremost a blueprint for coexistence. It is said to be an indispensable guide for getting along with other people here in this world--with
immediate family and more distant relatives, friends,
neighbors, strangers, the poor, all mankind. Almost
unanimously, the first and most promptly given answer to
a question about what God wants of people elicits such
answers as, "not to lie", "not to steal", "not to talk
in a bad way about others". Without religion, people
say, there would be anarchy, mayhem, terror; brothers
would be afraid of brothers, sons would fight fathers,
one's life and land would be in jeopardy. Compared to
social prescriptions, the observation of ritual and any
orientation toward the transcendental or mystical rank
low in the village's hierarchy of religious duties. It
is said, for example, that animosity toward a relative
or neighbor cannot be balanced with even the most con-
scientious observation of ritual or prayers. In fact,
just the opposite is true according to village theology:
the sin of bad relationships with others cancels the
merits gained from prayer and fasting.

Women are quick to point out that conditions of
peace and goodness have gone from bad to worse in the
village. Indeed, the so-called revival of religion has
changed people's characters for the worse: there is more
unrest, dishonesty, and fighting than ever before. The
religion as now propagated is not right, cannot be right,
because it is obviously ineffective in bringing about
better interpersonal relationships.

On a national level things appear even worse. A
true Muslim is honest, peaceful and empathetic--a perfect
social companion. In the eyes of most village women
this is a fundamental message of Islam, and they see it
flouted by the present state of affairs in Iran. The
message that comes from the religious authorities is one
of fear, blood, war, and death. True Muslims are generous; a religious leader ordering the execution of a
young Communist accused of throwing a bomb is blood-
thirsty and revengeful, regardless of the evil the Communist has done. True Muslims are kind; a religious
leader who sends scores of young men to be killed in war
and thereby throws thousands of mothers, wives, and
daughters into grief and despair is cruel, even though
Iraq is an aggressor. True Muslims are protective and
compassionate; a religious leader who orders a prostitute
to be stoned is committing a crime worse than hers.
Although the Communist's, Iraq's, and the prostitute's
actions are crimes by any local standards, they cannot be
rectified by other crimes, even when committed in the
name of religion. The proud announcements of executions
for various crimes horrifies all the village women, without exception. To them, executions are devilish and

heathen. They produce the paradox of religious leaders
who engage in abhorrent anti-religious activities in the
name of religion. These leaders' proclamations of faith
are suspected to be mere lip service and a mockery of
Islam. The piety they project is rendered a perversion by
their acts. Their moral credibility, their religious
authority are questioned and, more often than not, denied.
The more zealous, the more fervent the religious authorities become, the more the women distance themselves from
the symbol system the mullahs manipulate; indeed, the less
women identify with the religion. If this is Islam, the
women argue, the killing, the murder, the tears, then I
am not a Muslim.

On the village level, executions do not happen, even
the beturbaned mullahs are a rarity. Here, the watch-
your-neighbor attitude demanded of everybody by the
mullahs, the implicit distrust of others' willingness to
live up to the religion's prescriptions is resented.
It is seen as a threat to the social web that traditionally was based on a good deal of tolerance for different
opinions and on punctilious expression of mutual respect.
Now, sons argue with fathers over matters of doctrine and
politics; brothers denounce each other, encouraged by
religious authorities; common sense is violated by the
creation of petty rules in the name of religion. The
narrow-minded uniformity of behavior and beliefs now
demanded by agents of the state-religion is obvious and
provocative, even to illiterate village women. The state-
religion is recognized as an ideology that serves political and not religious ends, and its enforcement is criticized as a misuse of religious authority. Again the
women say if this is Islam, then I am not a Muslim.

No matter how emphatically the women might disagree
with the system, it is not possible to escape it entirely.
The whole legal-bureaucratic apparatus of the village
claims to be implemented Islam. In fact, however, the
return to Islamic law had surprisingly little effect on
legal conditions of everyday life for village women. Up
to August 1981 there was only relatively mild interference
in village affairs by outside agents, political, legal, or
otherwise, except for heavy propaganda efforts.[4] In the
absence of heavy-handed legal authorities, customary local
law has stayed in effect for most practical purposes.
Villagers conduct their affairs as best they know how and
as they have always done. For example, the Muslim inheritance laws so unfavorable to women (they inherit half as
much as men) actually are much better than traditional
local inheritance laws, under which daughters inherit
nothing. Still, just as the more favorable Family Protection Law under the Shah was never implemented in the
village, so the Islamic law is being ignored now. A few
exceptions aside, women don't claim their legal inheritance, and nobody cares; where there is no complaint,

there is no judge.

The legal marriage age for women is dealt with similarly. In the past, the Shah's 18-year minimum age for
girls had been circumvented successfully whenever it was
thought to be necessary. In a society where marriage-
ability for women is defined as preceding sexual maturity
and birth certificates are much a matter of parental
discretion, legal age measured in years means very little.
The marriage age for both girls and boys has been rising
steadily in the village over the past ten years, due to
factors of changing economic and educational routines.
The recent lowering of the legal marriage age for girls
to 13, therefore, does not upset many people in the
village and does not seem to affect actual marriage age
patterns.

The harsh legal stance against adultery and prostitution does not ruffle any feathers locally either. There
is no prostitution in the village; the rare illicit relationships are disapproved of and quietly handled between
the families involved. The only official action taken
locally within the last decade against an adulterous pair
involved two strangers to the village. The affair had
been gossiped about for several years without much consequence. In the end the lovers behaved indiscreetly; there
were rows in public, and after much melodrama which both
scandalized and amused the village, the man was finally
forced to leave. The woman, who is married locally,
continues to live in the village with her husband.
Although illicit sexual relationships have always been
regarded as grave sins, villagers argue that it is not
man's business to meddle judgementally with the sins of
others. God Himself will mete out punishment for one's
sins, either here or hereafter.

The stringent demands on sexual propriety in general,
although not expressed in any particular single law, are
felt throughout the village. The newly tightened code of
ethics has the most noticeable consequences for women on
the level of interpersonal, day-to-day interaction with
men. Never free and easy, male-female relationships
other than those between closest relatives are now tor-
tuous. The separation of public and private is complete,
with women extremely reluctant to transgress the boundary
lest they be labelled "immoral". In principle, any place
a man occupies, however temporarily, is restricted for
women. Thus, even one's own house is "private" only as
long as no man other than a closely related household
resident is present. A girls' school is "public" because
a man could potentially be on the premises. Indeed, female students above fifth grade and all female teachers
are veiled in school.[5] To move unreproachably in public
space a woman must be properly attired, must observe
extreme self-effacement, and must have good reason for
being there. For instance, a widow out shopping has a

good reason for being in public--she has no husband to do
it for her--but a married woman does not. Indeed, very
few women are now seen in the village lanes or shopping
areas. Those who are out are carefully veiled in dark
heavy veils, in contrast to a short time ago when veiling
was casual and the light veil was treated almost like an
ornament. To match the prevailing somber atmosphere,
colors of skirts have changed from bright hues to dark
ones. Even young girls dress like old women. "We are
all in mourning now," women comment only half-jokingly.
     The group most affected by these tightened restric-
tions on movement is the unmarried teen-age girls.
In accordance with general Islamic attitudes toward the
subject, female sexuality traditionally was seen in the
village as a potential threat to the moral well-being of
men and thus to the community. Like all potentially
dangerous powers, it had to be checked in order to be put
to good use. The only proper check was marriage; the
only good use, producing children. Girls ideally were
married before they reached sexual maturity. Although
socio-economic conditions have been working against early
marriages for a decade in the village, no alternative way
of dealing with female sexual power developed. Unmarried
sexually-mature girls were kept out of circulation, so to
speak, so that one hardly ever saw them. Reinforcing
this local trend in regard to married women, the recent
incessant official pronouncements on proper conduct for
women has fallen on open ears. For example, the customary spring expeditions by groups of girls for gathering
wild edible plants have become much smaller as fathers,
mothers, or brothers forbid their daughters/sisters to
go because of the potential challenge to propriety. Likewise, high school attendance by girls has dropped: to
walk to school in public, no matter how tightly veiled,
to be outside the house most of the day, has become
morally risky. In addition, since boys and girls can no
longer be taught together nor by teachers of the opposite
sex, the few girls in high school have limited choice in
their course selection--no science, for example. This in
turn severely limits their future career opportunities,
which have always been meager. The fact that jobs for
women have all but disappeared--practically as well as
ideologically--has turned formal education of girls beyond the fifth grade into an eccentricity: it is of no
practical value and is morally compromising.
     Many women express the suspicion that these restric-
tions serve the ideological end of enforcing male dominance over women. It seems paradoxical that despite their
insight and the fact that all women suffer under the constraints, women themselves are the most scrupulous guardians of their meticulous observation. There are two
possible explanations for this. By checking each other,
women avoid a potentially much more painful and embarrassing attention by men or even outsiders. Moreover, by

fashioning themselves into specialists of these rules, older women can use them to keep younger female members of their social circle in check and thereby strengthen their own authority over others. This system works all the way down to the level of children, as when a seven-year-old threatens to tattle on her four-year-old sister's "indecent" behavior, thereby asserting the superiority of her own wisdom and power. Although all women, without exception, comply with the limits set by religious authorities, most of them deny that it would be sinful to do otherwise. The tight prescriptions are seen as socially oppressive but morally neutral. From the theological point of view of the women, they are useless. "No woman will go to heaven on the color of her veil," it is said.

Restrictions on women's movements have other consequences, too. Since the traditional outings and public dances at weddings have been forbidden--all dancing and music are declared sinful--there are no morally acceptable diversions for women outside the house except for occasional unpopular public sermons by itinerant preachers.[6] Indeed, only visits to the health clinic and weekly visits to the cemetery are legitimate, uncompromising outings. As both lack the ideological overtones the women are so quick to perceive, they have become very popular. While visits to the doctor are naturally somewhat restricted, graveside visitations, locally rare prior to the revolution, have become elaborate to an unprecedented degree. Grief is pronounced morally good; it now provides the most visible social dimension of religion for village women. Since the prolonged and fervent expression of grief has become the only regular religiously sanctioned activity for women outside the house, for many women religion has become grieving.

On Thursday afternoons, clusters of dark-clad women carrying bowls with fruits or sweets under their all-encompassing veils gather around the graves of close relatives. Singing, chanting, wailing, sobbing fill the air. Food is passed around in honor of the dead. Between the lamentations, news is exchanged, counsel given, affairs discussed. Some women join other mourning groups around other graves. After two hours or so of this, the women drift homewards, emotionally drained and filled with news.

It is easy to detect an element of defiance, protest even, in these mourning rituals gone public. Toward the end of the summer of 1981, many women who joined the parties had not recently lost any close relatives at all. They mourned because they "felt like it"; they used the catharsis of crying to ease the burden of unspecified unhappiness or of some particular discontent. The wailing crowds of women in the cemeteries all over the country focused attention on this-worldly misery in general, an attention the regime tried hard to play down in

favor of a promised bright future either eventually in
this or at least in the next world. Honoring of the dead,
an important and meritorious religious duty, thus threatened to become a danger to the very ideology that had
fostered it by turning the people's eyes toward the world
beyond in the attempt to wean them from petty, sinful
preoccupations with this-worldly affairs. After some ugly
incidents in several different places in Iran, mourning
rituals too became restricted and the public expression
of grief for "martyrs", the dead of the war, was outlawed
in some places. Although this did not happen in the
village, it was known to happen elsewhere, was perceived
as a manipulative distortion of a religious domain by
political agents, and was grimly added to the list of
governmental wrongs against both the religion and women.

The return to Islamic law brought an easing of procedures for polygyny and divorce of women. Legally, a
man now can be married to four wives simultaneously, and
to even more consecutively. This causes local women much
anxiety, although neither the number of polygynous marriages nor the rate of divorce has actually increased
locally; both rates were and still are low. The mere fact
that a man can now divorce his wife virtually whenever he
wants to or can just as easily take an additional wife
causes resentment and bitter talk, as well as sarcastic
jokes, among women. The legal clause that a man cannot
take a second wife without the consent of his first is
no solace. Many sob-stories circulate in the village
about women who were tricked and browbeaten by their
husbands into consenting to a co-wife or were divorced if
they resented her. Fact or fiction, they express real
anguish and dread. Women fail to see any moral good
connected with these laws, no redeeming religious or
spiritual value whatsoever, either in this or in the
next world. Rather, they take the laws very practically
as an effective undermining of their position vis-a-vis
their husbands and a strengthening of the man's position
at the woman's expense. No matter what the mullah's say,
religion is thus seen as being used to support men and to
oppress women.

One of the immediate practical results of the changed
political atmosphere in the village has been a marked increase in the birthrate. In regard to regulation (or
absence of regulation) of pregnancies, religious ideology
and wider socio-cultural factors again reinforce each
other in such a way that most women feel resentful yet
unable to resist the pressure. Pregnancy is not proclaimed religiously meritorious unless it results in
death: the only women who are said to go straight to heaven without interrogation are those who die in childbirth.
However, according to religious tradition a woman's foremost function, her God-ordained basic purpose, is to be a
producer of offspring for a man. Consequently, religious

authorities refuse women the right to limit pregnancies--
only a man as the owner of his children and responsible
head of the family is to make such a decision. Aside
from religious pressures, there are social ones. A woman
who practices birth control without the consent of her
husband not only is committing a grave sin but can also
legally be punished by her husband.

Barrenness is and always has been an uncontestable
reason for divorce and polygyny (although in the village
it very rarely resulted in either). A childless couple
is socially impaired; their power position vis-a-vis
other relatives is low, and they have no children to rely
on for support in old age. In the absence of other
legitimate status-conveying activities for village women,
childbearing is the main determinant of a woman's social
standing in the community. Therefore, she will strive to
have as many pregnancies as possible, no matter how much
she might personally resent the burden of bearing and
raising children. Considerations of personal comfort,
even of health, lose out time and again, especially if
the husband wants more children, even if contraceptives
are available.

Although their use has not been proclaimed sinful,
contraceptives are much more difficult to obtain now.
Their use has markedly decreased since they are no longer
distributed by the midwife in the village--woman to woman. They must be requested from the male physician at
the clinic in the next village. The request might be
granted readily, or the woman might be put through a
pious cross examination that would embarrass her. Thus,
women are discouraged from requesting contraceptives.
As for other methods of avoiding childbearing, abortion
is outlawed, and it is a grave sin for a woman to refuse
sex to her husband.

Women in the village don't like to be pregnant; many
don't even like children very much. Beyond the third or
fourth child, pregnancies and infants are treated as
routine events, burdensome to be sure, yet as unavoidable
as other burdens of life. Again, religion is not held
responsible for this state of affairs but is perceived
as supporting it. No help, not even spiritual solace,
is offered by religious authorities for pregnancy or
child-rearing unless a woman dies in the process of fulfilling her foremost earthly purpose: providing for a
man.

All-in-all, on the practical level of day-to-day
social intercourse, men are seen to be able to (re)assert
nearly absolute dominance over women by using the same
moral idiom of the fundamentalist religion which they
reject in many other areas. This double standard in the
use of ideology does not escape women, even if they are
powerless to change it. The most important reasons for
successful male assertion and women's docile acceptance

226

of the consequences, however, lie outside the sphere of
religion. As men have become more and more dependent on
wages, salaries, and outside markets over the last twenty
years, women have been inched out of their productive
niches in the village economy; their dependence on men as
breadwinners has increased, and their power domain has
diminished. Formerly valuable producers of necessary
goods, women have become primarily homemakers and producers of children. Although this development has nothing to do with religion as such, the image of woman as
the dependent, child-producing keeper of a man's house
is the one proclaimed by religious authorities to be the
only legitimate one for women. Linked to it, the para-
meter of acceptable conduct for women has constantly been
narrowed over the last year, limitations demanded and
justified in the name of religion and propageted as the
God-ordained order of things in this world. In this
dilemma--and there is no doubt that most women see it
as a dilemma--women see only dismal choices: to protest
their position means to protest the official religion and
its powerful executive; to accept it means to abandon
common sense, time-tested cultural traditions, and practical experience, and to stop thinking rationally for
the sake of a system of ideas that are seen as the pure
self-serving ideology of a politically oppressive worldly power.

There is, of course, no question as to the prudent
choice. On countless occasions all through their history, villagers in general and village women in particular have survived by formally giving in to oppressive
forces: landlords, tax-collectors, soldiers, gendarms,
rogues, fathers, husbands. But never before, they
claim, was powerful evil so closely connected with
religion.

Aside from changes in the socio-legal sphere, village women now also have to deal with ideologically tint-
ed methphysical of Shi⁻i Islam. An orientation towards
martyrdom, towards the other world, and towards considering the present life to be but a preparation for a
better one to come is very much stressed officially. All
soldiers killed in the war with Iraq are declared martyrs, religious heroes enviably reposing in heaven.
Worldly amusements--as few and as innocent as they were
in the villages--have been declared frivolous, immoral,
and a threat to one's other-worldly well-being. Food and
other shortages are declared unimportant concommittants
of the implementation of a truly Islamic social order.

Village women, although unimpressed by the fervent
puritanical tones of these messages, have found it easy
to accept the image of general this-worldly misery, of
life as a perpetual cycle of poverty, hard work, and
sickness. The present message of earthly life as pain
and gloom falls on ready ears. In the religious order

of things, existential hardships are balanced by other-worldly eternal pleasures. But while these pleasures are visualized vividly for men, other-worldly bliss for women traditionally has been described vaguely; heaven simply is synonymous with a place of rest and peace. For women heavenly bliss is not sensually elaborated as it is for men; the fragrances of paradisical flowers, the heavenly taste of paradisical fruits, the pleasing sights and sounds are muted and faint. Paradise for men is described as pleasure; for women, it is the absence of pain. The present ideologues have not made heaven any more attractive for women. Consequently, women perceive heaven simply as a less ugly but much harder to attain alternative to hell.

Hell is much more real and better defined than heaven for women; it is a place of gory tortures, intense and detailed suffering. For men, it is defined vaguely as a "bad" place. Just as a painful life here on earth is more easily attained and more likely than a good one, so it is hell more easily attained and more likely than heaven, women claim. This is so because ordinary people are sent to hell not so much as severe punishment for spectacular crimes committed on earth-- these are rare, they conclude in realistic self-appraisal --but rather for their failure to live up to the high standards for routine day-to-day behavior set by religious authorities. In this respect women are much more vulnerable than men; declared morally weaker than men, and being more exposed to a boring and hum-drum daily existence, they are more likely to sin in small ways than men are. Many little sins, however, add up to a heavy burden on the scales of judgement.

If they believe religious authorities, women feel they have little to hope for either in this world or in the next world. The only way out of the dilemma thus created is to question the ultimate authority of the religious leaders in such doctrinal matters: after all, women say, the mullahs are only men. We'll find out soon enough how God, the merciful, will really judge us.

There is yet another conceptual problem for women connected with the afterlife. Even before the revolution heaven was always slightly suspected of being a "public" place where women don't quite fit, a place where a male God resides like a king, surrounded by male angels, a place where human men frolic not with human women (at the thought of this, women giggle in embarrassment) but with celestial maidens, far superior to earthly women and seemingly not bound by restrictions of propriety. Now, with thousands of so-called martyrs from the war declared to have been admitted to heaven without as much as a question by the angels of judgement, heaven is seen as totally a man's place. Women are hopelessly outnumbered in paradise. Their grief over the deaths of their men

and the hardships these cause are seemingly not rewarded
in this life, nor in the next.

All this, however, although so clear to the women
that they are able to talk about it explicitly, does not
alarm them greatly. Rather, with the black humor of the
underdog, they turn officially nurtured expectations for
heaven and fear of hell to mockery in countless jokes,
and render both heaven and hell an absurdity and a man-
made fiction. "You know why we have a shortage of ce-
ment? Because they have to build a house for each martyr
in heaven." "The angels are getting deaf because the
martyrs sing nothing but revolutionary songs." "Heaven
must be as boring as television: full of wounded heroes
and preaching mullahs."

This critical distancing from official pronouncements on the other world, however, does not mean that
women no longer believe in an afterlife. Heaven and hell
still exist in the common sense order of things; only
their natures are not well defined. Rarely are they
believed to be what religious authorities claim them to
be. "God alone knows what heaven and hell is." "We'll
find out about it when we get there." Again, the
religious specialists' assertions are doubted at best
and often rejected altogether.

There are only a few women in the village able to
read the Qur'an, the hadith, or religious treatises.
Fewer yet have the opportunity to obtain religious
literature. The vast majority of women get the "truth"
in bits and pieces--interpreted, edited, and simplified--
from sermons, over television, in folkloristic stories
and anecdotes. There is a profound skepticism among
women toward anything spread by word of mouth. This
skepticism has an important consequence for the acceptance of religious doctrine by women: anybody's claim
to present the truth can be easily challenged--a neighbor's, an itinerant preacher's, a mullah's on television,
or Khomeini's himself. It is all hearsay.

Even without knowing first hand the extent and the
nature of the directives pertaining to a woman's place in
an ideal Islamic society as laid down in the hadith or
the Qur'an, most women perceive traditional religious
doctrine as unsympathetic to them.[8] In concordance with
the implementation of hadith ideas and Islamic law since
the revolution, this opinion has intensified, especially
among the many women who see these laws and ideals mis-
used as ideological tools. The typical reaction is outward compliance--after all, legal authorities enforce
religious rules, and opposition, although not likely to
be a sin, still means opposing an increasingly ruthless
worldly power. Besides, the social fabric of a village
does not lend itself easily to the organization of protest by women.[9] But outward compliance for most women
only masks an inward rebellion. Despite the overt and
seemingly fervent religiosity displayed in public every-

where, religious beliefs in the village have taken a different turn. They are characterized by denial of most official religious proclamations and the adherence to a homemade minimal theology in which God-demanded personal integrity and honesty and the acceptance of hardships sent for unknown and unknowable reasons by God, together with a vague hope that on the Day of Judgement God will indeed be merciful to His humble sinners, are the major parameters. This religion is largely stripped of ritual because ritual is linked with the religious powers-that-be, and these are suspected of using the religious idiom to further their own interests. Thus, traditional rituals of the Islamic calendar are boycotted. Prescribed fasts are no longer observed: "God would not be pleased with my fast because my heart is full of anger." Many women don't even pray any more: "The mullahs have stolen the prayers."

The facts that religious rituals are fast becoming meaningless, that religious symbols are muddled, that hypocrisy in religious matters is widespread, and that unrest and hostility rule the day are taken by many women as a signal for the imminent end of the world. Existential hardships in the past were endurable and philosophically manageable because they were seen as resulting from an established order. Poverty, pain, and oppression were by-products of life itself. Now, they are seen as man-made, as telltale signs that the universe is crumbling at the core.

The role of the theo-political elite's ideology thus is not only marginal to the cultural web--the time-tested rule of life in the village--but is seen as a threat to its survival. The ideology, which is probably an answer to great cultural-economic stress in the cities, produces an enormous strain in the village. The very fact that the clerical regime in Iran is resorting to ever stronger methods of social control can be taken as an indication that its ideology is losing touch--or perhaps never was quite in touch--with the cultural reality of the country as a whole. While the young men in the cities try to curb its disastrous development with violence, the women in the village reject it quietly and try to hold on to the shreds of their traditions.

NOTES

1. AZ, "The Women's Struggle in Iran," Monthly Review 32 (no. 10, 1981): 22-30; Guity Nashat, "Women in the Islamic Republic of Iran," Iranian Studies 13 (Nos. 1-4, 1980): 165-94. Almost every issue of the Newsletter has a piece on the exalted position of Muslim women.
2. Clifford Geertz, Interpretation of Cultures

(New York: Basic Books, 1973) (see especially chapter 8. "Ideology as a Cultural System"); Mary Hegland, "Religious Ritual and Political Struggle in an Iranian Village," MERIP Reports, no. 102, January, 1982

3. See, for example, Newsletter (no. 38, November-December 1981).

4. These mainly take the form of public speeches blasted over the village through loudspeakers, sermons in mosques and, occasionally, at funerals, and daily radio and television broadcasts. Since the village was connected to an electrical power network in 1977, about 70 percent of all households have acquired television sets. Nearly all villagers are avid, if disenchanted, television watchers.

5. Although this situation produces mostly awkward or embarrassing encounters, it does have its funny moments. For instance, a male inspector of schools was refused entrance to the girls' grade school by the female principal, who brandished the inspector's own letter in his fact. The letter stated that men are not allowed in a girls' school under any circumstances.

6. For a variety of reasons there were no religiously oriented get-togethers for women in the village in the past, and there are none at present either. For religious gatherings in cities, see Anne Betteridge, "The Controversial Vows of Urban Muslim Women in Iran," in N.A. Falk and R.M. Gross, Unspoken Worlds (San Francisco: Harper and Row, 1980).

7. See also Jane I. Smith and Yvonne Y. Hadad, "Women in the Afterlife: The Islamic Tradition as Seen from Qur'an and Tradition," Journal of the American Academy of Religion 43 (no 1, 1975): 39-50.

8. See, for example, the chapter by Adele K. Ferdows and Amir H. Ferdows, "Women in Shi^{c}i Fiqh: Images Through the Hadith," in this volume; and Shireen Mahdavi, "Women and the Shi^{c}i Ulama in Iran," Paper prepared for the 15th Annual Meeting of the Middle East Studies Association, Seattle Washington, November 1981. Even the few women who do not complain usually argue only that Islam bettered the status of women in Muhammed's time. "It could be much worse," they say.

9. Even women in a large village close to an urban center had great difficulties in organizing participation in an already ongoing, sweeping protest movement, as Mary Hegland describes in "The Village Women of Aliabad and the Iranian Revolution," RIPEH 4 (no. 2, Fall 1980) and 5 (no. 1, Spring 1981): 47-57.

13
The Institution of Mut'a Marriage in Iran: A Formal and Historical Perspective

Shahla Haeri

My objective in this chapter is to describe a temporary type of marriage that is currently receiving much support from the present leaders of the Iranian regime. I will discuss how temporary marriage (mut^{c}a or sigheh), a culturally stigmatized institution with ambiguous boundaries of meaning and action, has been historically employed as a solution both to the problems generated by rules of segregation of sexes, as well as to those policies devised to integrate the sexes. I will also discuss how the present Iranian regime attempts to transform and sanction this form of marriage through education of the public.

Prior to the Revolution of 1979, although most people knew about mut^{c}a, however vaguely, those who contracted a mut^{c}a marriage often learned about it through a mullah, a friend, or a neighbor rather than through formal means. The Revolution of 1979 brought about a marked and socially significant change in the attitude of the state toward mut^{c}a. Whereas the Pahlavi regime had looked upon the institution of temporary marriage with disdain (although not openly discouraging its practice), the Islamic regime has taken a positive stand toward mut^{c}a, and is formally educating the public about the advantages of temporary marriage for the individual and society. The regime hails the idea of temporary marriage as symbolic of Islamic foresight and progressive views on sexuality. By educating the public and encouraging its practice, the regime has thrust the concept of mut^{c}a into the public arena, and into mass awareness, the consequences of which shall remain a test for further observation.

Religiously, mut^{c}a is a "contract" between a man and an unmarried woman in which both the duration of the union and the brideprice must be specified. Registration of the contract is optional; i.e., the agreement could be spelled out verbally by the temporary spouses. Similarly, no witnesses are required at the ceremony. From the beginning and throughout Islamic history, mut^{c}a has been a controversial issue and the subject of many heated debates and arguments between the members of different sects of Islam. At times it was discouraged; at other times permitted. Sometimes it functioned openly and without much restraint; at other times it was secret and discreet. Mutʿa has always had a controversial character due to its marginal and ambiguous status. Depending upon the policies and attitude of the ruling regime and its relationship with the religious community, the social acceptability (although not necessarily the legality) of mutʿa rose and fell, contributing to an increase or decrease in the number of mutʿa relationships. For example, the attitude of the Pahlavi regime toward mutʿa was one of disdain, and its policy was one of benign neglect. In contrast, the present Islamic regime has taken a positive stand on mutʿa by endorsing it publicly and encouraging its practice in the society.

Mutʿa is an Arabic term and, in the context of marriage, means that "a man agrees to give a woman something for a specified period in return for her sexual favors, with the understanding that there would be no marriage in the beginning nor a divorce at the end."[1] Theologians distinguish mutʿa from permanent marriage on the basis of the objective of sexual pleasure for the former and of procreation for the latter. All laws and regulations regarding mutʿa marriage are rooted in this distinction.

A mutʿa woman is religiously/legally referred to as a mustaʾjireh,[2] [the object of lease]; she is contracted for a fixed period, with a fixed payment, for the purpose of sexual pleasure,[3] underscoring the pleasure principle of mutʿa marriage. This dual transaction of sex and goods (often money) is the core of mutʿa marriage. Although such conditions are not unique to mutʿa, the significance of this institution lies in that, historically, it has been sanctioned, blessed, and encouraged by the Shiʿite religious hierarchy.

Contrary to what many Iranians, including some scholars, believe, mutʿa was not an Islamic innovation[4] devised for the welfare of the community of believers. Rather, mutʿa was an ancient pre-Islamic custom practiced by Arabian tribes.[5] According to Robertson Smith, mutʿa marriages were a medium for a "temporary alliance" between a man (often a stranger) seeking protection and the tribe which gave him refuge. This form of alliance was common at the time of the Prophet Muhammad.[6] The custom of mutʿa marriage was abolished in the mid-seventh century, A.D. by the Second Caliph, Umar, who condemned it as fornication. He assigned the harsh penalty of stoning for those who continued to practice it. Despite the Caliph's order and his policy of severe punishment, mutʿa marriage continued to persist among the Shiʿi Muslims, becoming shrouded in mystery and secrecy.[7]

In its original pre-Islamic form, the woman resided
with her own tribe; her kin maintained any rights they
had over her; and she continued to enjoy their support
and protection. The wife could dismiss her husband at
her pleasure, and any children born of mut^{c}a unions
belonged to the wife's lineage rather than to the husband's.[8] In its present Shi^{c}i form, however, mut^{c}a
marriage is entrenched in the Islamic ideology of patriarchy, and based upon the Islamic maxim of al-walad-u
lil-firash [the child is of the bed]; any child born of
one of these marriages is considered the father's legitimate descendant, with full legal rights--at least in
theory. Based on this similarity between permanent marriage and mut^{c}a, the Shi^{c}ites classify mut^{c}a as a form
of marriage. Despite these structural changes, the function of mut^{c}a marriage has remained basically unaltered:
a legal/religious and cultural alternative to permanent
marriage for sexual gratification.

Historically, mut^{c}a marriage was often associated
with long-distance trade and even more often with pilgrimages. Primarily an urban phenemon, it occurred most
frequently around the shrines of religious figures.[9]
Mut^{c}a is a contract requiring an act of offer, made
by the woman and an acceptance, made by the man. It must
include a precise statement, either verbal or written, of
the period of the union and the consideration or payment
(sometimes translated and interpreted as brideprice).
The length of a mut^{c}a marriage may vary from a few hours,
days, or months, to years. The contract differs significantly from permanent marriage in that mut^{c}a is a personal contract founded upon consent between a man and a
woman without intervention on the part of the woman's
family. Witnesses are not necessary nor is it necessary
to conclude the marriage before a notary public. According to Shi^{c}i doctrine, mut^{c}a is a type of marriage which
"nobody needs to know anything about."[10] Tusi, the great
Shi^{c}i theologian and religious scholar specifies that
"at no time taking witnesses of making it [mut^{c}a] public
are conditions of mut^{c}a, unless the man fears accusations
of fornication, in which case taking two witnesses is
recommended." At the end of the specified period the
partners separate without any divorce procedures.[11]

According to the Qur'an, a man is permitted up to
four permanent wives simultaneously, provided that he is
financially capable of supporting them and that he can
treat them fairly and justly. A Shi^{c}ite man is legally
permitted and religiously encouraged[12] to contract as
many mut^{c}a unions as he desires, simultaneously or seri-
ally. No restriction of any sort is placed on the man;
no Qur'anic moral appeal is made to his sense of "just-
ness and fairness." All is left to his descretion. The
conditions are radically different for women. Married
women are totally excluded from contracting a mut^{c}a

marriage. Unmarried women (never married,[13] widowed, or divorced) are permitted to select one temporary husband at a time; after the dissolution of each temporary marriage, no matter how short its duration, women must keep idda, a waiting period of two menstrual cycles, or 45 days. The reason for keeping idda is the determination of a possible pregnancy in order to prevent confusion of parentage. After menopause, mut^{c}a women need not keep idda since they cannot bear children. These women are permitted to marry temporarily as frequently as they wish. Interestingly, the idda of divorce is not two, but three months or three menstrual cycles. Explanations for this difference vary, but a very likely one is that if the divorce is of a revocable type the three months period is stipulated for the divorcee in case the husband changes his mind and decides to return to her. In the case of a temporary marriage, there is no right of return for the husband. A mut^{c}a wife is the object of lease, and so "Should be freed to go on after her own business."[14]

The unique thing about mut^{c}a is that it is not simply a form of concubinage or prostitution, despite striking resemblances. The problem is more complex than mere similarities might suggest. The basic difference between mut^{c}a and prostitution is that children born in mut^{c}a unions are their father's legitimate heirs and have equal status, theoretically, with children of permanent marriage before the law. A more important distinction, however, between mut^{c}a and prostitution is a religious and conceptual one: prostitution, in religious thinking, represents disorder, disobedience to the established rules, corruption, and indulgence in sinful and unlawful sexual activities. It is fornication, which is explicitly condemned in the Qur'an. It is viewed as detrimental to the society's general health and welfare, and goes against its stated ethics and ethos. While performing a similar function, mut^{c}a symbolizes social control and harmony with the social order. Although serving to gratify sexual needs, it is presumably not an anti-social behavior. Rather, participants are following a divinely-recommended way to gratify these needs. Significantly, not only is mut^{c}a not considered immoral, it is perceived to combat corruption and immorality.

At the cultural level, however, all is not that neatly clear between mut^{c}a and prostitution; in the spectrum from permissible to forbidden sexuality in Iran, cultural perceptions of mut^{c}a fluctuate widely between the two poles of permanent marriage and prostitution. Although religiously sanctioned and legally legitimized, mut^{c}a relationships--at least until the Revolution of 1979--never gained a general cultural approval. Outside of relgious circles, mut^{c}a had a somewhat stigmatized, ambiguous, and marginal status.

The two most fundamental and inalienable rights of the spouse in a permanent marriage are the wife's right to proper daily maintenance, which includes proper clothing and housing, and the husband's right to sexual pleasure. In return for the husband's unlimited right to sexual pleasure, the woman is entitled to the right of intercourse; that is, every four months her husband is obligated to have intercourse with her.[15] Of course, it is recommended that a husband go to his wife every fourth night; however, he is not obligated to intimacy with her unless he wishes.[16] In fact, women are advised to refrain from "hanging onto" their husbands, demanding intimacy.[17] The message conveyed here is that intercourse is not a matter in which pleasure is reciprocated in kind, but that is is transferred in one direction only; in exchange for sexual pleasure received by men, women ought to be compensated economically.[18]

In the same spirit the rights and obligations of the temporary spouses are stipulated. An exchange of capital and sexual favors is also the basic principle of mut^{c}a marriage. The distinction is that the "consideration" (fixed payment) is the only kind of payment a mut^{c}a wife receives. This is why specification of the consideration is essential in this type of marriage. Failure to specify the consideration in a contract of mut^{c}a marriage makes it void. Besides her consideration, a mut^{c}a wife is not legally entitled to daily expenses unless they are decided upon beforehand. Nor is she entitled to the right of intercourse.[19] She is the object of lease and is at her husband's service. He can decide whether or not to have intercourse with her. But, based upon the same principle, the woman's right to her consideration is not curtailed should he decide not to become intimate with her when the condition for nonsexual coexistence (discussed below) has not been agreed upon beforehand. The temporary wife should receive her consideration, regardless. "It is as if someone rents a house but chooses not to go there; he still has to pay."[20] But if he dismisses her without consummation before the expiration of the mut^{c}a contract, the woman is entitled to only half of her consideration, at least in the opinion of many of the ulama.

For her part, the mut^{c}a wife is not required to be as obedient to her husband as a permanent wife. Her activities are less restricted, and she need not secure permission for what she does. Ironically, in exchange for the privileges--for the most part financial--accorded a wife in a permanent marriage, a mut^{c}a wife seems to be compensated with a greater degree of individual freedom and autonomy--at least in theory. She may exercise her will, however, only as long as it does not interfere with the husband's right to sexual pleasure. In that case,

she must obey him; otherwise she has committed a sin.[21]
Arguing this point, Katuzian writes,

> In a mut^c a marriage the man agrees to pay the
> brideprice, and the woman is obliged to perform
> her wifely duties. Sexual intercourse, from
> the viewpoint of Iranian/Shi^c i law, is the man's
> right only, and the woman must obey him. So
> that is why only the husband has the right to
> dismiss his wife.[22]

Such a masculine perspective is at the core of Shi^c i
legal principles and concepts, particularly in the areas
of family and marriage.

Although temporary marriage existed at the time of
the Prophet, the rules and regulations pertaining to
mut^c a marriage developed piecemeal and at a much later
date. Its present procedures are the outcome of frequent
dialogues and debates between the Sunni and Shi^c i ulama.

A condition unique to mut^c a marriage is the possibility of agreement for nonsexual coexistence; the
temporary spouses may agree to enjoy each other's company
in many other ways without having sexual intercourse.[23]
In a case where sexual intimacy has not taken place, the
woman is not bound to keep idda (the waiting period)
upon the dissolution of the mut^c a marriage; she can
immediately contract another mut^c a marriage with another
man.

Another condition unique to mut^c a marriage is that
the man stipulates the specific time of day he wishes to
visit his mut^c a wife. It can be day or night, and the
agreement can include the number of times intercourse
will take place. If the partners decide only on the
number of times they will have intercourse without
specifying the time within which they will visit, then
the agreement is invalid and the mut^c a marriage is void.[24]

Unlike permanent marriage, "A mature girl, whether
a virgin or not, has the authority to give herself in a
mut^c a marriage, and her guardian does not have the right
to prevent her."[25] Maturity for girls is considered to
be age nine or ten.[26] Some of the ulama have recommended getting a father's permission for a mut^c a marriage
with a virgin, but all agree that mut^c a is not forbidden
if a guardian's permission is not secured.

In a permanent marriage, only the husband has the
right to divorce, and there are several types of repudiation of a wife in Islam. This one-sided exclusive right
to terminate a mut^c a marriage also belongs to the man,
provided that he has paid her the agreed-upon consideration. The woman has no right to alimony, but he does
not have the right of return as in a permanent marriage.
The mut^c a wife cannot legally dismiss her temporary
husband; should she decide to leave him or to refuse to
be intimate with him without the condition for a non-

sexual relationship, she must compensate him. The amount
of her consideration is computed on the basis of the time
she has spent with him minus the time she has taken away
from him.

A mut^{c}a marriage contract is renewable. If the
partners wish to renew, they first must take care of the
existing contract; just before the expiration of the
ongoing contract, the husband should make a gift of the
remaining time, however short, and release the wife from
her obligations. They then must agree on a new contract;
it can be either for another temporary marriage or for
a permanent one. In this special case the woman is not
bound to keep idda, since the marriage has been renewed
at once with the same person.[27]

Mut^{c}a has been one of the most controversial issues
in Islamic Shari^{c}a. Its status underwent many changes
during the time of the Prophet. According to one scholar
mut^{c}a was permissible in the beginning of Islam; it was
forbidden after the Khaybar war (628), permitted again
during the Awtas war (629), and prohibited once again
after that. Seven times mut^{c}a was permitted and then
forbidden--or vice versa.[28] While uncertainty surrounds
the Prophet's own actions and attitude, there is no
ambiguity about the fact that Umar, the Second Caliph,
did ban mut^{c}a in the seventh century and warned trans-
gressors that they would be punished by stoning.

The Sunnis, following the Caliph Umar's commandment
while looking to the time of the Prophet for justification, held that the Prophet's change of heart and mind
were necessitated by the perils of an ongoing war and
its impact on his soldiers long separated from their
wives.[29] The Shi^{c}i ulama, however, have maintained that
Muhammad never outlawed mut^{c}a.[30] In their view, the
Prophet sanctioned it as a form of marriage; they considered the Sunni reasoning tantamount to blasphemy on
the grounds that they attribute permission for fornication (explicitly forbidden in the Qur'an) to the Prophet,
as well as lack of a sound moral judgement and inconsistency of behavior on the Prophet's part.[31]

The Shi^{c}i ulama have been divided as to exactly
how to define mut^{c}a and how to interpret it in particular socio-historical contexts: Is it permanent marriage?
Is it concubinage? Is it something in between for the
sake of sexual pleasure? How is it to be distinguished
from prostitution? From slave marriage? Each kind of
relationship has its own set of rights and obligations.
As an illustration of the ambiguity of mut^{c}a marriage,
an early source, Imar al-Sharid, says,

> I asked Ibn al-Abbas [d. 689] whether mut^{c}a is
> fornication or marriage? Ibn al-Abbas said,
> "It is neither fornication nor marriage." I
> asked then what is it? He said, "It is mut^{c}a

that God has named it so in the Qur'an." I said,
"Do men and women inherit from one another?" He
said, "No."[32]

The confusion over the definition and status of mut^{c}a of
women has persisted ever since. The Sunnis maintained
that mut^{c}a, though a current custom at the time of the
Prophet, is not marriage by virtue of Umar's interpretation of the Prophet's intention but that its permission
at one point in history was due to unusual conditions of
hardship for individuals and society, i.e., long separa-
tions due to war. Mut^{c}a was then permitted to prevent
chaos and social disorder by soothing individual discom-
fort. The Shi^{c}i ulama do not dispute the fact that the
Prophet might have indeed recommended mut^{c}a to his
soldiers, but they take issue with the Sunni position
that it was meant to be only a temporary phenomenon. The
Shi^{c}i ulama turned their attention to some higher authorities who would lend virtue to their claim of the legitimacy of mut^{c}a: the Qur'an and the Tradition of the
Prophet. Rejecting Umar's ban on mut^{c}a, the Shi^{c}ites
resort to the proverbial statement, "That which has been
halal [permitted] by Muhammad is halal until the Day of
Resurrection, and that which has been haram [forbidden]
is haram until the day of Ressurrection."[33] They did not
feel they needed to justify this Divine sanction. It was
there to take care of male sexuality. This is the
attitude that is reflected in the earlier works of the
ulama.

However, in the twentieth century an increasing
number of those with modern education began to criticize
religious practices and leadership. One practice particularly attacked by modernist men and women was mut^{c}a. To
many women it represented the most flagrant exploitation
of young and poor women. In response to these attacks
the ulama gradually developed arguments in defence of
mut^{c}a. Since the practice could not be banned--it had
occupied too central a position in past controversies between Shi^{c}is and Sunnis--the only solution was to advance
convincing modern arguments in its defense. The undefin-
ed status of mut^{c}a provided the ulama with a way out of
the impasse.

The Shi^{c}i ulama argue that a part of the maintenance
of social order and prevention of anarchy and chaos is
recognition of the urgency of sexual drives and the
necessity of finding morally acceptable means of channel-
ing them.[34] But even here the Shi^{c}i ulama are not unani-
mous; some believe that mut^{c}a of women should be resorted
to only in times of necessity, i.e., long separation due
to trade or pilgrimage,[35] whereas others stress biological urges regardless of social conditions.[36] Still more
recently, some of the ulama emphasize the dual advantages
of mut^{c}a in the development of individuals on one hand
and in the gratification of sexual needs on the other.[37]

It is interesting to note that when explanations
and/or justifications for mut^{c}a marriage are given, they
are projected back into the time of the Prophet, making
mut^{c}a appear to be one of his Traditions and thus
legitimate and blessed.[38] The modern arguments follow
these justifications with radically different interpretations of mut^{c}a. Whereas in the past the ulama were under
no illusion about the implications of mut^{c}a marriage nor
of the nature of mut^{c}a relationships between the sexes,
leading contemporary ulama have tried to change the
traditional conceptualization of mut^{c}a and insist upon
depicting it as marriage only. They discourage the use
of the term mut^{c}a (sexual pleasure), and of terming the
women engaging in mut^{c}a as the objects of lease or hire.

An editorial critical of mut^{c}a in an Iranian
women's journal in 1974 asserting that mut^{c}a was a form
of hire and demeaning to women prompted this response
from Ayatullah Mutahhari:

What does it [mut^{c}a] have to do with hire and a
fee? Is the time limit in this marriage the
cause of its being excluded from definition of
marriage and acquiring for itself a form in
which "fee" and "hire" are appropriate terms?
And is it only because it is explicitly ordained
that the mahr [dower] must be "fixed" and
"definite" that this mahr is being depicted
as the rental charge? We ask whether, if
there were no dower and the man did not place
anything before the woman, she would then
regain her human dignity?"[40]

In the same spirit, Nasir Makarim-Shirazi charges:

Is not temporary marriage a "reciprocal
marriage contract," but for a specified
period, and with the observance of all the
other conditions? Does this reciprocal contract differ legally from any other agree-
ments and contracts?[41]

Mutahhari further argues in his response to the
editorial in the women's journal that it is not the
mut^{c}a woman but the Western woman (he apparently assumes
that the editorial had a Western bias) who is humiliated
and objectified because of her indiscriminate association with men.[42] He points out that temporary marriage
provides a woman with a moral way of providing for herself and possibly for her children.

Ayatullah Mutahhari is responsible for the current
regime's recent official policy and attitude toward
mut^{c}a. The present Islamic regime has mounted an intensive campaign of revitalization of insitution of
temporary marriage--the term "mut^{c}a" is never used--and
has attempted to reintroduce it to society from a com-

pletely new perspective. Inexpensive, readily available articles and books in its favor have appeared on the market. The regime is attempting to purify the institution of some of its negative cultural connotations by representing mutᶜa (or as it is now called, temporary marriage) as one of the most progressive and farsighted aspects of Islamic thought.[43]

In order to introduce temporary marriage to a much wider cross-section of society, it is the subject of a detailed article in the Religious Education textbook.[44] Intended for use by adolescent students from the tenth grade up, the text sets forth a number of reasons for the necessity of temporary marriage: youth have urgent sexual needs; sexuality is one of the most important motivating drives in human beings; permanent marriage is costly and includes all kinds of obligations and responsibilities; young people are at an age when they cannot afford permanent marriage, but they should not be burdened with a long sexual moratorium until they can afford it. So it is recommended that young people contract a mutᶜa marriage while they continue their educations rather than abandon education for marriage. The article makes one further suggestion:

> A man and a woman can in this type of marriage agree that their sexual pleasure be limited. For example, they can agree to refrain from sexual intercourse, and the man has to honor the agreement. Therefore, such marriages where non-intercourse is agreed upon can be interesting for the engagement period. In fact, it can be a trial marriage and a way for the would-be partners to get to know each other without any feelings of sin or guilt.[45]

Under the current regime, mutᶜa has gone through a conceptual metamorphosis, emerged with an almost completely new meaning, and is addressed to a completely different audience. The concept of trial marriage for the period of engagement--a concept unfamiliar to Iranian Muslims--is in fact ideologically congruent with the cultural requisite for virginity; it does resolve, theoretically, the cultural conflict over virginity by allowing for some degree of intimacy without the loss of virginity.[46] Here is the crux of the matter. While the Islamic position on sexuality is celebrated as being positive, self-affirming, and cognizant of human needs, it is at the same time viewed as disruptive and disturbing to the social order if not controlled and regulated.

Elaborate etiquettes and customs in conjunction with formal laws have developed to ensure separate spheres of male and female control and influence. Symbols of segregation are evident everywhere in Iran: high walls that separate family units from each other and

from the larger society; veils that separate men from
women, curtains that determine the place of men and
women in public and private domains, and certainly not
least, psychological barriers. The institution of
temporary marriage is not an aberration in Iranian society where segregation of the sexes is the law of the
land. Sexual segregation and temporary marriage are not
contradictory to each other but are in fact complemen-
tary aspects of the ideology that celebrates sexuality
but permits it only within certain religious boundaries.
Bahunar spoke for the Islamic regime in Iran when he
said,

> Unlike those who believe that recommending
> temporary marriage contributes to free and
> unlimited relationships and the prevalence
> of prostitution, this plan [the recommenda-
> tion of mut^{c}a] would be an effective means
> of preventing the spread of prostitution and
> family instability, . . . and those who
> verbally criticize this type of marriage,
> in practice do the same thing themselves,
> but in different ways.^{47}

Makarim-Shirazi answers objections raised to the institution of mut^{c}a by asserting that manipulation of the
law, which he agrees is occurring, should not be confused
with the intention of the law.^{48}
    The Islamic regime's official policy and positive
attitude toward mut^{c}a is compatible with the Shi^{c}i doctrinal perspective on segregation of the sexes and the
nature and extent of male/female relationships. In
essence, the message conveyed here is two fold. On the
one hand, sexuality--primarily male sexuality--is
religiously favored and recommended; on the other hand
people will be punished if they step out of the religiously prescribed boundaries. Repeatedly one reads (or
hears from clergy and laymen alike) that Islam is an
easy religion, divinely prescribed to solve human problems and to take care of human needs. It is to make
life easy for people. Mut^{c}a is frequently mentioned as
a case in point. It is easily accessible and divinely
blessed. That is to say, despite (or perhaps because of)
all the walls, veils, and barriers--cultural and psycho-
logical--a man and a woman can conceivably come together
in a temporary marriage by simply uttering the mut^{c}a
formula in any language they know.

APPENDIX

    Men and women agree to a mut^{c}a marriage for a
variety of reasons. The two most commonly articulated
by the religiously learned and echoed by laymen is that
men contract such a marriage motivated by sexual desire,
whereas women do it for financial motivations. Although
there is some truth to such popularly-held beliefs, the

financial motive for women is not as pervasive as one
might think. Brief studies of several differnt women
indicate that they have other reasons to enter mut^ca
marriages as well.

Mahvash

Mahvash, 44 years old (in 1978), was the eldest of
six children. At age 13 she was married in order to
relieve her family of some of its financial burdens. However, the marriage was not successful; her husband
divorced her and forbade her to see her children. She
moved to Iraq and subsequently married an elderly Iraqi
whom she claims was impotent. She left him and returned
to Iran--to Qum, which has long had a reputation as a
mut^ca city. She uses the shrine of Ma^csumeh as a residence, not having a room of her own, and earns her living
by reading the Qur'an for women for a fee.

Her reason for contracting mut^ca marriages is sexual
satisfaction. Her great complaint is that keeping idda
is unfair to women--that after even the briefest mut^ca
marriage a two month waiting period is commanded before
another such relationship can begin. It is her claim
that she receives many invitations to mut^ca; she accepts
only those from men to whom she is physically attracted.
Her attitude toward mut^ca is very positive; quoting
the Shi^ci authorities to me, she went to some length to
describe the spiritual reward of temporary marriage.

Ma^csumeh

Ma^csumeh is a friend of Mahvash, but lacks Mahvash's
positive attitude. Rather she seems disoriented and
bears a grudge against some unknown enemies. Like
Mahvash, she was married off when she was very young to
a man much older than she. He was hot-tempered and beat
her for no reason. He threw her out suddenly, using as
an excuse that she had been seen laughing with the
shish-kabob seller at the local store. He refused to
listen to her side of the story or to give her another
chance. She has never again seen her three children.

The shish-kabob seller apparently was interested in
her; he offered her a mut^ca marriage for three months.
Although she did not know exactly what mut^ca entailed,
she accepted his offer because she could not go home.
Her father was ashamed of her and refused to take her in.
During the three month period, she conceived; terrified
of her father's reaction, she fled to Tehran without
telling anyone of her situation. She is now in Qum with
her six-year-old daughter--the child's father, the shish-
kabob seller, has denied her.

Fati

Fati is in her late thirties. She seems to have a
good knowledge about mut^ca rules and regulations, and she

fancies herself a matchmaker. She talked about the
great spiritual reward of mut^{c}a and about how she has
frequently prevented a sinful act by instructing the
couple to contract a mut^{c}a marriage. She has even written a pamphlet about the procedures of mut^{c}a marriage
which she distributes.

Fati was only three years old when her father,
a mullah [a religious preacher], divorced her mother,
retaining Fati's custody. Her subsequent life with a
step-mother was unhappy, and she was married at the age
of nine. Five years later she was divorced from her ill
husband. Her second marriage was to a rich 80-year-old
man; it lasted only two months. She claims that there
was no sexual contact between them; rather he expected
her to bring tea and sweets for his frequent guests and
to prepare his opium paraphenalia.

By the time of her third marriage, Fati had a good
idea of what she wanted from a relationship. She
approached a widower, 30 years her senior, and suggested
to him that they enter into a mut^{c}a marriage for 24 hours
to see if they were compatible temperamentally. They
agreed on a non-sexual mut^{c}a. She did not feel that
they were compatible, but faced with the man's eagerness
she suggested renewing the contract for 40 days, again
with the condition of a nonsexual relationship. She
moved into his house; after the 40 day period they again
renewed the contract. Finally he suggested permanent
marriage to her. She accepted and received a large
brideprice. However, she claims that she has often
begged her husband to divorce her and go back to the
mut^{c}a arrangement; she prefers that because she does not
like to be tied down.

Tuba

Tuba is in her late twenties. Her first marriage,
at age 16, ended in divorce after six months because of
her husband's deviant sexual preferences. She has had
two temporary marriages which ended in separation. There
were two children from the second temporary marriage, but
one of them drowned in the little pool at her parents'
house. She works (in 1981) as a low-ranking employee in
one of the offices affiliated with the Public Health
Department in Kashan, where she lives. She pays her
mother to take care of her six-year-old son; the mother
constantly scolds Tuba for her mut^{c}a marriage.

She met her first temporary husband in a bank where
he was working and fell in love with him. He pursued her
and expressed his love for her. After a few months he
asked Tuba to become his mut^{c}a wife. He told her that
he would divorce his wife but that he didn't want them
to have to wait until the divorce was finalized. He
also told her that she was his mut^{c}a for life. Tuba
herself didn't know anything about mut^{c}a beyond the fact

that it existed; her family didn't know much more than
that.

The temporary husband promised Tuba money and gave
her a promissory note which he later stole from her.
Fearing that his permanent wife, in Tehran, would discover his mut^c a marriage, he discouraged Tuba from
becoming pregnant. Indeed, Tuba feels that possibly the
reason he stopped liking her was that she became pregnant.
She says that he did not give her any brideprice, nor did
he give her money daily. He did not provide her with a
place of their own, but rather came to visit her now and
then at her parents' house.

Tuba now believes that she was deceived into a mut^c a
marriage, led to believe that it was for life and that
it would last forever. She accepted the mut^c a because
she was in love with him. He deserted her after three
years, and her court actions against him proved futile.
He had removed any documents that could be used against
him. Her only benefit from the court proceedings was
that it was ruled that she had waited long enough and
did not have to keep idda before she could remarry.

Mahin

In her early thirties, Mahin is the administrator of
a small clinic in East Tehran. Well dressed and having
the appearance of a successful career woman, she does
not always follow the current regime's requirement that
all women wear a scarf or veil outside the home. Her
appearance contradicts any stereotyping of a mut^c a woman.

Mahin met her mut^c a husband on a cold winter morning
in 1980 as she was going to work. He offered her a ride,
and she accepted. Attracted to each other they began to
go together. He was honest about being married and the
father of two small children. Mahin was divorced and the
mother of a small boy in her ex-husband's custody.
After a week they flew to Mashhad for a day to solemnize
their love for each other at the shrine. Early in the
summer they spent a month's vacation together in Europe.
However, there was no formal relationship between them
at that time.

After their trip, he suggested that she become his
mut^c a wife for six months. There were executions of
alleged adulterers each day, and neither of them wanted
trouble, so Mahin decided to enter into the relationship
although she thought the idea of mut^c a was "stupid."
He rented an apartment for her near his jewelry store and
arranged to meet her there. He picked her up each morning from her parents' home, took her to the apartment,
and then went on to work. She was no longer working, so
she would cook their lunch and wait there for him. They
normally had lunch and then spent the early afternoon
together before he returned to his shop. When he left
work, he picked her up, returned her to her parents house,
and went home to his wife and children.

Mahin found their life together pleasant. He was very generous, giving her much more money than they had agreed on, as well as jewelry and other gifts. However, two events disrupted the pleasure of their relationship. Despite his attempts to deceive her and to keep his mut^c a marriage a secret from his permanent wife, she found out and began to make his life miserable. To add to his woes, Mahin became pregnant. Her temporary husband prevailed upon her to get an abortion despite her desire to have the child on the grounds that his wife had just had a third child and that he had no peace at home. If Mahin had a child too, his argument went, he would also have no peace at their apartment. Furthermore, he said he could not afford to maintain two entire households. Mahin agreed to the abortion only if he would agree to marry her permanently. Not only did he not fulfill that promise, but he began to see less and less of her.

Mahin finally gave up their apartment, into which she had moved full time. She returned to her parents' house, living once again with her mother, her opium-addicted father, her brother and his wife, and her two younger brothers. She was disillusioned by the relationship and its outcome. Although she felt that his first (permanent) wife's rights had been abrogated by the mut^c a marriage, she also felt that she had been taken advantage of. She does not blame herself for what happened, but feels that her temporary husband ruined the lives of his three children as well as hers, his, and his wife's.

Despite the fact that all of these women had financial arrangements with their temporary husbands, as required by law, financial gain did not seem to be the primary motive in any of their mut^c a marriages. Mahvash seemed mainly motivated by sexual desires; Mahin and Tuba loved their temporary husbands and thought they were entering into long-term relationships. Fati preferred mut^c a to permanent marriage because of the greater degree of freedom it gave her. Ma^c sumeh needed someone to take care of her, but her need was at least as much emotional as pecuniary; furthermore, her emotional state after her break with her permanent husband has been such that nothing makes very much difference to her. Most mut^c a marriages are not economically advantageous, anyway, especially since women have to observe idda for 45 days after the relationship ends.

NOTES

The study resulting in this chapter was made under a fellowship granted by the Social Science Research Council and the American Council of Learned Societies. The conclusion, opinion, and other statements in this chapter are those of the author, and not those of the Councils.

246

1. From Muhīt ul-Muhīt, cited in Sachiko Murata,
"Izdivāj-i Muvaqqat va Āsār-i Itjtimā^cī-yi Ān" ["Temporary
Marriage and Its Social Effects"], M.A. thesis, Divinity
College, Tehran, 1357/1947, p. 37; M. Shafāhī, Mut^ca va
Āsār-i Huqūqī va Ijtimā^cī-yi Ān [Mut^ca and Its Legal and
Social Effects] (Tehran: Haidari Publishing, 1352/1973),
pp. 13-15. All translations from Persian into English
are mine, unless otherwise specified. Further, I shall
use the term mut^ca as both a noun and a verb, as the
Shi^cī ulama have done so in their texts.
2. It is interesting to note here that Shaikh M. H.
Tūsī (d. 1081 A.D.) refers to a mut^ca woman as a parastār
[nurse or attendant].
3. N. Kātuziān, Huqūq-i Madanī-yi Khānivādeh [Fam-
ily Civil Law] (Tehran: Tehran University Press, 1357/
1979), pp. 13-15; Murata, "Izdivāj," pp. 40, 47; Shafāhī,
Mut^ca, p. 15.
4. H. Haqqānī-Zanjānī, "Izdivāj-i Muvaqqat az Fahshā
Jilougīrī Mīkunad" ["Temporary Marriage Prevents Prostitution"] in N. Makarim-Shīrāzī, ed., Maktab-i Islām [Ideol-
ogy of Islam] (Qum: No. 9, 1348/1969), p. 31-33. He
writes that "in the beginning of Islam when decadence and
promiscuity were rampant" the Prophet would remind people
that Islam has permitted mut^ca and that they should use
this "healthy method" rather than unlawful means. See
also, S. H. Yūsifī-Makkī, Mut^ca dar Islām [Mut^ca in
Islam] (Tehran: 1342/1963), pp. 10, 12.
5. W. Robertson Smith, Kinship and Marriage in
Early Arabia (Boston: Beacon Press, 1903)., p. 35.
H.A.R. Gibb, et al., "Mut^ca," Shorter Encyclopaedia of
Islam (Leiden: E. J. Brill, 1953), p. 418.
6. Robertson Smith, Kinship, p. 82; Gibb, "Mut^ca,"
p. 418.
7. Apparently the custom has not completely died
out in Sunnī countries either; see M. T. Hughes, et al.,
"Mut^ca," The Encyclopaedia of Islam, v. III (Leiden:
E.J. Brill, 1936), p. 775.
8. Robertson Smith, Kinship, p. 85.
9. Gibb, "Mut^ca," p. 420.
10. Robertson Smith, Kinship, p. 84; M.A. Qazvīnī,
Sīyagh-i Uqūd [Forms of Contracts] (Tehran: n.d.).
11. Shaikh Muhammad ibn Hasan Tusī, al-Nahaya, Tr.
by M. Y. Danish-Pazhūh from Arabic to Persian (Tehran:
University of Tehran Press, 1343/1964), p. 498.
12. Mut^ca, it is often said, should be contracted
for its savāb [spiritual reward]. Stories about its
savab abound. Qazvīnī relates the following saying to
the Imam Sādiq, ". . . and God creates seventy angels
from each drop of ablution water of a man practicing
mut^ca in order to intercede on his behalf on the Resurrection Day [i.e., unless under extreme conditions,
ablution must be performed after sexual contact]. God
curses those who refrain from practicing mut^ca" (Qazvīnī,

Siyagh, pp. 59-60). In another saying also attributed to
the Imam Sādiq, Qazvīnī writes, "God has forbidden
alcoholic beverages for Shi^cites, but has instead recommended mut^ca" (Qazvīnī, Siyagh, p. 61).

13. Whether or not a virgin can be involved in a
mut^ca relationship or whether it is permitted for men to
mut^ca adolescent virgins has been a point of contention
among the ulama. Shaikh Tūsī states that "If a virgin
is mature--nine or ten years--then her father's permission is not necessary" (Tūsī, al-Nahāya, p. 499). But
in the following line he suggests that it is better to
acquire a father's permission when one wants to contact
a mut^ca marriage with a virgin. Shafāhī, noting the
controversy, attributes the following saying to the Imam
Sadiq, "Aba Abdullāh told the Imam, 'This virgin, unbe-
knownst to her parents has invited me to go to her and
expressed interest in a mut^ca marriage. Is it all right
for me to mut^ca this girl? The Imam said, 'Yes it is,
but refrain from having intercourse with her, because
mut^ca is shameful for virgins.' I asked, 'What if she
was willing herself?' Imam said, 'If she was willing then
it is not forbidden'" (Shafāhī, Mut^ca, p. 182).

14. Shafāhī, Mut^ca, p. 218; also, Kātūzīan, Huqūq-i
Madanī, p. 465.

15. M.B. Majlisī, Hulyat ul-Muttaqīn [Ornaments of
the Pious] (Tehran: Qa'im Publishing Co., n.d.), p. 70.

16. Tūsī, al-Nahāya, p. 490; A.J. Muhaqqiq-i Hillī,
Mukhtasar-i Nāfī^c [Useful Summary], Tr. by E. Yārshāter
and M.T. Dānish-Pazhūh (Tehran: University of Tehran
Press, 1343/1964), p. 437; Ayatullah R. Khomeini, Towzīh
ul-Masā'il [Explanations of Problems] (Tehran: n.d.), pr.
2418; Ayatullah S.A. Khu'ī, Towzīh ul-Masā'il [Explana-
tion of Problems] (Tehran: n.d.), problem 2418; Majlisī,
Hulyat, p. 82. The waiting period for a wife after the
husband's death is also four months.

17. Z. Qurbānī, "Huqūq-i Zan va Showhar beh yik Dīgar
["The Rights and Obligations of Wife and Husband"], in
Maktab-i Islām (no. 7, 1344/1965): 47-51; Khomeini,
Towzīh ul Masā'il, problem 2412; Khu'ī, Towzih ul-Masā'il,
problem 2412.

18. An often emphasized right of Muslim women is
their refusal of matrimonial intimacy in exchange for
their brideprice: at the start of the conjugal union,
the wife is legally permitted to demand her brideprice in
exchange for her consent. Should she, however, conform
to her husband's wishes before receiving her brideprice,
she cannot ever refuse him unless she has physiological
excuses (Tūsī, al-Nahāya, p. 483; Khomeini, Towzih ul-
Masā'il, problem 2420. Her right to her brideprice, however, is not curtailed.

It can be noted here that the overwhelming majority
of writers dealing with the role and status of Iranian
Muslim women have been men. In Mashhad I did not find

248

any books on the subject by women among all the books of
the Astāni-i-Quds Library on the card catalogue. One of
the few exceptions is Qudssiyeh Hijāzī, a lawyer, who has
written on women's legal status in marriage and family.
But she also argues and emphasizes the traditional aspects
of the law. In her view the exchange of capital and
sexual pleasure are among the fundamental rights of husband and wife. She writes, "A man's right is his right
to tamattu^C [sexual pleasure], and a women's is her right
to nafaqeh." See Q. Hijāzī, Izdivāj dar Islām [Marriage
in Islam] (Tehran: Haidari Co., 1345/1966).

    19. Muhaqqiq-Hillī, Muktasar, p. 525; Majlisī,
Hulyat, p. 82; Murata, "Izdivaj," p. 57; Shafāhī, Mut^{C}a,
p. 232. The ulama unanimously agree that a mut^{C}a wife
does not have the right of intercourse, but husbands are
instructed not to refrain from intimacy with their wives
beyond a four month period, be they permanent or temporary
marriages. Ayatullahs Khomeinī and Khu'ī acknowledge the
lack of a mut^{C}a wife's right to the every-fourth-night
[hamkhābigī] (problem 2425), but recommend that, "A husband should not refrain from intimacy with his mut^{C}a wife
beyond a four month period" (problem 2422). The mut^{C}a
wife, unlike the permanent wife, cannot demand vaty
[intercourse] as a right.
    20. Murata, "Izdivaj," p. 47.
    21. Ayatullah Khomeinī, Towzih ul-Masā'il, problem
2427; Ayatullah Khu'ī, Towzih ul-Masā'il, problem 2427.
    22. Kātūziān, Huqūq-i Madanī, p. 443.
    23. Tūsī, al-Nahāya, p. 502; Murata, "Izdivāj,", p.
54; M. J. Bāhunar and A. Gulzādeh-Ghafūrī, eds.,
Ta^{C}līmāt-i Dīnī [Religious Education] (Tehran: Ministry
of Education, 1360/1981), p. 40; Ayatullah Khomeinī,
Towzih ul-Masā'il, problem 2421; Ayatullah Khu'ī, Towzih
ul-Masā'il, problem 2421. The condition for non-sexual
relations in mut^{C}a marriage does not negate the basic
pleasure principle of this form of marriage. It perhaps
assumes a broader base for pleasure. It also provides
individuals with some options.
    24. A.J. Muhaqqiq-i Hellī, Sharāyi^C ul-Islam [Islamic
Law], Tr. by A. Ahmad-i Yazdī and M.T. Danish Pazhuh from
Arabic into Persian (Tehran: University of Tehran Press,
1347/1968), p. 524.
    25. Muhaqqiq-i Hellī, Sharāyi^C, p. 523.
    26. Tūsī, al-Nahāya, p. 499.
    27. Murata, "Izdivaj," p. 64; Shafāhī, Mut^{C}a, p.
219; Ayatullah Khomeinī, Towzih ul-Masā'il, problem 2432.
    28. Murata, "Izdivāj,", p. 85.
    29. Murata, "Izdivāj,", p. 70.
    30. Tūsī, cited in Murata, "Izdivāj," p. 95.
    31. Murata, "Izdivāj," p. 95; Kāshif ul-Ghitā',
A'īn-i Mā [Our Custom], tr. by N. Makārim-i Shīrāzī
(Qum: Hadaf Publishing, 1347/1968), pp. 263-70; Ayatullah
M.H. Tabatabā'ī, Shi^{C}ite Islam, Tr. by S.H. Nasr from
Persian into English (Albany: State University of New

York Press, 1975), p. 227.

32. Yusifi-Makki, Mut^c a dar Islām, p. 23.
33. Kāshif ul-Ghitā, A'īn-i Mā, p. 268. In a conversation I had with an Ayatullah who is also a professor at the University, he stated flatly, ". . . Yes, mut^c a is like prostitution except that one has the name of God and the other doesn't" (December, 1981, Tehran).
34. Kāshif ul-Ghitā', A'īn-i Mā, pp. 278-79; Ayatullah Tabātabā'i, Shi^c ite Islam, p. 229; Ayatullah M. Mutahhari, "The Rights of Women in Islam," part 3, Mahjubah [a journal for women in English] (1981), pp. 52-56; Ayatullah M. Mutahharī, Nizām-i Huqūq-i Zan dar Islam [The System of Women's Rights in Islam](Tehran: Zibā Publishing, 1353/1974). Makārim-i Shirāzi. cited in Kāshif ul-Ghitā, A'īn-i Mā, pp. 380-86; Shafāhī, Mut^c a, pp. 331-38.
35. Personal conversation with the Ayatullah Shari^c at-Madārī, summer, 1978.
36. Tabātabā'i, Shi^c ite Islam, 229; Makārim-i Shirāzī, cited in Kāshif ul-Ghitā, A'īn-i Mā, pp. 385-87. Shafāhī, Mut^c a, 327-30.
37. Ayatullah Mutahharī, "Rights of Women," p. 53; Bāhunar, Ta^c līmāt, 37-38.
38. Gibb, "Mut^c a," p. 419; N. Coulson, A History of Islamic Law (Ilkey, Yorks.: The Scholar Press, Ltd., (1964).
39. It is significant to note here the complete turnaround of the interpretation of ajr [consideration] to mahr [brideprice] in Ayatullah Mutahhari's message. When the Sunnī scholar, Fahkr-i Rāzī argued that the meaning of ajr in the Qur'an should be interpreted as mahr, the Shī^c ī ulama argued against it, and maintained that the two different forms of payments referred to two different types of marriage in the Qur'an. Ayatuallah Mutahharī's interpretation seems to be in direct conflict with the opinion of his Shī^c ī predecessors.
40. Mutahharī, "Rights of Women," p. 54.
41. Makārim-i Shirāzī, in Kāshif ul-Ghitā, A'īn-i Mā, p. 376.
42. Mutahharī, "Rights of Women," p. 55.
43. Mutahharī, "Rights of Women," pp. 52-53; Makārim-i Shîrazî in Kāshif ul-Ghitā, A'īn-i Mā, pp. 372-390; Bāhunar, Ta^c līmāt, pp. 37-41. The term currently used is izdivāj-i muvaqqat [temporary marriage] instead of mut^c a or sigheh, which have pejorative connotations.
44. The religious education textbook was edited by the late Dr. Bāhunar, a student and close associate of the Ayatullah Mutahharī. Also the Islamic Republic's Prime Minister, he was killed in a bomb explosion in the summer of 1981. The second editor of the text book is Mr. Gulzādeh-Ghafūri, a member of the present Parliament.
45. Bāhunar, Ta^c līmāt, p. 40.
46. What such trial marriages may do to the reputa- of a young woman in a culture where virginity is symbolically a girl's only "capital" shall remain a test for

250

future empirical studies.
   47. Bahunar, Ta^climāt, p. 39; also see Makārim-i
Shīrāzī, in Kāshif ul-Ghitā, A'īn-i Mā, p. 377.
   48. Makārim-i Shīrāzī, in Kāshif ul-Ghitā, A'īn-i
Mā, p. 378; see also Mutahharī, "Rights of Women," p. 55.

BIBLIOGRAPHY

Arberry, A.J., trans. The Koran Interpreted (New York
   MacMillan Publishing Co., 1955).
Bahunar, M.J. and Gulzadeh-Ghafuri, A., eds. Ta^climāt-i
   Dīnī [Religious Education] (Tehran: Ministry of Edu-
   cation, Dāvar-Panāh Publishing, 1360/1981).
Coulson, N. A History of Islamic Law (Ilkey, Yorkshire:
   The Scholar Press, Ltd., 1964).
Fayzee, A.A. Outlines of Muhammadan Law, fourth ed.
   (Delhi: Oxford University Press, 1974).
Geertz, C. Interpretation of Cultures (New York: Basic
   Books, Inc., 1973).
Gibb, H.A.R. "Mut^ca." Shorter Encyclopaedia of Islam
   (Leiden: E.J. Brill, 1953), pp. 418-20.
Haqqānī-Zanjānī, H. "Izdivāj-i Muvaqqat az Fahshā
   Jilowgīrī Mīkunad" ["Temporary Marriage Prevents
   Fornication"]. Maktabi-Islām (no. 9, 1348/1969):
   31-33.
_____. "Izdivāj-i Muvaqqat" ["Temporary Marriage"].
   Maktabi-Islām (no. 7, 1348/1969): 13-15.
Hijāzī, Q. Izdivaj dar Islām [Marriage in Islam] (Tehran:
   Haidari Publishing, 1345/1966).
Houtsma, M.T. "Mut^ca." Dictionary of Islam, vol. 3.
   (Leiden: E.J. Brill, 1936).
Hughes, T.P. "Mut^ca." Dictionary of Islam (Anarkali,
   Lahore: Premier Book House Publishers and Book-
   sellers, 1964).
Ja^cfarī-Lankarūdī, Dr. M.J. Huqūq-i Khānivādeh [Family
   Laws] (Tehran: Haidari Publishing, 1355/1976).
Kāshif ul-Ghitā, M.H. A'īn-i Ma [Our Custom] N. Makārim-i
   Shīrāzī, trans. (Qum: Hadaf Publishing, 1347/1968)
Kātūziān, N. Huqūq-i Madanī-yi Khānivādeh [Family Civil
   Laws] (Tehran: University of Tehran Press, 1357-1978).
Khu'ī, Āyatullāh S.A. Towzīh ul-Masā'il [Explanation of
   Problems] (Tehran: 1979).
Khomeīnī, Āyatullāh R. Towzīh ul-Masā'il [Explanation of
   Problems] (Tehran: n.d.)
Majlisī, M.B. Hulyat ul-Muttaqīn [Ornaments of the Pious]
   (Tehran: Qā'im Publishing, n.d.)
Muhaqqiq Hillī, A.J. Sharāyi^cul-Islām [Islamic Law],
   A. A. Yazdī and M.T. Dānish-Pazhūh, trans. from
   Arabic into Persian (Terhan: University of Tehran
   Press, 1347/1968).
_____. Mukhtasar-i Nāfi^c [Useful Summary], E. Yar-
   shāter and M.T. Dānish-Pazhūh, trans. (Tehran:
   University of Dehran Press, 1343-1964).

Murata, Sachiko. "Izdivāj-i Muvaqqat va Asār-i Ijtimāᶜī-yi An" ("Temporary Marriage and Its Social Effects"], Master's thesis, Divinity College, Tehran, 1353/1974.

Mutahhari, Ayatullah M. "The Rights of Women in Islam," part 3. Mahjubah 1 (no. 10, 1981): 52-56.

———. Akhlāq-i Jinsī dar Islām va Jahān-i Gharb [Sexual Ethics in Islam and in the Western World] (Qum: Sadrā Publishing, n.d.).

Pickthall, M.M., trans. The Meaning of the Glorious Koran (New York: New American Library, Inc., n.d.).

Qazvīnī, M.A. Sīyagh-i Uqūd [Forms of Contracts] (Tehran: n.d.).

Qurbānī, Z. "Huqūq-i Zan va Showhar Nisbat Beh Yik Dīgar" ["The Rights and Obligations of Wife and Husband"], Maktab-i Islām (no. 7, 1344/1965): 47-51.

Robertson-Smith, W. Kinship and Marriage in Early Arabia (Boston: Beacon Press, 1903).

Shafāhi, M. Mutᶜa va Asār-i Huqūqi va Ijtimāᶜi An, 6th edition [Mutᶜa and Its Legal and Social Effects] (Tehran: Haidari Publishing, Tehran, 1352/1973).

Tabātābā'ī, Ayatullāh M.H. Shiᶜite Islam, S.H. Nasr, trans. (Albany: State University of New York Press, 1975).

Tūsī, Shaikh M.H. al-Nahaya, M.Y. Dānish-Pazhūh, trans. from Arabic to Persian (Tehran: University of Tehran Press, 1343/1964).

Yusifī-Makkī, S.H. Mutᶜa dar Islām [Mutᶜa in Islam] (Tehran: 1342/1965).

14
Family Planning
in Post-Revolutionary Iran

Yasmin L. Mossavar-Rahmani

A group of male and female inmates of Qasr Prison in
Tehran were recently freed because they each agreed to
marry a fellow prisoner. They were allowed to select
their future mates by talking to them over the telephone
and viewing them from behind glass cases. Those who
selected spouses were able to walk out free--blessed
by the Bunyad-i Izdivaj [Foundation for Marriage], which
presented them with gifts of clothing and cash.[1]

Such scenes are not uncommon since the Islamic
government finds marriage a "panacea for all societal
ills." Now that Iran has become a society which propa-
gates marriage, is there any room for family planning?
This chapter will examine the effects of the revolution
on family planning in Iran, and the attitude of the present hierarchy toward family planning. The policies of the
previous regime will also be discussed briefly.

Pre-revolutionary Period

By the end of the 1960's Iran had a population of
around 25 million, which was growing at the rate of 2.8
percent per annum.[2] Since this rate of growth was judged
to be excessive, in 1970 the Iranian government embarked
on an aggressive population control policy aimed at reducing growth to 2 percent initially and to 1 percent
within twenty years.[3]

Accordingly, a number of government, nongovernment,
and voluntary agencies began to provide family planning
assistance to women of childbearing age, numbering about
five million at that time. Organizations involved in
family planning included the Ministry of Public Health,
the National Organization of Women, and the Family Planning Organization.[4]

As was customary at that time in Iran, the latest
techniques and devices were imported and distributed.
These modern contraceptive methods included the IUD, the
pill, sterilization (both tubal ligation and vasectomy),
menstrual regulation, and injections. And, like many
other forms of modern technology that poured into the

country, these devices were not put to proper, intelligent, or effective use. Hence, traditional methods such as azl [withdrawal] remained widely practiced alternatives.[5]

The pill was most widely circulated because it was easy to handle and did not require a gynecological examination. Eventually it became so common that family planning clinics operated by the various national organizations relied almost exclusively on the pill. In turn, the clinics, which became the primary distribution points for the pill, evolved into the focal point of family planning in Iran, replacing traditional channels such as the mosque and women's networks.

Clinics were so eager to distribute the pills that they failed to properly instruct and prepare the users, thereby leaving them with ill-conceived notions and an incorrect sense of how to utilize the contraceptives. One post-revolutionary official of the Ministry of Health recalled the pre-revolutionary procedure:

> They [family planning promoters] would sit back in their clinics and offices and wait for people to come to them . . . or they would drive into the villages with a loudspeaker on their car, while the women were in the fields. When the women did not respond to their calls, they would dispense pills out to whomever was standing around, usually children and old people, and then consider treatment for those women accomplished.[6]

The pill became more popular and was more readily accepted than other modern contraceptives because it did not interfere with the woman's abilities to perform her religious duties. In contrast, the IUD never became popular because it increased the level of bodily discharges and created a religious sense of impurity in women. (According to Shi[c]ite texts which describe the conduct of everyday life, a woman must follow specific guidelines of religious ritual in accordance with her level of bodily discharges. During menstruation, for instance, a woman may not attend a mosque, pray, read the Qur'an, or engage in sexual activity.[ ]) Another reason for the pill's popularity was that it resulted in water retention, which in turn increased body weight.[8] Since added weight was culturally considered attractive, women, particularly skinny women, were understandably eager to use it.

Sterilization (vasectomy and tubal ligation), which became legal in 1976, was a practice not readily accepted by the majority of the population.[9] It was especially difficult for men to accept vasectomy. In one study among Kurdish men, it was discovered that the condom was favored and used most often. Coitus interruptus [azl] was used, but was not liked, and vasectomy was seldom adopted or even considered.[10]

These attempts at contraception did not reduce the widespread practice of abortion. In 1972 it was estimated that in the city of Tehran alone there were 20 to 30 abortions per 100 live births, at a time when abortion was illegal.[11] As a result of these abortions, fertility in Tehran was estimated to be 25 percent lower than for the country as a whole. In recognition of this statistic, the government legalized abortion in 1973.[12]

The pre-revolutionary government's desperate attempts to lower the natural rate of population increase was not without irony, for at the same time the country was faced with a severe shortage of the skilled and unskilled workers needed to fulfill its ambitious development plans. Doctors, nurses, engineers, construction workers, and laborers were imported in large numbers from such countries as Pakistan, Korea, and the Philippines.

A more meaningful figure for comparison and concern would have been the infant mortality rate, an indicator measuring the number of infant (children under one year of age) deaths per 1000 live births during the same period. A low infant mortality rate is made possible by a low incidence of unhealthy obstetrical methods and by a low occurrence of debilitating disease and malnutrition. It is remarkable that in 1976 Iran had a relatively high infant mortality rate of 108, even higher than that of Egypt (98), a country which is more populated but poorer than Iran.[13] Furthermore, the infant mortality rate in Iran was highest among rural female infants. Even during the toddler and early pre-school years (ages one to four), girls had a higher mortality rate than boys (a weighted male age-specific death rate of 15.3 vs. 19.2 for females).[14]

Islam and Family Planning

Islamic history tells of many forms of family planning. These range from simple withdrawal and abstinence to complex potions and suppositories.[15] Contraception seems to have been a routine part of everyday life in the Middle East. An early tenth century writer, for example, recommends family planning for physically infirm women, especially those who are unable to bear the burdens of pregnancy. There is also a prohibition against imparting contraceptive information to women of low moral standards, lest the practice be abused.[16] In the eleventh century, the Iranian scientist Avicenna recommended the drinking of sweet basil infusions for birth control.[17] Still another imaginative authority recommended

. . . warm clothing and abstention from astringent, bitter, or cold food. In particular the woman should not eat melons or peaches but should choose eggs, onions, soups, leeks, mallow, saffron, tails of animals, and the flesh

of the legs of young fowls. She should engage
in vigorous exercise, violent sexual intercourse, and much laughter.[18]

It has also been hypothesized that the dramatic demographic decline in the Mamluk empire of Egypt and Syria
in the mid-fourteenth century during the Black Death may
have been caused by many adverse factors including the
use of birth control.[19]

These instances point to the flexibility of the
relationship between Islam and family planning. As a
rule, Islam places great emphasis on the family and its
welfare. The Qur'an, for example, recommends marriage
and procreation for those who are physically and economically able and advises abstinence for all others:

> Marry the spouseless amongst you, and your
> slaves and handmaidens that are righteous if
> they are poor, God will enrich them of His
> bounty; . . . And let those who find not the
> means to marry be abstinent until God enriches
> them of His bounty. (XXIV, 30-35)[20]

Child spacing and breastfeeding are other ways by
which the Qur'an attempts to insure family welfare. By
recommending that women nurse their infants for two full
years and that lactating women not become pregnant, the
Qur'an expresses concern for the health of both the
mothers and the infants by ensuring that enough time
elapses between the births and that infants receive
adequate maternal nutrition:

> Mothers shall suckle their children two years
> completely, for such as desire to fulfill
> suckling. But if the couple desire by mutual
> consent to wean, then it is no fault in them.[21]

The hadith [the prophetic traditions] is another
source for interpreting Islamic law. The authenticity of
this source, however, is subject to debate by the ulama.
For this reasons the conditions for the practice of azl,
for instance, differ from one legal school to another.
The Shafiᶜis permit azl without stipulation; the Hanbalis
and Malikis insist that the free woman give her permission for azl each time it is practiced.[22] According to
Shiᶜite texts, a wife may give her husband permanent permission by writing it in her marriage contract, thereby
avoiding having to give her permission each time. If azl
is practiced against the wishes of the wife, without a
stipulation authorizing it in her marriage contract, then
diya [damages] must be paid by the husband to the wife.[24]
It is interesting to note that the more conservative
Shiᶜites even denounce azl outright:

> . . . azl is evil and anyone practicing it has
> to pay for it--unless the wife is old, unable
> to bear children, has an evil tongue, or will

not nurse her children.[25]

Inherent in the stipulations for the practice of azl is the notion that a woman has rights to sexual fulfillment and childbearing and that azl eliminates these rights.

Family Planning in the Post-Revolutionary Period

In 1982 the population of Iran, estimated at 41.2 million, was growing at a rate of 3.1 percent per year. This rate was far above the projected 2 percent goal of Shah Muhammad Riza Pahlavi for the '80s and close to the rates for Egypt (3.1%) and Jordan (3.6%), two countries with historically high fertility rates.[26]

The leaders of the new regime, however, do not seem interested in population control. Their policies are designed to encourage just the opposite. After the revolution, Ayatullah Ruhullah Khomeini ordered family planning clinics to stop abortions and sterilizations. Furthermore, all other family planning activities were placed under the sole jurisdiction of the Ministry of Public Health, in the Division of Family Health. As already noted, the regime is taking steps that will facilitate marriage. The legal age for marriage has been lowered to 13 years for women and 15 for men. Perhaps most dramatic, polygamy has been reinstituted.

Such actions have aroused the objections of many educated and progressive women and men. However, this group was unable to stand against the tide of Islamic fundamentalism. Voicing objections was possible during the early days of the revolution, but has become increasingly difficult as Islamic circles gained power. Thus, Ayatullah Khomeini was able to continue with his programs, one of which was the creation of Bunyadi-Izdivaj [Foundation for Marriage]. This organization disburses funds to needy men and women who wish to marry; among those eligible for these funds are widows, prostitutes, prisoners, and the handicapped. Ayatullah Khomeini himself recently urged war widows to wed revolutionary guards:

> I give my sincere and fatherly advice to these
> young men and to women who have lost their
> husbands to consider marriage, this divine and
> valuable tradition, and to leave behind chil-
> dren to persevere like themselves.[27]

Ayatullah Khomeini criticizes the previous government for establishing laws such as the Family Protection Law which made it more difficult for a man to obtain a divorce or to marry a second wife:

> The Family Protection Law which has been recent-
> ly passed by the illegal parliament is against
> the tenets of Islam. Those who implement this
> law are guilty of an irreligious act. Women
> who have been divorced through this mechanism

are still considered married, and their divorces remain annulled. If they remarry, they are committing adultery.[28]

This is not to say, however, that Khomeini disapproves of family planning. His own statements and those of other officials indicate that the Islamic government recognizes the need to safeguard family welfare through family planning. However, as yet there has been no blueprint for family planners to follow.

It is not clear, for instance, whether the IUD falls in the category of abortives, which would render it unacceptable. The question of sterilization also remains unsolved and remains controversial among Islamic jurists because some consider vasectomy equivalent to castration or an impairment [naqs-i uzv]. In Islamic texts, castration is tantamount to the murder of an adult.[29] For those who realize that sterilization of the male and female does not impair sexual dirve and does not damage sexual organs, this method is legitimate and acceptable. Many Islamic countires, including such Arab states as Tunisia, have judged sterilization to be in accordance with the tenets of Islam.[30]

Abortions have always been available in the Middle East for a fee. Performed by private doctors or by quacks, abortions have persisted despite the unfavorable pronouncements of ruling hierarchies. In Iran abortions were available before they became legal in 1973, and are available today, despite Khomeini's pronouncement of their illegality in 1979. When abortions are illegal it is the poor who suffer because they have no access to good private doctors and can afford only the herbalist or the quack. The poor also often have little access to good family planning information. When a poor woman becomes pregnant, abortion is a well-known solution and is often done in unhygienic and dangerous circumstances.

The question of abortion in Islam is one of considerable controversy. Though they generally disapprove of it, Islamic jurists allow abortion as long as it is done prior to the 120th day of pregnancy, before the fetus is animated with life.[31] However, Ayatullah Khomeini disapproves of abortion so much that he disregards any notion of ensoulment; he finds abortion unacceptable regardless of the stage of pregnancy. In his treatise, there is only one mention of the subject, a passage in which he advises against seeking an abortion.[32] It is important to note that as the chosen Imam or leader, Ayatullah Khomeini may issue pronouncements which he feels are important for the prevailing times. In Iran today, doctors may perform abortions only in case of risk to the life of the mother, and then only if a panel of physicians agrees to such action.

Ironically, the late Dr. Muhammad Husain Bihishti, an active leader of the Islamic government, was instru-

mental in legalizing abortion in 1973. His action was
based on the notion of ensoulment, that is, animation
after the 120th day. Bihishti argued that a fetus' growth
proceeds in stages based on the following Qur'anic
interpretation:

> In enumerating the phases of growth in man's
> creation, the Holy Qur'an said: "Now of fine
> clay have we created man; then we placed him,
> a moist germ, in a safe abode. Then we made
> the moist germ a clot of blood; then made the
> clotted blood into a piece of flesh; then made
> the piece of flesh into bones; and we clothed
> the bones with flesh; then brought forth man
> of yet another make. Blessed therefore be God,
> the most excellent of Makers. (XXIII: 12-14)
> In which of these phases does the Qur'an
> regard the fetus as a human being? . . .
> From the verses cited above it is clear that
> the fetus was transformed into a human being
> when God "produced it as another creation,"
> a creation distinguished from all other ani-
> mals, namely man.[33]

Bihishti further stressed that prior to ensoulment, the
fetus is an animal because it is possessed by a life
which has the potentiality to turn human. It is only
after the point at which the fetus becomes human that
abortion would be considered a crime.[34] Ayatullahs Kazim
Shari[c]at-Madari and Abul-Qasim Khu'i follow Dr.
Bihishti's views on abortion.

In Islamic texts, the question of abortion is dominated by the subject of economic renumeration: paid to the
woman by the husband if he is responsible for initiating
the abortion, to the man by the wife if she requests the
abortion, and to the siblings of the unborn infant if
both parents are at fault. In practice, however, it is
not clear how these damages are paid.

The stages and penalties are assessed in the following manner: if a woman has an abortion when the egg is
fertilized (stage of nutfeh), the penalty is twenty units
of gold. It is sixty units when the embryo is developed
(stage of madagha, 2.5 months) and one thousand units
after the fourth month (after ensoulment). If the aborted
fetus is found to be female, then damages assessed for the
last stage are halved to five hundred units of gold.[35]

On the whole, the ruling Islamic hierarchy disapproves of abortion and sterilization; physicians who perform either are exposed to the danger of harsh punishment
by the government. Those contraceptives which require the
permission of both spouses are acceptable to the Islamic
government. These would include azl, the pill, the condom, the diaphragm, and breastfeeding. In the meantime,
while ideological opinion governs the rules of family

260

planning, the statistics concerning the infant mortality
rate have not improved since 1976. It is still estimated
at 108 and is higher than that of Egypt, Tunisia, and
Morocco.36

Conclusion

It is difficult to predict how the revolutionary
government will handle family planning in the future. It
is probable that men, as heads of government and heads of
households, will increasingly determine the course of
family planning. Concurrently, women may become restricted to the home, limited to the role of homemaker and
child-bearer.

Yet, despite the pronouncements of the ruling hierarchy, women will probably continue to seek abortions as
they have always done in the Middle East. Traditional
means of contraception such as spacing and azl will remain popular as modern contraception becomes less available and less competently used. In countries with rising
conservatism, such as Iran, modern contraception will be
more acceptable if it is correlated with family welfare
rather than undermining notions of modesty and propriety.
It is when such sacred beliefs are respected that doors
slowly open for new notions. It is hoped that Iran will
be able to reconcile fundamentalist ideology with the
health requirements of its growing population. Otherwise,
higher fertility rates and declining health standards will
place additional strains of its diminishing resources.

NOTES

1. Iran Times, August 7, 1981, p. 1.
2. National Census of Iran, 1966
3. John K. Friesen and Richard V. Moore, "Iran,"
in Country Profiles (New York: Population Council,
October 1972), p. 6.
4. Ibid., pp. 1, 8-12.
5. Ibid., p. 6
6. Iranian 1 (no. 17, 2 Aban 1358/October 24, 1979):
11-12.
7. For rules relating to menstruation, see "Ahkām-i
Hā'iz," in Towzih ul-Masā'il of Ayatullahs Khomeini,
Shari'at-Madari, and Khu'i.
8. Personal communication with former health corps
member, based on experiences in Luristan.
9. M.A. Bat-Haee. "Knowledge and Attitudes of Kurdish men in Iran with Respect to Vasectomy and Other Means
of Fertilization Control," Journal of Family Welfare 33
(no. 4, June 1977): 3-22.
10. Ibid.
11. T.B. Larsen, "Estimates of Induced Abortion in
Some Middle Eastern Countries," in I.R. Nazer, ed., Induced Abortion: A Hazard to Public Health? Proceedings

of the First Conference of the International Planned Parenthood Federation, Middle East and North Africa Region, Beirut, Lebanon, February 1971 (Beirut, Lebanon: IPPF Middle East and North Africa Region, 1972), p. 78-101.

12. Ibid.

13. Population Growth Survey of Iran, Final Report, 1973-1976, serial number 777 (Tehran: Plan and Budget Organization, Statistical Centre of Iran, June 1978), p. 93.

14. Ibid., pp. 98-99.

15. Cyril Elgood, Safavid Medical Practice (London: Luzac & Co., 1970), pp. 234-44.

16. Ibid., p. 236.

17. Ibid., p. 237.

18. Ibid.

19. Michael Dols, "The General Mortality of the Black Death in the Mamluk Empire," in A.L. Udovitch, ed., The Islamic Middle East: 700-1900: Studies in Economics and Social History of the Middle East (Princeton, NJ: The Darwin Press, 1981), p. 417.

20. A.J. Arberry, The Koran Interpreted, vol. 2: Suras XXI-CXIV (London: Allen & Unwin, Ltd., 1955), XXIV, 30-35.

21. Ibid, vol. 1: Suras I-XX, II, 33.

22. Al-Ghazāli, Ihya' Ulūm al-Dīn, vol. 2 (Cairo: Thaqafat al-Islamiyya, 1938), p. 41.

23. Al-Hillī, Sharica, vol. 2. (Tehran: n.d.), p. 172.

24. Ibid.

25. Jacfar Shaikhul-Islāmi, Parvarish-i Kūdak dar Islām (Tehran: Shirkat Sahami Intishār, 1352/1974).

26. World Data Sheet for 1982, Population Reference Bureau.

27. Los Angeles Times, April 16, 1982, p. 20.

28. Ayatullah Ruhullah Khomeini, "Khātimeh" in Towzīh ul-Masā'il (Tehran: n.d.), pp. 463-64.

29. For stipulations concerning abortion, see "Ahkām-i Dīyeh," in Towzih ul-Masā'il of Ayatullahs Sharicat-Madari and Khu'i.

30. L.S. Sodhy, G.A. Metcalf, and J.S. Wallach, "Islam and Family Planning: Indonesia's Mohammadiyah," Pathpaper, no. 6 (1980): 13.

31. "Ahkām-i Dīyeh" in Towzih ul-Masā'il of Ayatullahs Sharicat-Madari and Khu'i. Also see Muhammed Bihishti, "Rules of Abortion and Sterilization in Islamic Law," in I.R. Nazer, H.S. Karmi, and M.Y. Zayid, eds., Islam and Family Planning, vol. 2 (Beirut, Lebanon: IPPF, Middle East and North Africa Region, 1974), pp. 402-425.

32. Ayatullah Ruhullah Khomeini, "Masā'il Mutifariq-eh-yi Zanashu'i," in Towzih ul-Masā'il, p. 391

33. Bihishti, "Rules of Abortion," p. 409.

34. "Draft Press Release and Its Discussion," in Nazer, Karmi, and Zayid, eds., Islam and Family Planning, p. 490.

262

35. "Ahkām-i Dīyeh," in Towzīh ul-Masā'il of Ayatullahs Shariᶜat-Madāri and Khu'i.
36. World Data Sheet for 1982.

15
Women Imprisoned in the Kingdom of the Mullahs[*]

Cynthia Brown Dwyer

Introduction

The purpose of this chapter is to present an eyewitness account of one explicit effect of the Iranian
Revolution upon what I took to be a cross-section of the
women in Islamic Iran. These were the three hundred or
so prisoners (chiefly political) held for varying lengths
of time in Evin Prison, Teheran, between July, 1980 and
February, 1981.

That effect was punishment by incarceration, with
little hope of justice (although a fair measure of mercy
after the fact was apparent during my imprisonment).
Arrests were made on the flimsiest of suspicions by irregular, untrained, and often ignorant Pasdaran (Revolutionary Guards); imprisonment was generally without trial
and lasted for periods ranging from a few days to many
months; the few women who were tried received sentences
ranging from 18 months to 12 years. A woman cabinet
minister during the Pahlavi monarchy had been executed
shortly before I was taken to Evin.

Side effects of imprisonment included extortion and
severe beatings--the latter for "crimes of corruption,"
for interrogation purposes, or as punishment for behavior
within the prison. Two women claimed to have been tortured before they were brought to Evin; I have reason to
believe these women were truthful. In November, 1980 a
presidential commission turned up hundreds of allegations
of torture in Iranian prisons.

Most punishment in Iran seemed to stem from offend-
ing the political or religious views (and new Islamic
"laws") of a relatively small group of narrowminded men
who had seized and consolidated their power over the year
and a half after the Islamic Revolution toppled the
Pahlavi regime in January, 1979. These new rulers were
aided in getting a fanatical grip on the country by means
of the hysteria stirred during the American hostage
affair.

I met no one in prison who, whether she had favored

---

[*] *See note, p. 182.*

the Revolution or not, could have forseen in February,
1979, as the crowds cheered the arrival of their hero,
Ayatullah Khomeini, that her political views, ethnic ties,
or private behavior would bring about her arrest so soon
after the demise of a thoroughly repressive state.

   Although I met some women with no apparent political affiliation, many others adhered to various political groups--the Mujahidin-i Khalq, the Fida'iyan-i Khalq,
the Communists, and the Furqan, National Front, and
Kurdish Kumileh parties. I lived, at various time, with
Kurds, Persians, Turkic-speakers, an Armenian, and
nationals of Germany, Greece, and England, as well as with
one French citizen of Iranian birth and Bakhtiari tribal
affiliation and a German-born woman who was an Iranian
citizen by marriage. From time to time, we were joined
by young children of prisoners.

   In this chapter I shall explain the resason for my
trip to Iran and imprisonment at Evin in 1980-81; I shall
convey some idea of the conditions and daily routine that
prevailed at that time in Evin; finally I shall describe
some of the women with whom I spent my months of incarceration.

   I must note that I do not speak Persian. Although I
picked up a vocabulary of perhaps two hundred words, most
information and conversation was channeled through English-speaking Iranians. Nonetheless, two years later I
retain vivid recollections of women I loved at Evin with
whom I could communicate only through sign language,
facial expressions, and hugs and kisses. Iranian women
are the most affectionate I have ever met; and the memory
of their affection colors my recollections.

Reasons and Impressions

   In April, 1980 I travelled alone to Iran for a close
look at the Iranian Revolution. The American Embassy
hostage crisis, then in its sixth month, was the episode
that finally riveted my attention on Iran, though in
truth it was the great ferment taking place there that
interested me the most. As a freelance writer, I was
dissatisfied with the narrow focus of the massive news
coverage from Teheran. The American media in particular
confined their investigative reporting to questions of
the hostages and to the Embassy environs on Takht-i
Jamshid street. Consequently, complex revolutionary
phenomena were treated as though the Revolutions's sole
raison d'etre was to hold Americans hostage. Further,
the media barely concealed its distaste for the Revolution, for the so-called religious fundamentalism sweeping
the Mideast, and for Iranians in general, whether they
were holding hostages and shouting anti-American slogans
or politely serving as translators to non-Persian speaking newsmen.

   I hoped to find answers to two important questions:

How was the average Iranian faring under the new government? How successful was the Islamic Revolution in meeting the aspirations and needs of Iranians?[1] I began to find my answers in the streets, offices, and homes of Tehran. I mingled comfortably in crowds that weren't at all like the menacing mobs portrayed on American television; I quizzed everyone I met about their work and their hopes for Iran. But my real answers came at Evin Prison, with the benefit of much closer observation and personal experience than I had thought possible.

My imprisonment was a direct outcome of the attempted military raid ordered by President Carter ostensibly to rescue the hostages during the night of April 24-25. The failure of the rescue mission triggered a chain of events that undermined a democratic revolution with solid religious underpinnings and prepared the way for the domination of the hardline faction of mullahs [clergymen] within the Islamic Republican Party and their allies, the ultra-fanatical Party of God and the Society for the Propagation of Islam.

In what was a parody of the Western concept of "clear and present danger," the mullah-run Majlis [Parliament] and the Revolutionary Council were able to use the American raid and the subsequent "discovery" of an alleged large-scale armed-forces "plot to overthrow Khomeini" (the so-called Hamadan coup) as an excuse to trample violently on the civil liberties and human rights of Iranians. These included great numbers of people--including many women--who had opposed the Shah and helped bring about the Revolution. Those doing the trampling included heretofore invisible or nondescript mullahs and their hangers-on, as well as several who appeared out of nowhere to seize great power; these were men who had not fought against or suffered under the Shah.

Silenced were the voices of clerics like the Grand Ayatullah Shari^c at-Madari, who did not approve, on Islamic grounds, of great political power being wielded by one sole Grand Ayatullah--Khomeini. Powerful clerics also moved against the tribal and ethnic minorities, especially the Kurds and Azerbaijanis.

Moderate and centerist nonclerical Nationalist politicians like Mihdi Bazargan were crushed in the violent in-fighting during the 15 months after the American raid. Left-of-center groups, the Fida'iyan and Mujahidin, who had fought long and hard against the Shah during many years preceding February 11, 1979, were disarmed, shut out of power, imprisoned, tortured, executed. They were foreced into an opposition stance that gave the Pasdaran and Revolutionary Courts an excuse for ever heavier oppression.

Like many of the other women in Evin Prison, I was caught in the wave of totalitarianism that was growing in Iran. On May 5 I was arrested for espionage.

After the failed American raid the Iranians, possibly with good reason, were looking for spies under every hotel bed, especially those occupied by foreign-passport holders. These were the hysterical days in late April. Some revolutionary faction or group of agents I have not yet been able to identify arrested me, and I was charged, along with a number of others--American, British, and Iranian--with working for the Central Intelligence Agency. I had not. What I actually did was what any good journalist would have done--followed a story that could have been an incredible scoop. I had listened to a purported scheme by an alleged dissident Iranian group (claiming to be patriotic), which wanted to act before the final round of Majlis elections scheduled for the middle of May. The group said they planned to rescue four or five hostages and thereby--in some manner I did not grasp--influence the outcome of the elections in favor of moderates and away from hardline clerics. I telephoned this information to Washington, attempting to put the group in touch with someone who could help plan a safe transfer of the hostages if they were smuggled out of Iran by this scheme. Though wild and dangerous, it struck me as no more so than the U.S. National Security Council's recent failure at Desert One, near Tabas, in central Iran.

I did not consider myself a plotter or an accomplice of the dissident Iranians. My only motive other than the journalistic one was humanitarian--I thought it might be possible to save lives. I do not believe that the scheme unfolded to me "in confidence" by a young Iranian student was a plan to entrap me, as was later widely suggested by both Iranian and American officials.

I was interrogated for perhaps fifty hours at three different detention centers over a period of two-and-a-half months by members of the Kumiteh-yi Markaz [Central Committee]. Then I was forced to agree to a secretly televised interview by the Kumiteh, using a prepared and rehersed script. Finally I was accused in the press of several capital crimes, transferred to Evin Prison on July 20, and there held under the jurisdiction of the Revolutionary Courts. I spent the next seven months awaiting trial--a one-sided farce that "convicted" me, without witnesses and using hearsay and perjured testimony, of spying. I was sentenced to the nine months I had already served in jail while awaiting trial and expelled from Iran. My "beat" had been Evin; my fieldwork was done from a cell.

Evin Prison and Women Prisoners

For the first fourteen days I was at Evin I was locked in a four-cell isolation unit. After that, except for ten days when I requested isolation,[2] I lived in the ten-room women's unit, where almost every prisoner was allowed to move freely most of the time. I also had occasion to visit the clinic and four administrative buildings in the huge compound. As far as I knew, all women prisoners were confined to the unit I was in, which held approximately fifty women at any one time while I was there. It was never overcrowded, although that situation must have changed in the summer of 1981, as mass arrests were stepped up. I must emphasize that I speak only of one unit of Evin, and only for the time I was an eyewitness.

There was no such thing as a "typical prisoner" among the women I met in Evin. There was great variety in age, social and economic status, education, occupation, ethnic heritage, religious affiliation, and political belief. The crimes for which they were imprisoned were as different as the lives they had led before becoming prisoners.

One woman was from the poverty-stricken streets of south Tehran, arrested and held more than a week after a dispute with a male neighbor over a package of cigarettes. It was her opinion of this regime that had sent her, frightened and sobbing, into the dreaded Evin (which had acquired its fearsome reputation during the SAVAK days of the monarchy) which suggested to me that the mullahs and their Revolutionary Guards must be in serious trouble with the Iranian masses if they needed to send such people to prison. For this woman came from the very class that Khomeini purported to be protecting and elevating in Iranian society. (Incidentally, she had a good opinion of Americans because she said a diplomatic family had befriended her crippled son a few years previously and had obtained medical attention for him.) A few of the prisoners, some as young as 16, accused of prostitution, and two older women, accused of adultery, appeared to have also come from the lower class.

I met six woman who were from wealthy and/or prominent families, and six others who appeared well-to-do, judging from their clothes, reported life-styles under the monarchy, and travel and education abroad. All were termed taquti, [aristocratic] by the Communists. These women were kind and generous to the poor women; they socialized with the Furqan and accused prostitutes alike, and they got along well with the women guards, who probably came from a class that had provided them with servants in other days.

The Mujahid and Fida'i women preferred to keep a distance from the taquitis. Still, everyone stripped completely in front of whoever else was in the hammam [bath], which accommodated eight bodies at one time, and everyone showered in perfect democratic fashion twice a week. And everyone took her turn scrubbing the halls, sinks, and toilets with no grumbling. I observed that the wealthiest women were the most diligent cleaning ladies, perhaps from having commanded troops of housemaids in the old days. Class consciousness seemed to disappear before everyone's desire to live in good sanitary conditions.

One of the upperclass women, from a diplomatic family, had held a middle-level position in the Iranian Foreign Ministry until her arrest; one had been a mayor of a Teheran suburb; one was the wife of a former cabinet officer and diplomat; one had held a high position with the Iranian Red Lion and Sun Society; one was a wealthy midwife with considerable landholdings. One woman had been a minor television personality; one, a teacher; one, director of a home for the retarded. The others were wives of officers or businessmen.

The great majority of the prisoners came from Kurdistan or from the middle class of Tehran. Almost everyone past 18 had completed high school, I believe, and one or two had been to school abroad. Some of the Mujahidin were college students; one Communist was a teacher, one, a would-be actress and poet, one, a nursing student. I believe only four women were illiterate; also a few of the Kurds and older Mujahid women may have been unlettered. I was generally impressed with the intelligence of the prisoners and enjoyed watching many of the Kurds and all the Fida'is read, study, and argue politics into the night. However, I suspect that their political tracts were sharply limited in outlook and information. Some of these studious young women had been shop girls before their arrests, and they appeared to regard imprisonment as conferring some mark of distinction which might be useful in their political parties when they were released.

It is possible that a government official had formulated a policy of simply holding these minor political detainees for "re-education." If this were the case, the occasional haphazard class in Arabic or the Qur'an could hardly be counted as efficacious; no training or work of any sort was provided anyone.

Among the prisoners was a professional madam, sent up to Evin from Khuzistan during the bad days of the Iran-Iraq War to serve out her five-year sentence. She was a self-contained woman who, like most prisoners, knit constantly. Many of us cheered the release of the American hostages while watching her six-inch television set.

My fellow prisoners' ages ranged from a 12-year-old Kurd to a 72-year-old woman sentenced to 18 months for allegedly running a gambling operation in her home. (Judging from her gentility and fastidiousness, I could not imagine that to be true.) A 14-month-old baby boy and three girls, ranging in age from four to six years, either lived there during their mothers' incarcerations or visited for a week at a time.[5]

The women prisoners were generally polite to one another and to the guards and most were even-tempered, although there were several people, myself included, who broke down and cried from time to time, out of loneli-

ness, fear, frustration, and the strain of having no
privacy. Generally we were sociable and happy enough,
and at teatime, we could be merry, momentarily forgetting
where we were. Two prisoners were verbally aggressive
and had violent tempers, and the Kurds and some of the
Mujahidin shouted in derision or anger at the guards. No
one fought physically, but there were many verbal skir-
mishes. One prisoner I was very close to appeared sui-
cidal on one occasion, and when I explained my fears to
the doctor, he emptied her purse of a large quantity of
sleeping pills. One girl was thought to be slightly
crazy, although she appeared to me to be more of a clown;
she was scorned by her Kurdish roommates and protected by
the Communists.

I met three prsioners who were pregnant and one who
had been arrested while pregnant but who had miscarried
at the hospital before I arrived. One woman was pregnant
by her husband, a fellow prisoner with whom she was
allowed conjugal visits; one was said to be pregnant by
her half-brother; and one young Mujahid woman, frail and
ailing, claimed to be married.

I met no one who had actually been raped, and no one
ever touched me, although I was held in a house with
young and middle-aged bachelors for more than two months.
One prisoner said she had been tortured and claimed that
she was threatened with rape. I did hear stories of a
special small prison where prostitutes were invited to
serve their terms as mut^ca [temporary] wives.[5] However,
I did not know anyone who was actually sent there.

In general I got along quite well with the Iranians,
developing affection for many and a deep love for a few
friends that I made there. In the beginning the Kurds
were either very curious or teased me about being a
jasus [spy], which hurt deeply. But I learned to tease
them in return and to yell back when they were bad-tem-
pered. Bad moods seldom lasted long, and women did not
bear grudges, except in a few cases. I admired the
Mujahidin for their political and religious views, although my closest acquaintances were the English-speaking
taqutis. Some of my fellow prisoners trusted me enough
to confide their hatred of Khomeini, and one or two
appeared to wish for a Pahlavi restoration.

And why were approximately three hundred women in-
carcerated in this maximum security prison located in the
foothills of the snow-capped Elburz Mountains northwest
of Teheran? About half were members of the Mujahidin
organization; most had been arrested during protest
demonstrations at the trials of party leaders. Another
fifty were Kurds whose "crime" was never clear to me or
to other prisoners who talked to them. Perhaps thirty
were members of the Fida'i organization or of various
splinter Communist groups, generally picked up for selling party newspapers or for demonstrating.[6] Seven others

were members of the terrorist group Furqan; their husbands had assassinated some prominent clergymen (in the
interests of separation of church and state, according to
the prisoners). The Furqan men had been executed, and
their wives were sentenced to terms of up to twelve years.
Three of us were foreign nationals accused of spying (all
were eventually released). Three more were Nationalists
who had been arrested and tried along with the officers
accused of planning the Hamadan coup, a "crime" they
denied.

Seven seemingly wealthy women appeared to have been
arrested only to force their families to pay large sums
or deed properties to obtain their freedom. Three women
were accused of alcohol offenses (one was beaten severely,
another was beaten less severely because she was not a
Muslim). Six were accused of drug-taking, a charge most
of them admitted; one of these was pardoned and later
became our favorite guard. About fourteen were imprisoned for prostitution; I believe all of these women had
been beaten: one was actually rubberhosed 100 strokes
while I was there. (It was customary for the guards to
shout, "God is great!" with each blow.) Two women had
admitted to adultery; both of them were under a possible
death sentence, but apparently the warden had managed to
get their cases delayed, and there appeared to be
real hope at the time I kissed them good-by that they
would be released eventually, inshallah [God-willing].

Five women thought they were held because their
husbands were wanted or had been arrested. One of the
grimmer episodes concerned Jaleh, whose paratrooper husband was tried for treason. She was told she would be
released when he was executed. She cried for weeks, then
seemed to forget her misery: one day she was released,
and we heard that her husband had faced the firing squad
the night before.

Then there were women detained for various minor,
sometimes inane, reasons. These detentions might be for
a week, or a month, or four months. Jealous relatives
had maliciously reported several of the women for trivial
offenses. A Baha'i woman was caught at the airport with
a Baha'i book considered heretical. Two young women said
they were caught with their boyfriends in a hotel lobby
and were innocent of any wrongdoing. Four were juvenile
runaways.

One woman had arrived at the Tehran airport with a
suspicious letter from a London bank; after days of
refusing to sign a paper saying she was guilty of some
crime, she was released. A customs guard at the airport
was accused of taking bribes and jailed. A woman had an
argument with a Pasdar in a gas station queue and was
locked up as a result. A Greek girl ran away from her
Iranian husband, was reported, picked up, and detained
until he "forgave" her and took her home to Mama, who
was the cause of her flight in the first place. Two

teenagers claimed to have gone to the Khuzistan front to
fight the Iraqis and gotten into some trouble they never
revealed. Perhaps the most unusual case was a woman whose
house had been raided by the Pasdaran. When she came to
Evin to register a complaint, she was detained for a
month.

It is possible that some of these women had committed serious crimes. If so, it was not likely that they
would have admitted it, nor did I want to know about it.

The possibility that an interrogator might get rough
during questioning existed, and one could not tell what
one did not know. Once, it was hinted that I could help
myself by giving testimony the interrogators wanted to
hear. However, I experienced no physical brutality at
Evin although some episodes at the two detention centers
would constitute psychological "battering." Apparently
few serious crimes were proven, for most women were
released within six months, without going to trial.

Of the three hundred or so prisoners I knew, only
one was known to be a "stoolie." Everyone knew that
Laila liked to "report" us to the guards, but they didn't
seem to take her seriously because I know of no punishment that resulted from her tale-bearing. Besides, the
guards spent so much time visiting with us that they
didn't need her gossip to know what was going on. From
time to time, other prisoners tried to channel Laila's
energy and teach her to read, and I went from active dislike of her to an amused admiration of her "originality."
I am almost certain that she feared execution for adultery.

It is possible that I met three prisoners placed in
the prison to try and learn if the Englishwoman and I
were actually foreign agents. Since two of them spoke
almost no English, they could learn little. The third
had several mysterious sessions with prison officials
shortly before my trial, but if she did discuss me, I
believe she helped me because she believed me to be
innocent of spying.

Although most of the prisoners in the section of
Evin where I was held had little hope of being treated
with what we call justice in the West, the atmosphere in
the "harem" was informal, humane, and at times it seemed
the safest place to be. However, the sound of the firing
squad from the courtyards of other areas of the prison
complex were continual reminders of where we were and of
what was happening beyond our walls. Then there was the
clothing of the executed cabinet minister, worn by poor
prisoners, a tangible suggestion of the worst that could
happen under this erratic "justice".

The food was generally good, especially the fresh
bread, yoghurt, rice, and tea. Prisoners' families
supplied ample quantities of fresh vegetables, fruit,
nuts, and sweets; and we could buy canned food, good
soap, shampoo, tissues, creams and lotions, and station-

ary at the prison PX.[7] Nail polish, henna, lipstick, and
eye makeup were forbidden. Prisoners wore whatever
clothes and jewelry they were wearing when arrested unless they were able to obtain others from relatives.

The usual procedure was to confine a prisoner in a
tiny, hot isolation cell for the first two weeks. Then
she was transferred to one of the six large bedrooms of
the women's unit. There was also a shower room, a kitch-
en-bathroom, a guards' office, and an interrogation room.
Stairs led down to an enclosed but unroofed garden where
we picnicked, exercised, sunned ourselves, and hung out
laundry. The rooms were kept clean by the prisoners and
vermin-free by exterminators and a roaming cat. I saw no
bugs and only one mouse, which was amazing considering
the amount of food we kept in our rooms and on the window
sills. The worst messes were caused by the hugh quantities of food thrown away every day and an occasional
overflowing toilet, probably deliberately stopped up with
sanitary napkins by protesting leftists.

A doctor, himself a life-prisoner, ran a small
clinic and supplied a sizable variety of European medi-
cines and vitamins. Shots were given for arthritis;
gynecological problems were treated at a downtown hospital clinic. In the cases of two women epileptics, however, treatment was neglected. Although we complained
about aches and pains, many trips to the doctor were to
exchange news with him; he covered the entire prison and
knew more than most prisoners. Once there was a rumored
outbreak of typhus among the men, but it proved to be
severe diarrhea. As for myself, except for two bouts of
diarrhea, probably from great anxiety, and a prior meno-
pausal condition, I was not ill.

Recreation included knitting, reading, conversation,
celebration of religious feasts, afternoon and evening
tea breaks, letter-writing, and television. We were
allowed books, newspapers, and radios; we were forbidden
foreign broadcasts, but we listened anyway. Visitors
were allowed once a week for brief, closely supervised
visits; they were allowed to bring clothes, money, books,
clean sheets, food, and hurriedly whispered news of the
world outside. Our hopes were kept up by continual
rumors of an expected mass attack on the prison, when we
would be freed by brave relatives!

The prison provided foam mattresses, rough sheets,
and woolen blankets; we sat, and ate, on the floor,
carpeted in clean indoor-outdoor carpeting, in Iranian
village fashion. Although the hundreds of knitting
needles were ample weaponry, had we been so inclined,
we were not supplied with forks or knives. We ate with
tablespoons. We acquired hot plates and brewed huge
quantities of tea. We made candles from orange skins and
oil, and occasionally we stayed up half the night praying
and chanting a special religious chant for our freedom.

We endured one small earthquake, the bombing of Tehran by the Iraqis, some artillery exchanges, and long tedious months of blackouts at 6:00 p.m., when there was nothing to do but go to bed. All who were physically capable donated blood for Iranian troops in Khuzistan.

Although squabbles broke out among prisoners or between prisoners and guards, punishments for behavior within the prison were rare. A few prisoners once staged a sitdown strike and were dragged away to isolation cells. The spirited Kurds, who often defied guards and prison officials alike, were transferred to a less desirable prison, as was one woman, a violent-tempered girl who flirted with the Pasdaran, and a woman accused of being a Lesbian. On the whole, the women guards were humane and tolerant. Several of them joined us at tea-breaks; an outsider would have been hard-pressed to distinguish the gossiping, knitting guards from their gossiping, knitting prisoners.

Some prisoners claimed there were guns in the guards office, but I never saw them. However, the male guards at the door downstairs were armed, as were all the men in other locations around the Evin grounds and buildings. Our guards were mostly lower-class, motherly women. Occasionally, they even cried on our shoulders about their troubles with their families or with prison administrators. During my internment, some of the guards were married, widowed, promoted, and demoted; a released prisoner married the son of one guard, and a woman prison-office worker who socialized with us married a reportedly handsome prisoner. However, we were not entirely free of harassment. One guard's favorite sport in the evening was to toss a rubber spider onto the lap of the smallest prisoner, who routinely obliged by squealing and jumping about.

It is indicative of the basic decency of these women guards that they were happy with me when letters arrived from home, rejoiced at my release, and kissed me goodbye. I would enjoy visiting even with them were I ever to return to Iran.

A typical day's routine: breakfast, cleaning the room, reading, knitting or socializing, dinner, nap, supper, washing up, evening snacks, bedtime. A day rarely varied except in ways I have indicated: a visitor, a stroll in the garden, a trip to the doctor or downtown to the hospital, an interrogation, an occasional movie or class. It was an odd mixture of boredom, anxiety for the future, restlessness, and sedentary socializing.

The grim reality of what was happening in Iran was also a part of our lives. Perhaps the most shattering reminder took place over several weeks. Two hundred men, convicted of treason, were shot by firing squads outside our rooms, at midnight.

Portraits from Prison

   The members of the Mujahidin organization were among
the more stimulating women at Evin. Strong-minded and
well-disciplined, they were members of the highly motivated and most active resistance organization in Iran
apart from the Kurds. Their cadres had participated
actively in the drive to overthrow the Shah, and they
felt cheated by Khomeini of a chance to help govern Iran
according to their tenets of a modern, socialist Islam.
Because they refused to be co-opted as the Communist
Tudeh Party had been and because of their courageous
defiance of Revolutionary Guards, resulting in widespread
demonstrations, street fighting, and assassinations of
hardline religious figures, they seemed to be popular
with Iranians. This probably made their influence extend
well beyond their estimated membership of 20,000 at the
end of 1981.
   A mild-mannered Pasdar who took me to the hospital
after my arrest said to me, "We love the Mujahidin; they
are our brothers and sisters, but they must not have
arms." I think their refusal to surrender their weapons
was one of the earliest open acts of defiance of Khomeini.
Evin began to fill up with their rank and file in the
summer of 1980, and from then on they bore the brunt of
mass arrests and indiscriminate executions.
   There was no Mujahid or any other prisoner I admired
more than 15-year-old A^{c}zam. During the month of Ramazan
[fasting], beginning in July, I often watched her rising
in the middle of a hot night from a blanket on the floor
where she slept to begin the daily observance of the
fast. She donned a dark chadur to pray. After she knelt
to touch her forehead to the clay prayer stone and stood
and bowed in the prescribed Muslim fashion, she solemnly
read aloud her favorite chapters of the Qur'an. Then she
fell hungrily on the heavy meal served at 3:30 a.m.
   Though only a teenager, A^{c}zam seemed as mature, both
physically and emotionally, as a woman twice her age.
She was strong, happy, beautiful, full of fun to the
point of being a tease, and proud. Her fiance, in his
twenties, was also in prison. She had been arrested
during a street demonstration in her native city of Arak
for carrying a protest banner. She showed the same
spirit when, along with three secular leftists and a few
Kurds, she defied the zindanbans [women guards] to stage
a brief sit-down strike. All were quickly dragged along
the hall to the isolation unit by hastily summoned
Pasdaran, but A^{c}zam was the only one who shouted Allah-u
akbar! [God is great!] as they were being dragged.
Roughly treated by a Pasdar and thrown into solitary,
she nonetheless steadily refused to apologize or to
renounce the Mujahidin.
   I got to know her better after I requested a transfer to isolation to escape the rancor in my room.[8] I

found A^{c}zam peacefully studying for her high school math exam. "What happened to you?" I asked as we hugged each other. For an answer she displayed a set of x-rays-- rather proudly, I thought--that showed what she claimed were injuries from a beating.

During our brief time together, A^{c}zam was as active as a large puppy, despite the close confinement in the 6' x 8' cell exactly the width of our two mattresses. The cell, indeed all of sprawling Evin, was too small for her joyous and active nature, but she did not complain. Nor did her spirits droop, except for a few hours when she suffered from menstrual cramps. When she was feeling pensive she sang a poignant lullaby about a martyr's widow crooning to her baby of the father's brave death.

Sometimes A^{c}zam would put aside her Qur'an or math and bend over the small stainless steel basin in our cell with her mouth near the drain. Giggling, she would call, "Girls!" until someone in the next cell answered. A lengthy conversation then took place via the pipes connecting the four cells in our row. When no guard was nearby, A^{c}zam would stand on tiptoe to peer out the small barred window which a child's handkerchief could have curtained. She led everyone in singing Mujahid marching songs so spiritedly that the Pasdaran outside the building sent in orders for her to shut up.

She felt triumphant at that point, and I am certain that she regarded prison as a time of testing of her strength and convictions. Arrest was welcome; time served would raise her in the eyes of comrades when she went home.

A^{c}zam refused repeated chances to win freedom by signing a statement promising to cease activities with the Mujahidin organization. "No! I'll stay right here and study my math," she told me firmly in a tone that suggested what fools our jailers were. But one afternoon, following our lunch of bread, cheese, tea, and fresh salad vegetables, A^{c}zam was released anyway. She had won! Her goodbye touched me deeply; she appeared apologetic to leave me alone in the stifling little cell.

Later I discovered how girls grew to be as staunch as A^{c}zam. One small child, four-year-old Gulshid, had been caught with her mother in a roundup of the Mujahidin. The mother refused to let Gulshid be sent home. The child played for several months as best she could in an environment without children's books or toys. Sometimes she seemed frightened or tired, but generally she held up well in what could only have been for her a harsh environment. With the first heavy snow, someone made her a snowman in the garden. Having quickly learned the Mjuahidin's stirring march songs and slogans, she sometimes pattered down the hall and stopped at the locked door to the guards' room. Rap, rap, rap went her small voice, "Darud, Darud, Mujahidin, darud!" [Salute, salute, Crusaders, salute!].

Shahrzad, secular leftist, poet, and would-be film personality (also said to have been a night-club dancer), was a larger-than-life personality. She fought with everyone at one time or another, but wooed those she wanted as friends. She led many violent quarrels with the zindanbans; however, they preferred drinking tea to carrying out any threat that would give them more work.

I never discovered to which of Iran's many leftist parties Shahrzad belonged, but political affiliation did not stay her tongue. In fact, she charged one of the more outspoken Communists, who had had the "distinction" of having studied in East Germany, with Lesbianism. Later she withdrew the accusation rather than get a fellow prisoner into that kind of deadly serious trouble.

I first noticed Shahrzad because she was sullen and withdrawn, unlike most of the prisoners, who were sociable, cheerful, and nonstop knitters. She sat on the dirty bare floor outside a dreary room reading most of the day and sometimes half the night. Then suddenly she came to life and began collecting names on a petition supporting Miss Shirazi, the women's warden, who was unfailingly kind to everyone but had had some sort of difficulty with the administration. That was soon followed by the sit-down strike, of which she seemed to be a ringleader. She ducked out, however, and did not go to solitary with A^czam and the others.

When I returned from my ten days of self-exile in isolation, she spoke kindly to me for the first time and said, using a mixture of Persian, Italian, and English, that she had circulated a petition supporting me, saying that I was a good person, was not a spy, and so forth. Finally, she recounted why she would do anything to stay out of solitary herself: "Once Pasdars took me blind-folded into the men's part and pushed me into a dark elevator. It went far, far down under the ground. They shoved me into a cell. It was too, too black. I didn't see anyone or hear anything except a Pasdar who brought me food. It was hot every minute and I stayed there many, many days." This was the first indication I had that women were punished outside our unit in Evin.

A glamorous picture of a younger Shahrzad appeared on the dust jacket of a small book of poems. She claimed authorship; others made fun of her claim. She was fond of one of Iran's favorite poets, Hafiz, and sometimes told our fortunes with his "help." She would close her eyes, open the thick book of classical verse at random, and put her finger down on a passage. This she would read aloud as the prediction of one's Fate. (Other women did this with the Qur'an and with the Bible; one Armenian told fortunes from coffee dregs.)

Shahrzad met her match, however, in the manipulative

and sly Simin, leader in another room that was home to most of the secular leftists. One shouting match lasted all night over the faint light of a kerosene lantern. The next morning Shahrzad called everyone divaneh [crazy] and threatened to transfer. I tried to talk sense into her by pleading, "Don't leave this floor. We need you here. You're a good leader, the liveliest one of us all."

Indeed, this volatile woman in her early thirties did not have enough to do. She tried hard to fill the interminable days and was forever organizing us--a clean-up of the garden, daily scrubdowns of the halls and bathrooms, shopping expeditions to the prison PX. Her energy was enormous, and prison a painful constriction on her freedom of movement and association. I believe it is possible that some women feared losing the love of their husbands or boy friends while in prison; Shahrzad may have had this on her mind.

When the Iraqis invaded Khuzistan province and briefly bombed Tehran in September, her patriotism soared. She became abusive of non-Iranians, specifically myself and a newly arrived Englishwoman, refusing the latter a cup of tea. Such behavior was unheard of among the unfailingly polite Iranians. She screamed at me to "shut up and stay out of the way. This night [of the heaviest shelling] belongs to Iran."

Increasingly hysterical fights over boiling water for tea between Shahrzad, now called in derision the Empress of Hot Water, and another foul-tempered woman finally got her transferred to the old Qasr Prison, a dreaded place presided over by the "hanging judge," the fanatical Ayatullah Khalkhali. The Shahrzad who returned to Evin shortly before I left was completely changed; she was a model prisoner, but I never found out what had happened to make her so. She was so calm I wondered if she had been beaten or had found a supply of tranquilizers.

But it is the earlier Shahrzad that I best remember --resplendent in a pair of shocking-pink Persian bloomers made of taffeta coupled with a black cotton blouse given her by a wealthy prisoner just before release; she wore a borrowed fringed shawl wound round her curly dark hair. Her eyes flashed; she sang gaily and pranced around our tiny walled garden with a hose, watering the scraggly rose bushes and tomato vines, trying to revive the parched plants at the end of a hot summer. Though she was not a typical prisoner, I like to think that she represented the spirits still caged within most Iranian women suffering under yet one more new repression in Iran.

Perhaps Kurdish men are indeed the fierce mountain tribesmen beloved of Western newsmen who periodically set out for the Zagros Mountains in search of colorful copy.

But their daughters and sisters at Evin were a complete
surprise. Suraya, Kali, Shabu, Kubra, and most of the 45
or so other young Kurds, nearly all still teen-agers, wore
flowing organza gowns that trailed along the prison's
dingy hallway. To wash their red plastic teacups in the
greasy sink and to mop floors they tied up their long
full sleeves and worked in their finery. By day they
produced enough baby booties, sweaters, houseshoes,
scarves, and doll clothes to earn our section the nickname
of Evin Boutique; at night they drank tea and studied.

Tuba was a short, round-cheeked, placid young woman
of about 18, neat but not well-dressed. She was one of
the few Kurds without a pretty gown. Although most Kurds
I met did not appear to be religious, Tuba was a devout
Sunni Muslim who fasted for Ramazan and prayed in a
black chadur.

Many prisoners claimed that one of the Kurdish women
had killed a man in a guerrilla action, but it could not
have been Tuba; she was too gentle. Another Kurdish
girl had fallen in love with the doctor's assistant, pursuing him by passing notes through friendly guards. When
he refused her offer of marriage, she threatened to kill
him, whereupon he locked himself into an isolation cell
until her rage passed. Again, this could not have been
Tuba; she was the embodiment of a modest Muslim woman.

Tuba's friends said she had worked in a factory in
the Kurdish city of Sanandaj and was the sole support of
a large family of younger sisters and brothers. I asked
why she was in prison. "She was on her way to buy bread
when she was stopped by a Revolutionary Guard." It seemed that most of the Kurds had been arrested arbitrarily
and hustled aboard a bus, where they were given sentences
of five or ten years apiece by a mere guard. Then they
were dumped at Evin. Some of my friends speculated that
they were being held as hostages for male relatives in
hiding during guerrilla activities. From time to time
some of the Kurds got into heated arguments with Mr.
Kajuai, the warden, about their sentences, but Tuba
never joined in.

Everyone was stunned one afternoon when a guard told
Tuba to get ready to leave at 4:30 the next morning to be
returned to the jail in Sanandaj. When the word spread,
every woman prisoner fell silent. The anxiety for Tuba
reflected on everyone's face was unprecedented. I was
told that a few weeks earlier another Kurdish woman had
been returned to Sanandaj in the same manner; shortly
thereafter, on a visiting day, a relative brought news
that she had been summarily shot. Tuba appeared to know
this rumor, but she said her goodbyes that evening smil-
ing placidly. Everyone, even the hard-boiled Simin,
kissed her again and again with tears in their eyes.
Tuba was the only one who did not cry. I never learned
what happened to her.

Early one morning, about the 12th of September, I watched three women carrying small bundles silently enter our room. They huddled in one corner, their faces drawn, their thin bodies in soiled and wrinkled clothes. They seemed weary, and they looked infinitely more frightened than any other newcomers. Picking my way across the room over several sleeping Kurds wrapped in blankets, I spoke to one of the newcomers and offered her tea. The small blond woman answered in perfect English, "My name in Minu."

Over the course of the morning we learned the story of the three women, the most horrible of the prison stories that I heard. The three, Farideh and Shahla, who were half-sisters, and Minu, were nationalists. Farideh, a blond of medium height, was the first to be arrested. She was blindfolded and tortured in a place she did not know. Then her tall brunette sister, Shalah, and Minu were taken into custody, and Minu was the torturer's next victim. Minu whispered that her tormentor had twisted her head around on her neck until she thought it would snap. A male voice had jeered, "Do you want to be raped?" but the threat was not carried out. The cell where she had been held was dark and suffocatingly hot, and a metronome-like device ticked loudly, day and night. Minu lost track of the time; hours stretched into days, days into weeks.[10] The three Nationalist women were brought to Evin and put on trial immediately with a group of men they did not know. They were pronounced guilty without being allowed to defend themselves and were awaiting sentencing.

This trial had been held near the end of a series of trials of men accused in the alleged Hamadan conspiracy. Many officers had been executed before the women arrived. During this period, each morning there would be headlines over a lineup of haunted faces in newspaper photographs announcing the number shot at midnight the night before. No one talked to me about these executions, although much later one of the guards, in a moment of the blackest humor, mimicked how, after she had tied a blindfold, a body riddled with bullets slumped to the ground. So when Minu ended her story of the torture and trial of the three of them with the calm announcement, "We will be shot tonight," all of us believed her and shuddered. It was one of the worst moments of my imprisonment, as horrifying as the time a Pasdar threatened to shoot me in an early detention center, where I was unprotected by regular guards, court officials, or even a kindly interrogator.

The hours of that long September day and evening wore on, but the three Nationalists were not summoned. They did not eat, but drank only a little tea. That night I rearranged my long foam mattress to give the four of us a place to put our heads. They were still there the next morning.

During the next few days the two sisters scarcely spoke. Tears streamed effortlessly down their cheeks. Farideh even fainted once. Minu did not cry but sat staring into space. She asked me if I knew who Joan of Arc was. "Maybe I'll be a Joan for my country," she mused aloud, trying to comfort herself. On the second day their pictures were in the paper with their co-defendants, who were unknown to the women.

As the days dragged by, many women paced the halls and prayed for the three. A fellow prisoner, a handsome and motherly Zoroastrian nurse-midwife, brought medicine "for the nerves." Even Khanum [Miss] Bakhtiari, a guard I had feared and disliked until that moment, sat with them for a long time assuring them that women never left our section for the execution yard.

But there were voices of hatred also. At first, I thought Simin, the leftist, was trying to tease them out of their fear, grinning and laughing in their direction. Shahla and Farideh listened for a minute, then began to cry soundlessly. I was stunned when someone translated for me. "You dirty monarchists, I hope you're shot," Simin sneered. "I'll sing and dance on your grave when that happens."

In a few days Shahla was sentenced to two-and-a-half years, and Minu to three (she would serve twenty months before being given amnesty). But Farideh's fate was still unknown; we were seized with fear.

In gratitude, Minu and Shahla held a sufreh, a religious feast that commemorated the courage of Zainab the daughter of Imam Ali, the first Shi^cite leader (d. 661). Minu spread two white sheets on the floor, Shahla lit candles, and we all sat cross-legged around the sufreh [tablecloth; feast]. A new guard, the motherly Khanum Tavakuli, was invited to read the young martyr's story aloud. Since the feast took place in the prostitutes' room, she thought we were all prostitutes, but hoping to reform us, she accepted and read with a marvelously expressive face and weepy voice. All the Muslim women wept, as on cue. But the tears were very real, and I was surprised to see the most stoical of prisoners weeping.

Since this was also the first night Iraqi planes shelled the airport, five miles away, non-Muslims had reason to weep also. The only person amused was Marzieh, a 17-year-old reformed runaway and drug user. She hopped about among the kneeling and swaying bodies passing out paper towels. (Marzieh was always an original; when she was betrothed to a guard's son, she asked that her dowry be a complete set of the writing of the late Dr. Ali Shari^cati^ll--even though his work was falling into disfavor with the mullahs.)

Story and prayer chants ended, tears dried on

Marzieh's paper towels, and the war temporarily forgotten,
we all fell to eating the nuts and fresh fruit, dates and
sweets, cheese and greens rolled in small pieces of un-
leavened bread. Even anxious Farideh, her hand still
bandaged from her torture, ate with us.

Custom calls for the sufreh to be repeated in a week.
The long reading had just begun when Farideh was summoned
out of the room, told to put on her chadur, and follow
the Pasdar. When she returned, limp with relief, she
brought news from the court: her sentence of execution
had been commuted to life imprisonment.

With their fates no longer hanging precariously, the
three relaxed and became prisoners like the rest of us.
We could all be sad or silly, bored or lonely, tired or
sick, hopeful or despairing. I remember Farideh, in a
green sweat suit, knitting with one bandaged hand and
singing a folk song from her native province of Luristan
or teaching us the old Persian national anthem. Her
fierce love of Iran appeared to sustain her.

I remember Minu, also intensely patriotic, well-edu-
cated and cultured, sipping her evening hot chocolate and
giving two Westerners an informal history lesson; we
tried to cover more than 2000 years of Persian history in
a few weeks. She gave me prayer beads and a colored
picture of Imam Ali, and she tried to teach me to say the
first sura, which is equivalent to the Lord's Prayer, in
Arabic.

And I remember Shahla, a welcome companion on a trip
to the gynecological clinic in a downtown Tehran hospital, in one comic episode (there were actually several
during my nine months as a prisoner). On the way back to
"home sweet home," as we called it (I found that Iranians
had an ironic sense of humor that appealed to me), the
Pasdaran let us stop at a grocery store to shop. Feeling
free as birds for the moment, flapping our way through
the supermarket pushing American-style shopping carts
before our heavily chadured bodies, we grabbed chocolates
and sardines, fresh mushrooms and Chef Boyardee spaghetti
before the armed zindanban herded us through the checkout
counter.[12] I think we actually sang on the way back.

Several women pooled their money at Christmas, 1980,
and asked a friendly guard to buy a turkey and all the
trimmings. With what delighted eagerness they surprised
the Englishwoman and me with a magnificent feast. It
made the pain of separation and spending a Christmas in
prison bearable.

Before I left Evin a motherly guard said: They've
ruined the Revolution--they've arrested too many people,
they've tortured and executed too many people. This
isn't what the people fought for." Hers was a more
definitive judgment of the state of Iran in February,
1981 than perhaps I can give, but I offer this chapter
and the poem[13] that follows in loving memory of the women

I knew briefly in Iran.

Evin Prison, 1981

Who knows what evil lurks in the
hearts of my guard, khanum?
Evil, Nein, Hannah,
banality's all that's stamped on their
hypocritically chadured hard hearts
like flowers on tombstones.
No massive fraulein stalks
the seven Kurdish beauties
locked in this stale old Persian harem.
But freshly showered and chadured in flowers
the young girls wait to visit their mothers,
their fathers, brave brothers;
their little sisters bring oranges
and wait under plane trees.

Still a shadow of fear floats into our cells.
somebody's been tried and led out in the night;
pictures appear, sounds ring out while I sleep,
and I saw one tall woman
proud as a witch
wrapped all in black
hooded in black
blindfolded in black
grasp a long dirty rag
attached to a Pasdar,
who heeled her away
to the Evin tucked away
from commissions that probe,
and I heard someone scream
and I saw someone's blood
on some stairs that I climbed,
and I think disinterested bullets
are finding their mark
tonight at Evin.

NOTES

    *This expression was used by a bookstore clerk in
April, 1980 to express his feelings for the regime. I
was seeking information as to whether Persepolis was open
for tourists. He thought not, and when I voiced amaze-
ment, "Why ever not?" he replied sourly, "Because we are
living in the Kingdom of the Mullahs."
    1. Although I went to Iran as a freelance writer,
with no formal assignments, several editors had expressed
an interest in articles I planned to write.
    2. I was living in a room with two elderly women,
whose bossiness and selfishness were hard for me to
adjust to after three months of living peacefully alone
(when actually left alone by the interrogators I called
the Gang of Three). There was also another prisoner who

questioned me a lot, and since there were rumors that she was a prison "spy," I wanted to put a lot of distance between us. The precipitating factor for my request, however, occured the day I muttered "Marg bar Iran" in response to "Marg bar Amrika" [Death to America]. I was overheard and reported to the guards. The guards said nothing, but I desperately wished for time alone, although I hated being confined 24 hours a day, most days, to a 6' x 8' windowless cell.

I had to raise quite a storm to be transferred back into the regular unit, but as in most matters except release, making a loud fuss was effective with the guards and higher prison authorities. Later, I never hesitated to scream or weep to win important concessions. It was both a game and an important release for pent-up feelings. From sociological reading, I understand that strong expressions of feeling are permitted lower-class and village women in Iran in retaliation for indignities from men that become unbearable. In this respect, I fit easily into the Kurdish-Mujahid milieu.

3. Apart from the fact that their mothers may have had no reason to be imprisoned, it seemed somewhat humane to allow the children to stay with their mothers. Still, prison life must have been very boring except when there was another child to play with. Once, when I was taken out of the prison for medical treatment and allowed to buy medicine at a Teheran pharmacy, I purchased a book for one child. Ironically, since I injudiciously bought a Western fairy tale with kings and princesses, I never saw the Mujahid child reading it.

4. I do not wish to convey the impression that anyone enjoyed being at Evin. But in those days, before Evin was turned into what a Swiss consular official told me was called "The Butchery" because of mass executions following the summer of 1981 assassinations of high government officials and Majlis members, we prisoners tried to enjoy each other's company in a civilized manner. The point is that we were allowed the opportunity to do so.

5. Temporary marriage is allowed under Shi^{c}i law. For more on the subject, see the chapter by Shahla Haeri in this volume.

6. For more on the Mujahidin and Fida'i organizations see the chapter by Eliz Sanasarian in this volume.

7. After the war with Iraq began, surprisingly there was no drop in the amount of fresh food brought in as gifts, although I think prices had gone up. The huge quantities of rice and beans cooked at the prison did not diminish either. It is probably fortunate that I like vegetarian meals and rice cooked well with a variety of sauces, for rice and bread kept us filled. Also see note 12.

8. See note 2.

9. Mr. Kajuai, who had been a prisoner under the Shah, according to A^{c}zam, whose brother had known him then, was polite and appeared genuinely concerned about our welfare. I was never afraid of him and would have found him approachable had I known Persian. He had a good reputation among the women, and some occasionally addressed him ru-beh-ru [face-to-face] with passionate pleas for his help. He was fatally shot in the summer of 1981, allegedly by a prison guard he fired. I remember his tired, unshaven face, back from a tour of duty on the Khuzistan front; his curious eyes watching over a Christmas service conducted by an Armenian priest for the Englishwoman and myself; and his soft apology for not speaking English when I lamented my "little Persian." I did not consider him personally responsible for the executions or beatings ordered by the mullah-dominated courts, and I felt a measure of safety with him in daily charge of our section.

10. Many prisoners told me they believed ex-SAVAK agents were being used by the hardliners in the government. I have read, in an article by Khosrow Fatemi, that "General Fardowst, the Shah's childhood friend and probably his most trusted confidant, who . . . directed the Shah's Special Intelligence Bureau . . . has become Khomeini's chief security advisor and the de facto head of his secret police, SAVAMA." [Leadership by Distrust: The Shah's Modus Operandi," Middle East Journal 36 (no. 1), p. 60, footnote 13].

11. For a discussion of a work by Dr. Shari^{c}ati, see the chapter in this volume by Marcia K. Hermansen.

12. More recent reports coming out of Iran indicate that there are now shortages of every kind, even of daily items such as sugar, soap, and meat; people must stand in line for hours to procure these necessities.

13. Knowledge of Hannah Arendt's The Banality of Evil, on the Holocaust and Adolf Eichmann, and the Italian film Seven Beauties, which depicts a Nazi concentration camp, will clarify allusions.

Epilogue

It might appear that the leaders of the present regime in Iran have succeeded in convincing women to be only mothers and wives. Within a relatively short time the regime was able to abrogate the laws it considered contrary to the Shari‘a and replace them with laws it believed in keeping with the laws of Islam. This has resulted in the drastic reduction of women's personal, political, cultural, legal, and social rights. The legally permitted age of marriage for women has been reduced to thirteen. Temporary marriage, even with women as young as age nine, is being touted as one of the signs of Islam's progressiveness. Women's ability to seek divorce has been restricted, and their right to gain custody of their young children after divorce has been removed from them. In the event of the husband's death, the custody of the children goes not to their mother but to the husband's male relatives. Polygamy has been revived, and women have been executed on charges of adultery while the men so charged have been allowed to go free after being lashed. Women have been removed from judge-ships and other important executive posts, and laws have been passed to ensure that they will not fill such positions in the future. Women are encouraged in every way to retire from work--early retirement laws have been passed, day care centers have been closed, and maternity leave for women has been abolished. Finally, the success of the government is manifest in the imposition of the Islamic hijab for women. Legislation passed in April, 1983 prosecutes women who fail to adhere to the dress code with imprisonment or a fine.

Nevertheless, it is too early to determine the long-term success or failure of the regime's policies toward women. In assessing the long-term impact of these poli-cies, several important factors must be kept in mind. First, the immediate impact of the regime's policies has been felt mainly by the educated professional and sec-ular women and by female students, primarily in urban areas, and they constitute only a small part of the

286

female population. The vast majority of the traditional
non-working women have not been affected by these policies as yet. This is even more true of rural women,
whose involvement in national life and politics has been
minimal. This may be best exemplified by the controversy
surrounding the forcible imposition of the hijab. For
most Iranian women the chadur is already the accepted
mode of dress. Their lack of political awareness and the
inability of the more educated women to publicly express
their views has prevented the majority of Iranian women
from realizing that at issue here are more fundamental
rights of women than merely their choice of dress. Furthermore, some of the major laws that were abrogated,
such as the Family Protection Law, had not been in effect
long enough to prove their usefulness for those who need
them the most: the poorer women.

An even more important reason for lack of sympathy
toward the modern working women by the more traditional
women has been the absence of strong feminist consciousness and political awareness among the masses of Iranian
women. As the various chapters of this work reveal, the
participation of traditional urban women in the revolution was prompted by their over-riding conception of this
activity as religious duty. The effective use of religious symbolism, equating Ayatullah Khomeini with Imam
Husain and the Shah with Husain's adversary, Yazid, was
instrumental in bringing out the masses of men and women
into the streets.

The lack of forceful opposition by professional
women and female student activists, the victims of many
of the regime's policies, may at first seem surprising.
Several factors account for the failure of educated women
to counter the increasing pressures brought to bear on
them. The most important is that the majority of the
women who opposed the Shah's regime lacked an ideological
framework--either political or feminist. They were
active merely to fight corruption and despotism. This
lack of a specific platform was exacerbated by the women's
ignorance of traditional religious teaching about women.
Furthermore, few secular women, or men, anticipated quick
emergence of a religious government from the ashes of the
Shah's regime. Therefore, when clerical leaders called
an early referendum to profit from their popularity with
the masses, women merely boycotted the constitutional
assembly (later known as the Assembly of Experts).

In the early days of the revolution some women who
had played an active role in the women's rights movement
under the previous regime tried to warn women of the
iminent danger directed at them by the regime's ideology
and policies. However, they were unable to generate
sufficient support among the women, both the more modern
professional or the politically active female students
and working women.

The ideological stance of the politicized women may

explain their failure to oppose the policies of the
regime. In the Tudeh Party, the principal Marxist group
represented, the women acquiesced in the policies of the
predominant male leadership; hence, until recently they
not only withheld criticism, but even supported the clerical regime. Presumably their support of a regime so
repressive of women's rights was based on the anti-American and anti-imperialist attitudes of the present regime.
The silence of other Marxist and Socialist female activists was caused at first by their belief that women
would not be liberated until the whole social structure
was changed. However, many of these women activists are
beginning to realize that women are discriminated against
not only on the basis of class but on the basis of sex,
and centuries of cultural patriarchy and rigid socialization will not be eliminated even after a working-class
takeover (in fact, many men in power today are from lower-
middle class backgrounds). Consequently, some women
activists have begun to voice discontent with the attitude that prevents their male colleagues from expressing
stronger public opposition to the plight of women. Some
activists have called for women to unite in the face of
"universal male chauvinism."
     The only political group that has openly opposed the
policies of the government toward women is the Mujahidin
organization. Once more banned by the regime in power and
the only effective guerilla movement in the country, the
Mujahidin has a much larger female membership than in the
past. The group has consistently addressed the issue of
women's rights. They recognize the importance of women
as part of a revolutionary force and show awareness of the
sexist biases against women in society. They are particularly critical of the deterioration of women's rights
under the present regime. Their vocal condemnation of the
policies of the Islamic Republic may have been the principal reason for the regime's decision in September, 1980
to close the universities which provided the Mujahidin
with havens in which to organize and recruit.
     The various penalties the regime imposes on the
opposition has ensured the silence of the majority of the
women opposed to the growing restraints that are being
placed on them. These penalties range from public harassment of women demonstrators and loss of employment to the
recent punishment for non-compliance with the Islamic
veil. Siyyid Husain Musavi-Tabrizi, the attorney general
of the revolutionary courts announced that violators would
be whipped, imprisoned and fined if they do not comply
with the Islamic mode of dress. Finally, the war with
Iraq may also have led some women to put their grievances
against the government aside while their country faces
threat from the outside. Obviously it would be incorrect
to assume that all educated and professional women oppose
the regime's policies. However, not everyone in agreement
with the government and its general ideology approves of

the punitive measures taken against women who refuse to
comply with these policies. One of the most outspoken
critics has been Mrs. A^czam Taliqani, one of two members
of Parliament. She has repeatedly criticized the government for its harsh treatment of women who refuse to comply
with the veil code. She also has questioned the regime's
discriminatory effort to impose a specific mode of dress
on women but not on men.

The lack of open opposition by women should not be
interpreted as a sign of their defeat and surrender nor
as a governmental victory in imposing its particular
vision of what women should be. Beneath the surface calm
a new awareness seems to be emerging among a growing number of Iranian women about the condition of women and the
discrimination practiced against them as women. This
growing awareness can be detected among women from different social and ideological backgrounds. Even women
who staunchly support the government sometimes express
this awareness. One such woman was Mrs. Munireh Gurji,
the only woman member of the Assembly of Experts. Although she was in full agreement with the need for re-
storing women to their Islamic role, she regretted the
lack of more women members in the Assembly "so that
women's fate would not be determined by the men." She
also was critical of the punishment of young prostitutes
by death while their male customers went free.

Even more revealing are signs of dissatisfaction
among the more traditional types of women, who are
beginning to voice objections to the discrimination
practiced against them in the name of Islam. Many letters to the editors in women's magazines indicate the
growing unhappiness about the restoration of <u>Shari^ca</u> laws
concerning marriage, divorce, and child custody. Woman
after woman complains of her fears of a second wife, of
being suddenly divorced, or of loss of her young children.
"What kind of justice is this that deprives me of seeing
my two-year-old son for three months?" one such letter
asks. Female high school students write, "What kind of a
system tells girls that they don't need to study mathematics but provides mathematics classes for boys of much
lesser ability?"

This growing realization of the need for women to
look after their own welfare is also expressed by a
growing number of articles in the press directed at
women. Although the authors pay lip service to the
higher ideals of the regime and express gratitude to the
Islamic State "for having improved and elevated women's
role in society," they repeatedly remind women that any
change in their status must originate from them through
their own efforts. These writers discuss the need for
women to extend helping hands to each other and to educate each other. The message that comes through is of
the need for women to try themselves to correct the
inequities imposed on them by a patriarchal culture. One

author, taking a great risk, advises women to "scream and demand that the new Islamic Parliament listen to you."

Although most women have apparently been supporting the regime, there are many indications that dissatisfaction is building among them. Not as many respond to the regime's call for support, and many more young women are joining the Mujahidin guerrilla organization.

It may be too soon to determine whether the majority of Iranian women, the traditional and the more secular, could be mobilized once more by another opposition group. But it would be safe to suggest that the lessons of their revolutionary activity will not be permanently lost on women. So far, the revolution seems to have been a sobering experience. A slowly growing number of women are beginning to realize that they cannot afford to have their fate determined by men, even by men of good will, that they are the best judges of their needs and their welfare as women, and that unless they actively participate in deciding the laws and conditions that affect them, they will not achieve real equality and full dignity as human beings.

The self-interest of the present regime would mandate a reconsideration of its policies toward women, even aside from moral considerations. Many women helped overthrow the previous regime, and they look back to their involvement in the revolution with pride. Their involvement in the social process has become an important asset to the present regime. Probably women will continue their commitment to the regime if they are treated as equal citizens and not as inferiors who must leave important matters to men.

Reassessment of policies toward women is required if the regime wants to build a viable economy that can compete successfully in the world economy. As the experience of many countries has shown, the human resources of both men and women are ultimately more important to development than a country's natural resources. In Iran, most women, including professional women, put the care of their families first. Therefore, the regime must find ways to encourage women to make effective contributions to the development process by joining the labor force and in other ways. Consequently, it must devise policies that will enable women to take part along with men in rebuilding the country. This role of women is in no way inconsistent with the fundamental tenets of Islam.

As the experience of some contemporary peoples suggests, a state can often silence opposition by brute force. The Islamic Republican regime must decide how far it intends to depart from the moral ideals of Islam in order to stay in power.

Contributors

Janet Bauer is an anthropologist. She teaches at the University of North Carolina, Chapel Hill, and is also a research associate of the Population Center at that University. She conducted research in Iran in 1977 and 1978 and has written about her research on migrant women in Tehran. She is currently writing a book on her research.

Anne H. Betteridge is an anthropologist; she lived in Shiraz from 1976 to 1980. She has conducted research on women's religious beliefs and rituals and has written several articles on this subject.

Cynthia Dwyer is a free-lance journalist living in Buffalo, New York. She went to Iran in 1979, and learned about Evin Prison first hand.

Adele Ferdows teaches political science at the University of Louisville in Kentucky. She has written about Islamic Fundamentalism and about the condition of women in Iran.

Amir Ferdows teaches political science at Indiana University, Southeast. He has conducted research and written about Islamic political thought and about the position of women in Islam.

Erika Friedl teaches anthropology at Western Michigan University. She lived in Iran for five years and conducted research on various aspects of rural culture. She has visited Iran several times since the February 11 revolution.

Shala Haeri is currently completing her doctoral work in anthropology at the University of California at Los Angeles. She has conducted field work on mut^ca at the Shrines of Qum, Mashhad, and in Tehran.

Mary E. Hegland is an anthropologist. She has conducted research in Iran from June 1978 to December 1979. She has written about her research and experiences.

Farzaneh Milani holds a degree in comparative literature. She has taught Persian literature at the University of California at Los Angeles and has written on modern Persian literature.

S. Kaveh Mirani is completing his doctoral work in economics at the University of Chicago. His research deals with the economic analysis of revolution.

Yasmin Mossavar-Rahmani has studied anthropology and has conducted research on family planning in clinics in Tehran both before and after the revolution.

Guity Nashat teaches Middle Eastern history at the University of Illinois at Chicago. She has published a book and several articles on social and economic history of Iran in the nineteenth century.

Fazlur Rahman is professor of Islamic thought in the Department of Near Eastern Languages and Civilizations at the University of Chicago. He has written numerous books and articles on Islamic philosophy and modern trends in the Islamic world.

Eliz Sanasarian is a political scientist. She has taught at the University of California at Los Angeles and at California State College, San Bernardino. She has conducted research and written a book and several articles on women's political participation in Iran in the twentieth century.

Index